To Renew Books
PHONE (925) 258-2233

Namkee G. Choi, PhD
Editor

Psychosocial Aspects of the Asian-American Experience: Diversity Within Diversity

Psychosocial Aspects of the Asian-American Experience: Diversity Within Diversity has been co-published simultaneously as *Journal of Human Behavior in the Social Environment,* Volume 3, Numbers 3/4 2001.

Pre-publication
REVIEWS,
COMMENTARIES,
EVALUATIONS . . .

"**P**rofessors of many disciplines, from ethics studies to psychology, sociology and social work, will certainly adopt this book for their college courses. Rarely does one encounter a book on Asian Americans that covers such a broad range of subjects and includes diversity of the population like this book.

Students, practicers, researchers, policy makers and academics will want to retain this book in their personal libraries. This timely book is an important resource for today, and it will be a value source of reference for many years to come. "

Rita Takahashi, PhD
Professor
San Francisco State University

"The new book, *Psychosocial Aspects of the Asian American Experience*, edited by Dr. Namkee Choi, is a much needed addition to the literature of the helping professons in general. Although Asian Americans are one of the fastest growing populations in the United States, they have received significantly less attention in social work literature than other populations of color. The book takes an important step towards filling this void. The book begins with demographic and historical information that provides a context for understanding heterogeneity within this population.

In particular, this book makes great strides towards helping the reader to understand the diversity that exist within the Asian American population. As a number of authors in this book point out, there are at least 26 different nationalities that fall under the umbrella of Asian/pacific Islander. This book provides information on such diverse population such as Chinese, Japanese, Filipinos, Koreas, Asian Indians, Vietnamese, Hmong, Cambodians, and Native Hawaiians. These groups often differ in terms of language, customs, era and circumstances of immigration, religion, socialeconomic status, and other variables. Likewise, this book examines issues at different stages of the lifestyle and among different generations of immigrants, illustrating that even with one Asian population there is often extensive diversity.

This book challenges the myth of Asian Americans as a model minority. Important empirical information on various Asian American populations in terms of factors such as socioeconomic status, mental health, and domestic violance. Additionally, information is presented. on issues such as cultural orientation, help seeking behavior, and responses to treatment. In a particularly thought provoking chapter, Lee, Lei & Sue explore some of the challenges in doing empirial research with Asian Americans and speculate on reasons for discrepancies in existing studies.

Psychosocial Aspects of the Asian-American Experience will be a great asset to social work students and practicers. This book is one of the few places where readers can find some much high quality, imperial information on Asian American populations. The book covers a variety of social issues and covers content on many different Asian population. The information in this book provides a more balanced, comprehensive, and multidimensional picture of the diverse populations we know as Asian American that is available elsewhere in the human services literature.

Hilary N. Weaver, DSW
Associate Professor
School of Social Work
State University of New York
at Buffalo

More pre-publication
REVIEWS, COMMENTARIES, EVALUATIONS . . .

"**P**sychosocial Aspects of Asian-American Experience makes a significant contribution to knowledge and research on Asian-Americans in the United States. The book contributes to knowledge areas in the identity development, psychosocial functioning, cultural adjustment, academic achievement, victimization, and aging. While it addresses issues relevant to the Asian-American population in general, it also stresses the diversity within this population by illuminating issue areas specific to sub-groups such as Chinese, Japanese, Korean, Filipino, Vietnamese, Cambodian, Whooping, Asian/Pacific Islander, and Asian Indian.. The historical demographic overview of Asian-Americans and the discussion of the current state of mental health research on this population are particularly noteworthy for their appeal to both practitioners and academicians.

Psychosocial Aspects of Asian-American Experience employs both qualittative and quantitative methodologies to uncover the realities confronting this group. Some experiences are better addressed through use of structural equation models and other statistical techniques of multivariate analysis. Some experiences are better revealed through focus groups, in-depth interviews, and narritives. Each chapter is a snapshot into the complex, and often ignored, world of Asian-Americans. Thus, the book itself represents a comprehensive and revealing album that chronicles the uniqueness of the groups categorized as Asian-Americans.

This book also has a significance that goes beyond Asian-Americans. It serves as a model for conducting theoretical and methodological inquires into the experiences of other populations that represent heterogeneous sub-groups. By disentangling the broad category, the diversity between the sub-groups can be more richly understood. Thus, his book represents the direction in which research in diverse populations should continue to move.

Alfreda P. Iglehart, MS.W, PhD
Associate Professor, UCLA

The Haworth Press, Inc.

Psychosocial Aspects
of the Asian-American Experience:
Diversity Within Diversity

Psychosocial Aspects of the Asian-American Experience: Diversity Within Diversity has been co-published simultaneously as *Journal of Human Behavior in the Social Environment,* Volume 3, Numbers 3/4 2001.

The *Journal of Human Behavior in the Social Environment* Monographic "Separates"

Below is a list of "separates," which in serials librarianship means a special issue simultaneously published as a special journal issue or double-issue *and* as a "separate" hardbound monograph. (This is a format which we also call "DocuSerial.")

"Separates" are published because specialized libraries or professionals may wish to purchase a specific thematic issue by itself in a format which can be separately cataloged and shelved, as opposed to purchasing the journal on an on-going basis. Faculty members may also more easily consider a "separate" for classroom adoption.

"Separates" are carefully classified separately with the major book jobbers so that the journal tie-in can be noted on new book order slips to avoid duplicate purchasing.

You may wish to visit Haworth's website at . . .

http://www.HaworthPress.com

. . . to search our online catalog for complete tables of contents of these separates and related publications.

You may also call 1-800-HAWORTH (outside US/Canada: 607-722-5857), or Fax 1-800-895-0582 (outside US/Canada: 607-771-0012), or e-mail at:

getinfo@haworthpressinc.com

Psychosocial Aspects of the Asian-American Experience: Diversity Within Diversity, edited by Namkee G. Choi, PhD (Vol. 3, No. 3/4, 2001). *Examines the childhood, adolescence, young adult, and aging stages of Asian Americans to help researchers and practioners offer better services to this ethic group. Representing Chinese, Japanese, Filipinos, Koreans, Asian Indians, Vietnamese, Hmong, Cambodians, and native-born Hawaiians, this helpful book will enable you to offer clients relevant services that are appropriate for your clients' ethnic backgrounds, beliefs, and experiences.*

Voices of First Nations People: Human Services Considerations, edited by Hilary N. Weaver, DSW (Vol. 2, No. 1/2, 1999). *"A must read for anyone interested in gaining an insight into the world of Native Americans. . . . I highly recommend it!" (James Knapp, BS, Executive Director, Native American Community Services of Erie and Niagara Counties, Inc., Buffalo, New York)*

Human Behavior in the Social Environment from an African American Perspective, edited by Letha A. (Lee) See, PhD (Vol. 1, No. 2/3, 1998). *"A book of scholarly, convincing, and relevant chapters that provide an African-American perspective on human behavior and the social environment . . . offer[s] new insights about the impact of race on psychosocial development development in American society." (Alphonso W. Haynes, EdD, Professor, School of Social Work, Grand Valley State University, Grand Rapids, Michigan)*

Psychosocial Aspects
of the Asian-American Experience:
Diversity Within Diversity

Namkee G. Choi, PhD
Editor

Psychosocial Aspects of the Asian-American Experience: Diversity Within Diversity has been co-published simultaneously as *Journal of Human Behavior in the Social Environment,* Volume 3, Numbers 3/4 2001.

The Haworth Press, Inc.
New York • London • Oxford

Psychosocial Aspects of the Asian American Experience: Diversity Within Diversity has been co-published simultaneously as *Journal of Human Behavior in the Social Environment,* Volume 3, Numbers 3/4 2001.

The development, preparation, and publication of this work has been undertaken with great care. However, the publisher, employees, editors, and agents of The Haworth Press and all imprints of The Haworth Press, Inc., including The Haworth Medical Press® and Pharmaceutical Products Press®, are not responsible for any errors contained herein or for consequences that may ensue from use of materials or information contained in this work. Opinions expressed by the author(s) are not necessarily those of The Haworth Press, Inc.

Cover design by Thomas J. Mayshock Jr.

Library of Congress Cataloging-in-Publication Data

Psychosocial aspects of the Asian-American experience: diversity within diversity/Namkee G. Choi, editor.
    p. cm.
    "Co-published simultaneously as Journal of human behavior in the social environment, volume 3, no. 3/4 2001."
    Includes bibliographical references and index.
    ISBN 0-7890-1049-6 (alk. paper)–ISBN 0-7890-1150-6 (alk. paper)
    1. Asian Americans–Psychology. 2. Asian Americans–Ethnic idenity. 3. Asian Americans–Social conditions. 4. Life cycle, Human. 5. Developmental psychology–United States. I. Choi, Namkee G., II. Journal of human behavior in the social environment.

E184.O6 P79 2001
305.895073–dc21
                                                                           00-047217

Indexing, Abstracting & Website/Internet Coverage

This section provides you with a list of major indexing & abstracting services. That is to say, each service began covering this periodical during the year noted in the right column. Most Websites which are listed below have indicated that they will either post, disseminate, compile, archive, cite or alert their own Website users with research-based content from this work. (This list is as current as the copyright date of this publication.)

Abstracting, Website/Indexing Coverage .... Year When Coverage Began

- *Cambridge Scientific Abstracts (Health & Safely Science Abstracts, Risk Abstracts* **1998**

- *caredata CD: the social & community care database* **1998**

- *Child Development Abstracts & Bibliography* **1998**

- *CINAHL (Cumulative Index to Nursing & Allied Health Literature), in print, also on CD-ROM from CD PLUS, EBSCO, and SilverPlatter, and online from CDP Online (formerly BRS), Data-Star, and PaperChase. (Support materials include Subject Heading List, Database Search Guide, and instructional video)* **1998**

- *CNPIEC Reference Guide: Chinese National Directory of Foreign Periodicals* **1998**

- *Criminal Justice Abstracts* **1998**

- *Family Studies Database (online and CD/ROM)* **1998**

(continued)

- *FINDEX www.publist.com* **1999**
- *FRANCIS, INIST–CNRS* **1998**
- *Index to Periodical Articles Related to Law* **1998**
- *Mental Health Abstracts (online through DIALOG)* **1998**
- *Social Services Abstracts www.csa.com* **1999**
- *Social Work Abstracts* **1998**
- *Sociological Abstracts (SA) www.csa.com* **1998**

*Special Bibliographic Notes related to special journal issues
(separates) and indexing/abstracting:*

- indexing/abstracting services in this list will also cover material in any "separate" that is co-published simultaneously with Haworth's special thematic journal issue or DocuSerial. Indexing/abstracting usually covers material at the article/chapter level.
- monographic co-editions are intended for either non-subscribers or libraries which intend to purchase a second copy for their circulating collections.
- monographic co-editions are reported to all jobbers/wholesalers/approval plans. The source journal is listed as the "series" to assist the prevention of duplicate purchasing in the same manner utilized for books-in-series.
- to facilitate user/access services all indexing/abstracting services are encouraged to utilize the co-indexing entry note indicated at the bottom of the first page of each article/chapter/contribution.
- this is intended to assist a library user of any reference tool (whether print, electronic, online, or CD-ROM) to locate the monographic version if the library has purchased this version but not a subscription to the source journal.
- individual articles/chapters in any Haworth publication are also available through the Haworth Document Delivery Service (HDDS).

Psychosocial Aspects of the Asian-American Experience: Diversity Within Diversity

CONTENTS

Introduction   1
Namkee G. Choi

Asian Americans in the Twentieth Century   7
Harry H. Kitano
Susan Nakaoka

Adoptive Parents and Identity Development
for Chinese Children   19
Rowena Fong
Anne Wang

Asian American Adolescents' Academic Achievement:
A Look Behind the Model Minority Image   35
Peter Allen Lee
Yu-Wen Ying

Depression Level in Inner-City Asian American Adolescents:
The Contributions of Cultural Orientation
and Interpersonal Relationships   49
Sandra L. Wong

Causal Modeling Predicting Psychological Adjustment
of Korean-Born Adolescent Adoptees   65
Dong Pil Yoon

Network Composition, Social Integration, and Sense
of Coherence in Chinese American Young Adults   83
Yu-Wen Ying
Peter A. Lee
Jeanne L. Tsai
Yu J. Lee
Malisa Tsang

Cultural Orientation of Hmong Young Adults   99
    Jeanne L. Tsai

Filipino American Dating Violence: Definitions,
    Contextual Justifications, and Experiences
    of Dating Violence   115
    Pauline Agbayani-Siewert
    Alice Yick Flanagan

"Being Indian,""Being American": A Balancing Act
    or a Creative Blend?   135
    Shobha Srinivasan

The Current State of Mental Health Research
    on Asian Americans   159
    Jennifer Lee
    Annie Lei
    Stanley Sue

Is an Independent Self a Requisite for Asian
    Immigrants' Psychological Well-Being
    in the U.S.? The Case of Korean Americans   179
    Kyoung Ja Hyun

Model Minority Demystified: Emotional Costs
    of Multiple Victimizations in the Lives
    of Women of Japanese Descent   201
    Mieko Yoshihama

Acculturation, Premigration Traumatic Experiences,
    and Depression Among Vietnamese Americans   225
    Dung Ngo
    Thanh V. Tran
    Judith L. Gibbons
    Joan M. Oliver

Somatic Complaint and Social Suffering
    Among Survivors of the Cambodian Killing Fields   243
    Edwina S. Uehara
    Paula T. Morelli
    Jennifer Abe-Kim

Culturally Competent Substance Abuse Treatment
   for Asian/Pacific Islander Women   263
      Paula T. Morelli
      Rowena Fong
      Julie Oliveira

Stress, Coping, and Depression Among Elderly
   Korean Immigrants   281
      Ada C. Mui

Diversity Within Diversity: Research and Social Work Practice
   Issues with Asian American Elders   301
      Namkee G. Choi

Index   321

ABOUT THE EDITOR

Namkee G. Choi, MSW, PhD, is Professor in the Graduate School of Social Work at Portland State University. Her research interests include social policy and program analysis and gerontological social work. She has published extensively in the area of minority aging with particular emphasis on racial and gender differences in economic status, retirement patterns, living arrangement, and long-term care service utilization. Dr. Choi coauthored *Long-Term Care and Ethnicity* (1998, Auburn), a comprehensive research report on cultural diversity and differential informal and formal service utilization patterns among White, African American, and Hispanic frail elders. Dr. Choi has also done important work in the area of family homelessness. Her recent book, *Homeless Families with Children: A Subjective Experience of Homelessness* (1999, Springer), has been praised by reviewers as one of the most significant studies on homeless families as the problems of homelessness and shelter life are presented from the families' own perspectives. Currently, Dr. Choi is doing research on the relationship between minority group membership and health outcome among pre- and early retirement populations. In conjuction with her research, Dr. Choi has also provided extensive consultation to regional and local social service agencies serving children, adolescents, families, and older persons.

Introduction

In the fall of 1998, John Wodarski, co-editor of the *Journal of Human Behavior in the Social Environment,* asked me to serve as the editor for a book about the experiences of Asian-Americans. (The Haworth Press has previously published books about the experiences of African Americans and Native Americans.) I gladly accepted the challenge because I believed such a special issue would serve an important scholarly function of disseminating state-of-the-art research findings and educating the readership about the current problems and issues faced by the rapidly growing Asian-American population.

After reviewing the existing books and journal articles on Asian Americans, I decided to organize the book to (1) cover issues across the life span–childhood, adolescence, young adulthood, adulthood, and aging–that both researchers and practitioners find useful in their research on and practice with Asian-American population groups; (2) reflect the ethnic and cultural diversity within the Asian-American population; and (3) focus on empirical research–both quantitative and qualitative–reports that have potential for impacting social policies for and social services to Asian Americans.

Since I announced the focus and direction of this work in the Asian-American research communities, mostly in social work and psychology, I received enthusiastic response from a number of Asian-American researchers. They not only sent in high-quality manuscripts for review and possible inclusion in this publication but also provided much encouragement and support for my endeavor to produce an issue that would leave a mark on both research and practice. Most contributors showed endless patience and a collaborative spirit throughout the arduous review, revision, and resubmission processes. The fruits of their enthusiasm and hard work are presented in this work.

[Haworth co-indexing entry note]: "Introduction." Choi, Namkee G. Co-published simultaneously in *Journal of Human Behavior in the Social Environment* (The Haworth Press, Inc.) Vol. 3, No. 3/4, 2001, pp. 1-6; and: *Psychosocial Aspects of the Asian-American Experience: Diversity Within Diversity* (ed: Namkee G. Choi) The Haworth Press, Inc., 2001, pp. 1-6. Single or multiple copies of this article are available for a fee from The Haworth Document Delivery Service [1-800-342-9678, 9:00 a.m. - 5:00 p.m. (EST). E-mail address: getinfo@haworthpressinc.com].

As shown in the table of contents, the text contains four articles on issues and problems pertaining to childhood and adolescence, four on young adulthood (mostly investigating college students), six on adulthood in general, and two on elders. The population groups covered represent the diversity of the Asian-American/Pacific Islander population: Chinese, Japanese, Filipinos, Koreans, Asian Indians, Vietnamese, Hmong, Cambodians, and native-born Hawaiians. The topics dealt with are also comprehensive, including ethnic identity development and psychological adjustment of adoptees, adolescents' attitudes and behavior regarding academic achievement, cultural orientation, dating violence, social network composition, acculturation, depression and other mental health problems, domestic violence, substance abuse, and more. Considering the comprehensive range of population groups and topics covered, I believe this work fills the gap in the knowledge base on current problems and issues faced by Asian Americans. I, along with all the contributors, hope that it will serve as a valuable resource for researchers, practitioners, and policy makers.

ORGANIZATION OF THE ISSUE

The lead article, on Asian Americans in the 20th century, by Harry H. Kitano and Susan Nakaoka, is intended to provide background information on the demographic and socioeconomic status of the Asian American population. Specifically, the article covers the brief history of Chinese and Japanese immigration in the mid- and late-19th century. Then, based on census data, it introduces readers to the demographic changes among Asian Americans between 1900 and the 1990s. In conjunction with the rapidly increasing number of Asian Americans, the article also discusses their socioeconomic status in the 1990s.

The next 16 articles are arranged to correspond to life span developmental stages ranging from childhood to old age. So, the second article, by Rowena Fong and Anne Wang, is on the identity development issues faced by Chinese-born baby girls adopted by American parents. The article first describes the socioeconomic and political environment in China that created the pool of abandoned baby girls and the dramatic increase in the number of American families who adopted Chinese baby girls in the 1990s. Then this exploratory study reports the findings from in-depth interviews with 10 adoptive parents of China-born baby girls in regard to the parents' concerns about their daughters' ethnic and cultural identity development and the parental efforts to help their daughters retain their cultural identity.

The third article is on Asian-American adolescents' attitudes and behavior regarding academic achievement from the perspectives of the 153 adolescent subjects. The authors, Peter Allen Lee and Yu-Wen Ying, analyzed entries to an essay contest, "Growing Up Asian American," and found that fewer than half the adolescents reported a positive attitude toward academic achievement. In contrast, a great majority of them reported that they engaged in behaviors that would enhance their academic achievement. In the authors' analysis of the essays, however, they also found significant distress among the adolescents who were striving to achieve academically.

The fourth article, by Sandra L. Wong, examines the effects of cultural orientation and interpersonal relationships on depression among Asian-American adolescents. With a sample drawn from an inner-city school, this study presents a rare picture of Asian-American children growing up in poverty and the psychosocial problems they face. The findings show that adolescents with a high orientation toward ethnic culture and a low orientation toward mainstream culture experienced greater depression than those who were assimilated. More positive relationships with parents and peers also predicted lower depression levels. Further, those who had immigrated after the age of 12 were more depressed than their American-born counterparts.

The fifth article, by Dong Pil Yoon, reports the findings of the author's survey research on the psychosocial adjustment problems of Korean-born adolescents who had been adopted by American parents. Specifically, the author tested the causal relationship, using structural equation modeling, among the parents' support of ethnic identity development, the parent-child relationship, and the adolescent adoptees' psychological adjustment. The findings show that a positive parent-child relationship in which parents support their children's ethnic identity development is the key to the children's successful social and personal identity development.

The sixth article, by Yu-Wen Ying, Peter Allen Lee, Jeanne L. Tsai, Yu J. Lee, and Malisa Tsang, is about the social network composition, social integration, and sense of coherence in a group of 353 Chinese American college students. The authors found that a little more than half of the sample had a Chinese-only network while the remainder had either ethnically and/or racially mixed networks. American-borns and those who had immigrated by age 13 were more likely than late immigrants to have ethnically/racially mixed networks, and those with such networks enjoyed the highest sense of coherence. The findings suggest that more diverse networks offer the reward of increased competence and better person-environment fit.

The seventh article is on the cultural orientation of Hmong young adults. Unlike previous researchers who focused on the cultural adjustment of refugees, the author, Jeanne L. Tsai, focuses on the cultural adjustment of the refugees' children, who have been raised primarily in the United States. Specifically, the study examines the differences between American- and overseas-born Hmong young adults in levels, models, and meanings of cultural orientation. Although both groups reported being more oriented to American than to Hmong culture, the groups differed in their underlying models of cultural orientation.

The eighth article, by Pauline Agbayani-Siewert and Alice Yick Flanagan, examines gender differences in physical, sexual, and psychological definitions and contextual justifications of and experiences with dating violence among Filipino American graduate students. The findings show significant gender differences in contextual justifications and definitions of psychological abuse. The authors discuss the findings in the context of Filipino American culture and history.

The ninth article, by Shobha Srinivasan, explores differences among young Asian Indian women in the United States, their counterparts in India, and their European American counterparts in their attitude toward gender equality and level of ethnic identity. In addition, the study reports on the predicaments young Asian Indian women experience in their struggle to balance traditional Indian cultural expectations with the desire to be accepted as Americans by majority members of the society. Given that little research has been done on Asian Indians in general, this exploratory study provides an invaluable opportunity to understand some issues faced by young Asian Indian women.

The tenth article, by Jennifer Lee, Annie Lei, and Stanley Sue, reports the current state of mental health research on Asian Americans. Based on a comprehensive review of existing research, the authors report that, although the prevalence rate of anxiety disorder has been equivocal, those of depression, somatization, and posttraumatic stress disorder among Asian Americans are at least as high as those for white Americans. These findings indicate that Asian Americans are not particularly well adjusted, in contrast to their stereotypical image as a model minority group. In addition, the authors point out methodological and conceptual problems that hindered researchers in determining the rates and distribution of mental disorders among Asian Americans. Suggestions for research directions are provided.

The eleventh article, by Kyoung Ja Hyun, examines the effect of interdependent (representing traditional Asian cultural values) and independent (representing the European American cultural norm) self-construals on Korean immigrants' psychological well-being, measured by depressive symptomology and life satisfaction. The findings show that those with a highly independent self-construal expressed significantly fewer depressive symptoms and significantly higher life satisfaction than those with a less independent self-construal. However, it was also found that an interdependent view of self did not hinder their psychological well-being. The author discusses the need for future research focusing on the potential benefits of both types of self-construal for Asian immigrants.

The twelfth article, by Mieko Yoshihama, is based on a population-based study of the prevalence of domestic violence and other types of interpersonal victimization among Japanese American women. The study reports a high prevalence of domestic violence as well as other types of victimization perpetrated by nonintimates. The findings also show a significant relationship between the immigration status and the proportion of respondents who experienced partners' emotional violence as well as the proportion who witnessed their fathers' domestic violence against their mothers. The author discusses the need for assessing the history of domestic violence and other types of interpersonal victimization when working with Japanese American women.

The thirteenth article, by Dung Ngo, Thanh V. Tran, Judith L. Gibbons, and Joan M. Oliver, investigates the role of acculturation as a potential mediator (mediating the negative impact) or moderator (buffering the impact) for premigration traumatic experiences (PTE) and depression among 261 Vietnamese Americans aged 25 and older. The findings show support for the moderator effect of acculturation but not for its mediator effect. It was found that PTE had a much stronger effect on depression among those with lower levels of acculturation than those with higher levels.

The fourteenth article, by Edwina S. Uehara, Paula T. Morelli, and Jennifer Abe-Kim, reports on the conflicts between western medical perspectives and Cambodian Killing Fields survivors' perspectives on somatic complaints. Illness narratives from two Cambodian women, intertwined with their experiences at the Killing Fields and their postimmigration adjustment problems in the United States, powerfully convey the women's resistance to and frustration at the psychopathological framing of their *authentic embodied pain* by health care professionals. The article make us think about the role of care systems in understanding and respecting survivors' perspectives and alleviating their suffering.

The fifteenth article, by Paula T. Morelli, Rowena Fong, and Julie Oliveira, is based on an analysis of in-depth interviews with 21 Hawaiian and other Asian-American women who participated in a culturally-based, women-centered substance-abuse treatment program in Hawaii. The analysis reveals factors that the women participants found vital to their treatment process: having their children with them in a nonpunitive, mutually respectful treatment milieu; working with consistent, competent residential staff and culturally sensitive interdisciplinary professionals; and involvement in a range of substance-abuse interventions, including cultural healing practices. The article underscores the importance of culturally competent interventions and practice models when working with Asian/Pacific Islander women.

The sixteenth article, by Ada C. Mui, examines the effects of life stresses and social support on depressive symptoms among 67 older Korean immigrants, who were recruited at senior centers and meal sites. The findings of the study, in confirmation of previous studies, show that the Korean elders admitted to depressive symptoms at a rate much higher than that found in other ethnic elders. The factors significantly associated with the Korean elders' depressive symptoms included poor health, stressful life events, dissatisfaction with help received from family members, and few good friends. The author states that the impact of these factors on the Korean elders' quality of life can be understood in the context of their immigration experience and Korean cultural values.

The seventeenth and final article, which I authored, provides an overview of the internal cultural and socioeconomic heterogeneity within the Asian-American elderly population and identifies those who experience multiple stressors affecting their quality of life. Then its discusses barriers to formal service utilization as well as strengths and deficits of informal support systems. To better serve Asian-American elders with their multiple needs for health, mental health, and social services, I stress the importance of increased funding for research on the group, diversification of social services programs in coethnic communities, and increased cultural competence in mainstream social service agencies.

Namkee G. Choi

Asian Americans
in the Twentieth Century

Harry H. Kitano
Susan Nakaoka

SUMMARY. At the close of the century, Asian/Pacific Islander Americans comprise a rapidly growing and diverse population in the United States. This population consists of ethnic groups that have been here for up to five generations, as well as recent immigrants and refugees. The Chinese and Japanese were the two groups that were identified by the United States census just before the beginning of the 20th century; by the end of the 1900s, Asian Indians, Filipinos, Koreans, Vietnamese, and Pacific Islander groups were added. It is a population that has many internal differences, with some groups faring relatively well, achieving income, educational and occupational gains, while other groups are far from achieving them. The purpose of this article is to look at the Asian Americans at the beginning of the 1900s and to assess the changes in their demographic and socioeconomic status by the end of the century. The descriptive data in this article provide a background for understanding the Asian American experience in the 20th century. *[Article copies available for a fee from The Haworth Document Delivery Service: 1-800-342-9678. E-mail address: getinfo@haworthpressinc.com <Website: http://www. HaworthPress.com> © 2001 by The Haworth Press, Inc. All rights reserved.]*

KEYWORDS. Asian Americans, population growth, sociodemographics

Where were Asian Americans in 1900 and where are they now? This article starts with a brief history of Asian immigration in the 19th century

---

Harry H. Kitano, PhD, and Susan Nakaoka, MA, MSW, are affiliated with the Social Welfare Department, School of Public Policy and Social Research, University of California, Los Angeles (E-mail: hkitano@ucla.edu).

[Haworth co-indexing entry note]: "Asian Americans in the Twentieth Century." Kitano, Harry H, and Susan Nakaoka. Co-published simultaneously in *Journal of Human Behavior in the Social Environment* (The Haworth Press, Inc.) Vol. 3, No. 3/4, 2001, pp. 7-17; and: *Psychosocial Aspects of the Asian-American Experience: Diversity Within Diversity* (ed: Namkee G. Choi) The Haworth Press, Inc., 2001, pp. 7-17. Single or multiple copies of this article are available for a fee from The Haworth Document Delivery Service [1-800-342-9678, 9:00 a.m. - 5:00 p.m. (EST). E-mail address: getinfo@haworthpressinc.com].

and provides an overview of the growth of the Asian American population between 1900 and the present time. In addition to the demographic changes, descriptive information on selected socioeconomic variables is provided as a background for understanding the history of Asians in this country and the progress they have made in the 20th century. The data are drawn primarily from the United States census.

As shown in Table 1, the Asian American categories in the United States census have been expanded to include different ethnic groups as persons belonging to the various ethnic groups become more numerous. The Chinese were formally included in the census in 1870, and the Japanese were included in 1890. In the 1990 U.S. census, the Asian/Pacific Islander (A/PI) groups included at least 26 different ethnic categories, including Chinese, Filipino, Japanese, Asian Indian, Korean, Vietnamese, Hawaiian, Guamanian, Samoan, and other A/PI. In this article, the focus will be on the largest Asian ethnic groups: Chinese, Filipinos, Japanese, Asian Indians, Koreans, and Vietnamese, although the other A/PI ethnic groups are included when necessary.

ASIAN AMERICANS IN THE NINETEENTH CENTURY

Although there were some isolated cases of Chinese, Japanese, and Filipinos entering North America at earlier times, the initial significant Asian

TABLE 1. The United States Census: Asian/Pacific Islander Categories, 1790-1990

Censal Year	Asian/Pacific Islander Category
1790	First Census includes whites, slaves, other.
1870	Chinese category added.
1890	Japanese category added.
1950	Filipino category added.
	Other Race (specify) _____. Added.
1960	Hawaiian category added.
	Part Hawaiian category added.
1970	Hawaiian and Part Hawaiian categories combined.
	Korean added.
1980	Vietnamese added.
	Asian Indian added.
	Guamanian added.
	Samoan added.
1990	Other A/PI (specify) _____. Added.

Source: Gall & Gall (1993: Original Source: Interview with Fred Bohme, U.S. Bureau of the Census. History Division, March, 9 1993)

immigration occurred about the time of the discovery of gold in California in 1849, with an influx of Chinese immigrant laborers. By 1860, there were more than 34,000 Chinese in North America, and by 1890, the number had grown to over 107,000 (see Table 2). Occupations of these early Chinese immigrants included gold mining, agriculture, and the building of the western leg of the first transcontinental railroad. They were primarily adult males and were viewed as sojourners with the goal of working, accumulating savings, and then returning to their homeland for a better life (Siu, 1987; Yang, 1999). Kitano and Daniels (1995) indicate that this orientation was common among all immigrants of the time; many European immigrants also showed a high rate of return migration to their native countries.

As their numbers grew, these immigrants soon became targets of harassment and racially motivated attacks. This hostility led to the Chinese Exclusion Act of 1882, which barred the immigration of Chinese laborers for ten years and was made permanent with additional legislation in 1902. At the time of the Act, there were some 125,000 Chinese in the U.S., but, due to the effect of the legislation, their numbers decreased to 89,000 in 1900 (Kitano & Daniels, 1995). The Chinese in the 19th century were primarily a male population; there were 27 males for every female. (This imbalance went down steadily so that by 1940 there were 2.9 males for every female.)

Significant Japanese migration began in the 1890s, and by 1900 the U.S. census counted over 85,000 Japanese. In some ways, the Japanese immigrants were parallel to the Chinese: they were predominantly males who worked at difficult, low paying jobs; they faced racism; and they were relegated to the bottom of the society (Glenn, 1986). But there was one major difference: China was viewed as a declining national power, and her desire to protect her immigrants was ignored while Japan had begun the transition to a modernized society, and there was a growing respect for the strong, armed nation. As a result, Japan initially received some latitude in the restrictive

TABLE 2. Chinese and Japanese Population by Sex, 1860-1900

Year	Chinese		Japanese	
	Males	Females	Males	Females
1860	33,149	1,784	–	–
1870	58,633	4,566	47	8
1880	100,686	4,779	134	14
1890	103,620	3,868	1,780	259
1900	85,341	4,522	23,341	985

Source: U.S. Bureau of the Census (1973a).

policies, allowing for the significant immigration of Japanese women in the 1910s and the 1920s (Kitano & Daniels, 1995).

In summary, the Asians in the United States in the 19th century had to face multiple barriers. Asians were often viewed as an "inferior race," and discrimination was present on every front. They were not allowed to become citizens and were relegated to the bottom of the political, economic and social structure. Their numbers were small, and their educational level was low; most could not communicate in English, and, thus, were unfamiliar with the norms and values of the host society. Because the number of female immigrants was so small, the predominantly male Asian immigrants had little hope of creating families and building communities (Chan, 1991).

ASIAN AMERICAN POPULATION GROWTH IN THE TWENTIETH CENTURY

Data in Table 3 show the total Asian population and the largest Asian ethnic groups of the United States by decade, from 1900 to 1990. In 1900, the Chinese were the most numerous, followed by the Japanese. But the Chinese population, as reported in the census, decreased between 1900 and 1920

TABLE 3. Population of the United States by Asian Ethnicity, 1900-1990

Year	Total, U.S.	Total Asian[b]	Chinese	Filipino[a]	Asian Indian	Japanese	Korean	Vietnamese
1900	76,212,168	204,462	118,746	–		85,716	–	–
1910	92,228,531	249,926	94,414	2,767	–	152,745	5,008	–
1920	106,021,568	332,432	85,202	26,634	–	220,596	6,181	–
1930	123,202,660	489,326	102,159	108,424	–	278,743	8,332	–
1940	132,165,129	489,984	106,334	98,535	–	285,115	8,568	–
1950	151,325,798	599,091	150,005	122,707	–	326,379	7,030[c]	–
1960	179,323,175	877,934	237,292	176,310	–	464,332	–	–
1970	203,211,926	1,429,562	436,062	343,060	–	591,290	69,150[d]	245,025
1980	226,545,805	3,446,421	812,178	781,894	387,223	716,331	357,393	245,025
1990	248,709,873	7,273,662	1,645,472	1,406,770	815,447	847,562	798,849	614,547

Note: A dash(–) refers to the absence of data for the ethnic group category in that census year.
[a]Included with "other race" for the United States in 1900 and for Alaska in 1920 and 1950.
[b]The 1980 and 1990 numbers include other A/PI groups not listed in the table, such as Cambodian, Hmong, Laotian, Thai, Hawaiian, Guamanians, Samoans, and other A/PI.
[c]Data for Hawaii only.
[d]Excludes Koreans in Alaska.

Source: Gall & Gall (1993); U.S. Bureau of the Census (1963, 1973a, 1973b, 1981, 1993a, 1993b, 1995).

when it numbered only 85,202, as the 1882 exclusion law affected the numbers of Chinese immigrants. In contrast, the Japanese population showed growth, from 85,716 in 1900 to over 220,596 in 1920. There were also 26,634 Filipinos recorded in 1920.

Since the Chinese Exclusion Act was in place, and with the number of Japanese growing and making significant strides in agriculture, attempts to limit Japanese immigration became a high priority in the early 1900s. The attitude of the Asiatic Exclusion League is illustrated in a copy of their proceedings in 1910–that Japanese could not be assimilated; that they lowered the standard of living, and that public policy should deny them marriage to white women (Daniels, 1962). The Gentlemen's Agreement signed in 1907 stopped the migration of Japanese laborers, and President Calvin Coolidge signed the 1924 National Origins Act, which virtually banned the immigration of all Asians to the United States.

The decade from 1930 to 1940 showed a slow increase in the number of Chinese (102,159 to 106,334) and Japanese (278,743 to 285,115). The significant migration of Japanese women by 1930 led to the birth of native-born children, the Nisei, and the development of a wide range of community structures in their new country. However, Strong (1934), in his book entitled, *The Second Generation Japanese American Problem*, wrote that although American born and American educated, the Nisei faced racism and discrimination as major barriers to their political, economic, and social progress.

World War II had a drastic effect on the status of Asian Americans. The Japanese were removed from the West Coast and placed in concentration camps (1942-1945). California and the coast of Oregon and Washington had no "free" Japanese, whether citizens or aliens. There was a leave policy that allowed government clearance for select groups of individuals to be released to the Midwest and East, and presently, there remain pockets of Japanese Americans in cities such as New York, Chicago, and Minneapolis. However, the majority returned to the West Coast after the end of World War II (Maki, Kitano & Berthold, 1999).

Other Asian groups fared better during wartime. Since China and the Phillipines were U.S. allies, Chinese exclusion was repealed in 1943, and, in 1946, Congress made Filipinos eligible for naturalization and added a token immigration quota of 100 (Kitano & Daniels, 1995). Chan (1991) discusses additional positive changes for these groups during the period: "The images held by the general public of these groups improved, some of their members finally managed to get jobs in the technical professions and skilled trades and sizable numbers of Chinese and Filipinos joined and served in the armed forces." The passage of the 1947 amendment to the 1945 War Brides Act, which allowed veterans to bring war brides into the country, also marked an important legislation concerning immigration. This act led to the migration of non-quota Asian women (Glenn, 1986; Hing, 1993).

From 1950 on, there were several significant policy changes that affected Asian Americans. The McCarran-Walter Act of 1952 granted naturalization to Japanese, and Japanese nationals were given an immigration quota of 100 (Hing, 1993). Hawaii became the fiftieth state in 1959, allowing the presence of individuals of Asian American ancestry in the halls of Congress. The 1965 Immigration Law abolished "national origins" as a basis for immigration quotas so that Asian immigrants were theoretically equal to Western Europeans. The Vietnam War and the Refugee Act of 1980 created a large influx of Southeast Asians, which is reflected in the censuses from 1970 through 1998.

The increased immigration from Asia since 1965 has created a different migration pattern from that of the beginning of the century. Changes in legislation and varying push and pull factors have created a very diverse population in the latter half of the century. In 1900, Asian immigrants consisted of Chinese and Japanese and were 1.5% of the total foreign-born U. S. population. In 1990, A/PIs consisted of over 26 different ethnic groups, and made up 25.2% of the total foreign-born U.S. population. Table 4 shows the percent of each Asian ethnic group's population in 1990 that was foreign-born. The population of all Asian groups, with the exception of the Japanese, was overwhelmingly foreign-born. Sharp increases in foreign-born Asians after the 1960 census reflect the post-1965 immigration wave.

According to the Current Population Survey, in 1997, 55% of A/PIs lived in the West and 95% in metro areas. California had the largest number (3.8 million), followed by New York (952,736), Hawaii (748,748), Texas (523,972), and New Jersey (423,738). The A/PI population is young, with an estimated median age in 1998 of 31.2 years; four years younger than the total population. It had a higher population growth between 1990 and 1998 than any other race/ethnic group, and A/PI children were more likely to live with both

TABLE 4. Percent of Population that Was Foreign Born, 1960-1990

Year	Chinese	Filipino	Asian Indian	Japanese	Korean	Vietnamese
1990	69.3	64.4	75.4	32.4	72.7	79.9
1980	63.3	64.7	70.4	28.4	81.9	90.5
1970	47.1	53.1	–	20.9	–	–
1960	39.5	48.9	–	21.5	–	–

Sources: U.S. Bureau of the Census (1963. Tables 11-13 and 25-27; 1973b, 1981, 1993b).

parents (84%) than were white children (77%) (U.S. Bureau of the Census, 1999).

PROGRESS MADE IN THE TWENTIETH CENTURY

From 1950, the census provides detailed information on select Asian American groups with respect to their level of education, type of occupation, and income, as shown in Tables 5-8. (Inconsistencies in the census–wording, sampling methods, and reporting of the data–limit the data available for previous decades and comparability for certain variables.) These socioeconomic indicators, along with some significant gains in the civil rights movement, show progress made by Asian Americans in the latter half of the 20th century.

Education: Data in Table 5 show median years of schooling attained by Chinese, Japanese, and Filipinos from 1950 to 1980. The dramatic rise in the median years of schooling for Chinese and Filipinos between 1960 and 1970 reflects the different profile of immigrants who arrived after 1965. Data for

TABLE 5. Median Years of Schooling: Persons 25 Years and Older, 1950-1980

Year	Chinese	Filipino	Asian Indian	Japanese	Korean	Vietnamese
1980	13.7m/12.8f	12.9m/13.4f	16.9m/13.0f	13.2m/12.7f	14.4m/12.5f	12.4m/12.0f
1970*	12.4	12.2	–	12.5	–	–
1960**	10.7m/11.7f	8.3m/11.1f	–	12.2m/12.1f	–	–
1950	8.4m/10.3f	6.7m/9.0f	–	12.2m/12.3f	–	–

Note: m = male, f = female.
*Source: U.S. Bureau of the Census (1973b: Data based on gender not available: 1981).
** Persons aged 14 years and over.

TABLE 6. Median Family Income, 1970-1990 (in current $)

Year	Chinese	Filipino	Asian Indian	Japanese	Korean	Vietnamese	All U.S. Families
1990	41,316	46,698	49,309	51,550	33,909	35,550	35,225
1980	22,559	23,687	24,993	27,354	20,459	12,840	19,917
1970	10,610	9,318	–	12,515	–	–	9,586

Sources: U.S. Bureau of the Census (1973b, 1981, 1993b).

TABLE 7. Percent of Families in Poverty, 1960-1990

Year	Chinese	Filipino	Asian Indian	Japanese	Korean	Vietnamese
1990	14.0	6.4	9.7	7.0	13.7	25.7
1980	10.5	6.2	7.4	4.2	13.1	35.1
1970	10.3	11.5	–	6.4	–	–

Sources: U.S. Bureau of the Census (1973b, 1981, 1993b, 1995).

Asian Indians and Koreans are available for 1980 only, and they also indicate that more educated immigrants entered the country after 1965. The gradual improvement among the Japanese, with fewer recent immigrants, reflects the progress of the second and third generation population. However, it should be noted that significant differences among ethnic groups exist. For example, according to the 1990 data, the more recent Asian immigrant groups and Pacific Islanders were not faring as well. The percentage of those who had a high school or higher education varied from 31% for Hmongs to 88% for Japanese. Among Pacific Islanders, the proportion with at least a high school diploma ranged from 64% for Tongans to 80% for Hawaiians (U.S. Bureau of the Census, 1995).

Educational achievement among Asian Americans continued to improve in the mid-1990s. According to the Census Bureau's Statistical Brief of 1994, 85% of A/PI's had a high school diploma, in comparison to 81% of the total population. Forty one percent of A/PIs had a bachelor's degree, compared to only 25% of the total U.S. population. In 1997, one out of every two A/PI adults aged 25 to 29 years were college graduates, compared to one in three whites, one in seven African Americans, and one in ten Hispanics (U.S. Bureau of the Census, 1999).

Occupation: Changing patterns in types of occupation and employment were difficult to measure over time because of the changing categories used by the Census Bureau. Hing (1993) reports that before 1950 Chinese, Japanese, Asian Indians, and Filipinos were primarily employed in rural, farmworker, or service jobs. Indeed, Japanese, and Filipinos have a long history of work in agriculture, and images of Chinese, Japanese and Filipino "houseboys" and domestics (females) were commonplace in the early 1900s. However, the 1965 amendments to the immigration law and gains made by nativeborn Asian Americans brought forth a significant increase in the proportion of professionals in most Asian groups. Figures from the 1990 census show considerable changes from the beginning of the century. Asians were more likely to be in "technical, sales, and administrative support jobs," and "man-

agerial and professional specialty jobs" (33% and 31%, respectively) than
the total population (32% and 26%, respectively). Again, differences between
and within groups are quite pronounced in the occupational distribution.

Income: Data in Table 6 show median family income for the major Asian
American groups in 1970, 1980, and 1990. Comparisons between the total
population and the Asian American groups show that significant progress had
been made for the latter. Again, however, the differences between the more
established groups and the more recently arrived Vietnamese group are worth
noting. The median family income for Japanese was more than double that
for Vietnamese in 1980 and remained much higher in 1990. The proportion
of families with 3 or more workers also distorts the data. In 1990, for
instance, Filipinos and Vietnamese had the highest proportion of families
with three or more workers (30% and 21%, respectively, compared with 13%
of the total U.S. families.)

In 1997, the A/PI's had the highest median household income, $47,249,
for all race groups. However, because the A/PI households on average had
more members than white households (3.17 vs. 2.58 people), the average
income per A/PI household member was lower ($18,569 compared with
$20,093) than that for white household members (U.S. Bureau of the Census,
1999).

The difference among ethnic groups in income status is the most pronounced in the poverty rates. As shown in Table 7, in 1990, 11% of all Asian
and Pacific Islander families lived in poverty, higher than the 8% for white
families (U.S. Bureau of the Census, 1995). The poverty rates for Chinese at
14%, Koreans at 14%, and Vietnamese at 26% were well above the rate for
White families, and indicate significant between-group differences. Other
refugee and Pacific Islander groups are faring even worse. Cambodians,
Laotians, and Samoans in Los Angeles County, for example, had higher
poverty rates (in 1990) of 46%, 40%, and 27%, respectively (United Way of
Greater Los Angeles, 1996).

Civil rights: Significant progress has been made in the civil rights movement, beginning in the 1960s. The election of Daniel Inouye to the U.S.
Senate in 1962 also marked the event that gave Asian Americans access to
Congress. One impressive positive indication of progress during this time,
however, was the passage of the Civil Liberties Act of 1988, which granted a
payment of $20,000 and an apology to surviving Japanese Americans (and
surviving relatives of the deceased) of the WWII era for their incarceration
during the war (Maki et al., 1999). The passage of the bill was significant not
only because of the government's admission of wrongdoing, but also because
of community solidarity created throughout the Redress Movement. Nevertheless, discrimination and injustice against Asian Americans has continued
in the latter half of the century. For example, in June 1982, Vincent Chin, a

Chinese American, was clubbed to death by two White Americans, and the murderers had to pay a fine of $3,000 without serving jail time, implying that a license to kill Asians cost only $3,000.

SUMMARY AND CONCLUSION

The pessimism that was a part of the Asian American experience at the end of the 1800s carried over to the early part of the 1900s. Exclusion was the reality, and the 1924 Immigration Act ceased all Asian immigration. World War II saw the forced removal of 120,000 Japanese Americans into concentration camps, but, ironically, also saw the beginning of change in the U.S. immigration laws. Immigration and naturalization became a part of the Asian American experience so that by the 1960s there was the inclusion, rather than the deliberate exclusion of Asian immigrants in American society.

The census itself had changed so that from the latter part of this century, more detailed statistics became available to chart changes among Asian Americans in American society. By the time of the 1970 census, demographic data on Asian Indians, Chinese, Filipino, Japanese, Koreans, and Hawaiians were available. It was also a reminder that the groups making up the Asian American category are not homogeneous, although, because of their relatively small numbers, Asian Americans are still lumped together for statistical and political purposes.

Socioeconomic indicators for Asian Americans in the latter half of the twentieth century show that certain segments of some ethnic groups have made considerable strides, while the other groups still face an uphill battle. We must also remember that even those who are on the "upper" ends of the socioeconomic scale still face issues such as the "glass ceiling," underemployment, unequal returns on their education, blatant discrimination, and hate crimes. But in general, the 20th century has seen progress for Asian Americans, and they have reason to look forward to the 20th century with optimism.

REFERENCES

Chan, S. (1991). *Asian Americans*. Boston: Twayne

Gall, S. B. & Gall, T. L. (1993). *Statistical record of Asian Americans*. Detroit: Gale Research Inc.

Glenn, E. N. (1986). *Issei, nisei, war bride*. Philadelphia: Temple University Press.

Daniels, R. (1962). *The politics of prejudice*. Berkeley, CA: University of California Press.

Kitano, H. & Daniels, R. (1995). *Asian Americans*. Englewood Cliffs, NJ: Prentice Hall.

Maki, M., Kitano, H., & Berthold, M. (1999). *Achieving the impossible dream: How Japanese Americans obtained redress.* Urbana, IL: The University of Illinois Press.

Hing, B.O. (1993). *Making and remaking Asian America through immigration policy, 1850-1990.* Stanford, CA: Stanford University Press.

Siu, P. (1987). *The Chinese laundryman: A study of social isolation.* New York: New York University Press.

Strong, E. (1934). *The second generation Japanese American problem.* Stanford: Stanford University Press. U.S. Bureau of the Census. (1963). *1960 Census of the population: Subject reports: Nonwhite population by race.* PC(2)-1C. Washington, DC: Government Printing Office.

U.S. Bureau of the Census (1973a). *1970 Census of the population: Population by sex and race, 1790-1970.* Series A 91-104. Washington, DC: Government Printing Office.

U.S. Bureau of the Census (1973b). *1970 Census of the population: Subject reports: Japanese, Chinese, and Filipinos in the United States.* Washington, DC: Government Printing Office.

U.S. Bureau of the Census (1981). *1980 Census of the population: The United States summary.* PC80-S1-3. Part 1, Volume 1, Chapter C. Washington, DC: Government Printing Office.

U.S. Bureau of the Census (1993a). *We the American Asians.* Washington, DC: Government Printing Office.

U.S. Bureau of the Census (1993b) *1990 Census of the population: Asians and Pacific Islanders in the United States.* CP-3-5. Washington, DC: Government Printing Office.

U.S. Bureau of the Census (1995). *Statistical brief: The Nation's Asian and Pacific Islander population, 1994.* SB/95-24. Washington, DC: Government Printing Office.

U.S. Bureau of the Census (1999). *Current population survey: Statistical abstract of the United States, 1998.* Washington, DC: Government Printing Office.

United Way of Greater Los Angeles. 1996. *Asian Pacific profiles: Los Angeles County.*

Yang, P. Q. (1999, February). Sojourners or settlers: Post-1965 Chinese immigrants. *Journal of Asian American Studies, 2,* 61-91.

Adoptive Parents and Identity Development for Chinese Children

Rowena Fong
Anne Wang

SUMMARY. In 1991, the People's Republic of China passed an Adoption Law that legalized the adoption of abandoned female infants. The majority of adopted parents were from the United States, which caused a major impact on parental childrearing practices. The lack of birth information forced these adoptive parents to prepare for questions concerning the shaping of identity development and formation. Research has documented the Chinese policy changes, parents' initial adjustment to bonding, and problems with special needs. But little attention has been paid thus far to identity development. This qualitative study examines the anticipated concerns and projected strategies in addressing the lack of birth information and identity development. The study found parents focusing on creating a birth heritage, instilling pride in Chinese culture, nurturing American backgrounds, addressing the orphan identity, and coping with special needs. Practice implications for theory building, practice innovations, and new research developments are discussed. *[Article copies available for a fee from The Haworth Document Delivery Service: 1-800-342-9678. E-mail address: <getinfo@haworthpressinc.com> Website: <http://www.HaworthPress. com> © 2001 by The Haworth Press, Inc. All rights reserved.]*

KEYWORDS. Chinese, children, adoptions, special needs, orphans

---

Rowena Fong is affiliated with the University of Hawaii at Manoa, School of Social Work, Honolulu, HI 96822 (E-mail: rowena@hawaii.edu).

Anne Wang is affiliated with the University of Hawaii at Manoa, Anthropology Department, Honolulu, HI 96822.

[Haworth co-indexing entry note]: "Adoptive Parents and Identity Development for Chinese Children." Fong, Rowena, and Anne Wang. Co-published simultaneously in *Journal of Human Behavior in the Social Environment* (The Haworth Press, Inc.) Vol. 3, No. 3/4, 2001, pp. 19-33; and: *Psychosocial Aspects of the Asian-American Experience: Diversity Within Diversity* (ed: Namkee G. Choi) The Haworth Press, Inc., 2001, pp. 19-33. Single or multiple copies of this article are available for a fee from The Haworth Document Delivery Service [1-800-342-9678, 9:00 a.m. - 5:00 p.m. (EST). E-mail address: getinfo@haworthpressinc.com].

INTRODUCTION

In 1991, the People's Republic of China passed an Adoption Law and since then major efforts have been made to facilitate foreign adoptions of mostly female infants. As a result, in 1996, China was the most popular country for adoptions. Statistics in 1997 indicate that infants from China were granted (56% of the world's total immigrant visas issued to orphans coming to the United States (Fong, 2000; *International Adoption and Child Abduction*, 1997; Yontz, 1997). Chinese infants continue to be abandoned primarily in front of orphanages located throughout China for multiple reasons: deceased parents, unusual family financial hardship, incapacity to care for special needs infants, and gender-biased political imperatives (Johnson, 1993; Johnson, 1996; Johnson, Huang, & Wang, 1998; Mosher, 1993; Riley, 1997).

The lack of birth knowledge, as a result of abandonment, has reportedly caused problems for adoptees when adulthood arrives. Historically, the adoptees' search for identity and assertion of birthrights forewarned that the inaccessibility to parents' genetic history could cause harm to adoptees and their children (Bender & Leone, 1995; McColm, 1993; Strauss, 1994). Driven by the need to know critical health information, adult adopted persons have succeeded in obtaining open adoption practices in many states but they may not have legal access to their original birth certificates. Recently, a county circuit court in the state of Oregon upheld Measure 58 that ruled in favor of *Doe vs. State*, restoring the right of adult adopted citizens to obtain their birth certificates. However, the availability of birth information is not an option in the Chinese adoptees' situation, mainly because it continues to be unlawful for these birth parents to give up their infant daughters. To try to have a second child without governmental permission violates the restrictions of China's 1979 single child policy (Croll, Davin, & Kane, 1985; Fong, 1990).

Missing birth information is a concern to adopted persons, foster care parents, adoptive parents, social workers, and other professionals, especially when the adoptee begins his or her search for identity. Although tense situations frequently exist between adoptive parents and birth parents, adoptees need to have birth information in order to facilitate the search for self or group identity (Grotevant, 1997; Grove, 1996; Liptak, 1993; Marcia, 1991; McRoy, Grotevant, & White, 1998; Phinney & Chavira, 1992). Grotevant (1997) concluded from his research: "In coming to terms with themselves as adults, individuals need to know who they are as adopted persons" (p. 12). He asserts, "Searching is an attempt to heal the sense of separation and loss brought through disconnection from one's family of birth" (p. 11). The lack of birth contact or information may result in low self-esteem, depression, or dysfunctional behaviors in the cases of some adoptees (Bender & Leone,

1995; McColm, 1993; Strauss, 1994). But, ultimately, the question of birth origin must be addressed and resolved in a manner suitable to the individual adoptee.

These potential problems of the adopted persons' identity search will surely exist for current Chinese-born adoptees. Although the adopted persons are only infants or preschoolers at the time of adoption, adoptive parents are cognizant of the fact that access to Chinese birth information is not possible (Cecere, 1998; Klatzkin, 1999). Yet, very little is known about how parents have been planning to cope with that impending problem. This study was designed to explore how parents of adopted Chinese girls have been shaping the identity of their adopted daughters and what measures they have been taking or planning to take to address the issue of lack of birth information and its impact on identity development. A brief review of China's single child policy and adoption law will be given to contextualize the current adoption situation in China. The description of the research study and its implications for social work practice follows.

BACKGROUND:
CHINA'S SINGLE CHILD POLICY
AND ADOPTION LAW

In 1979, the People's Republic of China enacted the controversial single child policy restricting families to having one child with the primary intent of controlling population. In order to avoid predicted disasters of food shortage and other natural resources, China needed to maintain its total population at a billion people through the end of the twentieth century (*China Daily*, 1986; Croll, 1985; Li, 1987; Mu, 1986). However, in the ensuing 20 years, the fate of female infants has been problematic, if not fatalistic. Although there were exceptions to the single child policy, in keeping with the Chinese tradition of producing a male heir, Chinese couples would birth their one allotted child but would find ways not to keep the baby if she were female. Human rights watchers focused on maltreatment practices, and, in the 1980s, reports of forced abortions alarmed political activists, scholars, and many professionals. This pressured the Chinese officials to instigate penalties for those couples who aborted innocent fetuses (*The Economist*, 1983; Greenhalgh & Bogaarts, 1987). Reports of forced abortions, or female infanticide practices, decreased as reports of orphaned female infants increased. Soon, abandoned infants were filling the orphanages in China at an alarming rate. Reports of mortality rates in orphanages ranged from 59.2% to 72.5% in certain provinces of China (Human Rights Watch, 1996). Even China's well run orphanages in Shanghai had estimated mortality rates as high as 90% in the late 1980s and early 1990s (Human Rights Watch, 1996).

Initial reports of the maltreatment practices toward these mostly girl babies in orphanages included physical and medical neglect, starvation, and lack of stimulation for special needs infants. The overcrowded conditions in Chinese orphanages caught national worldwide attention and put pressure on China to change its human rights policies (Johnson, 1993; Johnson, 1996; Johnson, Huang, & Wang, 1998; Riley, 1997). As a result, the 1991 Adoption Law of China presented itself as a humane way of allowing abandoned female infants to be lawfully adopted by parents, single or married. Between 1982-1992, China approved 13,630 foreign adoptions (Cecere, 1998). Of that number, American parents adopted approximately 1,188 children. Since 1992, close to 14,500 children have been adopted in the U.S. (Cecere, 1998).

METHOD

The research study was conducted in 1998-1999 on a purposive sample of ten parents of adopted Chinese girls: a Caucasian single parent mother; two Caucasian couples; three Japanese parents; and a mixed Caucasian and Japanese couple whose adopted daughter had severe special needs. Four of the mothers were Caucasian; two were Japanese. Two of the fathers were Caucasian, and the other two were Japanese. The families were primarily located in Hawaii, with the exception of one couple from the East Coast. Parents' ages ranged from 37 to 66 years old. Most of the parents adopted their first child from China, with the exception of the 65-year-old father who already had an adult son and the mixed couple who already had a preschooler adopted from Korea. The Japanese couple was adopting their second child from China. The Chinese female infants in the study when adopted ranged in age from 18 months to four years old. Three infants had experienced foster care in China, while all six had been abandoned to orphanages.

Since the volunteer parents were recruited through university and church contacts to conduct an exploratory pilot study, limitations to the study are acknowledged because of sampling size and selection. However, discussions and findings of this pilot study are intended to be used to replicate longitudinal research studies on the identity formation of Korean adoptees conducted on larger random samples in Hawaii and on the Mainland (Bergquist & Kim, 1999; Kim, 1976; Kim, 1978).

Using a semi-structured interview guide, the interviewer focused on the adoptive parents' intended ways of developing their daughters' identities and the parents' projected plans to address the lack of birth information. The parents were interviewed mostly in their homes in taped sessions that lasted two to four hours. The interview data were transcribed and cross-checked in follow-up conversations with the participants themselves.

The data gathered through the semi-structured interviews allowed for depth in the analysis of anecdotal responses and inductive discovery but forfeited generalizability. The parents' narratives were analyzed using grounded theory, coding in data analysis with five major conceptual categories emerging from the data. Interviews' were also conducted with social service providers in Hawaii, who worked primarily in the area of adoptions. To check for reliability and validity, data from the social service provider interviews and additional information from other adoptive parents' reports in the written literature (Klatzin, 1999; Tessler, 1999; Youtz, 1997) were used to triangulate the findings of the narratives shared by the adoptive parents in this study.

FINDINGS

The adoptive parents reported their intentions of developing their adopted daughters' identities in the following ways: (1) create a birth heritage; (2) instill pride in the child's Chinese identity; (3) integrate the adoptive parents' background; (4) explain the abandonment; and (5) cope with medical and physical special needs.

Creating Birth Heritage

Parents wanted to create birth heritages for their daughters not only to celebrate diversity but also to facilitate an early exposure to ancestral heritage. To fill the void of birth information, some parents sought to prepare their infants about their Chinese cultural background, so that later possible trauma could be minimized. A Japanese father reported that "the more she understands about her Chinese culture the more she's gonna be able to identify with that . . . I always say remember who you are and where you came from" (F1). Parents want to make sure that the adopted daughters will have coping tools and resources. A Japanese mother mused: "We would have to provide her with resources but we are not of Chinese descent . . . the parents' role is to provide her with resources and allow the child to flourish . . . " (M1).

By promoting and creating cultural heritages, some parents wanted not only to preserve the Chinese infants' cultural heritage but also to be sensitive to other issues. This concern was the need to achieve balance. Some adoptive parents did not want to overdo the Chinese input for fear the infant would become too sensitive and feel different. A Caucasian father shared, "We try to ensure that feeling Chinese is a positive thing but we want to downplay its importance in relation to her being our daughter" (F2). Other parents disputed the need for balance and wanted their daughters to be in touch with their Chinese heritage and to integrate daily the language, customs, and history into their lives and routines. A Japanese father married to a Caucasian wife explained:

> Usually when we identify stuff, we'll see stuff and point out saying, "that's Chinese, that's Korean. They do this in China." A lot of the

education is pretty matter of fact. It's like we are structuring stuff or whatever. (F3)

Parents may support this integrative approach in creating a birth heritage but admit it is the daughters' choice and their own ethnic background may limit them. A Caucasian mother conceded:

> I can't make her Chinese. I don't know how. I am not Chinese. I don't want people to think that Chinese language and dance is it. I don't want people to feel like I was trivializing the culture . . . we want to be respectful of the depth and richness of that culture. (M3)

Parents were supportive and offered their adopted daughters language classes and Chinese activities that reflected customs and norms but they didn't pretend to be Chinese. As one Caucasian parent confessed, "I wouldn't know how to facilitate her immersion . . . but however far she wants to go with that, we'll support her" (M4). Parental support was available to help the daughters create a birth heritage but with limitations and hesitations.

Instilling Pride in Chinese Identity

Parents wanted their daughters to have a source of pride in their Chinese identity and recognized the need for cultural support to accomplish this in some family situations. Many of the adoptive parents, both Caucasian and Japanese, defined their adopted daughters' ethnic identities as racially Chinese but culturally American. A fourth generation Japanese mother analogized, "I think she is a Chinese seed planted in American soil . . . yeah, she was transplanted" (M2). However, because of racial differences between Chinese daughters and non-Chinese parents, the adoptive parents felt an urgent need to foster their daughters' ethnic identity. Some of the interviewed parents concluded that the racial identity of being Chinese American played a significant part of their daughters' permanent identity. A Caucasian, single mother wanted her daughter "to feel great about herself . . . have pride in whom she is as a human being, as a woman, as a Chinese woman, as a person. I want her to realize her absolute magnificence and part of that is being Chinese" (M5).

Aware of race relations in the U.S., several adopted parents acknowledged that because of racial appearance, their adopted daughters would probably be labeled "minority" women and have to contend with Asian stereotypes. A Caucasian mother pondered, "I wonder if she will be challenged with some of the stereotypes of Chinese American kids, like being a "brain" or being good at math or science" (M3). Parents also wondered if their adopted daughters might need assistance in integrating into the non-adoptive Chinese community in the United States. A Caucasian mother with two adopted children surmised, "the children from China, no doubt, will have their own different versions of the Chinese American experience. But they also overlap with the broader segment of the population that is adopted, internationally or in the United States. Again, the experiences have been extremely diverse and may not lend themselves to easy journeys" (M3). Some parents realized that they might have to help their daughters face racism. As one Caucasian parent acknowledged, "those of us who are white parents of Chinese children will have to learn to see the world from a different perspective because our kids will, sooner or later, face racism and they will need our support" (M2). Racism, minority status, stereotypes, and integration into the non-adoptive Chinese community were all issues parents might have to contend with in instilling pride in their daughters' Chinese identity and helping them create their own versions of being adopted Chinese Americans.

Integrating Adoptive Parents Background

Parents wanted to embrace their adopted daughters' Chinese ethnicity and integrate their own cultural and religious backgrounds with the adopted daughters'. But some parents admitted limitations in knowledge about their own customs and norms. The Japanese couple in the study conceded that, being fourth generation, they had minimal knowledge about their heritage and they hardly had any first-hand knowledge about the Chinese culture. The Japanese mother reported, "I am so terrible with my Japanese heritage. I have no heritage. It's just embarrassing. I am fourth generation Japanese so I don't even speak any Japanese . . . You know I feel more Chinese than I do Japanese because I am studying it more. I have been to China but I have never been to Japan" (M1).

A Caucasian parent held the conviction that it was important for her daughter to be proud of her white background:

> We can't make ourselves Chinese and why should we? I'm proud of my parents just as he (the husband) is proud of his. And I'm sure she (the adopted daughter) will be proud of hers. And we'll help her in that venture. But we can't become Chinese because her ancestry was. (M4)

The same Caucasian mother added, "although I have ethnicity as part of my identity, the essential part of my identity is that I am a self-reliant, capable individual and that's how I really want to raise her" (M4).

Other parents felt it was important to acknowledge their religious identity to their children. A mother explained, "I'm very happy we have our Christian beliefs because when we talk about identity . . . we are children of God so it doesn't matter how you came to be because that is our identity . . . I just want her to find her identity in Christ" (M1). Her husband added, "we are Christians and we believe it is important for her (their adopted daughter) to understand that" (F1).

Supporting birth heritage and instilling Chinese identity were compounded by parents' wishes to include their own sources of identity or ethnic backgrounds. Some parents had very strong senses of their ethnic backgrounds; others did not. But most adults agreed that they did not want their infant daughters to be resentful toward China or their birth parents.

Explaining the Abandonment

All parents were aware that as orphans their daughters faced unprecedented challenges. Little birth information was available to them unless notes or mementos were attached to the abandoned infants. At the time of adoption, adoptive parents did have opportunities to ask questions of Chinese officials, but they themselves had scant information about the children's origins. Although most of the female orphans were given Chinese names at birth, many of the adopted parents have changed all or parts of the name after the adoption occurred. This further eliminated any connections to birth.

Parents anticipated difficulties for their daughters and themselves when birth questions would arise. The most dreaded question the adoptive parents feared was why the Chinese mother did not want her baby. Parents' responses to this question varied. One perspective was not to romanticize it but to tell the facts. Parents would attempt to tell their daughters the historical and social circumstances and how the families were limited to one child in China at the time the child was born. One set of parents prepared their response as follows:

> Our intention is to tell the truth about what we know and not romanticize things. If she says stuff like did my mommy love me, we are not going to say yes. That's not really the truth. The truth is we really don't know. We don't know about your mommy. It's a difficult situation. Something has to be done. We plan to tell her the truth appropriate to her age. (F4, M4)

Another parent mentally rehearsed her explanation:

> Well, I think the way I understand it from hearing all those stories about those parents who so-called abandoned their kids. It's more like in China, they put their kid on the side of the road. We believe that although the parent put her on the side of the road, she probably gave her a blanket and checked the weather. She was probably hiding somewhere to make sure someone picked her up. (F1)

Another parent's interpretation is that the adopted daughter was not abandoned because her birth parents did not care about her, but instead they were doing a good thing for her:

> My guess is they (the birth parents) knew she would be found and taken to an orphanage and given to a good family that could provide for her better than they could. And that's the ultimate sacrifice. (M5)

Some parents planned to tell their daughters a lot of "I don't knows." Other parents are trying to rationalize a plausible scenario of abandonment. All adopted parents struggled to present their answers to their abandoned daughters in a manner that minimizes resentment toward China and birth parents.

Coping with Physical and Medical Special Needs

Not all parents who have adopted children from China faced the set of challenges that accompany raising a child with special needs. These parents bore the additional burden of discerning correct medical diagnoses and treatments for their daughters' disabilities and debilitating physical conditions. Without this information, for some families there can be dire consequences. A mother of a special needs infant recalled the shock of their daughter's condition at the time of adoption.

> She was sick, so painfully skinny. She wouldn't eat; wouldn't sleep. I don't think they could have prepared us for that. I went back and read my contract. I know they will have institutional effects. I know there's malnourishment. But until you see it and feel it you don't know what it's like. (M3)

She was distressed because her adopted daughter was gravely ill, and they did not know whether it was due to inadequate institutional care or genetic dysfunctioning. The father recalled that he initially did not attach to or bond with his adopted daughter. His role was more of a custodian rather than adoptive parent. He felt that, because of her special needs, he was coping with life and death survival. He reported: "I think for a time period we felt more like her custodians than her parents . . . We signed on as her parents but it's our obligation to get her healthy" (F3). After that challenging first year, the couple no longer regarded her as an obligation but applauded her resiliency and strength as a survivor of many traumas. Another couple coped with the burdens of their special needs daughter by turning to their religion. They saw their child as being "in God's hands." Their second adopted daughter, who had a serious heart condition, was considered a "provision to them and all her needs would ultimately be met" (F1, M1).

Most parents with children who have special needs probably preferred a healthy child but eligibility requirements may have prevented it. The couple with the husband aging in his 60s adopted a special needs child who is functioning normally. The two couples who already had another child were only eligible for special needs infants. One of the fathers whose daughter was receiving chemotherapy admitted the following:

> I think if we didn't have the first adoption, I don't know how we would have coped in this whole situation. It's a little easier because we have a healthy child. If we hadn't been through that [the first adoption], it would have been more difficult. Our coping would not have been the same. (F3)

DISCUSSION

The parents in this study were concerned about their daughters' identity as adopted persons, orphaned at birth without identified family origins. To plan for the anticipated problems concerning the lack of birth information, they considered several strategies. They wanted to instill a sense of pride in some kind of Chinese identity but recognized that, for some parents, their own limited knowledge about Chinese history, language, and customs might be a handicap. With cultural traditions of their own, parents sought to integrate their ethnic heritages with their daughters' Chinese backgrounds. However, ethnic language or traditions were unknown to some parents. In these cases, the adopted parents acknowledged the need for support.

Explanations about abandonment were fashioned in each parent's understanding of Chinese history and political events. But nearly all the parents grappled with rationales for the birth parents' desertion of their infant daughters. Parents whose adopted daughters struggled with special needs were forced to seek medical treatments planned with no genetic history or family medical information. These and many more unknown challenges faced these parents and their daughters.

The findings in this study affirm the critical importance of birth information in the identity development of adopted individuals. Ingersoll (1997), in her study on psychiatric disorders among adopted children, found environmental factors such as post-adoption events contributed to psychiatric problems. She warns:

> Adoptees are particularly likely to develop identity conflicts, since they must grapple with the same issue of unknown ancestry as well as what have been called "covert" and "status" losses that affect adoptees. Covert loss refers . . . to relinquishment by birth parents . . . Status loss

is being perceived as different from other children in the community or in the adoptive family. (p. 64)

Ingersoll's research (1997) may be used to understand the projected concerns of the adoptive parents in this study about the lack of birth information. Adopted parents worried about the feelings of abandonment and rejection their birth daughters may experience when grown. The research on adoptees' feelings of rejection when birth issues are not resolved suggests potential problems with intimacy and family relationships (Reitz & Watson, 1992; Rosenberg; 1992; Schooler, 1993). Schooler (1993) noted:

Rejection ranks as one of life's most painful experiences. For some adopted children, especially in the vulnerable adolescent years, feelings of rejection and abandonment from their birth parents can override the positive and nurturing love of their adoptive family. (p. 170)

Losses, grief, and mistrust become some of the main issues needing therapeutic help as a result of rejection. Other losses, such as lack of control over one's health, birth situation, and political history, could be considered "status losses." According to Ingersoll's cited definition of status loss, the Chinese infants are different in status from the children in the community. This may be because the adoptees in the study have the composite identity of having special needs, being orphans, and becoming Chinese Americans born in communist China but who are raised by non-Chinese parents in democratic America. Status losses and the losses of birth parents and birth culture were in the minds of the adoptive parents but other challenges also prevailed related to the identity development of their daughters.

The findings in the study strongly suggest monitoring the development of the ethnic identity of these adoptees. Their experiences may contribute to identity development theory and Asian American studies when adoptees begin to construct their Chinese identity in a meaningful way. Because the Chinese adoptees are born in the People's Republic of China and because Chinese culture there is different from America, Hong Kong, or Taiwan, this heralds a new Chinese-American experience completely different from the "Chinatown" or "model minority" Chinese Americanness. For the most part, the adoptive parents are in effect constructing a different kind of Chineseness for their daughters, depending on their own religious, ethnic, and marital backgrounds, and on their exposure to the culture and norms of the People's Republic of China.

Grotevant (1997) mentions the "core-context model of identity development" which forewarns that "major challenges to identity will occur when contextual shifts take place, since identity involves the ongoing negotiations between the psychological interior and social context" (p. 21). The adoptive parents' concern about the need to instill pride in their daughters' Chinese identity raises "core-context" questions. Parents vary in their knowledge of "core" Chinese values and beliefs pertinent to the People's Republic of China, which could affect their daughters' psychological functioning. Yet the "context" of the child's own non-Chinese, adoptive parents' backgrounds complicates the identity development process. Contextual shifts may occur in the adoptees' identity development process as they adopt the various identities of Chinese, Asian, Chinese-American, overseas Chinese, Chinese orphan, American-born Chinese, local Chinese, and American throughout their exploratory years. Bergquist and Kim (1999) conclude the following from their research on the identity formation of adopted Korean adults:

> Ethnic identity is a social construct rather than an inherent attribution, nurtured and sustained by the family and community through the instilling of cultural traditions, mores, and values. A transracially placed adoptee is socialized in the culture of their adoptive family with varying degrees of exposure to their birth culture. How can, or should, an individual attempt to develop an ethnic identity, which is congruent to his or her physical appearance defined by society? The theoretical research would suggest that congruency is important because we are social beings, and therefore, do not function in isolation. (p. 21)

How the social construction of these adoptees' identity develops is to be documented in future research studies.

IMPLICATIONS FOR SOCIAL WORK PRACTICE

New research is warranted in the field of international adoptions from China. More documentation is needed as parents of Chinese adopted infant girls find ways to create a myriad of information based on mastering Chinese language, attending Chinese cultural events, visiting China towns, and interacting with Chinese born families in order to create a unique birth heritage for each individual adoptive situation. How these adoptees create their identity and how parents shape their development of this search for self will become unique experiences to be documented in research endeavors longitudinally or short-term so that identity development theory building is modified to refit "core-context models of identity development" (Grotevant, 1997).

As adoptees search for their identity integrating the various roles of orphan, daughter, adopted, Chinese, American, Chinese-American, Asian American, local living in Hawaii, special needs child, and American daughter, they will need new understandings of how to make meaning and create contexts for these various parts of their lives. The research literature in Asian American Studies, Ethnic Studies, and Chinese Studies will acquire new knowledge bases to guide social workers and other professionals in their services to these women and their families. Family studies in the area of adoptions may also be affected as adoptees and their parents seek to blend ethnicities and lifestyles. The language of adoption, for instance, including terms such as birth parents, birth culture, and birth children, adds new meaning to the construct of family and ethnicity. Multiple identities will intersect, such as adoptee, orphan, daughter, female, Chinese, American, and Chinese-American. The added intricacies of adoption, abandonment, foreign birthplace, and a second set of invisible parents call for new research endeavors. The mixedness of being born in China and acculturated in Americanized Chineseness by Caucasian parents constitutes its own ethnicity. Each family and adoptee is, nevertheless, unique in different identities, experiences, and backgrounds.

Social work services will have to develop new practice innovations to handle adoptive placements who have no birth information. Assessments and interventions without birth histories will require new skills and trainings in the areas of adoptions and child welfare. Special needs adoptees will require better medical explanations to understand the diagnoses, treatment interventions, and preventions which originated in a Chinese world view whose etiologies may not be based upon western orientations but more on ancient Asian philosophies and orientations.

New longitudinal research is mandatory to monitor the impact of the Chinese adoptees' adjustment to their new social environments. Replication studies of research done on Korean and Romanian adoptees are possible but with the understanding that China's situation is very different. As a Communist society with a 5,000 year-old history of discrimination against women, comparisons to other countries are needed but difficult to extrapolate given the differences in social environments.

REFERENCES

Bender, D. & Leone, B. (1995). *Adoption: Opposing viewpoints.* San Diego, CA: Greenhaven Press.

Bergquist, K. & Kim, D. (1999). *Long-term impact on identity formation of intercountry adopted adults: Korean American Case.* Paper presented at the Council on Social Work Education Annual Program Meeting in San Francisco, California.

Cecere, L. (1998). *The children can't wait: China's emerging model for intercountry adoption.* Cambridge, MA: China Seas.

China Daily. (1986). Little suns need down-to-earth help. Vol. 6, No. 1514. June 2.

Croll, E., Delia, D., & Kane, P. (1985). *China's one child family policy.* New York: St. Martin's.

Erikson, E. (1968). *Identity, youth, and crisis.* New York: W.W. Norton & Co.

Fong, R. (2000). The sociocultural context of infant mental health in the People's Republic of China. In H. Fitzgerald & J. Osofsky (Eds.). *WAIMH handbook of infant mental health,* (pp. 181-202). New York: John Wiley & Sons.

Fong, R. (1990). *China's only child: The impact on early childhood education and childrearing.* Cambridge, MA: Harvard University. Unpublished doctoral dissertation.

Greenhalgh, S. & Bongaarts, J. (1987). Family policy in China. *Future Options in Science.* March 6. 1167-1172.

Grotevant, H. (1997). Coming to terms with adoption: The construction of identity from adolescence into adulthood. *Adoption Quarterly,* 1, 3-27.

Grove, V. (1996). *Successful adoptive families: A longitudinal study of special needs adoption.* West Connecticut: Praeger.

Human Rights Watch. (1996). *Death by default: A policy of fatal neglect in China's state orphanages.* New York: Author.

Ingersoll, B. (1997). Psychiatric Disorders Among Children: A Review and Commentary. *Adoption Quarterly,* 1, 57-73.

International Adoption and Child Abduction. (1997). Immigrant visa issued to orphans coming to the U.S. (http://travel.state.gov/orphan_numbers.hmtl).

Johnson, K. (1993). Chinese orphanages: Saving China's abandoned girls. *The Australian Journal of Chinese Affairs,* No. 30 (July) 61-87.

Johnson, K. (1996). The politics of the revival of infant abandonment in China with special reference to Hunan. *Population and Development Review.* 22(1):77-98.

Johnson, K., Huang, B., & Wang, L. (1998). Infant development and adoption in China. *Population and Development Review,* 24(3) 469-510.

Kim, D. (1976). *Intercountry adoptions: A study of self-concept of adolescent Korean children who were adopted by American families.* Chicago, IL: University of Chicago. Unpublished doctoral dissertation.

Kim, D. (1978). Issues in transracial and transcultural adoption. *Social Casework,* (Oct.) 477-486.

Klatzin, A. (ed.) (1999). *A passage to the heart: Writings from families with children from China.* St. Paul, MN: Yeong & Yeong Book Co.

Li, H. (1987). Population policy key to China's future. *Beijing Review* (July 20), 5-6.

Liptak, K. (1993). *Adoption controversies.* New York: The Changing Family, Franklin Watts.

Marcia, J. (1991). Identity and self-development. In R. Lerner, A. Petersen, and J. Brooks-Gunn. (Eds.). *Encyclopedia of Adolescence.* Vol. 1. New York: Garland.

McColm, M. (1993). *Adoption reunions: A book for adoptees, birth parents, and adoptive families.* Toronto, ON: Second Story Press.

McRoy, R., Grotevant, H., & White, K. (1998). *Openness in adoption.* New York: Praeger.

Mosher, S. (1993). *A mother's ordeal: One woman's fight against China's one-child policy.* London: Warner Books.

Mu, A. (1986). A family's smallness is its strength. *Beijing Review* 29 (December 1), 19-20.

Phinney, J. & Chavira, V. (1992). Ethnic identity and self-esteem: An exploratory longitudinal study. *Journal of Adolescence* 15, 271-81.

Reitz, M. & Watson, K. (1992). *Adoption and the Family System: Strategies for Treatment.* New York: The Guilford Press.

Riley, N. (1997). American Adoptions of Chinese Girls: The Socio-political Matrices of Individual Decisions. *Women's Studies International Forum* 20(1), 87-102.

Rosenberg, E. (1992). *The Adoption Life Cycle: The Children and Their Families Through the Years*. New York: The Free Press.

Schooler, J. (1993). *The Whole Life Adoption Book*. Colorado Springs, CO: Pinon Press.

Strauss, J. (1994). *Birthright: The guide to search and reunion for adoptees, birth parents, and adoptive parents*. New York: Penguin Books.

Tessler, R., Gamache, G., & Liu, L. (1997). Challenges of raising Chinese Americans. *FCC-New England China*. Connecticut Newsletter.

The Economist. (1983). China's she-cull baby. April 18. p. 36.

Yontz, D. (1997). American parents, Chinese children: A Sino-American experience for the 1990's. *Yale China Review*. 5(2), Fall.

Asian American Adolescents' Academic Achievement: A Look Behind the Model Minority Image

Peter Allen Lee
Yu-Wen Ying

SUMMARY. This investigation examined the attitudes and behavior regarding academic achievement from the perspective of 153 Asian American adolescents who participated in an essay contest entitles "Growing Up Asian American." Less than half the adolescents (42.5%) reported a positive attitude toward academic achievement, while over half expressed either negative attitude (13.1%) or mixed positive/negative attitude (44.4%). In contrast, an overwhelming majority (83%) of the adolescents exhibited embracing behavior toward academic achievement, while only 1.3% rejected and 15.7% showed mixed embracing/rejecting behavior. In addition, attitude and behavior were significantly correlated. All of the adolescents with positive attitudes exhibited embracing behavior. Adolescents with non-positive attitudes (negative or mixed) were more likely to show embracing behavior (70.5%) than non-embracing (rejecting or mixed) behavior (29.5%). The findings

Peter Allen Lee and Yu-Wen Ying are affiliated with the University of California at Berkeley, School of Social Welfare, 120 Haviland Hall, Berkeley, CA 94720-7400.

The authors wish to thank the Asian American adolescents who wrote the essays which served as data for this study, and the Asian Pacific American Community Fund for granting us access to them. Yukie Fujimoto, Shino Kimura, Le V. Lam, and Carol Peng provided assistance with library research and data coding.

The study was supported in part by a faculty grant from the University of California at Berkeley to the second author.

[Haworth co-indexing entry note]: "Asian American Adolescents' Academic Achievement: A Look Behind the Model Minority Image." Lee, Peter Allen, and Yu-Wen Ying. Co-published simultaneously in *Journal of Human Behavior in the Social Environment* (The Haworth Press, Inc.) Vol. 3, No. 3/4, 2001, pp. 35-48; and: *Psychosocial Aspects of the Asian-American Experience: Diversity Within Diversity* (ed: Namkee G. Choi) The Haworth Press, Inc., 2001, pp. 35-48. Single or multiple copies of this article are available for a fee from The Haworth Document Delivery Service [1-800-342-9678, 9:00 a.m. - 5:00 p.m. (EST). E-mail address: getinfo@haworthpressinc.com].

suggest significant distress among Asian American adolescents even though, behaviorally, they may be embracing academic achievement. *[Article copies available for a fee from The Haworth Document Delivery Service: 1-800-342-9678. E-mail address: <getinfo@haworthpressinc.com> Website: <http://wwwHaworthPress.com> © 2001 by The Haworth Press, Inc. All rights reserved.]*

KEYWORDS. Asian American adolescents, model minority, academic achievement

Growing up Asian in America, for me, is something that I consider an advantage and a disadvantage. I often find myself trapped between the expectations of others and of myself. Asians are expected by other people of different cultures to be at the top when it comes to academic achievement because of their background. Many Asian parents of the previous generation immigrated to the U.S. from Asia, where students are pushed to excel because of the immense competition. So they brought those experiences down to the next generation–my generation. As a result, we kids are expected to study and succeed.

–13 Year-Old U.S.-born Korean Female

Asian Americans have been labeled as the "model minority" because they are believed to have overcome the challenges of racism, low socioeconomic status, unfamiliarity with American culture, and limited English language skills to attain educational and economic success comparable to or even exceeding that of Whites (Crystal, 1989; Suzuki, 1977; Tang, 1997; Yun, 1989). There is significant evidence of the academic achievement of Asian Americans, which will be reviewed below. However, there is virtually no research on how the journey toward educational achievement is experienced by Asian American youth. The popular media's portrayal of Asian American students as "whiz kids" suggests a process that is easy and effortless (Brand, 1987; Kasindorf, 1982). At the same time, scholars have noted their social and psychological needs in spite of the "model minority" image (Chun, 1980; Crystal, 1989; Tan, 1994; Ying, Lee, Tsai, Hung, Lin, & Wan, in press; Yun, 1989). The current investigation empirically examines the subjective experiences of Asian American adolescents, in particular, their attitudes and behavior with regard to academic achievement.

ASIAN AMERICAN ACADEMIC ACHIEVEMENT

Evidence of Asian Americans as the "model minority" appeared as early as the 1930s when the proportion of school enrollment of Chinese and

Japanese youths in the 16 to 20 year old range began to exceed that of their white counterparts (Hirschman & Wong, 1986). Since then, these two Asian ethnic groups have risen in affluence despite racial prejudice (Hirschman & Wong, 1986; Sowell, 1981), and other Asian American groups have followed their example (e.g., Koreans, Filipinos, Indians, and Vietnamese). The 1990 U.S. Census found Asian Americans to be overrepresented among those with college and post-bachelor degrees (U.S. Bureau of the Census, 1992). Specifically, 22.7% of Asians/Pacific Islanders, 13.9% of non-Hispanic Whites, 7.5% of African Americans, 6.4% of Hispanics, and 6.1% of Native Americans held bachelor's degrees; and 13.0% of Asians/Pacific Islanders versus 7.7% of non-Hispanic Whites, 3.8% of African Americans, 3.6% of Hispanics, and 3.2% of Native Americans held post-bachelor's degrees (O'Hare, 1992). These numbers support the high educational achievement of Asian Americans, but need to be viewed with the caveat that they disguise the significant variation in education and income levels across and within Asian ethnic groups (Oliver, Gey, Stiles, & Brady, 1995).

While the "model minority" image generates pride for some Asian Americans, it also incites competition, envy, and prejudice from members of other racial groups (Chun, 1980; Hurh & Kim, 1989). This is not surprising as the creation of the "model minority" stereotype was partially intended as a reprimand to non-Asian American racial minorities. Thus, a 1966 *U.S. News and World Report* article stated that "At a time when it is being proposed that hundreds of billions be spent to uplift Negroes and other minorities, the nation's 300,000 Chinese Americans are moving ahead on their own–with no help from anyone else . . ." (cited by Suzuki, 1977). The pitting of Asian Americans against other non-White Americans is unfortunate and distracts attention from the fact that Asian Americans, like other racial minorities, continue to be subjected to racial discrimination. As such, despite their higher educational attainments, Asian Americans have a lower mean per capita income than Whites ($13,638 vs. $15,687, U.S. Bureau of the Census, 1992) and are more likely to live below the poverty line (14.6%) than White Americans (9.5%; De Vita, 1996). After testing various possible explanations, Barringer, Takeuchi, and Xenos (1990) concluded racial discrimination was the most likely cause for this discrepancy.

Two major views have been proposed to explain high academic achievement among Asian Americans. One is primarily cultural and attributes achievement to traditional values, such as filial piety, diligence, and effort (Freeman & Morss, 1993; Kim & Chun, 1994; Sue & Okazaki, 1990). The other is specific to the American context and attributes achievement to relative functionalism, i.e., Asian Americans are turning to education as primary means for social mobility in a society that discriminates against racial minorities (Sue & Okazaki, 1990).

Current Study and Its Significance

In spite of the substantial literature on academic achievement in Asian Americans, very few studies have examined the process toward achievement from the youths' perspectives. This investigation addresses this gap in the literature by assessing (1) the presence of positive and negative attitudes toward academic achievement, (2) the presence of embracing and rejecting behavior regarding academic achievement, and (3) the relationship of attitude and behavior toward academic achievement in Asian American adolescents.

It is important to empirically study the process toward achievement as, in spite of the positive outcome of success in many cases, anecdotal evidence suggests some Asian Americans do report negative attitudes and significant psychological distress, such as anxiety and depression, in response to the tremendous pressures they experience from their parents and teachers (Lee, 1994). Certainly, if Asian American students are found to hold negative attitudes toward the pressure to succeed, the question of "success at what cost" arises. This finding would be important to parents, educators, and other professionals who may assist with the modification of extreme expectations and development of effective coping strategies. Even at the larger societal level, an exaggerated image of Asian Americans as "whiz kids" may need to be counter-balanced by an awareness of their struggles and the psychological costs of their success.

Asian American Adolescents' Attitudes and Behaviors Toward Academic Achievement

The first research question examines Asian American adolescents' attitudes toward academic achievement. Their attitude may be positive, negative, or a mixture of the two. Those with positive attitudes value learning and academic accomplishments and/or share their parents' belief that education is an important means for upward mobility (Kao, 1995; Lee, 1994; Tan, 1994). Other adolescents with negative attitudes devalue academic achievement and/or resent their parents' overemphasis of perfect grades, their lack of interest in the child's non-academic pursuits, and their non-negotiable expectations regarding career goals (Rousseau, Drapeau, & Corin, 1996; Schneider & Lee, 1990). This may be particularly disturbing as, in contrast, White parents, who represent the majority society's norm, hold a broader perspective, encourage achievement across a range of activities (sports, music, or other hobbies, as well as academics), and afford their children greater freedom in career choice (Schneider & Lee, 1990). Finally, Asian American adolescents may also hold both positive and negative attitudes toward academic achievement, as they may concurrently value achievement but also resent the pressures to which they are subjected.

The second research question examines Asian American adolescents' behavior with regard to academic achievement. These may be embracing, rejecting, or a mixture of both. Asian American adolescents may exemplify embracing behaviors by studying diligently and by planning to attend college. Others may reject academic achievement by refusing to study or by missing class (Lee, 1994). A mixture of embracing and rejecting behaviors may also co-exist. For instance, adolescents may plan to attend college (to fulfill parental expectation) but may fail to study and go to classes regularly.

The third research question examines the association of attitude and behavior toward academic achievement. In general, it is expected that a positive attitude would be associated with embracing behavior and a negative attitude would be associated with rejecting behavior. It is unlikely that a positive attitude would be associated with a rejecting behavior. However, it is possible for a negative attitude to be associated with an embracing behavior. Given the importance of academic achievement to Asian American parents, it is plausible that adolescents who hold negative attitudes will nonetheless feel obliged to behave in a manner consistent with their parents' expectations.

METHODS

Sample

The data utilized for this study were derived from essays submitted to the 1995 San Francisco Bay Area "Growing Up Asian American" Essay Contest sponsored by the Asian Pacific American Community Fund. The contest was publicized in local newspapers and schools. Names and addresses were removed from all essays prior to their release. A total of 705 essays were submitted by Asian American youths aged 6 to 22. From this total, 153 essays from the 13-22 year old category identified attitudes and behaviors toward academic achievement, and served as the data for this investigation.

The sample of essay authors consisted of 73.9% East Asians (Chinese, Japanese, and Koreans), 11.1% Southeast Asians (Vietnamese, Cambodian, Thai, and Burmese), 8.4% South Asians (Indians and Filipinos), 2.0% ethnically mixed Asians, and 4.6% Asian-non-Asian mixed adolescents. About two-thirds (64.1%) of the participants were born in the United States, and the rest (35.9%) were born overseas. Their mean age was 16.73 years (SD = 2.54). Almost three-quarters of the sample were female (73.2%), and about one quarter were male (26.8%).

Measures

Attitude. Attitudes toward academic achievement were operationalized as positive, negative, or mixed attitudes. A positive attitude was coded if adolescents valued education, academic achievement, and/or studying hard in school. A negative attitude was coded if adolescents devalued academic achievement and/or resented the parents/teachers/peers' expectations and pressures to succeed. A mixed attitude was coded if adolescents expressed both positive and negative attitudes.

Behavior. Behavior toward academic achievement was operationalized as embracing, rejecting, or mixed. Embracing behavior was coded if adolescents pursued academic achievement by studying diligently and/or intending to pursue higher education. Rejecting behavior was coded if adolescents did not pursue academic achievement by refusing to study, by skipping class, and/or by not intending to pursue a higher education. Mixed behavior was coded when adolescents exemplified both embracing and rejecting behaviors.

Procedure

Four Asian American undergraduate students served as raters for this study. They reviewed all essays submitted by 13-22 year olds for inclusion into the sample. From this evaluation, the selected 153 essays were divided into two piles, and each pile was coded independently by two raters regarding attitude and behavior toward academic achievement. The interrater reliability was .75. Disagreements were discussed and reconciled.

RESULTS

Distribution of Attitude and Behavior Toward Academic Achievement

To answer the first two research questions, distributions of attitude and behavior toward academic achievement were calculated. With regard to attitude, 65 (42.5%) were positive, 20 (13.1%) were negative, and 68 (44.4%) were mixed. With regard to behavior, 127 (83.0%) were embracing, 2 (1.3%) were rejecting, and 24 (15.7%) were mixed.

Common codes found in the essays and examples of six out of the nine possible combinations of attitude and behavior are illustrated in the following excerpts. The combination of positive attitude with rejecting behavior, positive attitude with mixed behavior, and mixed attitude with rejecting behavior were not found.

Excerpt 1 (17 Year-Old Immigrant Vietnamese Male)

As a child growing up, life was very brutal and cruel to my family. My mother had to work excessively hard to meet the emotional and financial needs of my siblings and I. It is undeniably difficult for a mother who was illiterate in English and five young children to survive in a society reserved only for the rich, powerful, and educated. Witnessing the dilemmas that my mother endured, I made a sacred vow to succeed in life because I was determined to not be in the same predicament that my mother was trapped in. She consistently reminded me that, without a good education, my future will be diminished. Her support, expectations, and encouragement assisted me in succeeding academically.

Coding: Attitude is positive and behavior is embracing.

Excerpt 2 (18 Year-Old U.S.-born Chinese Male)

I studied hard and got good marks but I seemed to be the most unhappy person in the room. I was so hard on myself. I would feel guilty and stupid if I could not figure out a math problem. I felt so pressured to do better than everyone else, because I felt I had to prove something. Because I lacked a social life, I felt that my grades were the only thing I had going for me. . . .

I began to break down in my junior year of high school. The pressure was just too much with such high expectations of my parents, and more importantly, myself, I had to hit rock bottom. I found it increasingly hard to concentrate. It seemed like my entire world was falling apart–I started to think that all my work was worthless because I was so unhappy.

Coding: Attitude is negative and behavior is embracing.

Excerpt 3 (16 Year-Old U.S.-born Japanese-Chinese Female)

I feel as if I am as much "American" as any of my other classmates, yet I know that I am still thought of as just an Asian. It is because of this type of thinking that stereotypes have been labeled on me which I seemed doomed to carry. Others of my race seem to have a higher academic status so therefore I am expected to have one too. America has set aside special expectations especially for us Asian teens, which are usually very hard to live up to. As a young Asian adult, I break all characteristics of the "typical Chinese/Japanese" woman. In my sixteen years, I have seen many academic opportunities pass by that I was expected to take.

Coding: Attitude is negative and behavior is rejecting.

Excerpt 4 (17 Year-Old U.S.-born Chinese Female)

[D]ealing with stereotypes from other non-Asians can become tiring occasionally. Ever since I won third [in a math contest], it seems all I did was reinforce the belief that all Asians are good in math. During my past high school years, I, along with many other Asian kids, often would have to deal with comments such as, "Worried you got an A-?" when I was anxious about my grades. It soon was to the point where receiving good grades was more of a relief than an accomplishment. Many of my peers would expect me to be a stereotypical Asian and cease to see me as an a person. The fact is that I avoid math when possible and I prefer cheerleading over studying . . . Cheerleading for example, was not in my parents' plan for me. Doing well in history and English were contrary to my parents' belief that math would be the subject that came easy to me.

Coding: Attitude is negative and behavior is mixed.

Excerpt 5 (15 Year-Old Immigrant Vietnamese Male)

I have always felt a great deal of pressure to succeed for [my father]. Though this can sometimes be maddening since it is an extra burden to my hectic existence, I feel that my goals [have elevated] from a mediocre level to a higher, more rigorous standard. I have been challenged to do the most possible rather than the minimum expected. I see myself as an extension of my father, a vessel through which he can relive his own lost childhood. In succeeding, I begin to repay my father for his lifelong investment in me for he and I both share in the pride and triumph of my successes.

Coding: Attitude is mixed and behavior is embracing.

Excerpt 6 (17 Year-Old Immigrant Indian Male)

In India, education is believed to be the most important thing in a child's life. A boy who succeeds in school will bring respect to his family, earn a high paying job, be able to marry a rich girl, and subsequently bring in a large dowry. My parents held on to these traditional Indian beliefs and applied them to me. From the beginning of my education to the present, my parents always pushed me to the limits. In fifth grade when I received a "B+" in science, I was spanked and grounded. My parents had already decided on the fact that I was to be a science major in college, and a "B+" in this subject was unacceptable to them. As the years progressed, I grew accustomed to the pressure my parents put on me, and gradually began to apply it on myself. Not only do I want to earn an "A," but I wanted to have the highest grade in the class. If anybody did better than me, I felt as if I was a failure. This attitude of mine developed me into a highly competitive yet nervous person. The constant fear of failure was always lurking in the back of my mind. There was only one way to succeed: to be the best. However, there were infinite ways to fail. . . .

In order to prove to my peers that I was much more than a scholar, I began affiliating with gangs during my junior year in high school. I enjoyed the respect and authority I gained, but made sure that my parents did not find out about my new lifestyle. During the week I would study as usual, but my weekend excursions to the library became trips to the mall and various parties. Fighting, drinking, and smoking, all became commonplace. During the weekends, I could break the mold my parents had put me into and become someone else. For the first time in my life, I felt as if I was making my own identity.

Every parent dreams of raising successful, caring children who become pillars of society. While stressing the traditional values and academic success to the highest degree, Asian parents tend to neglect the hardships their children face. Being a minority who is trying to find identity in a diverse and constantly changing society requires support at home, not stress.

Coding: Attitude is mixed and behavior is mixed.

The Relationship of Attitude and Behavior Toward Academic Achievement

To highlight the association of positive versus non-positive attitude with embracing versus non-embracing behavior in answering the third research question, we combined the two attitude categories of "negative" and "mixed" into "non-positive," and the two behavior categories of "rejecting" and "mixed" into "non-embracing." This increased the cell size and the power of the test. The collapsed "non-positive" and "non-embracing" categories included essays that expressed attitudes or behaviors which were unsupportive toward achievement. Using this recategorization, 88 (57.5%) had non-positive attitudes and 26 (17.0%) had non-embracing behaviors.

After the recoding, a chi-square analysis was conducted to determine the relationship between the adolescents' attitudes and behaviors regarding academic achievement. As Table 1 shows, the overall chi-squared was significant ($\chi^2 = 23.14$, df = 1, p = .00001). All 65 adolescents with positive attitudes exhibited embracing behavior. Interestingly, of the 88 adolescents with non-positive attitudes, 62 (70.5%) exhibited embracing behavior, while

TABLE 1. The Relationship Between Attitude and Behavior

	Embracing Behavior (n = 127)	Non-Embracing Behavior (n = 26)	Totals (N = 153)
Positive Attitude	n = 65 100%	n = 0 0%	n = 65 100%
Non-Positive Attitude	n = 62 70.5%	n = 26 29.5%	n = 88 100%

The overall chi-squared is significant (χ^2 = 23.14, df = 1, p = .00001); those with non-positive attitude are more likely to exhibit embracing than non-embracing behavior (χ^2 = 14.73, df = 1, p = .0001).

26 (29.5%) exhibited non-embracing behavior. To test whether this distribution occurred by chance, an additional chi-square analysis was conducted for adolescents with non-positive attitudes. The results show they were significantly more likely to embrace than not embrace academic achievement (χ^2 = 14.73, df = 1, p = .0001).

DISCUSSION

Distribution of Attitude and Behavior Toward Academic Achievement

While a significant number of Asian American adolescents held positive attitudes toward academic achievement (42.5%), the majority held non-positive attitudes (13.1% were negative and 44.4% were mixed). Excerpt 1 illustrates that a positive attitude toward education is an important means for future success. Those with negative attitudes often shared the sentiment expressed by the writers of Excerpts 2, 3 and 4. The writer of Excerpt 2 experienced immense pressure to succeed and was dependent on grades for his sense of self-worth. He felt "unhappy," "guilty," and "stupid." These comments suggest severe negative psychological consequences secondary to perceived unrealistically high academic expectations. Similarly, the writer of Excerpt 3 felt "doomed" to carry the stereotype of an academically successful Asian American student. In excerpt 4, the author was tired of stereotypes depicting Asians as good in mathematics, expressed "receiving good grades was more of a relief than an accomplishment," and preferred cheerleading over studying.

Excerpts 5 and 6 reflect mixed attitudes. In Excerpt 5, the pressure to succeed was "sometimes . . . maddening," juxtaposed with a positive attitude acknowledging the functions of academic achievement. In Excerpt 6, the writer acknowledges wanting "the highest grade in the class," but also needing "support at home, not stress [due to the pressure to succeed]."

The overwhelming majority of Asian American adolescents (83%) exhibited behaviors which embraced academic achievement (see Excerpts 1, 2, and 5). The writer of Excerpt 1 was "succeeding academically." The author of Excerpt 2 "studied hard," and the author of Excerpt 5 pursued and achieved success. Only 1.3 % of the sample exemplified rejecting behavior. The author of 3 allowed "many academic opportunities pass by that [she] was expected to take." A few of the essays (15.7%) reflected mixed behaviors (see Excerpts 4 and 6). The author of excerpt 4 avoided mathematics but did well in English and history. In the case of Excerpt 6, the writer continued to excel academically, but also affiliated with gang members and partied with friends instead of going to the library.

The Relationship of Attitude and Behavior Toward Academic Achievement

All adolescents with positive attitudes exhibited embracing behaviors toward academic achievement. They are most representative of the Asian American "model minority" image. They valued and pursued academic excellence, as illustrated by Excerpt 1. In contrast, those with negative/mixed (non-positive) attitudes and rejecting/mixed (non-embracing) behaviors (17%) exemplify an image opposite to that of Asian Americans as model minorities. This is illustrated by Excerpt 3, as the writer dreaded the stereotype of the high achieving Asian American and chose not to pursue academic opportunities.

Perhaps most interesting are the 62 adolescents who expressed a non-positive attitude but an embracing behavior toward academic achievement. Based on their behavior, they may be viewed as model minorities, as they seek, and may attain, academic success. However, their negative/mixed attitude is associated with unhappiness and dissatisfaction. Thus, the author of Excerpt 5 "always felt a great deal of pressure to succeed," which "can sometimes be maddening," but also embraced success as a means to honor his father. The author of Excerpt 2 "studied hard and got good marks" but felt like "the most unhappy person in the room." He began to "break down" from the pressure to succeed, but continued to invest his sense of self-worth in his grades. In the end, "It seemed like my entire world was falling apart–I started to think that all my work was worthless because I was so unhappy." Since a large proportion of the sample (40.5%) falls into this category, this finding suggests that a significant number of Asian American adolescents striving to achieve academically are experiencing significant distress.

Study Limitations and Directions for Future Research

Several limitations may affect the generalizability of this study's findings while also suggesting directions for future research. East Asians (Chinese, Japanese, and Koreans) were overrepresented, while other Asian American subgroups (Southeast Asians and South Asians) were underrepresented in the sample. Although Asian Americans share some similar experiences as a racial minority group, differences do exist across the subgroups, especially in migration history. Also, there was an overrepresentation of females, who composed almost three-quarters of the sample. Future research should include a more heterogeneous sample of Asian Americans.

Asian American adolescents skilled in English, accomplished academically, familiar with mainstream society, and invested in sharing their experiences as Asian Americans were more likely to enter this essay contest. In contrast, underachievers or those not enrolled in school (where recruitment for the contest was primarily conducted) were less likely to participate. Thus, it is likely that our results are biased in favor of positive attitude and embracing behavior. It is possible that in the general population of Asian American adolescents, more youth hold negative or mixed attitudes and/or show rejecting/mixed behaviors toward academic achievement. Inclusion of a more representative sample would better reflect the distribution of attitude and behavior toward academic achievement and their association.

Given the cross-sectional nature of the current study's design, it is unclear if attitude preceded behavior (as we assume) or vice versa. Longitudinal studies and more elaborate qualitative methods are needed to accurately assess the developmental processes of academic achievement. Also, the interrater reliability was acceptable, but lower than desired. This was due in part to the difficult task of coding and delineating multiple themes contained within the essays, and our inability to directly question the adolescents. Future studies ought to utilize an interview format to better assess Asian American youth's attitudes and behaviors toward academic achievement.

Implications and Conclusion

The study findings provide important implications for professional practice. Although many Asian American adolescents continue to strive for educational excellence, a significant proportion hold negative attitudes and suffer from the tremendous pressures they experience. Excerpts from the essays suggest symptoms of psychological dysfunction. Parents, educators, and mental health professionals should be aware of the significant distress these adolescents experience in spite of their embracing behaviors. Not all Asian American adolescents are able to attain exceptional achievements. Parents' and teachers' expectations ought to incorporate a realistic assessment of an adolescent's abilities.

In conclusion, this is one of the first studies to provide a behind the scenes look at the process behind Asian American adolescent achievement using a large sample. The most striking finding was that many Asian American adolescents with a non-positive attitude nonetheless exhibited embracing behaviors toward academic achievement. This suggests significant struggle and ambivalence around achievement and deserves attention from parents and professionals serving this population.

REFERENCES

Barringer, H., Takeuchi, D., & Xenos, P. (1990). Education, occupational prestige, and income of Asian Americans. *Sociology of Education, 63*, 27-43.

Brand, D. (1987). The new whiz kids: Why Asian Americans are doing so well and what it costs them. *Time, 130*(9), 42-51.

Chun, K. (1980). The myth of Asian American success and its educational ramifications. *IRCD Bulletin*, 1-12.

Crystal, D. (1989). Asian Americans and the myth of the model minority. *Social Casework, 70*(7), 405-413.

De Vita, C. J. (1996). The United States at mid-decade. *Population Bulletin, 50*(4), 2-44.

Freeman, V. S., & Morss, J. (1993). Study habits and academic achievement among Asian students. *College Student Journal, 27*, 352-355.

Hirschman, C., & Wong, M. (1986). The extraordinary educational attainment of Asian-Americans: A search for historical evidence and explanations. *Social Forces, 65*(1), 1-27.

Hurh, W., & Kim, K. (1989). The "success" image of Asian Americans: Its validity and its practical and theoretical implications. *Ethnic and Racial Studies, 12*(4), 512-538.

Kao, G. (1995). Asian Americans as model minorities? A look at their academic performance. *American Journal of Education, 103*(2), 121-159.

Kasindorf, M. (1982, December). A model minority. *Newsweek*, pp. 39-51.

Kim, U., & Chun, M. B. (1994). Educational success of Asian Americans: An indigenous perspective. *Journal of Applied Developmental Psychology, 15*, 329-343.

Lee, S. (1994). Behind the model-minority stereotype: Voices of high- and low-achieving Asian American students. *Anthropology & Education Quarterly, 25*(4), 413-429.

O'Hare, W. P. (1992). America's minorities–The demographics of diversity. *Population Bulletin, 47*(4), 1-47.

Oliver, J. E., Gey, F. C., Stiles, J., & Brady, H. (1995). *Pacific Rim States Asian demographic data book*. Berkeley, CA: University of California Pacific Rim Research Program.

Rousseau, C., Drapeau, A., & Corin, E. (1996). School performance and emotional problems in refugee children. *American Journal of Orthopsychiatry, 66*(2), 239-251.

Schneider, B., & Lee, Y. (1990). A model for academic success: The school and home environment of East Asian students. *Anthropology & Education Quarterly, 21*(4), 358-377.

Sowell, T. (1981). *Ethnic America: A history.* New York: Basic Books.

Sue, S., & Okazaki, S. (1990). Asian-American educational achievements: A phenomenon in search of an explanation. *American Psychologist, 45*(8), 913-920.

Suzuki, B. (1977). Education and the socialization of Asian Americans: A revisionist analysis of the "Model Minority" thesis. *Amerasia Journal, 4*(2), 23-51.

Tan, D. L. (1994). Uniqueness of the Asian American experience in higher education. *College Student Journal, 28*(4), 412- 421.

Tang, J. (1997). The model minority thesis revisited: Counter evidence from the science and engineering fields. *Journal of Applied Behavioral Science, 33*(3), 291-315.

U.S. Bureau of the Census (1992). *1990 census of population and housing, 1990 CHP-1-1. Summary population and housing characteristics.* Washington, DC: U.S. Government Printing Office.

Ying, Y., Lee, P. A., Tsai, J. L., Hung, Y., Lin, M., Wan, C. T. (In press). Asian American college students as model minorities: An examination of their overall competence. *Cultural Diversity and Ethnic Minority Psychology.*

Yun, G. (1989). *A look beyond the model minority image: Critical issues in Asian America.* New York: Minority Rights Group (New York) Inc.

Depression Level in Inner-City Asian American Adolescents: The Contributions of Cultural Orientation and Interpersonal Relationships

Sandra L. Wong

SUMMARY. This study examines the effects of cultural orientation and interpersonal relationships on depression among inner-city Asian American adolescents, controlling for demographic variables. Data were obtained from 144 high school students. The mean CES-D was 19.24. Cultural orientation and interpersonal relationships were significant predictors of depression. Individuals who were separated (had a high orientation towards ethnic culture and low orientation towards mainstream culture) experienced greater depression than those who were assimilated (had a high orientation towards American culture and low orientation towards ethnic culture). In addition, the presence of a more positive parent and peer relationship predicted lower depression levels. None of the demographic variables were significant predictors of depression in the overall model, although late immigrants (those who immigrated after the age of 12) were more depressed than American-born adolescents in the bivariate analysis. Implications of findings are discussed. *[Article copies available for a fee from The Haworth Document Delivery Service: 1-800-342-9678. E-mail address: <getinfo@haworthpressinc.com> Website: <http://www. HaworthPress.com> © 2001 by The Haworth Press, Inc. All rights reserved.]*

Sandra L. Wong, PhD, is affiliated with the Oakland Unified School District.

Address correspondence to Sandra Wong, Psychological Services, 495 Jones Avenue, Oakland, CA 94603 (E-mail: swong@ousd.k12.ca.us).

The author would like to thank Yu-Wen Ying and Raymond Chan for reviewing earlier drafts of the paper.

[Haworth co-indexing entry note]: "Depression Level in Inner-City Asian American Adolescents: The Contributions of Cultural Orientation and Interpersonal Relationships." Wong, Sandra L. Co-published simultaneously in *Journal of Human Behavior in the Social Environment* (The Haworth Press, Inc.) Vol. 3, No. 3/4, 2001, pp. 49-64; and: *Psychosocial Aspects of the Asian-American Experience: Diversity Within Diversity* (ed: Namkee G. Choi) The Haworth Press, Inc., 2001, pp. 49-64. Single or multiple copies of this article are available for a fee from The Haworth Document Delivery Service [1-800-342-9678, 9:00 a.m. - 5:00 p.m. (EST). E-mail address: getinfo@haworthpressinc.com].

KEYWORDS. Depression, cultural orientation, interpersonal relationships, Asian American adolescents

Depression in adolescents is a serious problem that is estimated to afflict as many as 10% to 20% of this population (Reynolds & Johnston, 1994). It is characterized by feelings of sadness, hopelessness, worthlessness, and guilt as well as a decrease in energy, changes in appetite, sleep, and psychomotor activity (Finch, Casat, & Carey, 1990). Adolescents may be more susceptible to depression than children and adults for a variety of reasons, including the myriad of biological, cognitive, affective, and social changes they experience during this period. It may be a time of turmoil for some as they strive to separate and individuate from their families. In the case of Asian Americans, adolescence may be exacerbated by migration experiences, cultural differences, and poor interpersonal relationships. Yet despite these risk factors, little research has focused on depression among Asian American adolescents. The current study addresses this gap in the literature by examining the effects of cultural orientation and interpersonal relationships on depression among Asian American adolescents, controlling for demographic characteristics.

SIGNIFICANCE

It is important to study the psychological well-being of Asian American adolescents because they have often been grouped together and viewed as the model minority. As a result of these misconceptions, many Asian American children and adolescents may suffer from psychological difficulties that are often overlooked. The model minority myth maintains a stereotypical perception that Asian Americans are well-adjusted with few social, psychological, or economic problems. However, closer examination of data used to promote the Asian American success story reveals a more complex picture. For example, while the 1997 median income for Asian Pacific Islanders (APIs) is $51,850, above the national median of $44,570 and the White family income of $49,640, a greater percentage of APIs live below the poverty level (14.0%) as compared to Whites (8.6%) (U.S. Bureau of the Census, 1998). Moreover, 20.3% of API children and adolescents live in poverty, as compared to 11.4% of White children and adolescents (U.S. Bureau of the Census, 1998). Similarly, low prevalence rates of psychopathology in the Asian American community have been reported based on clinical samples without taking into consideration the underutilization of mental health services by Asian Americans (Kuo, 1984). However, true prevalence rates of mental disorders within the Asian American community are difficult to determine because of its relatively small size, heterogeneity, and rapid changes in demographics (Sue, Sue, Sue, & Takeuchi, 1995).

Those most likely to be harmed by the model minority myth are Asian American adolescents in the inner-city. As is typical of the inner-city, this group tends to come from families with lower incomes, less education, and higher unemployment. They are recent immigrants or refugees who live in the inner-city for economic and cultural reasons (e.g., Chinatown provides them with the ability to shop, socialize, and conduct business in their primary language). These adolescents are susceptible to the same vices as other adolescents in the urban setting (i.e., drugs, gangs, and violence). In addition, they may face difficulties arising from limited English proficiency and cultural differences.

This study has practical implications for professionals working with Asian American adolescents. Findings may be used to inform and develop prevention and treatment programs. For example, if cultural orientation and interpersonal relationships impact psychological well-being, interventions directed at Asian American adolescents should target change in these variables. Below is a brief description of the experience of adolescence and depression in Asian Americans, followed by the study's hypotheses and the relevant literature review.

ADOLESCENCE AND DEPRESSION AMONG ASIAN AMERICANS

The major developmental task of adolescence is identity formation (Erikson, 1963). During this period, the individual faces the challenges of forming a coherent and stable identity. Failure to do so may result in confusion and/or psychological distress, commonly referred to as an "identity crisis." Identity formation within the European American cultural context entails individuation and separation from parents. This is incongruent within the Asian cultural context where the individual is defined by family and position in the family (Huang, 1997). Seeking an individual identity outside of the family is discouraged and may be viewed as a selfish act. This disparity in values makes it difficult for many Asian American adolescents who may desire to be like their mainstream European American peers on the one hand, and also meet family obligations and expectations on the other hand. The additional task of negotiating the delicate balance between two cultures during adolescence makes its developmental challenges more difficult and complicated.

Previous investigations have suggested a variance in factors contributing to depression between White and Asian American young adults. Aldwin and Greenberger (1987) found perceived parental traditionalism and three coping strategies (accepting the problem, trying to solve the problem, and expressing emotions) accounted for 44% of the variance in depression among Korean American college students. In contrast, two other variables (academic stress and respondent's own value system) were significant predictors of depression in their White American counterparts, accounting for 13% of the variance. This difference emphasizes the centrality of interpersonal relationships to Asian Americans. This current investigation further examines depression in Asian Americans and identifies factors that are of particular relevance to them.

HYPOTHESES AND LITERATURE REVIEW

The literature review is organized according to the following hypotheses:

1. Asian Americans adolescents are hypothesized to experience greater depression than White adolescents.
2. Cultural orientation will have an effect on depression with bicultural students reporting the least amount of depressive symptoms followed by assimilated, separated, and marginal students (i.e., marginal students are hypothesized to report the greatest level of depression).
3. Parental and peer interpersonal relationships will correlate negatively with depression.
4. Depression will vary by the demographic control variables of gender, migration status, SES, and ethnic group membership as follows: (a) girls are hypothesized to report greater depression; (b) late immigrants (those who immigrated after the age of 12) are hypothesized to report the greatest depressive symptomology, followed by early immigrants (those who immigrated before or at the age of 12), with American-born adolescents reporting the least depressive symptomology; (c) SES is hypothesized to correlate negatively with depression; and (d) Southeast Asian adolescents are hypothesized to report greater depression than Chinese adolescents.

Depression

The first hypothesis postulates that Asian American adolescents in this study will report greater depression than White adolescents in Radloff's (1991) high school sample. As mentioned earlier, in addition to the developmental challenges experienced by mainstream adolescents, inner-city Asian American adolescents have the extra task of maintaining a balance between two cultures in an environment with greater stressors (e.g., higher rates of poverty and crime) and fewer resources (e.g. fewer enrichment activities at home and at school). While some studies have found Asian American young adults to have lower depression levels (e.g., Roberts, Roberts, & Chen (1997), these studies have often focused on adolescents from middle class backgrounds. The experiences of these young adults may be vastly different from those of inner-city Asian Americans (e.g., parents have less education and poorer English language skills or families have more recent migration history), making them more vulnerable to cultural conflicts, poorer interpersonal relationships, and depression.

Cultural Orientation and Depression

The second hypothesis postulates the presence of a relationship between cultural orientation and depression. Bicultural individuals were hypothesized to enjoy better outcomes psychologically, followed by assimilated, separated, and marginal students. Berry's (1984) model of acculturation describes an individual with a bicultural orientation as one who embraces both the mainstream and ethnic cultures. An individual with an assimilated cultural orientation embraces the mainstream culture and rejects the ethnic culture. An individual with a separated cultural orientation embraces the ethnic culture and rejects the mainstream culture. A marginal cultural orientation describes rejection of both the ethnic and mainstream cultures.

Many researchers have argued that cultural orientation can have profound psychological consequences, including depression, anxiety, feelings of marginality and alienation, and psychosomatic symptoms (Atkinson, Morten, & Sue, 1989; Hovey & King, 1996). Many also suggested that biculturalism is the best cultural orientation, as it allows the individual to maintain pride in her culture of origin as well as function in the larger mainstream culture (e.g., Padilla, 1992). In a context such as the school, where mainstream values are promoted, an assimilated cultural orientation would provide greater psychological benefits than a separated orientation (Ying, 1995). In contrast, the marginal person has been described as having the greatest risk for psychological problems because he feels isolated and closed off from members of both the ethnic and mainstream cultures (Padilla, 1992).

Interpersonal Relationships and Depression

It was also hypothesized that there would be a negative association between parental and peer relationships and depression. Positive parental and peer relationships have been correlated with lower depression rates in adolescents (Aseltine, Gore, & Colten, 1998; Hurd, Wooding, & Noller, 1999). Differential rates of acculturation, problems due to miscommunication, lack of empathy, misunderstandings of ideas, different customs and values, and lack of common past experiences have been found to be sources of conflict between migrant parents and their children (Sluzki, 1979) and among their peers (Padilla, Alvarez, & Lindholm, 1986).

Demographic Control Variables and Depression

Girls were hypothesized to report a higher depression level, based on previous findings (Avison & McAlpine, 1992; Cuellar & Roberts, 1997). Beyond the gender inequalities experienced by girls and women in the mainstream society, traditional Asian cultures impose stricter gender roles and greater household responsibilities for girls and young women (e.g., earlier curfew, limited social activities, taking care of younger siblings, cooking).

In terms of migration status, late immigrants were hypothesized to report greater depression, followed by early immigrants, then American-born students. Research on distress experienced by immigrants and native born individuals is inconclusive. One study found that immigrant Hispanic adolescent boys (grades 6-7) reported greater stress than their U.S. born counterparts (Gil, Vega, & Dimas, 1994). Another found U.S. born Hispanic respondents, 18 years and older, to report significantly higher depression on the CES-D than immigrants from Mexico (Golding & Burnam, 1990). Participants in this study who have spent less time in the U.S. (i.e., late immigrants) were hypothesized to have greater distress because they have had less time to adjust culturally. Similarly, early immigrants were hypothesized to report greater depression than American-born students.

Socioeconomic status (SES) was hypothesized to have a negative correlation with depression. Low SES has been found to correlate with poorer psychological well-being (Cuellar & Roberts, 1997; Golding & Burnam, 1990). Asian American families from low SES backgrounds generally have fewer resources for social and economic support, resulting in greater strain on the family. Asian American adolescents from low SES backgrounds may also be expected by their parents to provide greater financial support and to have more responsibilities in the family, leading to greater stress and depression.

Southeast Asian adolescents in this study were hypothesized to report greater depression symptoms than Chinese adolescents. Differences in depression between Southeast Asian groups and Chinese Americans have not been studied. In this investigation, Southeast Asian adolescents were hypothesized to report greater depression levels because of their refugee background status. While many of these adolescents may not have personally experienced traumas from war torn countries or lived in refugee camps, a large majority of their parents may have encountered traumatic events before settling in the U.S. The distress experienced by Southeast Asian parents may affect their parenting skills, which may in turn impact the psychological well-being of their children (Ying & Akutsu, 1997).

METHOD

Sample

One hundred forty-four (144) students from an urban high school in the San Francisco Bay Area participated in this study. Ninth and eleventh grade students were targeted and recruited from core social studies classes. Participants ranged in age from 14 to 19 years with a mean of 15.7 years (SD = 1.35). There were roughly equal numbers of males (71, 49%) and females (73, 51%) in the sample (see Table 1). Seventy-nine participants were American-born (54.9%) while 65 were foreign-born (45.1%). Of the foreign-born, 39 were early immigrants (60%) (i.e., they immigrated to the U.S. before or at the age of 12), and 26 were late immigrants (40%) (i.e., immigrated to the U.S. after the age of 12). Socioeconomic status (SES) was measured using Hollingshead's two-factor index of social position (Hollingshead, 1957). A participant's father's occupation and educational level were used to calculate

TABLE 1. Demographic Variables by Depression

	n	CES-D	Significant Differences
Total	144	19.24 (10.39)	
Mean Age in Years	15.7 (1.35)		
Gender			
Male	71	19.42 (10.40)	
Female	73	19.07 (10.45)	
Migration Status			
American-born	79	17.51 (9.96)	Late Immigrants >
Early Immigrants	39	19.68 (11.32)	American-born;
Late Immigrants		23.84 (9.03)	$p < .05$
Mean SES † (SD)	63.06 (12.47)	$r = .10$	
Ethnic Group (n = 140)			
Chinese	92	19.53 (10.45)	
SE Asian	48	18.31 (10.25)	
Cultural Orientation			
Bicultural	83	18.67 (9.89)	
Assimilated	27	16.31 (9.03)	
Separated	28	21.53 (10.30)	
Peer Relationship (SD)	47.90 (15.32)	$r = -.4737$	$p < .001$
Parent Relationship (SD)	43.60 (16.67)	$r = -.4310$	$p < .001$

† Using Hollingshead's (1957) two-factor index of social position; scores range from 11 to 77, with lower numbers indicating highest SES.

an index with scores ranging from 11 to 77, with a lower number reflecting higher SES. The mean SES index for the group was 63.06 (SD = 12.47), indicating low SES. Further analyses (not shown in Table 1) revealed that a third (31.9%) of the respondents' fathers had 6 or less years of formal education and 12.8% had no formal education. Only 10.5% of respondents' fathers had at least one year of post-secondary education. A majority of the participants were of Chinese descent (92 Chinese, 20 Mien, 16 Vietnamese, 11 Cambodian, 1 Filipino, 1 Laotian, and 3 of Mixed Asian descent). Those from Mien, Vietnamese, Cambodian, and Laotian backgrounds were classified into the Southeast Asian group. The Filipino and "mixed Asian" students were dropped from analyses involving ethnic group membership.

Measurements

Cultural Orientation

Cultural orientation was assessed using the General Ethnicity Questionnaire-Abridged version (GEQ) (Tsai, Ying, & Lee, 2000). This questionnaire was constructed with two versions, one that referenced Chinese culture (GEQ-C) and one that referenced "American" culture (GEQ-A). The questionnaires assess participants' orientation to an ethnic minority and American culture. In this study, the GEQ-C was adapted to reference a general "ethnic" culture (GEQ-E). For example, the question "I was raised in a way that was Chinese" was changed to "I was raised in a way that was _____." When completing the GEQ-E, students were instructed to complete the GEQ-E by replacing the blanks with their ethnicity. The two scales (GEQ-E and GEQ-A) consist of 25 items and are the same except in referencing the different cultures. Using a Likert scale, subjects rate how much they agree with statements about their cultural orientation (e.g., "I was raised in a way that was Chinese"). For items about their cultural orientation, the scale ranges from "1" for "Strongly disagree" to "5" for "Strongly agree".

A cutoff score of 3.0 on the GEQ-E and GEQ-A was used to categorize students into four different cultural orientations. Students with high scores (mean of 3.0 or above) on both the GEQ-E and GEQ-A were categorized as bicultural (n = 83). Students with high scores on the GEQ-A and low scores (mean < 3.0) on the GEQ-E were categorized as assimilated (n = 27). Students with high scores on the GEQ-E and low scores on the GEQ-A were categorized as separated (n = 28), and students with low scores on both the GEQ-E and GEQ-A were categorized as marginal (n = 6). Internal reliability was high in this sample for both instruments (α = 0.88 for both).

Relationship with Parents and Peers

Participants' perceived quality of parental and peer relationships was measured using the Inventory of Parent and Peer Attachment (IPPA) (Armsden &

Greenberg, 1987). The IPPA has been used with adolescents and young adults ages 12 to 20 years and consists of 28 items for the assessment of parental relationships and 25 items for the assessment of peer relationships. Respondents rated on a 5-point Likert scale how often each statement (e.g., "My parents respect my feelings" and "My friends understand me"). The scale ranges from "1" for "Almost always or always true" to "5" for "Almost never or never true." Internal reliabilities were 0.71 for Parent Attachment and 0.83 for Peer Attachment.

Psychological Well-Being

The Center for Epidemiologic Studies Depression Scales (CES-D) was used to assess the psychological well-being of participants. The CES-D was developed by Radloff (1977) to measure depressive symptomatology in the general population and has been used to assess depression symptoms in adolescents (Radloff, 1991). The CES-D consists of 20 items in a self-report format (e.g., "I did not feel like eating; my appetite was poor."). Respondents are asked to mark each statement according to how often they felt or behaved this way during the past week. Response categories are: "rarely or none of the time" (less than 1 day); "some or a little of the time" (1-2 days); "occasionally or a moderate amount of time" (3-4 days); and "most or all of the time" (3-7 days). Each response is scored from 0 to 3. Higher scores indicate more symptoms. The CES-D has been found to have high internal consistency (0.85 in the general population) (Radloff, 1977) and high internal consistency within an Asian American adult population (Kuo, 1984; Ying, 1988). Internal reliability for this sample was also high ($\alpha = 0.87$).

Procedures

Participants were introduced to the project as a study on the type of stress high school students encounter. Parental consent forms were sent home with the students after the short presentation. Only students with signed consent forms allowing participation in the study were surveyed. Questionnaires were implemented in the classroom to students in a group setting. Students were advised that their participation was not mandatory nor would it have an effect on their grades. The questions were read aloud to participants who needed extra help while subjects marked their own answer sheets.

RESULTS

Findings from bivariate analyses are presented for each hypothesis, followed by an overall model that examines the predictive value of each variable. Given the small number of marginal students, they were dropped from all analyses involving cultural orientation.

Depression

The first hypothesis postulated Asian American adolescents would be more depressed than their White American counterparts. The mean CES-D score was 19.24 (SD = 10.39) in this sample. A one-sample t-test showed it did not differ significantly from Radloff's (1991) sample of White high school students (mean = 17.88, SD = 10.31) [t(143) = 1.57, p = .12].

Cultural Orientation and Depression

The second hypothesis postulated variation in depression level by cultural orientation, specifically that biculturals would have better outcomes than assimilated and separated students. The relationship was tested using analyses of variance tests. Results showed that the three cultural orientation groups did not differ significantly on depression level [F(2,135) = 1.96; p = .15]. Bicultural students had a mean of 18.67 (SD = 9.89) on the CES-D. Assimilated students had a mean of 16.31 (SD = 9.03), and separated students had a mean of 21.53 (SD = 10.30).

Interpersonal Relationships and Depression

The third hypothesis postulated a negative correlation between depression and parental and peer relationships. Pearson product correlations were used to test this hypothesis. As predicted, parental and peer relationships negatively correlated with depressive symptoms (r = −4310; p < .001 for IPPA-Parents and r = −.4737; p < .001 for IPPA-Peers).

Demographic Variables and Depression

To test the last hypothesis regarding the association of demographic control variables and depression level, analyses of variance, Pearson product correlations, and t-tests were used. While girls were hypothesized to report a higher level of depression, a one-tailed t-test revealed no gender difference in the rate of depression. Males reported a mean of 19.42 (SD = 10.40) on the CES-D, and females had a mean of 19.07 (SD = 10.45). (Please see Table 1.)

Late immigrants were hypothesized to report greater depression, followed by early immigrants, then American-born students. This hypothesis was partially supported. Analysis of variance and Scheffe post-hoc tests showed the three migration status groups differed significantly in their depression levels

[F(2, 141) = 3.83, p = .02]. Scheffe post-hoc tests showed late immigrant students reported significantly greater depression (mean = 23.84, SD = 9.03) than American-born students (mean = 17.51, SD = 9.96). There was no significant difference between late and early immigrants (mean = 19.68, SD = 11.32) nor between American-born and early immigrants.

Lower SES students were hypothesized to experience greater depression than higher SES students. Analyses showed SES was not significantly correlated with psychological well-being as measured by the CES-D (r = .10; p = .24). Also, Southeast Asian adolescents were hypothesized to report greater depression symptoms than Chinese adolescents. However, one-tailed t-test results show there was no difference between Chinese (mean = 19.53, SD = 10.45) and Southeast Asian students (mean = 18.31, SD = 10.25) in depression scores.

Overall Model

Because of its high correlation with cultural orientation, migration status was excluded from the overall model. Chi-square analyses showed American-born (see Table 2) respondents were more likely to be bicultural (χ^2 (1) = 30.00, p < .001) or assimilated (χ^2 (1) = 12.88; p < .001) while late immigrants were more likely to have a separated cultural orientation. A multiple regression analysis used to test the overall model was significant (Adjusted

TABLE 2. Beta Weights of Overall Model Predicting Depression

Variable	CES-D
Adjusted R^2	0.26
F-Ratio	6.02***
Gender	
Male vs. Female	0.02
SES	0.06
Ethnic Group	
SE Asian vs Chinese	−0.03
Cultural Orientation	
Assimilated vs Bicultural	−0.14
Separated vs Bicultural	0.08
Separated vs Assimilated	0.20†
Interpersonal Relationships	
IPPA-Parent	−0.35†††
IPPA–Peer	−0.29††

One-tailed tests: †p < .05 ††p < .01 †††p < .001
Two-tailed tests: *p < .05 **p < .01 ***p < .001

$R^2 = .25$, $F[7,121] = 7.00$; $p = .001$) with cultural orientation, parent, and peer relationships as significant predictors of depression. Respondents with a separated orientation had significantly higher scores on the CES-D than those with an assimilated orientation (beta = .20; $p = .03$, one-tailed test). However, respondents with bicultural orientations did not have significantly higher scores on the CES-D than respondents with assimilated (beta = $-.14$, $p = .09$, one-tailed test) or separated orientations (beta = .08, $p = .16$, one-tailed test). Adolescents with positive parent and peer relationships reported lower depression levels (beta = -0.35, $p = .001$, one-tailed test for parent relationships; beta = -0.29, $p = .01$, one-tailed test for peers). None of the demographic control variables (gender, SES, ethnic group) were significant in the model.

DISCUSSION

Contrary to the first hypothesis, there was not a significant difference in depression level between Asian American adolescents in this sample and White adolescents from Radloff's (1991) sample. However, Asian American respondents' level of depressive symptomology was slightly higher and approached significance. A significant difference may not have emerged because this study was based on a sample of convenience. Students with higher depression levels are more likely to have academic and behavior problems, including truancy. These same students, therefore, may not have participated in the study because (a) they were not in class to complete the surveys or (b) they did not return consent forms.

Consistent with the second hypothesis, cultural orientation was a significant predictor of depression. Individuals who were separated (i.e., those with a high orientation towards ethnic culture and low orientation towards American culture) experienced greater depression than students who were assimilated (i.e., those with a high orientation towards American culture and low orientation towards ethnic culture). However, contrary to the hypothesis, bicultural students (i.e., those with a high orientation towards both cultures) did not have the lowest depression level. Ying (1995) proposes that the relationship between cultural orientation and psychological well-being varies by the cultural context. Current findings suggest that the environment of these adolescents (i.e., the school, community, and the larger society) may support students who have a greater mainstream European American orientation and discourage students who have an orientation towards the ethnic culture.

Also as hypothesized, interpersonal relationships were significantly correlated with depression. Individuals with more positive parent and peer relationships experienced lower depression levels. In addition, results of one-sample t-tests showed parental and peer attachment scores for adolescents in this study (mean = 43.60, SD = 16.67 and mean = 47.90, SD = 15.32, respectively) were significantly lower than those reported by Armsden and Greenberg (1987) in their White adolescent sample (parent mean = 60.7, SD = 16.2; peer mean = 56.6, SD = 10.4) (parent: t(143) = − 12.31, p < .001; peer: t(142) = − 6.79, p < .001). This finding indicates that Asian American adolescents have poorer attachments with their parents and peers than White adolescents. Poorer attachment may be a result of intergenerational/intercultural conflicts specific to Asian American immigrant families. For example, communication becomes difficult when parents and children are not proficient in one common language (e.g., children are not fluent in their parents' native language and parents are not fluent in English). Conflicts may also arise as Asian American adolescents quickly adopt mainstream values (e.g., individualism vs. collectivism) and customs (e.g., asserting their opinions) at a much faster rate than their parents. While the effects of migration may influence the parent-child relationship, it does not adequately explain the lower quality of peer relationships reported by Asian American adolescents. Instead, it may be that even among their peers, Asian American adolescents do not have support for issues related to cultural conflicts. Future studies need to further examine the nature of Asian American adolescent peer relationships.

The last hypothesis examining demographic characteristics was only partially confirmed. While there were no differences in depression levels by gender, ethnic group, or SES, there was a difference by migration status. Gender differences may not have been evident because other factors such as cultural orientation or interpersonal relationships may be more pertinent to this population. That is, girls in this sample may find general cultural differences (e.g., behaviors, language) more problematic than issues related to gender roles and expectations. Chinese American adolescents may not have reported greater depression than Southeast Asian adolescents because inner-city Chinese Americans may suffer from significant distress due to economic and migration factors (e.g., loss of family's social and economic status in the U.S.) and thus do not vary in the *amount* of stress experienced by Southeast Asian refugees/children of refugees. Future studies need to examine whether there is a difference in the source of stress for different ethnic groups. SES may not have been a significant predictor of depression because of the homogeneity within the sample as will be discussed in the next section on limitations of the study. As hypothesized, late immigrants reported significantly greater depression than American-born students. There are at least two factors that may contribute towards this difference. First, it may be that migration during adolescence is especially stressful because it is a critical period for social and identity development. Second, late immigrants may report greater depression because they have had less time to adjust to the new culture. Although differences were not significant, as hypothesized, early immigrants reported depression levels in between American-born and late immigrants. This finding is supportive of the above two explanations.

Study Limitations and Directions for Future Research

This study had a few limitations that should be addressed in future studies. First, the sample was homogeneous in terms of generational status and SES. It is not representative of Asian Americans as a whole. These results, therefore, may not be generalizable to other Asian American adolescents. Future studies must address the diversity within the Asian American community by sampling adolescents from various generations (e.g., first, second, third, and later generations), ethnic groups (separating Southeast Asians into separate ethnic groups), SES, and cultural orientations (including marginal students). Also, the question of potential variation in depression level between Asian American and White American adolescents should be further examined using a more diverse and representative Asian American sample.

In addition, some students with poor English language skills had difficulty completing the survey. This may compromise the accuracy of their responses. Future studies should make surveys available in respondents' native languages to ensure better reliability and validity.

This study was designed to ascertain the contributions of cultural orientation and interpersonal relationships on depression. Future investigations need to assess the specific variables that influence cultural orientation and parent and peer relationships. For example, does classroom curriculum that includes Asian American content influence cultural orientation? Do differential rates of acculturation such as the acquisition of English language skills influence parent and child relationships? And does participation in structured social activities influence peer relationships? This information is essential in planning prevention and intervention programs.

IMPLICATIONS AND CONCLUSIONS

Results from this study indicate inner-city Asian Americans are in need of attention and appropriate mental health services, as suggested by the large number of respondents with high depression levels. Programs that help make smoother transitions into the American culture for recent immigrants and/or foster greater parent-child and peer relationships are essential. Examples of programs that can help ameliorate depression in youth include ones that work with immigrant parents on the one hand (i.e., teaching parents child rearing practices that bridge the gap between Eastern and Western cultures), and with their children and adolescents on the other (i.e., help them learn and appreciate their parents' traditional cultures). One such program is SITICAF (Strengthening of Intergenerational/Intercultural Ties in Immigrant Chinese American Families), which has shown that a parenting intervention program improves intergenerational relationships (Ying, 1999). Professionals working with adolescents also need to help those who have recently immigrated to this country in learning and adapting positively to the ways of their new home. One way to accomplish this may be to explicitly teach adolescents the differences in values, beliefs, and behaviors between their native culture and the culture of their new homeland. Discussing the process of acculturation and normalizing their feelings during the process may be helpful. More importantly, researchers and practitioners working with Asian Americans must take into account the heterogeneity of the community and the complexity of the problems they face in order to better understand and serve this growing population.

REFERENCES

Aldwin, C., & Greenberger, E. (1987). Cultural differences in the predictors of depression. *American Journal of Community Psychology*, 15(6), 789-813.

Armsden, G., & Greenberg, M. (1987). The Inventory of Parent and Peer Attachment: Individual differences and their relationship to psychological well-being in adolescence. *Journal of Youth & Adolescence*, 16(5), 427-454.

Atkinson, D. R., Morten, G., & Sue, D. W. (1989). A minority identity development model. In D. R. Atkinson, G. Morten, and D. W. Sue (Eds.), *Counseling American minorities: A cross cultural perspective*, (pp. 35-47). Dubeque: William C. Brown.

Aseltine, R., Gore, S., & Colten, M. (1998). The co-occurrence of depression and substance abuse in late adolescence. Development & Psychopathology, 10(3), 549-570.

Avison, W., & McAlpine, D. (1992). Gender differences in symptoms of depression among adolescents. *Journal of Health & Social Behavior*, 33(2), 77-96.

Berry, J. W. (1984). Cultural relations in plural societies: Alternatives to segregation and their sociopsychological implications. In N. Miller & M. Brewer (Eds.), *Group in contact.* New York: Academic Press.

Cuellar, I., & Roberts, R. (1997). Relations of depression, acculturation, and socioeconomic status in a Latino sample. *Hispanic Journal of Behavioral Sciences*, 19(2), 230-238.

Erikson, E. (1964). *Childhood and society.* New York: W. W. Norton & Co.

Finch, A., Casat, C., & Carey, M. (1990). Depression in children and adolescents. In S. B. Morgan & T.M. Okwumabua (Eds.), *Child and Adolescent Disorders: Developmental and Health Psychology Perspective* (pp. 135-172). Hillsdale, NJ: Lawrence Erlbaum Associates.

Gil, A., Vega, W. A., & Dimas, J. (1994). Acculturative stress and personal adjustment among Hispanic adolescent boys. *Journal of Community Psychology*, 22(1), 43-54.

Golding, J., & Burnam, M. (1990). Stress and social support as predictors of depressive symptoms in Mexican Americans and non-Hispanic Whites. *Journal of Social & Clinical Psychology*, 9(2), 268-287.

Hollingshead, A. (1957). Two factor index of social position. New Haven, CT: Yale University Press.

Hurd, K., Wooding, S., & Noller, P. (1999). Parent-adolescent relationships in families with depressed and self-harming adolescents. *Journal of Family Studies*, 5(1), 47-68.

Kuo, W. H. (1984). Prevalence of depression among Asian-Americans. *Journal of Nervous & Mental Disease*, 172(8), 449-457.

Padilla, A. (1992). Bicultural development: A theoretical and empirical examination. Unpublished.

Padilla, A., Alvarez, M., & Lindholm, K. (1986). Generational status and personality factors as predictors of stress in students. *Hispanic Journal of Behavioral Sciences*, 8(3), 275-288.

Padilla, A., Wagatsuma, Y., & Lindholm, K. (1985a). Acculturation and personality as predictors of stress in Japanese and Japanese-Americans. *Journal of Social Psychology*, 125(3), 295-305.

Radloff, L. S. (1977). The CES-D scale: A self-report depression scale for research in the general population. *Applied Psychological Measurement*, 1(3), 385-401.

Radloff, L. S. (1991). The use of the Center for Epidemiologic Studies Depression Scale in adolescents and young adults. *Journal of Youth and Adolescence*, 20(2), 149-166.

Reynolds, W. M., & Johnston, H. F. (1994). The nature and study of depression in children and adolescents. In Reynolds & Johnston (Eds.), *Handbook of Depression in Children and Adolescents*, (pp. 3-13). New York: Plenum Press.

Roberts, R., Roberts, C., & Chen, Y. (1997). Ethnocultural differences in prevalence of adolescent depression. *American Journal of Community Psychology*, 25(1), 95-110.

Sluzki, C. (1979, December). Migration and Family Conflict. *Family Process*, 18(4), 379-390.

Sue, S., Sue, D. W., Sue, L., & Takeuchi, D. T. (1995). Psychopathology among Asian Americans: A model minority? *Cultural Diversity & Mental Health*, 1(1), 39-51.

Tsai, J. L., Ying, Y., & Lee, P. A. (2000). The meaning of "being Chinese" and "being American" variation among Chinese American young adults. *Journal of Cross Cultural Psychology,* 31, 302-322.

U.S. Bureau of the Census (1998). Current population survey.

Ying, Y. (1988). Depressive symptomatology among Chinese-Americans as measured by the CES-D. *Journal of Clinical Psychology*, 44(5), 739-746.

Ying, Y. (1995). Cultural orientation and psychological well-being in Chinese Americans. *American Journal of Community Psychology*, 23(6), 893-911.

Ying, Y. (1999). Strengthening intergenerational/intercultural ties in migrant families: A new intervention for parents. *Journal of Community Psychology*, 27(1), 89-96.

Ying, Y., & Akutsu, P. D. (1997). Psychological adjustment of Southeast Asian refugees: The contribution of sense of coherence. *Journal of Community Psychology*, 25(2), 125-139.

Causal Modeling Predicting Psychological Adjustment of Korean-Born Adolescent Adoptees

Dong Pil Yoon

SUMMARY. Self-concept theory and ethnic identity theory imply causal relations among positive parent-child relationship, ethnic pride, and psychological adjustment of children who were intercountry adopted. This study used linear measurement and structural equation models to test the plausibility of the causal model dealing with the relations among indexes of parent's support of ethnic background, positive parent-child relationship, collective self-esteem, and psychological adjustment in a sample of 241 Korean-born adolescent adoptees. Consistent with the expectations of the self-concept theory and the ethnic identity development theory, the findings show that a more positive parent-child relationship, in which the parents support their children's ethnic identity development and share ethnic socialization experiences, predicts better psychological adjustment of the adopted children. Policy and practice implications of the findings are discussed. *[Article copies available for a fee from The Haworth Document Delivery Service: 1-800-342-9678. E-mail address: <getinfo@haworthpressinc.com> Website: <http://www.HaworthPress.com> © 2001 by The Haworth Press, Inc. All rights reserved.]*

Dong Pil Yoon, PhD, is Assistant Professor, West Virginia University, School of Social Work and Public Administration, Division of Social Work, B20 Knapp Hall, Morgantown, WV 26506. (e-mail: dyoon@wvu.edu)

The author would like to thank Chuck Cowger, Harry Triandis, and Rod McDonald for their support, encouragement, and insightful comments on the research. The author also wishes to thank David Lim and Clarice Aeby for their helpful contributions during the stages of the research.

[Haworth co-indexing entry note]: "Causal Modeling Predicting Psychological Adjustment of Korean-Born Adolescent Adoptees." Yoon, Dong Pil. Co-published simultaneously in *Journal of Human Behavior in the Social Environment* (The Haworth Press, Inc.) Vol. 3, No. 3/4, 2001, pp. 65-82; and: *Psychosocial Aspects of the Asian-American Experience: Diversity Within Diversity* (ed: Namkee G. Choi) The Haworth Press, Inc., 2001, pp. 65-82. Single or multiple copies of this article are available for a fee from The Haworth Document Delivery Service [1-800-342-9678, 9:00 a.m. - 5:00 p.m. (EST). E-mail address: getinfo@haworthpressinc.com].

65

KEYWORDS. Intercountry adoption, ethnic identity, structural equation modeling, psychological adjustment, collective self-esteem

Rigorous application of upper-level statistical measurement and analyses is necessary to understand the complex interaction of cultural and familial structures in identity formation, particularly for children raised in either intercountry or transracial adoptive families. A great deal of confusion and disagreement has long surrounded the issue of adoption across ethnic and racial boundaries. Heretofore, the complexity of different cultural and familial structures has brought broad definitions of ethnic identity and, therefore, the absence of more precise measurement and insufficient data analysis on intercountry adoption. As a result of these gaps in measurement and analysis, results yielded have been inconclusive (Kirk, 1965; Kim, 1978; Feigelman & Silverman, 1983; Smith, 1991). This lack of clarity is particularly troubling in understanding the importance of parent-child relationship in the development of adoptees' ethnic identity and collective self-esteem (i.e., ethnic pride).

Given the importance of understanding self-image of youth in a culturally diverse world, the small microcosm of intercountry adoption affords the opportunity to carefully study interaction among culture, ethnicity, and parent-child relationship. The purpose of this study is to raise the level of measurement and analysis typically reported in adoption literature and to statistically account for collective self-esteem and the interactive properties associated with its development. Specifically, the study reports the research process–the trajectory of inquiry–applied to the interaction of parents' support of children's ethnic backgrounds, parent-child relationships, and the children's ethnic identities and collective self-esteem on psychological adjustment of Korean-born adopted children. Structural Equation Modeling (SEM) is demonstrated as extremely useful in explaining more complex relationships between aspects of the adoptees' ethnic identity development process. As a result, this study yields more conclusive findings than those of previous studies.

BACKGROUND: ADOPTION OF KOREAN CHILDREN

For the past four decades, Korea allowed almost unrestricted adoption of its orphaned and abandoned children by foreigners. About 90,000 Korean-born children were adopted by American families since 1956 (Lee, 1996). In particular, during the 1980s, more than 40,000 Korean-born children were adopted by North Americans, representing the largest number of all transculturally adopted children. Korea has been the most frequently used source for Westerners, particularly U.S. citizens, seeking to adopt children from other countries.

Intercountry adoptions have been less politicized than transracial adoptions because many believe that issues such as ethnic identity and mental health of intercountry-adopted children are less important than the consequences of remaining in an orphanage or an economically depressed country (Ressler, Boothby, & Steinbock, 1988). Furthermore, intercountry adoptions have received less research attention than transracial adoptions in the United States because it is difficult for researchers to extrapolate and transfer research findings from one ethnic group to another, given that social identity formation can be changed according to social, environmental, and historical processes. Thus, despite the potentially significant role of ethnic identity for transculturally adopted children, empirical attention to the subject has been limited. Most past research has concentrated on a single factor, such as the self-esteem or mental health of adopted children, thereby neglecting the complex relationship between adoptive family structures and the children's ethnic identity formation processes. Moreover, most extant intercountry adoption studies in the U.S. are based on small sample sizes and only report on family demographic data and general initial adjustment patterns of adopted children. Only a few previous studies reported that intercountry-adopted Korean children and intraracially adopted children in the U.S. were not different in long-term adjustment patterns (Wood, 1972; Kim, 1977).

THEORETICAL FRAMEWORK AND PREVIOUS STUDIES

The analytical model in this study is based on two theories: the self-concept theory (Erickson, 1968) and the ethnic identity development theory (McGoldrick, 1982; Smith, 1991; Spencer & Marktrom-Adams, 1990). According to the self-concept theory, family support, including feelings of love and belonging, plays an important function in the lives of adolescents experiencing stress in their interpersonal environment. Bagley, Verma, Mallick, and Young (1979) and Coopersmith (1981), addressing issues of adjustment in the adopted children, found that love and the stability of the family structure led to positive self-esteem. In addition to the consistency and warmth of the family environment, previous studies have also shown that certain parental motivations for choosing to adopt a child with a different racial and ethnic background predict the child's healthy self-concept (Kim, 1978; Koh, 1988).

Identification with one's ethnic group is considered crucial for positive mental health of the ethnic individual. More specifically, Smith (1991) stated that acceptance of one's ethnic group as a positive reference group leads to positive self-esteem, whereas rejection leads to self-estrangement and maladaptive psychological behavior. An individual needs to have an ethnic sense of belonging (to any ethnic group) in order to prevent social alienation and self-estrangement. Thus, the identity that one constructs represents a set of internalized meanings attributed to the self in a social position or role. An identity, therefore, serves as a standard or reference for who one is. Therefore, it can be predicted that when ethnic identity provides a sense of positive rather than negative social identity, development through adolescence will see a consolidation of ethnic identity as a source of positive evaluation and self-definition.

Spencer and Marktrom-Adams (1990) define ethnic identity development as a process in which an individual is constantly assessing the "fit" between his/herself and his/her cultural environment. Especially for children, who are in the formative stage of their identity development, their sense of a good "fit" is likely to be crucially important for their psychological well-being. Both the facts of being adopted and of being ethnically different from most people in the surrounding community cause the adopted adolescent, in theory at least, to find identity development tasks substantially more difficult. Despite the assumed significant relationship between ethnic identity, ethnic pride, and psychological adjustment of adopted children, however, previous studies examining that relationship reported conflicting findings. By using factor analysis revealing factors of ethnic identification, ethnic pride, and ethnic shame variables, Feigelman and Silverman (1983) found these factors to be of considerable importance in the adjustment of Korean-born adolescent adoptees. In contrast, Kim (1978), Bagley and Young (1981), and Gill and Jackson (1983) failed to find any significant association between ethnic pride and psychological adjustment. However, as those studies merely attempted to find the child's level of ethnic identity and self-esteem separately, there are critical limitations to understanding the dynamics of how these factors can impact on intercountry-adopted children's psychological adjustment. In particular, while measurements of racial identity and self-esteem can be accepted as reliable, their validity remains questionable for this population. It is uncertain that these measurements really measure what the researchers set out to measure.

Reviewing previous intercountry adoption studies, there is no research which indicates whether or not parents' support of children's ethnic background is crucial for psychological adjustment of Korean-born adoptees. Because the family is the primary social system through which culture is transmitted (McGoldrick, 1982), parents' support for children's ethnic identity development is likely to be a significant factor for their psychological well-being. Phinney and Chavira (1992) found that familial support might be an important prerequisite for minority youths to explore their culture of origin.

To fill in some gaps in previous research, based on the findings of Feigelman and Silverman (1983), Smith (1991), and Phinney and Chavira (1992), this study posits a theoretical model that a positive relationship between adoptive parents and children in terms of sharing experiences of the children's ethnic socialization is the fundamental factor in the children's identity development process. In particular, based on the perspectives and experiences of adoptees, the reduction of racial or ethnic identity to a more specific and objective concept has been taken into account. Collective self-esteem or ethnic pride as an intervening variable is, therefore, determined to be a measurable indicator of ethnic identity.

METHOD

Sample and Data Collection

A purposive sample of 800 Korean adolescent adoptees identified through the Holt International Children's Service and were sent a survey instrument accompanied by a cover letter explaining the purpose of the study and an informed consent form. The subjects of this survey were both adoptive parents and adolescent adoptees. Data were collected from the middle of September through late November 1996. Completed mail questionnaires were obtained for 241 adolescent adoptees from 28 states of the U.S., representing a 30% response rate.

The mean age of the children was 14. The range of ages represented in the actual sample was 12 to 19. The majority of respondents (92%) had no physical or mental problems; only a small percentage (8%) of the subjects reported having a physical disability. In terms of ethnicity of the adoptive parents, a majority (95%) were Caucasian, and the rest were minorities (Asian, Hispanic, American Indian, and other). About 95% of the adoptive parents were married, with only a small percentage of them divorced (3%) or widowed (2%). Most adoptive parents had a high level of education; 27% had a college degree, and 21% had a master's degree or beyond. One half of the sample reported an annual income of $20,000 to $69,999, 21% fell within the $70,000 to $89,999 range, and 29% had an income over $90,000. In terms of racial composition of neighborhood, 77% of the respondents live in predominantly white communities compared to 23% in integrated communities.

Variables and Instruments

Based on the review of existing literature, exogenous latent variables (parental support of ethnic background and positive parent-child relationship) and endogenous latent variables (collective self-esteem and psychological adjustment) were constructed as independent and dependent variables for this study. Positive well-being, distress, personal self-esteem, ethnic pride, direct support of ethnic background, indirect support of ethnic background, warmth, and positive communication were constructed as observed variables.

Variable 1: Parents' Support of Child's Ethnic Background

The researcher had developed an eight-item scale to measure parents' direct and indirect support of child's ethnic background, with positive and negative modes. With factor analysis, however, one item was dropped due to lack of validity, and only seven items were adopted as indicators for the measurement of this exogenous latent variable. Respondents used a six-point Likert scale to indicate the extent of their agreement with the items. The scores for negative items were reverse scored.

Variable 2: Parent-Child Relationship

To measure positive parent-child relationships, items were selected from the Parental Acceptance-Rejection Questionnaire (PARQ; Barner & Olson, 1982) and the Parent-Adolescent Communication Scale (PACS). Subscales of the child version of PARQ (Rohner, 1986) assessed aspects of warmth in parent-child relationships. The rejection items were reverse scored and combined with the acceptance items to form a measure of parental warmth. The internal consistency reliabilities (Cronbach's alpha) were .77 and .75 for acceptance (20 items) and rejection (10 items), respectively. For this study, five items were selected from each dimension of acceptance and rejection according to the size of the factor loadings.

The PACS was composed of two scales–one that measured the degree of openness in family communication, and one that assessed the extent of problems in family communication. Each scale was composed of 10 items and used a 6-point Likert-type response format (1 = strongly disagree, 6 = strongly agree; the scores for negative items were reversed in value). Alpha reliabilities for each subscale were .87 and .78. For this study, the researcher selected five items from the Open Family Communication Scale and four items from the Problems in Family Communication Scale according to the size of the factor loadings reported. Parental warmth and positive parent-child communication were used as indicators of positive parent-child relationships.

Variable 3: Collective Self-Esteem

To measure children's collective self-esteem/positive ethnic pride, items were selected from the Multigroup Ethnic Identity Measure (MEIM) (Phinney, 1992). The MEIM, consisting of a single scale of 14 items, assessed three aspects of ethnic identity: positive ethnic attitude and sense of belonging, ethnic identity achievement, and ethnic behaviors or practices. The reliability of the MEIM is .81 with high school students (Phinney, 1992). In order to accurately specify and objectively measure collective self-esteem of adoptees, three dimensions were shifted to two dimensions: ethnic pride and ethnic involvement. In addition, a new indicator was developed: shame about ethnic origin, which was a negative dimension of ethnic pride (reversed scores of extent of shame about ethnic origin). In other words, the Collective Self-Esteem Scale (CSE) was composed of two scales–one that measured the degree of positive ethnic pride and one that assessed ethnic involvement. Based on the factor analysis, five items were selected for ethnic pride and seven items were selected for ethnic involvement, dropping three items due to low validity. The CSE used a 6-point Likert-type response format (1 = strongly disagree, 6 = strongly agree).

Variable 4: Personal Self-Esteem

To measure children's personal self-esteem, items were selected from the Rosenberg Self-Esteem Scale (RSE). The RSE (Rosenberg, 1965) is composed of two scales–one that measures the degree of self-regard and one that assesses the extent of self-derogation. Each scale consists of five items. These scales were developed as a multidimensional factor structure by Carmines and Zeller (1979) and Kaplan and Pokorny (1969). Alpha reliability for the single scale is .93. The self-derogation items were reverse scored in value. In order to decrease the number of items, four items were selected from each dimension of self-regard and self-derogation by dropping one item, respectively. The RSE uses a 6-point Likert-type response format. The RSE has been reported as having good reproducibility and scalability.

Variable 5: Psychological Adjustment

To measure psychological adjustment, items were selected from the State-Trait Anxiety Inventory (STAI), the Beck's Depression Inventory (BDI), the Affect Balance Scale (ABS), and the Satisfaction with Life Scale (SWLS). Psychological adjustment was composed of two dimensions–one that measured the degree of distress through anxiety and depression and one that assessed the extent of positive well-being through positive affect and satisfaction with life. The STAI (Spielberger, 1979), consisting of a single scale of 20 items and the BDI (Beck, 1961), consisting of a single scale of 21 items, measured the degree of psychological distress. Six items were selected from the first scale and six items from the second scale in order to decrease the number of items. Cronbach alpha reliabilities for each subscale were .85 and .86. These subscales measured the negative dimensions of psychological adjustment.

The ABS (Bradburn, 1969), consisting of 10 items and the SWLS (Diener et al., 1985), consisting of 5 items, measured the degree of positive psychological well-being. Five items were selected from the first scale by selecting positive items and all five items from the second scale. Cronbach alpha reliabilities for each subscale were .64 and .84. These were the positive dimensions of adjustment.

The STAI, BDI, and ABS used a 6-point Likert-type response format (1 = none of the time, 6 = all of the time) and the SL used a 6-point Likert-type response format (1 = strongly disagree, 6 = strongly agree).

Data Analysis

Causal relationships among the five latent variables as well as the relationship between latent variables and observed variables were examined by Structural Equation Modeling (SEM-PROC-CALIS:LINEQS), using a maximum likelihood method for the estimation of parameters of the proposed model. In the measurement model, the process of model modification was explained according to the goodness-of-fit index, along with a test of reliability and validity of all the variables. In the structural model, a theoretically meaningful and statistically accepted model was presented, including direct and indirect effects of latent variables.

In order to determine the appropriateness of the model fit, the chi-square test statistic for goodness-of-fit was used. The literature suggests that researchers should not rely solely on chi-square because it does not work equally well with various types of fit indices, sample sizes, estimators, or distributions (Bollen, 1989; Hayduck, 1987; Joreskog & Sorbom, 1992: La Du & Tanaka, 1989). Therefore, the alternative goodness-of-fit indices provided by the program included the Goodness-of-Fit Index (GFI), Adjusted Goodness-of-Fit Index (AGFI), Root Mean-Square Residuals (RMR), Bentler's Comparative Fit Index (CFI), McDonald's Centrality Index (MCI; 1989), and Bentler and Bonett's Normed Fit Index (NFI) and Non-Normed Fit Index (NNFI).

RESULTS

Model Revision

In advance of the model revision, two improper solutions were found, representing an unsuitable model for the data. First, the correlation between psychological adjustment (F1) and personal self-esteem (F2) was estimated over 1.0, representing negative eigenvalue in PHI matrix which consists of the residual terms paired with manifest variables or other residual terms. Therefore, these two factors were considered as one factor. In addition, factor loading (V6) was greater than 1.0. Therefore, according to Heywood cases, the factor loading was constrained at 1.0 and the residual variance was constrained at 0.0 to solve the problem (Bollen, 1989).

The chi-square value for the initial theoretical model (Figure 1) was statistically significant, $\chi^2 = 232.78$, $p < .0001$ (df = 25; $N = 241$). A number of other results, however, indicated that there was in fact a problem with the model's fit. The GFI was .819, and the AGFI was .675, not representing a "good" fit. The RMR, the square root of the average of the squared residuals, was .140. Bentler's CFI was .798 and Bentler and Bonett's (1980) NNFI was .709. Bentler and Bonett's (1980) NFI was .782, and MCI was .650, representing a "not good" fit (see Table 1).

In this respecified model, the improvement in fit is substantial if the error terms of V8 and V9 of the parent-child relationship are allowed to covary. These two variables are conceptually similar, both relating love and affection toward children, and, therefore, it is plausible that their error terms are corre-

FIGURE 1. The Initial Revised Theoretical Model

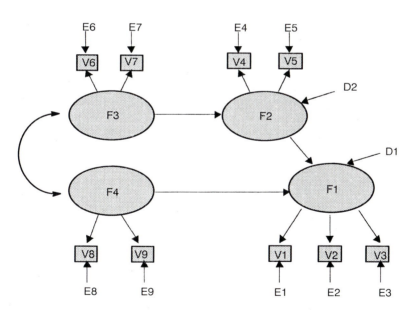

F1 = Psychological Adjustment V1 = Positive Well-Being; V2 = Distress; V3 = Personal Self-Esteem; F2 = Collective Self-Esteem; V4 = Ethnic Pride; V5 = Ethnic Involvement; F3 = Parent's Support of Ethnic Background; V7 = Indirect Support of Ethnic Background; F4 = Positive Parent-Child Relationship; V8 = Warmth; V9 = Positive Communication; D1 = Error of F1; D2 = Error of F2

lated. The resulting estimation yielded a model with $\chi^2 = 109.4$. In addition, covariation between the error terms of V4 and V5 of the collective self-esteem subscale yielded $\chi^2 = 24.2$. Conceptually, having ethnic pride and involvement in ethnic activity or ethnic group are believed to support each other in increasing collective self-esteem. With this theoretical support, the correlation between two residual variances was released to be estimated. The covariation of the error terms was added, instead of deleting one of the variables, because these variables were not as highly correlated but were conceptually related. With the combination of each pair of error terms of variables (E4 & E5 and E8 & E9), goodness-of-fit indices showed that the revised measurement model displayed values of .918 on GFI, .840 on AGFI, .088 on RMR, .926 on CFI, .907 on NFI, and .884 on NNFI. Though the value of model fit was increased, the revised measurement model was still unaccepted as the study's "final" theoretical model.

A review of the model's residuals revealed that the distribution of normalized residuals was asymmetrical and that two of the asymptotically standardized residuals were relatively large (in excess of 4.0). Furthermore, there was still one negative eigenvalue in the PHI matrix. Hence, V5 (ethnic involvement), having high asymptotically standardized residuals, was dropped from the revised model, simultaneously dropping covariations between both error variances between V4 and V5 and V8 and V9.

Table 2 presents the intercorrelations for the measured variables used in this study. Goodness-of-fit indices showed that the re-revised model displayed values of .944 on GFI, .894 on AGFI, .054 on RMR, .958 on CFI, .939 on NFI, .938 on NNFI, and .924 on MCI. Values on all goodness-of-fit indices of the revised model were well within the acceptable range (in excess of .90). As seen in Table 1, chi-square for the final revised model dropped from 232.78 (df = 25, p = .000) to 57.13 (df = 19, p = .000), representing a "good" fit. All other goodness-of-fit indices showed incremental improvement in overall model fit. Therefore, this re-revised model was accepted as the study's "final" theoretical model.

Evaluation of Measurement Model

In the study, one of its indicators of endogenous latent variables was fixed at 1.0 and variances of exogenous latent variables were standardized to 1.0 in order to set the scale of each latent variable. The t scores obtained for the coefficients in Table 3 range from -11.10 to 16.47, indicating that all factor loadings were significant ($p <.001$). Standard errors of factor loadings ranged from .071 for distress to .055 for parent's indirect support of ethnic background, representing reliable measures of latent constructs. The squared multiple correlations ranged from .500 (for distress) to .824 (for open communication).

TABLE 1. Overall Goodness-of-Fit Indices for Hypothesized Theoretical Model

Model	Absolute Indices					Incremental Indices			Parsimony Index	
	χ^2	df	p	GFI	RMR	CFI	NFI	NNFI	MCI	AGFI
1. Initial theoretical model (four factors with 9 variables)	232.8	25	.000	.819	.140	.798	.782	.709	.650	.675
2. Respecified model (combined two pairs of error terms: E4 & E5 and E8 & E9)	99.2	23	.000	.918	.088	.926	.907	.884	.854	.840
3. Respecified final model (8 variables: dropping V5 and covariance of E4 & E5 and E8 & E9)	57.1	19	.000	.944	.054	.958	.939	.938	.924	.894

Note: N = 241. GFI = Goodness-of-Fit Index; RMR = Root Mean-Square Residual; CFI = Comparative Fit Index; NNFI = Non-normed-Fit Index; AGFI = Non-Normed-Fit Index; AGFI = Adjusted Goodness-of-Fit Index; MCI = McDonald's Centrality Index

The path coefficients between parent's support of ethnic background and its indicators were: direct support of ethnic background, 1.0 (constrained), and indirect support of ethnic background, .73 (t = 16.47, p < .001) (Figure 2). Estimates indicated that these maximum likelihood paths were all significant (p < .001). Distress had a negative path parameter with the exogenous latent variable, psychological adjustment. Personal self-esteem had the highest path coefficient with the exogenous latent variable. The path coefficients between psychological adjustment and the measure for all indicators had high factor loadings.

Evaluation of Structural Model

All path coefficients were statistically significant (p < .05), ranging from 4.18 to 9.20 (t value). Squared multiple correlation (R-Square) for the structural equation was .067 on collective self-esteem, indicating that about 7% of the variance of the structural equation of collective self-esteem (F2 = PF2F3 F3) was explained by parent's support of the child's ethnic background (F3); R-Square was .593 on psychological adjustment, indicating that about 59% of the variance of structural equation of psychological adjustment was explained by collective self-esteem (F2) and parent-child relationship (F4). In addition, the correlation between two exogenous latent constructs (F3 and F4) was .36 (see Table 4).

The subsequent analysis supported that parent's support of the child's ethnic background had a direct positive impact on the child's collective

TABLE 2. Correlation Matrix Among Measured Variables for Re-Revised Hypothesized Model

Variable	V1	V2	V3	V4	V5	V6	V7	V8
V1								
V2	.50***							
V3	.69***	− .67***						
V4	.35***	.36***	.43***					
V5	.26***	− .11	.19**	.28***				
V6	.16*	− .10	.15*	.20**	.75***			
V7	.54***	− .38***	.40***	.11	.37***	.22***		
V8	.61***	− .41***	.51***	.15*	.34***	.20**	.72***	

Note: N = 241; *p < .05; **p < .01; *** p < .001

V1 = Positive Well-Being; V2 = Distress; V3 = Personal Self-Esteem; V4 = Ethnic Pride; V5 = Direct Support of Ethnic Background; V6 = Indirect Support of Ethnic Background; V7 = Warmth; V8 = Positive Communication

self-esteem, indicating that the coefficient between two factors is .26 ($t = 4.18$, $p < .05$) (see Figure 2). In this model, the parent's support of ethnic background can be a partial factor to increase the child's collective self-esteem, suggesting that a large portion of unexplained variances should be considered. The path coefficient between parent-child relationships and psychological adjustment was highly significant, (F4 ⇒ F1 = .63, $t = 9.20$, $p < .05$). The subsequent analysis supported that collective self-esteem as a mediator had a direct positive impact on the individual's psychological adjustment, indicating that the path coefficient between two factors is .39 ($t = 7.05$, $p < .05$). In this model, the indirect effect of parents' support of the child's ethnic background on psychological adjustment is insignificant [.101 = (.260 × 388)].

DISCUSSION

The psychological adjustment of intercountry-adopted children has not been examined previously in relation to the parental support of ethnic background. This study investigated the effects of parental support of ethnic identity development on the children's psychological adjustment while taking into account the mediating effect of collective self-esteem. The results of this study provide empirical evidence that a positive parent-child relationship had a direct positive effect on the child's psychological adjustment, suggesting that adoptive status alone is not likely to result in the child's negative identity development. Consistent with previous research (Feigelman & Silverman,

TABLE 3. Properties of the Re-Revised Final Measurement Model

Indicators	Standardized Loading	t [a]	Reliability	Error Variance
F1				
V1	.795		.632[b]	.368[c]
V2	−.707	−11.10	.500	.500
V3	.868	13.51	.753	.247
F2				
V4	1.000	d	1.000	.000
F3				
V5	1.000	1.000	.000	
V6	.728	16.47	.530	.470
F4				
V7	.795	13.39	.632	.368
V8	.908	15.76	.824	.176

a All t tests were significant at $p < .001$.
b Calculated as the square of the standardized factor loading (= R^2).
c Calculated as 1 minus the indicator reliability.
d PROC-CALIS does not provide t values for indicator measured variables (these factor loadings are to be constrained to 1.00).

F1 = Psychological Adjustment; V1 = Positive Well-Being; V2 = Distress; V3 = Personal Self-Esteem; F2 = Collective Self-Esteem; V4 = Ethnic Pride; F3 = Parent's Support of Ethnic Background; V5 = Direct Support of Ethnic Background; V6 = Indirect Support of Ethnic Background; F4 = Positive Parent-Child Relationship; V7 = Warmth; V8 = Positive Communication.

1983), the findings clearly demonstrate that parental support of ethnic socialization was associated with a positive sense of ethnic identity (a cluster of self-conceptions involving ethnic pride and negative image about ethnic origins). This indicates that a negative sense of ethnic identity may represent a vulnerability to psychological maladjustment. In other words, these findings highlight that Korean-born adolescents who describe their parents as supporters of ethnic socialization feel more positively about their ethnic origins. As hypothesized, collective self-esteem had direct effects on psychological adjustment, including mental health and self-esteem, demonstrating that the greater one's collective self-esteem, the less likely one is to have psychological problems. By differentiating collective self-esteem from the broad concept of ethnic identity and by utilizing Structural Equation Modeling (SEM), this study was able to find the causal relationship between collective self-esteem and psychological adjustment, along with moderate correlation between parental support of ethnic background and a positive parent-child relationship. In other words, this study shows that parental support of ethnic back-

FIGURE 2. The Re-revised (and Final) Theoretical Model (Involving Path Coefficents)

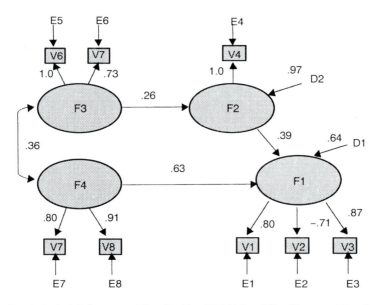

F1 = Psychological Adjustment; V1 = Positive Well-Being; V2 = Distress; V3 = Personal Self-Esteem; F2 = Collective Self-Esteem; V4 = Ethnic Pride; F3 = Parent's Support of Ethnic Background; V5 = Direct Support of Ethnic Background; V6 = Indirect Suppport of Ethnic Background; F4 = Positive Parent-Child Relationship; V7 = Positive Communication; D1 = Error of F1; D2 = Error of F2

ground plays a significant role in making a connection between a positive parent-child relationship and collective self-esteem.

Several limitations exist within this study. The first limitation is the lack of generalizability of the findings. The study sample may not be representative of all families who adopted Korean-born children. The second limitation is the validity and reliability of two measured indicators involving parent's direct and indirect support of ethnic background. Although item development, involving relatively few items, was based on the ethnic identity scale using psychometrically sound measurement procedures and the internal consistency coefficient was adequate, the measure's validity in the study was not directly evaluated. Finally, although the present model posits a causal influence in the context of intercountry adoption, directionality could not be asserted within the present study. Given the cross-sectional nature of the present investigation, it is quite possible that the direction of causality may be reversed.

TABLE 4. Structural Parameter Estimates for the Re-Revised Model

Path	Parameter		Standardized Coefficient	Standard Error
Direct Effect				
F2→F1	PF1F2	F2	.388	.035
F4→F1	PF1F4	F4	.630	.044
F3→F2	PF2F3	F3	.260	.062
Correlation between Exogenous Constructs				
F3↔F4	CF3F4		.361	.059
Indirect Effect				
F3→F2→F1			.101	
Squared Multiple Correlations for Structural Equations				
	F1 (Psychological Adjustment)		.593	
	F2 (Collective Self-Esteem)		.067	

F1 = Psychological Adjustment; F2 = Collective Self-Esteem; F3 = Parent's Support of Ethnic Background; F4 = Positive Parent-Child Relationship

The findings and limitations of the study provide some directions for future research. First, because of the exploratory nature of the modeling procedure conducted with the sample of the study, confidence in the findings relies on replication of the results in an independent sample. That is, after acceptable fit has been achieved with a series of respecifications, the final model should be cross-validated by another independent sample (Hatcher, 1994). Secondly, in order to establish the most acceptable causal relationships among the factors in the SEM, a longitudinal study needs to be conducted. Finally, though the present study identified the causal relationships among the factors, the outcomes are limited to only Korean-born adolescent adoptees. With the SEM, additional research needs to be conducted on the process of psychological adjustment of intercountry-adopted children, including different ethnic groups such as Chinese and other Asian country-born adoptees. In addition, not only should there be studies exploring the existence of the same process of psychological adjustment, but also studies that expand the boundary of the process of identity development for Korean-born adoptees.

CONCLUSION

The SEM appears to be a valid tool to help understand the role of parents of Korean-born adolescent adoptees and the dynamics of the adoptive family relationship. Given its proven utility in this study, the SEM may be the most powerful approach available at this time for evaluating and explicating the effects of intercountry adoption on children. There are several implications of these findings for practice and policy. First, provided that the notion of collective self-esteem is apparently supported, intercountry adoption agencies need to help adoptive parents to be more sensitive and knowledgeable about potential problems with respect to ethnic identity–the "who am I" question. In other words, parents need to understand that the enhancement of collective self-esteem can lessen problems of their adopted children's psychological adjustment, and sharing experiences of children's ethnic socialization is a significant factor contributing to their children's unique process of identity development. In particular, as adoptive parents have children experiencing a different dynamic state of identity development, they should get involved in the child's ethnic socialization process, simultaneously establishing a positive and open interaction. Secondly, in order to strengthen the functioning of adoptive families, all intercountry adoption agencies need to provide adoptive families with unique intervention and prevention programs. Social workers need to increase their effort to reach out to adoptive families and link them to cultural resources by sharing information and utilizing ethnic resources targeted to this population. Even for adoptive parents with plentiful informal supports or resources, the continuum from early stage of adoption to later stage of adoption needs solid international adoption policies and programs to supplement both formal and informal support systems. Finally, policymakers should address the larger issues involved in ensuring that Korean-born adopted children can have access to the cultural resources that can help them remain socially and psychologically healthy.

REFERENCES

Bagley, C., Verma, L., Mallick, M., & Young, L. (1979). *Personality, self-esteem and prejudice*. London: Aldershot Gower.

Bagley, C., & Young, L. (1981). The long-term adjustment of a sample of intercountry-adopted children. *International Social Work, 23*, 16-22.

Barner, H. L., & Olson, D. H. (1982). Parent-adolescent communication scale. In D. H. Olson & H. L. Barner (Eds.), *Family inventories: Inventories used in a national survey of families across the family life cycle* (pp. 33-48). St. Paul: Family Social Science, University of Minnesota.

Beck, A. T. (1961). An inventory for measuring depression. *Archives of General Psychiatry, 4*, 561-571.

Bentler, P. M., & Bonett, D. G. (1980). Significance tests and goodness-of-fit in the analysis of covariance structures. *Psychological Bulletin, 88*, 588-600.

Bollen, K. A. (1989). *Structural equations with latent variables*. New York: John Wiley & Sons.

Bradburn, N. M. (1969). *The structure of psychological well-being*. Chicago: Aldine.

Carmines, E. G., & Zeller, R. A. (1979). *Reliability and validity assessment.* Beverly Hills. CA: Sage.

Coopersmith, S. (1981). *The antecedents of self-esteem.* Palo Alto, CA: Consulting Psychologists Press.

Diener, E., Emmons, R. A., Larsen, R. J., & Griffin, S. (1985). The satisfaction with life scale: A measure of life satisfaction. *Journal of Personality Assessment, 49,* 71-75.

Erikson, E. H. (1968). *Identity: Youth and crisis.* New York: W. W. Norton.

Feigelman, W., & Silverman, A. R. (1983). *Chosen children: New patterns of adoptive relationships.* New York: Praeger.

Gill, O., & Jackson, B. (1983). *Adoption and race: Black, Asian and mixed race children in white families.* New York: St. Martin's Press.

Hatcher, L. (1994). *A step-by-step approach to using the SAS system for factor analysis and structural equation modeling.* Cary, NC: SAS Institute.

Hayduk, L. A. (1987). *Structural equation modeling with LISREL.* Baltimore, MD: Johns Hopkins University.

Joreskog, K. G., & Sorbom, D. (1992). *LISREL VIII: A guide to the program and applications.* Chicago: SPSS.

Kaplan, H. B., & Pokorny, A. D. (1969). Self-derogation and psychosocial adjustment. *Journal of Nervous and Mental Disease, 149,* 421-434.

Kim, D. S. (1977). How they fared in American homes; A follow-up study of adopted Korean children in the US. *Children Today,* 6(2), 2-6.

Kim, D. S. (1978). Issues in transracial and transcultural adoption. *Social Casework, 59,* 477-486.

Kirk, H. D. (1965). *A theory of adoption and mental health.* New York: The Free Press.

Koh, F. M. (1988). *Oriental children in American homes: How do they adjust?* Minneapolis, MN: East West Press.

La Du, T. J., & Tanaka, J. S. (1989). Influence of sample size, estimation method, and model specification on goodness-of-fit assessments in structural equation models. *Journal of Applied Psychology, 74,* 625-635.

Lee, C. I. (1996, December 15). Intercountry adoption: 40 years. *ChoSun IlBo,* p. 29.

McDonald, R. P. (1989). An index of goodness-of-fit based on noncentrality. *Journal of Classification, 6,* 97-103.

McGoldrik, M. (1982). Ethnicity and family therapy: An overview. In M. McGoldrick, J. K. Pearce, & J. Giordano (Eds.), *Ethnicity and family therapy* (pp. 3-30). New York: Guilford.

Phinney, J. S. (1992). The Multigroup Ethnic Identity Measure: A new scale for use with diverse groups. *Journal of Adolescent Research,* 7(2), 156-176.

Phinney, J. S., & Chavira, V. (1992). Ethnic identity and self-esteem: An exploratory longitudinal study. *Journal of Adolescence, 15,* 271-281.

Ressler, E. M., Boothby, N., & Steinbock, D. J. (1988). *Unaccompanied children: Care and protection in wars, natural disasters, and refugee movements.* New York: Oxford Press.

Rohner, R. P. (1986). *The warmth dimension: Foundations of parental acceptance-rejection theory.* Beverly Hills, CA: Sage.

Rosenberg, M. (1965). *Society and the adolescent self-image.* Princeton, NJ: Princeton University Press.

Rosenthal, D. A., & Feldman, S. S. (1992). The nature and stability of ethnic identity in Chinese youth: Effects of residence in two cultural contexts. *Journal of Cross-Cultural Psychology, 23,* 214-227.

Smith, E. J. (1991). Ethnic identity development: Toward the development of a theory within the context of majority/minority status. *Journal of Counseling and Development, 70,* 181-188.

Spencer, M. B., & Marktrom-Adams, C. (1990). Identity processes among racial and ethnic minority children in America. *Child Development, 61,* 290-310.

Spielberger, C. D. (1979). *Understanding stress and anxiety.* New York: Nelson.

Stein, L., & Hoopes, J. (1985). *Identity formation in the adopted adolescent.* New York: Child Welfare League of America.

Wood, J. (1972). *A study of the long-term adjustment of children of Korean heritage adopted by American families.* Eugene, OR: Holt.

Network Composition, Social Integration, and Sense of Coherence in Chinese American Young Adults

Yu-Wen Ying
Peter A. Lee
Jeanne L. Tsai
Yu J. Lee
Malisa Tsang

SUMMARY. This investigation examined the network composition, social integration, and sense of coherence in a group of 353 Chinese American students at a public university. About half (55.5%) of the sample had a Chinese-only (ethnically same) network while the remainder had either ethnically and/or racially mixed networks. Late immigrants (arriving after age 12) were more likely to have close relationships with other Chinese only, and American-borns and early immigrants (arriving before or at age 12) were more likely to have non-Chinese Asian and non-Asian members in their network. Greater racial/ethnic similarity among network members was associated with greater network integration. Individuals with a racially/ethnically mixed network enjoyed the highest sense of coherence, followed by those with an

Yu-Wen Ying, Peter A. Lee, Yu J. Lee and Malisa Tsang are all affiliated with the University of California at Berkeley, School of Social Welfare, 120 Haviland Hall, Berkeley, CA 94720-7400 (E-mail: ywying10@socrates.berkeley.edu).

Jeanne L. Tsai is affiliated with the University of Minnesota at Minneapolis.

The authors wish to thank John S. Huang, Yuan Hung, Melissa Lin, and Ching Tin Wan for their assistance with data collection.

The study was partially supported by a University of California at Berkeley faculty grant to the first author.

[Haworth co-indexing entry note]: "Network Composition, Social Integration, and Sense of Coherence in Chinese American Young Adults." Ying, Yu-Wen et al. Co-published simultaneously in *Journal of Human Behavior in the Social Environment* (The Haworth Press, Inc.) Vol. 3, No. 3/4, 2001, pp. 83-98; and: *Psychosocial Aspects of the Asian-American Experience: Diversity Within Diversity* (ed: Namkee G. Choi) The Haworth Press, Inc., 2001, pp. 83-98. Single or multiple copies of this article are available for a fee from The Haworth Document Delivery Service [1-800-342-9678, 9:00 a.m. - 5:00 p.m. (EST). E-mail address: getinfo@haworthpressinc.com].

ethnically same network, and those with either a racially-same or mixed network reported the lowest sense of coherence. Altogether, the findings suggest ethnically/racially similar networks afford a sense of comfort, but more diverse networks offer the reward of increased competence and better person-environment fit. *[Article copies available for a fee from The Haworth Document Delivery Service: 1-800-342-9678. E-mail address: <getinfo@haworthpressinc.com> Website: <http://www.HaworthPress.com> © 2001 by The Haworth Press, Inc. All rights reserved.]*

KEYWORDS. Inter-racial/inter-ethnic relationships and social networks, social integration, sense of coherence in Chinese Americans' network composition, Chinese American, social integration

At the dawn of the 21st century, the United States is one of the most racially and ethnically diverse nations of the world. Five major racial groups are represented: European, African, Hispanic, Asian, and American Indian. Within each racial group, various ethnicities may be found. For instance, in the case of Asian Americans, major ethnic groups include the Chinese, Japanese, Koreans, Filipinos, Indians, Pakistanis, Vietnamese, Cambodians, and Laotians. In 1990, of the entire American population, 75% were White, 12% were African American, 9% was Hispanic, 3% were Asian and Pacific Islander, and 1% were American Indian (U. S. Bureau of the Census, 1991). It is projected that by the year 2000 the number of White Americans will decline by 4%, while the Hispanic and Asian and Pacific Islander groups will increase by 2% and 1.5%, respectively, with smaller gains in the African American and American Indian populations (U. S. Bureau of the Census, 1992). The proportion of the non-White population will continue to grow such that within 50 years, it will comprise almost half of the American population: specifically, 16.2% will be Black, 21.1% will be Hispanic, 10.7% will be Asian, and 1.2% will be American Indian (U.S. Bureau of the Census, 1992).

With the growing diversification of the American population, the persistence of discrimination and prejudice toward cross-racial/ethnic groups poses a substantial threat to the unity of our nation. In *Race Matters*, Cornel West (1993, p. 4) stated, "There is no escape from our interracial interdependence, yet enforced racial hierarchy dooms us as a nation to collective paranoia and hysteria–the unmaking of any democratic society." The 1992 Los Angeles Race Riots pointed to the volatility of inter-racial anger in America. In 1997, a total of 4,710 hate crimes due to race and 836 hate crimes due to ethnicity/national origin were reported to the Federal Bureau of Investigation (*San Francisco Examiner*, 1999). These numbers are likely to be an underestimate, as not all race/ethnicity driven hate crimes were likely to be reported, and some were likely to be disguised and not identified as such. Due to cross-racial/ethnic mistrust and animosity, Americans cannot be said to share a sense of community as defined by Seymour Sarason (1974, p. 157), i.e., "the perception of similarity to others, an acknowledged interdependence by giving to or doing for others what one expects from them, the feeling that one is part of a larger dependable and stable structure." To achieve this sense of community, the formation of cross-racial/ethnic alliances is crucial. Existing research suggests that the ability to appreciate and embrace racial/ethnic diversity emerges not from fleeting acquaintances and casual contacts, but close and long-term personal associations (Ellison & Powers, 1994; Pettigrew, 1997).

The current study contributes to the literature of intergroup relations by focusing on the largest group of Asian Americans in the United States, i.e., Chinese Americans, and examines three specific questions: (1) What is the racial/ethnic composition of social networks among Chinese American young adults? (2) How does the racial/ethnic composition of their social network contribute to their network's integration? (3) How does the racial/ethnic composition of their social network contribute to a personal sense of coherence, i.e., the degree to which the world is experienced as comprehensible, manageable, and meaningful?

THE FOCUS ON CHINESE AMERICANS

The limited literature on interracial/ethnic relationships has focused primarily on White-Black associations (for review see Foster, Martinez, & Kulberg, 1996; Schneider, Smith, Poisson, & Kwan, 1997). With the growing diversification of the American population, understanding of cross-racial/ethnic interactions needs to be broadened to include other racial/ethnic groups. As 31.1% of America's current population increase is attributable to immigration, primarily from Asia and Latin America (De Vita, 1996), the question arises as to whether these newly arriving Americans and their descendants are forming cross-race/ethnic relationships as they adjust to living in their new homeland. Roberta S. Sigel (1991, p. 3) noted that "hosts and newcomers alike have to *learn* what it means to live democratically in a multi-ethnic world and, to accept diversity without fear or rancor." Among the major racial groups in the United States, Asian Americans grew faster in size (by 31%) between 1990 and 1995 than any other (De Vita, 1996). Chinese Americans make up the largest ethnic group among Asian Americans, and two-thirds of them are immigrants. Given this variation in migration status, focusing on Chinese Americans allows us to examine change in the racial/ethnic composition of their social network secondary to increased contact with non-ethnic Chinese Americans.

Most research on cross-racial/ethnic relationships has focused on school age children (for review, see Schneider et al., 1997). In contrast, relatively few studies have examined adults. In addition, it is particularly interesting to study Chinese American college students' interracial/ethnic relationships for two reasons. First, Western psychological theories suggest that during adolescence, significant exploration occurs across all life domains, including the social one (Erikson, 1968). This is a time when individuals may question their parents' and teachers' values and begin to form their own. As such, it is a time when their relationships, including the race/ethnicity of their intimate network, are more likely to result from conscious choice. While this exploration is usually associated with the junior high and the high school years for mainstream Americans, it may be delayed for many Chinese Americans until the college years due to pressures to conform to parental expectations. During college, they are exposed to members of other cultural backgrounds. As they share the common goal of an advanced education, Chinese American students may be likely to form cross-racial/ethnic associations. For those who live away from home to attend college, the physical separation further decreases parental influence. Thus, the social network of Chinese Americans is likely to better represent personal choice during college than at an earlier time.

Second, given the diversity of the student population at the study site, participants have ample opportunity to choose either same- or cross-race/ethnic relationships. Specifically, at the time of this investigation, 19.3% of this university's undergraduate population was Chinese American, 20.1% was non-Chinese Asian, 32.4% was White, 13.8% was Latino, 5.5% was African American, and 1.1% was American Indian, with the ethnicity of the remainder being other or unidentified. As such, the conditions promoting intergroup contact and reducing prejudice specified in Allport's (1954) contact hypothesis were present, i.e., (a) equal status contact between members of majority and minority groups (i.e., all are students) who are pursuing common goals (i.e., an education); (b) contact that is institutionally (i.e., university) sanctioned; (c) opportunity for majority and minority group members to interact as equals (i.e., all are students).

Racial/Ethnic Composition of Social Network

The first research question examined the racial/ethnic composition of the social networks in Chinese American young adults. The intergroup literature consistently shows a preference for same-race/ethnicity individuals due to apparent physical and cultural similarity (e.g., Antrobus, Dobbelaer, & Salzinger, 1988; Sagar, Schofield, & Snyder, 1983). Thus, it was hypothesized that Chinese American college students would show a similar preference for individuals most like themselves, i.e., other Chinese Americans (same ethnicity), followed by non-Chinese Asians (same race but different ethnicity), and the least preference for non-Asian Americans (different race).

In addition to identifying the distribution of same and cross-racial/ethnic networks, potential variation by migration status was of major interest. With increasing length of residence in the United States and exposure to diverse groups, individuals are more likely to form cross-racial/ethnic relationships. In addition, exposure to diversity during childhood enhances the probability of the formation of close cross-racial/ethnic relationship in adulthood (Ellison & Powers, 1994). Tsai, Ying, and Lee (2000) found that late immigrants (arriving in the US after the age of 12, or onset of adolescence) have the strongest sense of identification with being Chinese and the weakest identification with being American. This may be because of their childhood socialization (in particular, their primary school education) in a Chinese cultural context and their recency of migration. In contrast, American-borns have the strongest identification with being American, and the weakest identification with being Chinese, because they have lived their whole lives in the United States. Early immigrants (arriving in the US at or before the age of 12) occupied an intermediate position in their identification. Thus, we hypothesized that late immigrants would most prefer to associate with other Chinese Americans, while American-born Chinese would interact with both ethnically different (non-Chinese Asians) and racially different (non-Asians) individuals, with early immigrants falling in-between these groups. Age, socioeconomic status, and gender were included as control variables.

Social Network Integration

The second research question assessed the association of racial/ethnic composition of the social network and its integration. The ecological model of human development postulates that compatibility in role demands across settings promotes greater linkage and integration (Bronfenbrenner, 1979). Adapting this model to our investigation, rather than focusing on linkage across settings, we examine linkage among individuals who make up the participants' social network. Network members who share the same ethnic (i.e., Chinese) or racial (i.e., Asian) backgrounds are more likely to form linkages due to similarity in values and behaviors than if such similarity is absent (i.e., a mix of Asian and non-Asian associations). For instance, Chinese and Asian cultures have been found to vary significantly from European American culture, with the former characterized as collectivistic and interdependent, and the latter as individualistic and independent (Markus & Kitayama, 1991). Collier (1996) found Asian American college students most valued caring and positive exchange of ideas while Anglo American students emphasized individual needs in their friendships. Thus, it was hypothesized that individuals with ethnically-same networks (all Chinese American) would enjoy the greatest social integration, i.e., the members of their network would be most likely to know and interact with one another, followed by ethnically-different but still racially-same networks (all Asian, but not necessarily all Chinese American). In contrast, individuals with the most ethnically and racially diverse networks (i.e., including non-Chinese Asians and non-Asians) would be likely to report the least integration. As before, demographic characteristics, such as age, socioeconomic status, gender, and migration status were included as control variables.

Sense of Coherence

The third research question examined the relationship of racial/ethnic composition of social network and sense of coherence. Antonovsky proposed the construct of sense of coherence as a mediator of positive health and defined it as a "global orientation that expresses the extent to which one has a pervasive, enduring though dynamic feeling of confidence that: (1) the stimuli deriving from one's internal and external environments in the course of living are structured, predictable, and explicable; (2) the resources are available to one to meet the demands posed by these stimuli; and (3) these demands are challenges worthy of investment and engagement" (Antonovsky, 1987; p. 19). These components of sense of coherence were identified as comprehensibility, manageability and meaningfulness. Studies have found coherence to be associated with positive physical and psychological well-being (Antonovsky, 1979, 1987; Ying & Akutsu, 1997; Ying, Akutsu, Zhang, & Huang, 1997).

Bronfenbrenner (1979) proposed that participation in culturally different settings promotes development by enhancing cognitive functioning and social skills. Again adapting this to our study, it is likely that compared to those with ethnically and racially similar networks, individuals with ethnically/racially mixed networks would enjoy a greater sense of coherence as their diverse relationships help them to better understand the world and negotiate their life challenges in the context of an increasingly culturally diverse United States. Thus, it was hypothesized that racial/ethnic homogeneity in social network would diminish sense of coherence while racial/ethnic diversity would increase it.

In addition, strong social integration reflects cohesion in one's social support network, which in turn, has been postulated to enhance sense of coherence (Antonovsky, 1979, 1987). Thus, it was hypothesized that social integration would promote sense of coherence. As before, demographic characteristics, such as age, socioeconomic status, gender, and migration status, served as control variables.

METHOD

Sample

The sample consisted of 353 Chinese American college students at a major public university in the western United States. There were a total of 174 men and 179 women in the sample. Of these, 122 were American-borns (ABC), 121 were early immigrants (arriving at or before the age of 12), and 110 were late immigrants (arriving after the age of 12). More detailed sample characteristics are reported in the Results section.

Measures

Study participants completed three questionnaires. The Demographics Questionnaire assessed basic demographic background information, including, age, sex, and father's education and occupation. The participant's socioeconomic status (SES) was calculated from their father's education and occupation using Hollingshead's (1957) method (where the possible range of scores is from 11 to 77, with 11 being the highest socioeconomic level).

The Social Participation and Integration Questionnaire (SPIQ) was developed specifically for this study. It examined the racial and ethnic composition of the participant's intimate network and its integration. Social network composition was assessed by participants identifying the five people they felt closest to in their life, including their race/ethnicity and relationship to the participant. Social integration was assessed by the extent to which each member in their network knew every other member of the same network. Specifically, the question stated: "Please describe the relationship these people have with one another. Would you say (1) they have never heard of each other and have never met; (2) they have heard of each other but have never met; (3) they have met less than five times but are not close to each other; (4) they have met more than five times but are not close to each other; (5) they have met more than five times and are close to each other." In the case where the respondent identified five significant people in his or her social network, this question was asked ten times, regarding the relationship of the first person with each of the other four, the second person with each of the next three, the third person with each of the next two, and the fourth person with the fifth. To derive the overall degree of social integration, the mean of these responses was calculated.

Sense of coherence was measured using the Sense of Coherence Questionnaire (Antonovksy, 1987). The instrument consisted of 29 items which examined the extent to which the respondents felt their lives were comprehensible, manageable, and meaningful. Some sample items are: (1) When you talk to people, do you have the feeling they don't understand you? (reverse coded, measures comprehensibility); (6) Has it happened that people you counted on disappointed you? (reverse coded, measures manageability); (4) Do you have the feeling you don't really care about what is going on around you? (reverse coded, meaningfulness). Participants respond to the items on a seven point scale, expressing differential levels of endorsement. Items 1, 4, 5, 6, 7, 11, 13, 14, 16, 20, 23, 25 and 27 were reverse coded. The total sense of coherence score was derived by summing the item scores–with a possible range from 29 to 203. In over twenty studies, the instrument's Cronbach alpha of internal consistency has ranged from .82 to .95 (Antonovsky, 1993). The alpha reliability in our sample was .89. The criterion validity of the Sense of Coherence Questionnaire has also been established in numerous investigations by the presence of significant correlation with health and well-being (Antonovsky, 1993).

Procedure

Participants were recruited through the psychology subject pool, announcement at classes, Asian American student organizations, and dorms, by distribution of flyers, and by word-of-mouth. They completed consent forms for participation and the three paper-pencil questionnaires named above, either alone or in a group with other participants.

RESULTS

Sample characteristics by migration status are presented in Table 1. Intergroup variation was assessed using Analysis of Variance with Scheffe post-hoc tests and Chi-Square tests. Sample characteristics are presented by migration status. The groups varied significantly on age [$F(2,350) = 24.01$, $p = .0001$]. Scheffe post-hoc tests ($p < .05$) showed late immigrants were older (mean = 21.14, SD = 2.14) than the ABCs and early immigrants (mean = 19.71, SD = 1.48 and mean = 19.93, SD = 1.31, respectively). The groups differed significantly from one another in socioeconomic status or SES [$F(2,350) = 11.42$, $p = .0001$]. Scheffe post-hoc tests ($p < .05$) showed ABCs enjoyed better SES (mean = 23.38, SD = 13.74) than the early and late immigrants (mean = 31.23, SD = 15.40, and mean = 31.38, SD = 15.31, respectively), as a lower score reflected higher SES. The three groups did not vary by the distribution of gender, with roughly equal numbers of men and women represented in each group. The distribution of racial/ethnic composition of their network is reported in the next section.

TABLE 1. Descriptives of Study Variables by Migration Status

	Total	American-Borns	Early Immigrants	Late Immigrants	Significant Group Difference
	(N = 353)	(N = 122)	(N = 121)	(N = 110)	
Age	20.23 (SD = 1.77)	19.71 (SD = 1.48)	19.93 (SD = 1.31)	21.14 (SD = 2.14)	Late immigrants> ABC and Early Immigrants*
SES	28.56 (SD = 5.25)	23.38 (50 = 13.74)	31.23 (SD = 5.40)	31.38 (SD = 15.31)	ABC> Early and Late Immigrants*
Gender					
Male	49.3%	48.4%	46.3%	53.6%	
Female	50.7%	51.6%	53.7%	46.6%	
Composition of Social Network					
Ethnically Same	55.5%	33.6%	48.8%	87.3%	Late Immigrants> Others**
Racially Same	19.3%	30.3%	22.3%	3.6%	Late Immigrants< Others**
Racially Mixed	11.9%	13.1%	14.9%	7.3%	
Ethnically/ Racially Mixed	13.3%	23.0%	14.0%	1.8%	Late immigrants< Others**
Network Integration	3.52 (SD = .78)	3.51 (SD = .72)	3.52 (SD = .76)	3.52 (SD = .88)	
Sense of Coherence	127.55 (SD = 21.37)	129.20 (SD = 20.15)	125.42 (SD = 21.97)	128.06 (SD = 22.01)	

*$p < .05$; **$p < .004$

Racial/Ethnic Composition of Social Network

Of the 353 participants, 95.5% were able to name five people in their intimate social network. The remainder named two to four people. Of the sample, the overwhelming majority (79.6%) named both family and non-family members, 16.4% named only non-family members (mostly peers), and 4% named only family members. A total of 196 participants (55.5%) identified only Chinese people in their intimate social network ("Ethnically Same Group"), 68 (19.3%) named both Chinese and non-Chinese Asians ("Racially Same Group"), 42 (11.9%) named Chinese and non-Asians ("Racially Mixed Group"), and 45 (12.7%) named Chinese, non-Chinese Asians, and non-Asians ("Ethnically and Racially Mixed Group"). Only 2 individuals named non-Chinese Asian and non-Asians relationships, and they were included in the "Ethnically and Racially Mixed Group," making a total of 13.3%. The non-Chinese Asian ethnicities included Korean, Japanese, Filipino, Vietnamese, and South Asian Americans. The non-Asian races included European, Latino, and African Americans.

As hypothesized, racial/ethnic composition of social network varied significantly by migration status (χ^2 = 76.31, df = 6, p = .00001). Pairwise comparisons were conducted by migration status (ABCs vs. early immigrants, ABCs vs. late immigrants, and early vs. late immigrants) and social network composition category (each category vs. all other categories). A total of 12 pairwise comparisons were conducted, thus a more conservative p value of .004 (.05 divided by 12) was used. Late immigrants differed significantly from American-borns and early immigrants, but the latter two groups did not vary from each other. As Table 1 shows, while 87.3% of the late immigrants named only Chinese people in their network (Ethnically Same Group), only 33.6% of the American-borns and 48.8% of the early immigrants did so (χ^2 = 68.90, df = 1, p = .00001, and χ^2 = 38.71, df = 1, p = .0001, respectively). In contrast, only 3.6% of late immigrants had non-Chinese Asians members in their network (Racially Same Group), as compared to 30.3% of the American-borns and 22.3% of the early immigrants (χ^2 = 28.32, df = 1, p = .0001, and χ^2 = 17.30, df = 1, p = .0003, respectively). Also, only 1.8% of the late immigrants had non-Chinese Asian and non-Asian relationships (Ethnically and Racially Mixed Group), as compared to 23.0% of the American-born and 14.0% of the early immigrants (χ^2 = 22.94, df = 1, p = .00001, and χ^2 = 11.42, df = 1, p = .0007). The three groups did not vary on network integration (overall mean = 3.52, SD = .78) nor sense of coherence (overall mean = 127.55, SD = 21.37).

Social Network Integration

The contribution of racial/ethnic composition of social network to integration, controlling for demographic characteristics (age, socioeconomic status, gender, and migration status), was tested using multiple regression analyses. The deleted comparison group for migration status and racial/ethnic composition of social network was rotated to allow for exhaustive comparisons of all categories. As Table 2 shows, the overall model was significant (Adjusted R^2 = .06, F[8,334] = 3.93, p = .0002). Using the more conservative two-tailed test, only racial/ethnic composition emerged as a significant predictor. The "Ethnically Same Group" was better integrated than the "Racially Mixed" (b = .38, SE = .13, p = .004) and the "Ethnically and Racially Mixed" (b = .65, SE = .13, p = .0001) groups. The "Racially Same Group" was better integrated than the "Ethnically And Racially Mixed Group" (b = .48, SE = .15,

TABLE 2. Social Network Integration as Predicted by Demographic Characteristics and Racial/Ethnic Composition of Social Network

Adjusted R^2 = .06, F(8,344) = 3.93, p = .0002

	b	(SE)	p (two-tailed tests)
Age	−.04	(.03)	.14
SES	.01	(.01)	.44
Male vs. Female	.03	(.08)	.72
ABC vs. Early Immigrant	.06	(.10)	.56
ABC vs. Late Immigrant	.17	(.12)	.16
Early vs. Late Immigrant	.11	(.11)	.33
Ethnically Same vs. Racially Same	.17	(.12)	.15
Ethnically Same vs. Racially Mixed	.38	(.13)	.004
Ethnically Same vs. Ethnically and Racially Mixed	.65	(.13)	.0001
Racially Same vs. Racially Mixed	.22	(.15)	.15
Racially Same vs. Ethnically and Racially Mixed	.48	(.15)	.001
Racially Mixed vs. Ethnically and Racially Mixed	.27	(.16)	.10

p = .001). These findings support our second hypothesis. None of the control variables were significant contributors to the model.

Sense of Coherence

The contribution of racial/ethnic composition of social network and social integration to sense of coherence, controlling for demographic characteristics, was also tested using regression analyses. As before, the deleted comparison group for migration status and racial/ethnic composition of social network was rotated to allow for exhaustive comparisons of all categories. As Table 3 shows, the overall model was significant (Adjusted R^2 = .05, F[9,343] = 3.12, p = .001). Using two-tailed tests, racial/ethnic composition of social network and integration emerged as significant predictors. The "Ethnically and Racially Mixed Group" had a greater sense of coherence than the "Racially Same" (b = 13.91, SE = 4.05, p = .0007) and "Racially Mixed" (b = 9.13, SE = 4.49, p = .04) groups, and marginally more than the "Ethnically Same Group" (b = 6.40, SE = 3.78, p = .09). The "Racially Same Group" reported a lower sense of coherence than the "Ethnically Same Group" (b = −7.51, SE = 3.19, p = .02). In addition, greater integration was

TABLE 3. Sense of Coherence as Predicted by Demographic Characteristics, Racial/Ethnic Composition of Social Network and Social Network Integration

Adjusted R^2 = .051, F(9,343) = 3.12, p = .001

	b	(SE)	p (two-tailed tests)
Age	.53	(.68)	.44
SES	−.03	(.08)	.72
Male vs. Female	4.15	(2.26)	.07
ABC vs. Early Immigrant	3.65	(2.77)	.18
ABC vs. Late Immigrant	2.72	(3.27)	.41
Early vs. Late Immigrant	−9.33	(3.05)	.76
Ethnically and Racially Mixed vs. Ethnically Same	6.40	(3.78)	.09
Ethnically and Racially Mixed vs. Racially Same	13.91	(4.05)	.0007
Ethnically and Racially Mixed vs. Racially Mixed	9.13	(4.49)	.04
Racially Mixed vs. Ethnically Same	−2.73	(3.69)	.46
Racially Mixed vs. Racially Same	4.78	(4.13)	.25
Racially Same vs. Ethnically Same	−7.51	(3.19)	.02
Social Network Integration	4.88	(1.48)	.001

associated with greater sense of coherence (b = 4.88, SE = 1.48, p = .001). The control variables were not significant predictors of coherence.

DISCUSSION

Racial/Ethnic Composition of Social Network

The racial/ethnic distribution of social network composition in the Chinese American college sample reflected a strong preference, first, for ethnic similarity (55.5% had close associations with other Chinese Americans only), and, second, for racial similarity (19.3% had close relationships with Asians only). In spite of the racial diversity at the campus which served as the study site, only 11.9% of the participants reported a racially mixed network (Chinese and non-Asians), and only 13.3% reported both an ethnically and racially mixed network (Chinese, non-Chinese Asians, and non-Asians). These findings showed that, in general, Chinese American students in a multi-racial/ethnic context still preferred to associate with individuals of their own ethnic and racial background due to similar physical characteristics and cultural values, consistent with the existing literature (Antrobus et al., 1988; Sagar et al., 1983).

However, a longer length of residence in the United States increased the probability of association with non-Chinese Americans. Both American-borns and early immigrants differed significantly from the late immigrants by being less likely to associate exclusively with other Chinese Americans and more likely have close relationships with non-Chinese Asians and non-Asians. However, American-borns and early immigrants did not differ significantly from each other in their network composition. As no other variable emerged as a significant predictor, it appears that early exposure to diversity was crucial in enhancing cross-racial/ethnic associations in adulthood (Ellison & Powers, 1994). In addition, late immigrants may be more limited in their cross-cultural knowledge and English facility compared to their American-born and early immigrant peers, which further diminishes the likelihood of the formation of cross-ethnic and cross-racial relationships.

Social Network Integration

As hypothesized, social network integration was greater for ethnically and racially similar networks (i.e., Chinese only and Asians only) than for ethnically/racially dissimilar (Chinese, Asian, and non-Asian) networks, and was also greater for ethnically similar vs. racially mixed (Chinese and non-Asian) networks, suggesting that when members of the network were culturally similar, they were more likely to know of and interact with one another. This was consistent with Collier's (1996) finding of within-race consistency and across-race variation in what African, Asian, Latino, and Anglo American college students most valued in their friendships.

Sense of Coherence

As predicted, the "Ethnically and Racially Mixed Group" enjoyed the greatest sense of coherence. As their social network best mirrored the cultural diversity of their environment, they may be said to enjoy the best person-environment fit, which enhanced their sense of comprehensibility, manageability, and meaningfulness of their world. Unexpectedly, the "Ethnically Same Group" enjoyed greater coherence than the "Racially Same Group." This was likely to be due to a difference in reference group when responding to the sense of coherence items. Chinese Americans who associated only with other Chinese Americans (these were most likely students who migrated to the United States after the age of 12) may be separated from their ethnically/racially diverse context in other respects as well, and they may have been considering only this narrower Chinese American world when responding to the sense of coherence items. As such, their higher sense of coherence may not generalize to the larger environment, in which their score may be significantly lower. On the other hand, those with non-Chinese Asian associations (these were most likely to be American-born Chinese) may be more engaged with the larger non-Chinese American context. In spite of their lower sense of coherence score compared to the "Ethnically Same Group," because of the potential difference in reference, they may actually enjoy a higher sense of coherence in a broader, more diverse context. Clearly, this deserves further investigation.

Finally, also as hypothesized, controlling for the racial/ethnic composition of the network and demographics, a stronger social integration, i.e., a greater cohesion in the support network, promoted a positive sense that the world was comprehensible, manageable, and meaningful.

Study Limitations

By focusing only on college students, it is unclear whether the distribution of social network composition reported here generalizes to other Chinese American young adults. Further studies need to include a more diverse sample. Also, by choosing a campus where Asian American students represent the largest racial group (surpassing White Americans), it is possible that our findings are biased toward racial/ethnic similarity in social network composition. In a context with fewer same race/ethnicity individuals, Chinese Americans may tend to have more mixed networks. This deserves further investigation. Also, while this study makes a contribution by moving beyond the study of White-Black associations, much more research is needed to better understand not only how racial/ethnic minorities relate to Whites but also to one another. It is only by doing so that a complete picture of inter-racial/ethnic associations in our country will emerge.

CONCLUSION

Taken together, these findings show increased inter-racial/ethnic association with increasing length of residence in the United States among Chinese American young adults. Ethnically/racially-same networks afford a sense of comfort due to implicit understanding and sharing of values and expectations among its members, and yield better network integration. However, racially and ethnically mixed networks afford the reward of better person-environment fit and of an increased sense of competence in the world. Beyond the personal benefit, cross-racial/ethnic relationships are likely to enhance a sense of community and common destiny among Americans across racial and ethnic lines, which contributes to unity among Americans.

With increasing diversification of the population, the challenge of cross-racial/ethnic understanding continues to gain importance for every American and for the United States as a nation. The study findings point to the need for increased opportunities for dialogue and exchange among Americans from different racial and ethnic groups to overcome our withdrawal from and fear of difference. Specifically, the finding that American-borns and early immigrants (who arrived at or before the age of 12) are more likely to associate with racially and ethnically different individuals than are late immigrants (who arrived after the age of 12) suggests that interventions which target children under the age of 12 may be particularly effective. However, as adults play a pivotal role in children's lives (especially as parents and teachers) and serve as important role models for future generations, it is important that they, too, be assisted to develop an empathy and appreciation for cross-racial/ethnic individuals through cross-racial/ethnic relationships.

REFERENCES

Allport, G. W. (1954). *The nature of prejudice*. Garden City, NY: Doubleday.

Antonovsky, A. (1979). *Health, stress, and coping*. San Francisco, CA: Jossey-Bass.

Antonovsky, A. (1987). *Unraveling the mystery of health: How people manage stress and stay well*. San Francisco, CA: Jossey-Bass.

Antonovsky, A. (1993). The structure and properties of the sense of coherence scale. *Social Science and Medicine, 36*(6), 725-733.

Antrobus, J. S., Dobbelaer, R., & Salzinger, S. (1988). Social network and college success, or grade point average and the friendly connection. In S. Sulzinger & J. Antrobus (eds.) *Social network of children, adolescents, and college students* (pp. 227-246). Hillsdale, NJ: Lawrence Erlbaum Associates.

Bronfenbrenner, U. (1979). *The ecology of human development: Experiments by nature and design*. Cambridge, MA: Harvard University Press.

Collier, M. J. (1996). Communication competence problematics in ethnic friendships. *Communication Monographs, 63*, 314-336.

De Vita, C. J. (1996). The United States at mid-decade. *Population Bulletin, 50*(4), 2-44.

Ellison, C. G., & Powers, D. A. (1994). The contact hypothesis and racial attitudes among Black Americans. *Social Science Quarterly, 75*(2), 383-399.

Erikson, E. (1968). *Identity: Youth and crisis*. New York: W. W. Norton.

Foster, S. L., Martinez, C. R., Jr., & Kulberg, A. M. (1996). Race, ethnicity, and children's peer relations. In T. H. Ollendick & R. J. Prinz (eds.) *Advances in clinical child psychology, Volume 18* (pp. 133-172). New York: Plenum.

Hollingshead, A. B. (1957). *Two factor index of social position*. New Haven, CT: Yale University Press.

Markus, H., & Kitayama, S. (1991). Culture and self: Implications for cognition, emotion, and motivation. *Psychological Review, 98,* 224-253.

Pettigrew, T. F. (1997). Generalized intergroup contact effects on prejudice. *Personality and Social Psychology Bulletin, 23*(2), 173-185.

Sagar, H. A., Schofield, J. W., & Snyder, H. N. (1983). Race and gender barriers: Pre-adolescent peer behavior in academic classrooms. *Child Development, 54,* 1032-1040.

San Francisco Examiner (1999). *Hate crimes by the numbers.* April 11, 1999.

Sarason, S. B. (1974). *The psychological sense of community: Prospects for a community psychology.* San Francisco, CA: Jossey-Bass.

Schneider, B. H., Smith, A., Poisson, S. E., & Kwan, A. B. (1997). Cultural dimensions of children's peer relations. In S. Duck (ed.) *Handbook of personal relationships: Theory, research and interventions. Second Edition,* (pp. 121-146). Chichester, England: John Wiley & Sons.

Sigel, R. S. (1991). Democracy in the multi-ethnic society. In R. S. Sigel & M. Hoskin (eds). *Education for democratic citizenship: A challenge for multiethnic societies* (pp. 3-8). Hillsdale, NJ: Lawrence Erlbaum Associates.

Tsai, J. L., Ying, Y., & Lee, P. A. (2000). The meaning of "Being Chinese" and "Being American": Variation among Chinese American young adults. *Journal of Cross-Cultural Psychology,* 31, 302-322.

U. S. Bureau of the Census (1991). *1990 Census of population and housing–Summary tape file 1. Summary population and housing characteristics.* Washington, DC: U.S. Government Printing Office.

U. S. Bureau of the Census (1992). *Population projections of the United States by age, sex, race, and Hispanic origin: 1992 to 2000. Current population reports, P25-1092.* Washington, DC: U.S. Government Printing Office.

West, C. (1993). *Race matters.* Boston: Beacon Press.

Ying, Y., & Akutsu, P. D. (1997). Psychological adjustment of Southeast Asian refugees: The contribution of sense of coherence. *Journal of Community Psychology, 25*(2), 125-139.

Ying, Y., Akutsu, P. D., Zhang, X., & Huang, L. N. (1997). Psychological dysfunction in Southeast Asian refugees as mediated by sense of coherence. *American Journal of Community Psychology,* 25(6), 839-859.

Cultural Orientation
of Hmong Young Adults

Jeanne L. Tsai

SUMMARY. Most studies of Hmong Americans focus on the cultural adjustment of refugees who arrived in the United States immediately after the Vietnam War. Few studies have examined the cultural adjustment of the children of these refugees, who have been raised primarily in the United States. This study explored whether American-born [ABH] and overseas-born [OBH] Hmong young adults differed in levels, models, and meanings of cultural orientation. Fourteen ABH and 32 OBH college students were asked what "being Hmong" and "being American" meant to them and complete were asked to the General Ethnicity Questionnaire (American and Hmong versions). Both groups reported being more oriented to American culture than Hmong culture. Despite similarities in mean levels of orientation to Hmong and American cultures and in the meanings of "being Hmong" and "being American," ABH and OBH differed in their underlying models of cultural orientation. For ABH, "being Hmong" and "being American" were unrelated constructs, whereas for OBH, they were negatively correlated constructs. *[Article copies available for a fee from The Haworth Document Delivery Service: 1-800-342-9678. E-mail address: <getinfo@haworthpressinc. com> Website: <http://www.HaworthPress.com> © 2001 by The Haworth Press, Inc. All rights reserved.]*

Jeanne L. Tsai is affiliated with the University of Minnesota.

Correspondence related to this paper should be directed to Jeanne L. Tsai, Department of Psychology, University of Minnesota, Elliott Hall, 75 E. River Road, Minneapolis, MN 55455 (E-mail: tsaix024@tc.umn.edu).

The author would like to thank Ying Wong, Heather Mortensen, Dan Hess, and Theresa Ly for their contributions to this project and Yu-Wen Ying for her insightful comments and helpful suggestions regarding this paper.

This project was funded by NIMH grant MH59051-01.

[Haworth co-indexing entry note]: "Cultural Orientation of Hmong Young Adults." Tsai, Jeanne L. Co-published simultaneously in *Journal of Human Behavior in the Social Environment* (The Haworth Press, Inc.) Vol. 3, No. 3/4, 2001, pp. 99-114; and: *Psychosocial Aspects of the Asian-American Experience: Diversity Within Diversity* (ed: Namkee G. Choi) The Haworth Press, Inc., 2001, pp. 99-114. Single or multiple copies of this article are available for a fee from The Haworth Document Delivery Service [1-800-342-9678, 9:00 a.m. - 5:00 p.m. (EST). E-mail address: getinfo@haworthpressinc.com].

KEYWORDS. Hmong, cultural/ethnic identity, acculturation

INTRODUCTION

Although estimates vary, demographers approximate that between 90,000 to 120,000 Hmong currently live in the United States (U.S. Bureau of the Census, 1998; Taylor, 10/25/98), residing primarily in Minnesota, Wisconsin, and California (Southeast Asian Resource Action Center, 1998). Most studies of Hmong and other Southeast Asian groups have focused on the cultural adjustment and mental health of the refugee groups that first arrived in the United States at the close of the Vietnam War, approximately two and a half decades ago (Chung & Lin, 1994; Nicholson, 1997; Ta, Westermeyer, & Neider, 1996; Westermeyer & Her, 1996; Westermeyer, Schaberg, & Nugent, 1995; Ying, Akutsu, Zhang, & Huang, 1997). Significantly fewer studies have examined the cultural adjustment of the children of these refugee groups, many of whom have spent the majority of their lives in the United States. The present study attempts to fill this gap by examining cultural orientation processes in a sample of Hmong young adults living in the Midwest.

Hmong in the United States

Unlike other Asian groups (e.g., Chinese, Japanese, Filipinos), Hmong did not voluntarily immigrate to the United States with the goal of economic advancement. Most Hmong arrived in the United States as political refugees in the mid-1970s at the close of the Vietnam War. During the War, Hmong males of all ages were "hired" by the United States Central Intelligence Agency (CIA) to fight against the Communist North Vietnamese. Although the Hmong fought to protect their homeland, they also received assurances from the CIA that should their efforts fail, they would receive U.S. support as compensation for their military service. In 1975, Hmong military were forced by Communist Vietnamese troops to retreat from Laos. As a result, the United States airlifted Hmong military officers and their families and brought them to the United States. However, these comprised only a small percentage of Hmong who were driven from their homes. Thousands of Hmong were forced to flee to refugee camps in Thailand and lived there for years before finally being allowed to immigrate to the United States and other countries (e.g., France, Australia, Canada) (for a more comprehensive history of the Hmong, please see Chan [1994] or Fadiman [1997]).

In the United States, Hmong were originally dispersed throughout the country to curb the impact their arrival had on any one community. However, in an effort to reunite with their family members and to be near other Hmong, many refugees engaged in secondary migrations, and communities with large numbers of Hmong soon emerged. Up until 1997, the largest group of Hmong lived in Fresno, California. Since 1997, however, an estimated 10,000 to 15,000 Hmong have left Fresno because of poor employment opportunities, rising crime rates, poor schools, and few social services. Most have moved to Minneapolis-St.Paul, Minnesota, where Hmong have better employment opportunities (Taylor, 1998). As a result of this recent migration, Minneapolis-St. Paul has become the new "Hmong capital" of the United States, housing approximately 60,000-75,000 Hmong (Ronningen, 1999; Taylor, 1998).

Most of the existing research on Hmong groups focuses on the difficulties many Hmong refugees encountered during their settlement in the United States. These difficulties have been attributed to several sources. First, life in the United States is drastically different from that in Laos. In Laos, Hmong practiced slash and burn agriculture, lived with extended family members, and held religious beliefs and ceremonies that often involved animal sacrifice. In the United States, Hmong have had to find other means of subsistence. They often are not able to live with extended family members, and many Hmong have had to restrict their performance of traditional ceremonies because of complaints by surrounding non-Hmong communities (Chan, 1994). Second, many Hmong arrived in the United States with severe cases of post-traumatic stress disorder and other forms of mental distress due to the losses they suffered in the Vietnam War (Nicholson, 1997; Ta et al., 1996). Third, many Hmong hold strong cultural proscriptions against mixing with and assimilating to majority cultures in order to preserve their cultural traditions. In fact, Ying et al. (1997) found that in a large community sample of Southeast Asian refugees, Hmong were significantly more culturally traditional than the other Southeast Asians examined (Vietnamese, Laotians, Cambodians, and Chinese Vietnamese). However, Hmong adherence to cultural traditions and resistance to cultural assimiliation may also hinder their adjustment to American life (Fadiman, 1997).

Cultural Orientation Among Hmong Young Adults

But what about the children of the first generation of Hmong refugees, many of whom are currently in their early- to mid-twenties and have lived the majority of their lives in the United States? What is their cultural orientation? Have they retained their Hmong heritage, adopted the traditions and customs of mainstream American culture, or both? Do American-born Hmong have different cultural orientations than those who were born overseas? Remarkably little research has focused on this generation of Hmong. Therefore, this study had two main goals: (1) to examine cultural orientation in a sample of

Hmong young adults who have spent the majority of their lives in the United States, and (2) to identify variation within this sample of Hmong young adults. Four exploratory questions regarding the cultural orientation of Hmong young adults were addressed: (1) Are Hmong young adults more oriented to American culture than to Hmong culture? (2) Do American-born (ABH) and overseas-born Hmong (OBH) differ in their mean levels of orientation to Hmong and American cultures? (3) Do models of cultural orientation vary by place of birth? and (4) Are the meanings attached to "being Hmong" and "being American" different for ABH and OBH? Given the dearth of literature on cultural orientation in Hmong young adults, no directional hypotheses were posed a priori.

Are Hmong Young Adults More Oriented to American Culture Than to Hmong Culture? Hmong young adults may be more oriented to American culture than to Hmong culture because they have been raised primarily in the United States. For the most part, their exposure to Hmong culture is limited to home environments, whereas their exposure to American culture spans school, work, and other non-home environments. On the other hand, if these Hmong young adults are influenced by Hmong proscriptions against cultural assimilation, they may be more strongly oriented to Hmong culture than to American culture, like the first generation of Hmong refugees (Ying et al., 1997).

Do American-Born (ABH) and Overseas-Born Hmong (OBH) Differ in Their Mean Levels of Orientation to Hmong and American Cultures? It is possible that ABH and OBH vary in their orientation to Hmong and American cultures, with ABH being more oriented to American culture than OBH, and OBH being more oriented to Hmong culture than ABH. However, as both groups in this sample of Hmong young adults have spent the majority of their lives in the United States, it is also possible that they will not differ in their orientations to either culture.

Do Models of Cultural Orientation Vary by Place of Birth? In a previous paper (Tsai, Ying, & Lee, 2000), my colleagues and I proposed and found that American-born and overseas born Chinese American college students differed in their models of cultural orientation. For American-born Chinese, "being American" and "being Chinese" are highly contextualized concepts and, therefore, develop independently. Because they are born into American culture *and* into a Chinese home environment, their conceptions of "being Chinese" and "being American" develop simultaneously in different contexts. That is, their conception of "being Chinese" develops in Chinese contexts, and their conception of "being American" develops in American contexts. As a result, their models of cultural orientation are bidimensional or not correlated with each other.

For overseas-born Chinese, however, "being Chinese" and "being American" are dependent constructs. Because they are born into a Chinese context, their conception of "being Chinese," which is essentially their way of functioning in the world, develops first. When they migrate to the United States, however, they must adopt a different way of functioning. In order to be more American, they must be less Chinese. Their conceptions of "being American" develop relative to their pre-existing conceptions of "being Chinese." Thus, their models of cultural orientation are unidimensional, or negatively correlated with each other. The present study explored whether these findings generalized to American-born and overseas-born Hmong young adults, especially those who have spent the majority of their lives in the United States.

Are the Meanings Attached to "Being Hmong" and "Being American" Different for ABH and OBH? Existing cultural orientation inventories often assume that the meanings of or associations with being a member of a particular cultural group are similar for individuals within that group. However, as individuals within a cultural group may vary in their exposure to and experiences in that culture, it is possible that the meanings of being a member of a cultural group may differ within cultural groups as well. For example, for ABH, "being Hmong" may be associated more with specific cultural traditions and expectations, whereas for OBH, "being Hmong" may be associated more with the refugee experience. On the other hand, because most young Hmong have spent the majority of their lives in the United States, there may be few differences in what "being American" and "being Hmong" mean for these two groups. Thus, the present study explored what meanings young Hmong adults attached to "being Hmong" and "being American," and whether they differed for ABH and OBH.

METHOD

Participants

Forty-six bilingual Hmong (14 American born, 32 overseas born) college students at a large Midwestern university were recruited from the General Psychology subject pool and campus student organizations to participate in a larger study. Chi-square statistics revealed no differences between ABH and OBH in sex, major, and employment status. Univariate analyses of variance revealed no group differences in age, years in college, grade point average, and language proficiency in English and Hmong. However, there were significant group differences in time spent in the United States (F [1, 45] = 7.28, $p <$ .01). Overseas-born Hmong spent significantly less time in the United States than did American-born Hmong, although both groups spent the majority of their lives in the United States. On the average, overseas-born Hmong came to the United States when they were 2.79 years of age (SD = 2.12, Range = 9.6 months to 7 years of age). (Please see Table 1 for specific demographic information.)

TABLE 1. Demographics of American-Born and Overseas-Born Hmong Sample

	Means (SD)/Percentages Within Groups	
	American-Born	Overseas-Born
Age (years)	19.21 (1.12)	20.28 (1.95)
Sex–Female	57.1%	62.5%
Place of birth		
United States	100%	
Laos		46.9%
Thailand		53.1%
Citizen Status		
U.S. Citizen	100%	34.4%
Permanent Resident		53.1%
Unknown		12.5%
Time Lived in the United States (years)	19.21 (1.12)	17.23 (2.63)
Years in College	1.93 (1.14)	2.41 (1.29)
Grade Point Average	2.88 (.88)	2.74 (.40)
Major		
Social Sciences/Humanities	14.29%	18.75%
Physical Sciences/Engineering	21.43%	25.00%
Life Sciences/Medicine	21.43%	15.63%
Business	21.43%	9.38%
Environmental Sciences		3.13%
Undeclared/Other	14.29%	21.88%
Unknown	7.14%	6.25%
Employment Status–Working	57.1%	71.9%
Proficiency in English[a]		
Speak	4.64 (.50)	4.27 (.87)
Understand	4.64 (.63)	4.39 (.82)
Write	4.64 (.63)	4.39 (.82)
Proficiency in Hmong[a]		
Speak	4.00 (.68)	3.81 (.70)
Understand	4.50 (.65)	4.17 (.71)
Write	1.93 (1.21)	1.93 (1.51)

Note. [a] On a scale from 1 = not at all proficient to 5 = extremely proficient.

Procedure

Study participants arrived at the laboratory and were greeted by a female bilingual Hmong interviewer. Previous studies have found that study participants provide more complete and accurate responses when they are interviewed by experimenters of similar cultural backgrounds than of cultural backgrounds different from their own (Waid & Orne, 1981; Murphy, Alpert, Moes, & Somes, 1986). Participants completed a basic demographic information questionnaire in which they were asked their age, place of birth, ethnicity, grade point average, major, citizen status, language proficiency, and employment status.

Participants were then asked the following two questions by the interviewer: (1) What does "being Hmong" mean to you? and (2) What does "being American" mean to you? Participants' responses were videotaped. After completing procedures related to another study, participants then completed the General Ethnicity Questionnaire, a measure of cultural orientation (see below). All instruments and instructions were delivered in English. Students were paid $25 for their participation.

Measures

General Ethnicity Questionnaire (GEQ). To measure cultural orientation, participants completed the General Ethnicity Questionnaire-American version (abridged) (GEQ-A) (Tsai et al., 2000) and the General Ethnicity Questionnaire-Hmong version (GEQ-H) developed for this study. The GEQ-H and GEQ-A allow independent assessment of orientation to Hmong and American cultures, respectively, and were originally developed for use with different cultural groups to assess cultural orientation in various life domains (e.g., social affiliation, language, attitudes). Participants use a 5-point scale ranging from 1 = "very much" to 5 = "not at all" to rate 25 items pertaining to their social affiliation, activities, attitudes, exposure, and food ("I go to places where people are Hmong"). Participants use a 5-point scale ranging from 1 = "very much" to 5 = "not at all" to rate 13 items pertaining to their language use and proficiency (e.g., "How much do you speak Hmong with friends?"). The same items were used for the GEQ-H and the GEQ-A; however, the reference culture differed. For example, on the GEQ-H, participants rated how strongly they agreed with the statement "I engage in Hmong forms of recreation." A similar item appeared on the GEQ-A: "I engage in American forms of recreation." The reliability and validity measures of the GEQ-H in this study were comparable to those reported in Tsai et al. (in press) in their use of the instrument with Chinese American samples. Cronbach's standardized item-alpha for the Hmong sample was .88 for the GEQ-H and .81 for the GEQ-A. To assess the concurrent validity of the GEQ-H and GEQ-A for the Hmong sample, the relationship between years in the United States and average orientation score was examined. As in Tsai et al. (in press), the longer Hmong had lived in the United States, the more oriented they were to American culture ($r = .30$, $p < .05$). The number of years spent in the United States was *not* significantly correlated with orientation to Hmong culture.

Coding of Open-Ended Responses

Participants' responses to the interview questions were transcribed. Two female research assistants (one European American, one Chinese) coded the transcripts after extensive training in the coding system developed for this study. Responses were coded for content using 19 content codes[1]: (1) label/category, (2) physical characteristics, (3) social affiliation, (4) values/beliefs, (5) language, (6) political/economic ideology, (7) cultural exposure/understanding, (8) geographic origin, (9) minority status, (10) reference to self, (11) food, (12) personality/traits/expressions, (13) activities, (14) customs/traditional behavior, (15) group history, (16) family heritage, (17) ethnic pride, (18) citizenship, and (19) miscellaneous/other. These codes were based on domains represented in existing inventories of cultural orientation (Mendoza, 1989; Suinn, Rickard-Figueroa, Lew, & Vigil, 1987; Szapocznik, Scopetta, Kurtines, & de los Angeles Aranalde, 1978; Tsai et al., 2000) as well as on the types of responses provided by the participants. Table 2 provides a detailed description of each of the 19 content codes.

Participants' responses received multiple codes, depending on the response; however, individual parts of participants' responses could only receive one code. For example, one participant responded:

> Being Hmong to me means that . . . would say its more like . . . a family where like everyone supports everyone and also like . . . you're related to everyone . . . And we hold family very, very high. And I'm just proud to be Hmong.[2]

Thus, this participant used four content codes to describe "being Hmong": (a) customs/traditional behavior ("a family where like everyone supports everyone"), (b) social affiliation ("you're related to everyone"), (c) values/beliefs ("we hold family very, very high"), and (d) ethnic pride ("I'm just proud to be Hmong"). In response to the question "What does being American mean to you?" another participant responded:

> I think being American means that I live in America and I am a citizen of America and . . . it's a category of people . . . it's a category of where you live.

This participant used three content codes to describe "being American": (a) label/category ("it's a category of people . . . category of where you live"), (b) geographic origin ("I live in America"), and (c) citizenship ("a citizen of America"). Inter-rater reliability was .96 (SD = .04, Range = .88 to 1.00), as determined by the mean Cohen's Kappa coefficient across the 19 content codes. Discrepancies in coding were resolved by arbitration and consensus between the two coders.

TABLE 2. Coding System for Open-Ended Responses

Participants' responses were divided into their component parts. Each component part received only one of the following content codes.

Content Code	Example
1. Label/Category:	"It's kind of a classification" "A category"
2. Physical Characteristics:	"Race" "Caucasian" "White" "Having light skin"
3. Social Affiliation:	"Being surrounded by the Hmong community" "Being part of their country"
4. Values/Beliefs/Attitudes:	"My values, beliefs" "How parents view kids should be" "ideas"
5. Language:	"We speak our language" "speak the language"
6. Political/Economic Ideology:	"Opportunity" "Place where you can have great success" "Have equal rights"
7. Cultural Exposure/Understanding:	"Way I was raised" "Understand the culture"
8. Geographic Origin:	"Come from certain areas" "From the mountaintops of Laos"
9. Minority Status:	"Part of a minority culture" "Different from Americans"
10. Reference to Self:	"Who I am" "What I am"
11. Food:	"Eat Hmong [food]" "American food"
12. Personality/Traits/Expressions:	"Close-minded" "Caring" "Being able to express yourself freely"
13. Activities:	"Culture activities" "Festivals"
14. Customs/Traditional Behavior:	"Tradition" "Follow a certain rule" "Can do what you want"
15. Group History:	"You have a history of migration" "Melting pot"
16. Family Heritage:	"Roots of your family"
17. Ethnic Pride:	"It's an automatic feeling you're just proud of who you are"
18. Citizenship:	"Nationality" "Having citizenship"
19. Other:	"Hmong means stranger"

DATA ANALYSES AND RESULTS

Question 1: Are Hmong Young Adults More Oriented to American Culture Than to Hmong Culture?

Paired sample t-tests conducted on the entire sample and then on each group (ABH and OBH) revealed that Hmong young adults were more oriented to American culture than to Hmong culture (All: GEQ-H = 3.34 [.48], GEQ-A = 3.85 [.33], $t[44] = -4.83, p < .001$; ABH: $t[12] = -4.36, p < .001$; OBH: $t[30] = -3.71, p = .001$ [ABH and OBH means are presented below]).

Question 2: Do American-Born and Overseas-Born Hmong Differ in Their Mean Levels of Orientation to Hmong and American Cultures?

Univariate analyses of variance on mean GEQ-A and GEQ-H scores were conducted. Analyses revealed no significant group differences in mean GEQ-A (ABH = 3.92 [.34], OBH = 3.80 [.37]) or GEQ-H scores (ABH = 3.43 [.21], OBH = 3.30 [.55]).

Question 3: Do Models of Cultural Orientation Vary By Place of Birth?

Pearson correlation coefficients for mean scores on the GEQ-A and the GEQ-H were calculated for each Hmong group. For American-born Hmong, mean scores on the GEQ-A and GEQ-H were not significantly correlated with each other, supporting a bidimensional model of cultural orientation ($r = -.10, p = .74$). For overseas-born Hmong, mean scores on the GEQ-A and GEQ-H were significantly correlated with each other ($r = -.60, p < .001$), supporting a unidimensional model of cultural orientation. That is, for overseas-born Hmong, the more "Hmong" they reported being, the less "American" they reported being.[3] Thus, consistent with previous findings (Tsai et al., in press), ABH and OBH differed in their underlying models of cultural orientation.

Question 4: Are the Meanings Attached to "Being Hmong" and "Being American" Different for ABH and OBH?

Pearson chi-square analyses were conducted on the frequency with which each of the content codes was used in the open-ended responses provided by each group. Analyses revealed that there were no significant differences in the content of American-born and overseas-born Hmong descriptions of "being Hmong" or "being American." Please see Tables 3 and 4 for the breakdown of responses. To describe "being Hmong," the most common codes used by both groups were customs/traditional behavior (e.g., "Hmong tradition"), group history (e.g., "you have a history of migration"), and label/category (e.g., "It's a kind of classification"). For both groups, the most common codes used to describe "being American" were customs/traditional behavior (e.g., "can do anything you want"), geographic origin (e.g., "live in America"), and political/economic ideology (e.g., "have equal rights"). In summary, the bulk of the findings suggest that American-born and overseas-

TABLE 3. "Being Hmong": Percentage of Responses for Each Code

	Percentage of Responses Within Groups	
	American-Born (n = 14)	Overseas-Born (n = 32)
1. Label/Category	28.6	40.0
2. Physical Characteristics	14.3	23.3
3. Social Affiliation	14.3	13.3
4. Values/Beliefs/Attitudes	28.6	20.0
5. Language	28.6	23.3
6. Political/Economic Ideology	---	---
7. Cultural Exposure/Understanding	28.6	26.7
8. Geographic Origin	7.1	30.0
9. Minority Status	28.6	30.0
10. Reference to Self	14.3	23.3
11. Food	7.1	6.7
12. Personality/Traits/Expressions	7.1	6.7
13. Activities	7.1	10.0
14. Customs/Traditional Behavior	42.9	33.3
15. Group History	28.6	33.3
16. Family Heritage	21.4	20.0
17. Ethnic Pride	14.3	23.3
18. Citizenship	---	6.7
19. Other	21.4	13.3

born Hmong do not differ in the meanings they attach to "being Hmong" and "being American."

DISCUSSION

This exploratory study is the first step in understanding the cultural orientation of today's Hmong young adults. This sample of Hmong young adults was more oriented to American culture than to Hmong culture. This finding is not surprising, as this sample of Hmong young adults was educated primarily in the American school system and is currently attending college. What is perhaps more interesting is that despite their greater orientation to American

TABLE 4. "Being American": Percentage of Responses Within Specific Hmong Group for Each Content Code

| | Percentage of Responses Within Group | |
	American-Born (n = 14)	Overseas-Born (n = 32)
1. Label/Category	7.1	6.5
2. Physical Characteristics	7.1	6.5
3. Social Affiliation	---	3.2
4. Values/Beliefs	7.1	6.5
5. Language	7.1	12.9
6. Political/Economic Ideology	21.4	32.3
7. Cultural Exposure/Understanding	14.3	32.3
8. Geographic Origin	35.7	51.6
9. Minority Status	14.3	16.1
10. Reference to Self	7.1	---
11. Food	7.1	3.2
12. Personality/Traits/Expressions	7.1	3.2
13. Activities	---	---
14. Customs/Traditional Behavior	57.1	71.0
15. Group History	7.1	6.5
16. Family Heritage	---	---
17. Ethnic Pride	---	---
18. Citizenship	14.3	6.5
19. Other	7.1	3.2

culture, they retain a moderate level of orientation to Hmong culture. This may be because most of the Hmong sample continued to live at home with their parents. Future research should include samples of Hmong who live away from their parents or live in communities in which Hmong have a smaller presence to examine how orientation to Hmong culture is influenced by these factors.

ABH and OBH did not differ in their levels of orientation to either culture, suggesting that differences in place of birth and the length of time spent in the United States did not influence degrees of orientation to American and Hmong cultures. Future research should include overseas-born Hmong who migrated to the United States at later ages to examine whether over time, these individuals become more oriented to American culture than to Hmong culture.

Despite similarities in mean levels of orientation to Hmong and American cultures, ABH and OBH did differ in their underlying models of cultural orientation. ABH held bidimensional whereas OBH held unidimensional models of cultural orientation. Although this finding supported previous findings, it is particularly striking given the young age at which the OBH came to the United States. This finding suggests that other factors in addition to those outlined in the introduction and Tsai et al. (2000) may be at play in the development of models of cultural orientation. It is possible that simply knowing that one was born in another country changes one's perception of one's current cultural environment. It is also possible that the home environments of individuals who were born abroad are different from those of individuals who were born in the United States in ways that promote more unidimensional models of cultural orientation. Again, future research should pursue these avenues.

Finally, ABH and OBH did not differ in the meanings they attached to "being American" and "being Hmong." These findings support other study findings that ABH and OBH did not differ in their mean levels of orientation to Hmong and American cultures, as measured by the General Ethnicity Questionnaire. Future studies should include other samples of Hmong with different levels of orientation to Hmong and American cultures to examine whether the meanings they attach to "being Hmong" and "being American" differ. In addition, research should examine the sources of these meanings. For example, it would be interesting to assess whether Hmong young adults learn what "being American" means from their parents or from their teachers in the American school system.

Limitations and Future Directions

This study has a number of limitations that can be addressed in future research. First, it is possible that the similarities found in interview responses between the groups were artifacts of the experimental situation. That is, Hmong of both groups may have been very conscious of being evaluated and, therefore, were more concerned with providing the "right" response rather than what they actually felt. We attempted to increase participant comfort by having a Hmong female of a similar age as the interviewer; however, it is possible that this was not effective. Only studies that obtain open-ended responses using other methods (pencil and paper measures, different interviewers) will assess whether this was the case. Second, it is possible that the use of English in the experimental procedures biased participants' responses. Yang and Bond (1980) found that when Chinese-English bilinguals completed instruments assessing their cultural identification in English, they reported greater identification with Chinese culture than when they completed the same instruments in Chinese. Future research should assess cultural orientation using instruments that are administered in spoken Hmong or in written Hmong script. Third, future studies should include measures of psychological adjustment to examine whether cultural orientation is indeed related to health and psychological adjustment in this generation of Hmong. Finally, longitudinal studies are needed to examine how these cultural orientation processes change (or do not change) over time.

Clinical Implications

This study was based on a non-clinical sample of Hmong college-students; therefore, its clinical implications are limited. However, its findings illustrate the tremendous variation within the group called "Hmong." Although Hmong older adults are culturally traditional (Ying et al., 1997), Hmong young adults are more oriented to American than to Hmong culture. In addition, although place of birth does not influence levels of orientation to Hmong and American cultures, it does impact models of cultural orientation. In the therapeutic context, this may influence the meaning particular interventions hold. For example, the suggestion to affiliate more with Hmong in order to learn more about Hmong culture may not threaten an American-born Hmong's cultural orientation, whose notions of "being American" are independent of his engagement in Hmong culture. However, the same suggestion may be very threatening to an overseas-born Hmong whose notions of "being Hmong" are related to "being American." In the latter case, the overseas-born Hmong may feel that the therapist is trying to make him "less American." In sum, future research on Hmong cultural orientation processes and their relations to mental health will help researchers and clinicians determine whether clinical interventions are necessary for this group. If they are, such research will also further the development of interventions that meet the needs of this growing group of Hmong young adults.

NOTES

1. A 20th code, "media," was dropped from the original coding system because it was not used by any of the participants.

2. Ellipses indicate "filler words" used by participants such as "um," "I don't know," and "you know."

3. In order to ensure that the different correlations for ABH and OBH were not due to differences in sample size, analyses were conducted on a randomly selected group of 14 overseas-born Hmong. These analyses revealed that for this subset of overseas-born Hmong, mean scores on the GEQ-A and GEQ-H were negatively correlated ($r = -.76$, $p < .001$), as was found for the larger sample of 32 overseas-born Hmong.

REFERENCES

Chan, S. (Ed.). *Hmong Means Free: Life in Laos and America*. Philadelphia, PA: Temple University Press.

Chung, R. C., & Lin, K. M. (1994). Help-seeking behavior among Southeast Asian refugees. *Journal of Community Psychology, 22*(2), 109-120.

Fadiman, A. (1997). *The Spirit Catches You and You Fall Down: A Hmong Child, Her American Doctors, and the Collision of Two Cultures*. New York: Farrar, Straus, & Giroux.

Mendoza, R.H. (1989). An empirical scale to measure type and degree of acculturation in Mexican American adolescents and adults. *Journal of Cross-Cultural Psychology, 20*, 372-385.

Murphy, J., Alpert, B., Moes, D., & Somes, G. (1986). Race and cardiovascular reactivity: A neglected relationship. *Hypertension, 8*, 1075-1083.

Nicholson, B. L. (1997). The influence of pre-emigration and postemigration stressors on mental health: A study of Southeast Asian refugees. *Social Work Research, 21*(1), 19-31.

Ronningen, B. (1999, May). Estimates of immigration populations in Minnesota. *PopBites: Publication of State Demographic Center at Minnesota Planning, 99* (16).

Southeast Asian Resource Action Center. (1998). Southeast Asian Population By State. *The Bridge: 1998 Year in Review*.

Suinn, R.M., Rickard-Figueroa, K., Lew, S., & Vigil, P. (1987). The Suinn-Lew Asian Self-Identity Acculturation Rating Scale: An initial report. *Educational and Psychological Measurement, 47*, 401-407.

Szapocznik, J., Scopetta, M.A., Kurtines, W., & de los Angeles Aranalde, M. (1978). Theory and measurement of acculturation. *Interamerican Journal of Psychology, 12*, 113-130.

Ta, K., Westermeyer, J., and Neider, J. (1996). Physical disorders among southeast Asian refugee outpatients with psychiatric disorders. *Psychiatric Services, 47*(9), 975-979.

Taylor, K. (1998, October 25). The Hmong: A New Wave. *Star Tribune*, A1-6.

Tsai, J.L., Ying, Y., & Lee, P.A. (2000). The Meaning of "Being Chinese" and "Being American": Variation Among Chinese American Young Adults. *Journal of Cross-Cultural Psychology, 31*, 302-322.

U.S. Bureau of the Census (1998). *1990 Census of Population, General Population Characteristics, United States (CP-1-1)*. Washington, DC: U.S. Government Printing Office.

Waid, W.M., & Orne, M.T. (1981). Cognitive, social, and personality processes in the physiological detection of deception. In L. Berkowitz (Ed.). *Advances in experimental social psychology (pp. 61-106)*. New York: Academic Press.

Westermeyer, J., & Her, C. (1996). Predictors of English fluency among Hmong refugees in Minnesota: A longitudinal study. *Cultural Diversity & Mental Health, 2*(2), 125-132.

Westermeyer, J., Schaberg, L., & Nugent, S. (1995). Anxiety symptoms in Hmong refugees 1.5 years after migration. *Journal of Nervous and Mental Disease, 183*(5), 342-344.

Ying, Y., Akutsu, P.A., Zhang, X., & Huang, L.N. (1997). Psychological dysfunction in Southeast Asian refugees as mediated by sense of coherence. *American Journal of Community Psychology, 25*(6), 839-859.

Yang, K.S., & Bond, M.H. (1980). Ethnic affirmation by Chinese bilinguals. *Journal of Cross-Cultural Psychology, 11*(4), 411-425.

Filipino American Dating Violence: Definitions, Contextual Justifications, and Experiences of Dating Violence

Pauline Agbayani-Siewert
Alice Yick Flanagan

SUMMARY. This study examined 171 Filipino American undergraduate students on physical, sexual, and psychological definitions and contextual justifications of and experiences with dating violence. A blended methodology that combined survey and focus group data was used. Filipino Americans tended to define dating violence as physical and sexual abuse. Perceptions of psychological abuse were more narrowly defined than physical and sexual violence. Conversely, focus group data indicated that Filipino American students are very cognizant of what comprises psychological abuse. Scaled score findings showed no significant differences between Filipino males and females. However, closer examination of the items comprising the scales revealed significant gender differences in contextual justifications and definitions of psychological abuse. Contextual justification was the only variable to have a significant effect on experiences of dating violence. Filipino

Pauline Agbayani-Siewert, MSW, PhD, is Assistant Professor, School of Public Policy and Social Research, Department of Social Welfare and Asian American Studies, University of California, Los Angeles, 3250 Public Policy Building, Box 951656, Los Angeles, CA 90095-1656 (E-mail: paui@ucla.edu).

Alice Yick Flanagan, MSW, PhD, is affiliated with Research Insights, Pasadena, CA.

The authors would like to acknowledge Cynthia Lopez Alcott, MSW, for reviewing an earlier draft of the article and the Institute of American Cultures Grant at the University of California, Los Angeles (UCLA) and the Senate Faculty Grant at UCLA for their support of this research.

[Haworth co-indexing entry note]: "Filipino American Dating Violence: Definitions, Contextual Justifications, and Experiences of Dating Violence." Agbayani-Siewert, Pauline, and Alice Yick Flanagan. Co-published simultaneously in *Journal of Human Behavior in the Social Environment* (The Haworth Press, Inc.) Vol. 3, No. 3/4, 2001, pp. 115-133; and: *Psychosocial Aspects of the Asian-American Experience: Diversity Within Diversity* (ed: Namkee G. Choi) The Haworth Press, Inc., 2001, pp. 115-133. Single or multiple copies of this article are available for a fee from The Haworth Document Delivery Service [1-800-342-9678, 9:00 a.m. - 5:00 p.m. (EST). E-mail address: getinfo@haworthpressinc.com].

115

American culture and history are used to assist in explaining the findings and formulate implications for practice. *[Article copies available for a fee from The Haworth Document Delivery Service: 1-800-342-9678. E-mail address: <getinfo@haworthpressinc.com> Website: <http://www.HaworthPress.com> © 2001 by The Haworth Press, Inc. All rights reserved.]*

KEYWORDS. Filipino-Americans, dating violence, psychological abuse

INTRODUCTION

In the last two decades, the literature on dating violence has grown. Terms such as "courtship violence," "dating violence," and "premarital abuse" have surfaced. Many scholars and researchers have asserted that this social problem needs further investigation since it provides a unique opportunity to understand the linkages between child victimization and later aggressive behaviors (Bernard & Bernard, 1983). Others (e.g., Suarez, 1994) have argued that the courtship phase is a developmental period that provides a vehicle for adolescents and young adults to rehearse adult roles and problem-solving skills in intimate relationships. Although the empirical base in dating violence has grown, there is a scarcity of empirical information on dating violence among ethnic minority adolescents and young adults. We know, for example, very little about this phenomenon in the Filipino community. The social science field has long recognized the importance of ethnicity and gender as social categories. The impact of ethnicity and cultural belief systems on attitudes and behaviors has long been acknowledged (Green, 1982). In addition, Bem (1993) maintained that gender serves as an organizing principle for every human interaction. Consequently, the goal of this paper is to describe Filipino American students' perceptions of dating violence and to identify significant factors related to the experience of dating violence. Similarities and differences between Filipino women and men will also be described. Specifically, this paper (1) describes definitions of psychological, physical, and sexual violence and contextual justifications for dating violence and (2) while controlling for gender examines the effect of perceptions of violence on experiences of dating violence.

REVIEW OF THE LITERATURE

Prevalence of Dating Violence

Almost two decades ago, Makepeace's landmark study (1981) on dating violence launched empirical attention among social scientists to further examine this topic. Over the years, researchers have struggled with the definition of dating violence, and, ultimately, developing precise instruments to measure the concept of dating violence has been difficult. Consequently, numerous studies have yielded a range of prevalence estimates. White and Koss (1991), for example, reported that during a woman's lifetime, one-third to one-half will experience physical violence by an intimate partner. In another study, Arias, Samios, and O'Leary (1987) found that physical violence among dating couples ranged from 20% to 66%. In general, it is estimated that about 33% of all females under 20 years of age have experienced some form of dating aggression or will experience it before they are adults (Suarez, 1994).

Psychological abuse has received less attention in domestic and dating violence research compared to physical and sexual abuse. However, when researchers examine acts of psychological abuse, findings suggest a high prevalence rate. One study found that over three-quarters of college women experienced psychological abuse during a six month period and 91% over their dating lifetime (Neufeld, McNamara, & Ertl, 1991). Sexual assault in the context of dating is also a common occurrence. One national study of college females found that 54% had experienced some form of sexual aggression by a dating partner at least once since the age of fourteen (Koss, Gidycz, & Wisniewski, 1987). The above figures may be underestimated because individuals are generally reluctant to report being involved in shameful behaviors (Clark, Beckett, Wells, & Dungee-Anderson, 1994). Asian Americans are especially averse to recounting experiences that may result in a loss of face for themselves and their families.

Dating Violence Among Asian Americans

Since Makepeace's study in the early 1980s, minimal empirical studies have examined dating aggression with ethnic minorities, particularly with Asian Americans. The stereotype of Asian Americans being "passive" has led many individuals to believe that intimate violence or dating violence does not exist in Asian American communities (Masaki & Wong, 1997). However, findings from Yick and Agbayani-Siewert's (2000) study with Chinese American college students found that 18.5% reported having experienced a form of physical violence in a dating relationship since they started dating. Unfortunately, an extant literature search has not yielded any empirical studies on Filipino American dating violence. Notwithstanding the important contributions of anecdotal (Agtuca, 1992) and conceptual literature (Santos, 1983; Agbayani-Siewert, 1994), an empirical understanding of Filipino American intimate violence and gender roles is nonexistent. An extensive review of the literature uncovered only one empirical work conducted in Australia on Filipino marital violence (Tan & Davidson, 1994). It has generally been assumed that Filipino American perceptions and attitudes towards intimate violence are similar to other Asian Americans, i.e., patriarchal. Descriptive, conceptual, and anecdotal literature provides inconsistent information on Filipino American sex role structures, which have been described as either egalitarian (Aquino, 1994), patriarchal (Actuga, 1994), or historically based on a matriarchal sex role structure (Pido, 1986). This inconsistency is not unique to Filipino Americans in the United States, but is found in literature from the Philippines as well.

In social science research, some scholars have argued that many paradigms and values in the field do not reflect social realities of ethnic groups (Padilla, 1990; Collins, 1989). Because of racism, discrimination, differential access to services, language barriers, and different cultural belief systems, the life experiences and social realities of ethnic minority members will differ significantly from those in Western mainstream communities. Consequently, many scholars advocate for a distinct epistemology that more accurately depicts the social realties and conditions of subordinate groups (Stanfield, 1993). This is particularly crucial as the Asian American population in the United States continues to grow. Since 1980, it has doubled to 2.9% of the total U.S. population (Kang & Kang, 1995). In terms of the demographic shift, the U.S. population has increased to a total of 9.8% and during the same time period, the number of Asian Americans has grown by 107.8%, a growth rate eleven times higher than the total growth rate of the U.S. population (U.S. Census, 1991).

Filipino Americans

Filipino Americans are the second largest Asian group in the United States, comprising 19.3% of all Asian Americans (Uba, 1994). Second to Mexico, the Philippines provides the United States (U.S.) with its largest group of immigrants. Filipinos share similarities with other Asian American groups; however, there are distinct differences which may affect Filipino attitudes and beliefs about gender roles and intimate violence. Filipino Americans, for example, are predominantly Catholic (over 80%) (Chan, 1992), and post-1965 immigrants represent a relatively homogenous background of professionals. In the United States, Filipino American women possess the second highest level of education compared to all other ethnic and gender groups, including White males and females (Agbayani-Siewert & Jones, 1997).

Historically, Filipino culture and society has been influenced by numerous cultures, most notably American, Spanish, and Chinese. The Philippines was colonized for over 350 years under Spanish rule, immediately followed by American occupation in 1899 (Agoncillo, 1990). Euro-American colonialism has had and continues to have a profound effect on Filipinos, both in the Philippines and in the United States (Santos, 1990; Rimonte, 1997). Filipinos have been inculcated with American ideals of individualism and democracy.

They come to the U.S. with the ability to speak, read, and write English. It has been said that Filipinos in the Philippines begin the acculturation process before immigration to the U.S. (Santos, 1990).

According to historical literature, Filipino sex role structure in pre-Spanish colonial rule was characterized as egalitarian (Castillo, 1942). Women assumed the role of chief and priestess equal to men, retained their surname after marriage, traced relatives bilaterally (Pido, 1986), and owned and disposed of property without permission from men. In contrast to European religion where Eve was created from Adam's rib, Filipino legend describes a male and female emerging simultaneously from a bamboo stalk (Andres & Illada-Andres, 1987). The first consonant of the ancient Tagalog word for God, *Bathala*, refers to woman (Mananzan, 1985). At birth, male and female offspring were equally accepted into the community (Mangahas, 1987). Today, this sentiment continues to be expressed, as Filipino families will give recognition, opportunities, and deference to any member who shows the potential to increase the family's resources or standing in the community, regardless of sex (Pido, 1986). Filipino men's and women's role structures were considerably altered under Spanish colonial rule. Women were not permitted to own property, retain their maiden surname, undertake leadership roles, or assume roles outside the home (Angangco, Samson, & Albino, 1980). On the other hand, Spanish colonial norms dictated that males should adopt patriarchal authority and display "machismo" mannerisms and behaviors (Yap, 1986).

Culture is shaped by environmental and situational factors that subsequently have an impact on individual attitudes and beliefs that influence goals and behaviors. One would expect that Filipino culture is not an archetype of Asian culture given over 400 years of historical Spanish and American interventions which brought about changes in religion, education, politics, and ideology. One would surmise, for example, that Filipino gender roles would be more egalitarian, similar to that of White Americans. Likewise, due to the influence of Spanish colonialism, one would speculate that Filipinos would possess a more traditional sex role structure. However, in addition to American and Spanish influences are indigenous Filipino cultural values and beliefs that are still evident today (Agoncillo, 1967). These indigenous values have also shaped perceptions of gender roles. Early Filipino culture appears to have been characterized by a horizontal collectivism (Triandis, 1993), of interdependency and egalitarianism that is still evident today. According to Enriquez (1993) the Filipino value of *pakikipagkapwa* (self and others) represents the core principles of humanity in the acceptance and treatment of others as equals. Current laws in the Philippines reflect indigenous egalitarian rather than patriarchal politics. For example, it is illegal to publicly denigrate women (Ho, 1987); places of employment are required by law to offer maternity and paternity leave; and women have the same legal rights as men to inherit, sell, and own property (Veloso, 1997).

Considering the historical mix of Filipino indigenous culture with the political, religious, and cultural influences of other countries, it would be expected that Filipinos hold a unique conception of gender roles similar to, yet unlike, Spanish and Euro-American and other Asian American groups. An assumption that Filipinos are similar to other Asian American groups, such as Chinese and Japanese Americans, may reduce our understanding of Filipino Americans and may result in practice and policy implications that may or may not be relevant or appropriate.

METHODOLOGY

Research and Sampling Design

This study used a blended methodology, cross-sectional survey design combined with focus group data. The survey sample analyzed in this paper is a subset (n = 171) of a larger study (n = 1,356) of undergraduate students from a large urban university during the 1996-97 academic year. The sampling design employed was purposive. Ethnicity was determined by the respondent's self-report. The survey was administered to both males and females. Classes known to have a large number of ethnic minority students were targeted. This recruiting method was chosen for two reasons. First, the goal of the study was to understand how ethnicity and culture shape perceptions of and experiences with dating violence. Second, ethnic minority students make-up a relatively small proportion of the university population (e.g., Filipino students comprise 4.8% of the student body). However, all students, regardless of ethnicity and race, were surveyed. Instructors of the targeted classes were contacted by letter for permission to distribute the self-administered questionnaire during scheduled class sessions. A total of 26 classes in the humanities, ethnic studies, history, language, social welfare, and social sciences were surveyed. Graduate students monitored the data collection process.

Focus groups were held one year after the collection and preliminary analysis of data was completed. To recruit Filipino student focus group participants, flyers were distributed throughout the university, and presentations were made at several Filipino American student organizations. Students were provided with a phone number to call if they were interested in participating in a focus group on Filipino American dating violence. To help create an environment where participants would feel comfortable in disclosing opinions and experiences, two focus groups (male, n = 4, and females, n = 4) were held separately. Each group lasted for approximately two hours. The focus groups were facilitated by a Filipino male researcher and a Filipino female researcher. All of the groups were tape-recorded.

Instrumentation

The Perceptions of and Attitudes toward Intimate Violence instrument was (Yick, 1997) modified for use in this study to include questions on dating violence. The development of the original questionnaire was based on a review of the literature and in-depth interviews with service providers knowledgeable about domestic violence in the Asian American community. It was piloted with a community sample (n = 30), and its psychometric properties were established (Yick & Agbayani-Siewert, 1997). Once the original questionnaire was revised, it was piloted with 128 college students of various racial/ethnic backgrounds.

The instrument has two scales–Definitions of Dating Violence and Contextual Justification. The Definition of Dating Violence scale has 3 subscales that measure perceptions of dating violence: verbal/emotional abuse (5 items), physical violence (4 items), and sexual violence (1 item). Respondents were asked on a six point Likert scale how much they agreed or disagreed that a particular behavior is dating violence. A high score indicates agreement that a particular behavior is violent. The Cronbach alpha for the Filipino sample was .80. The Contextual Justification Scale assesses the extent to which respondents agree or disagree whether certain situations warrant the use of dating violence by men. Statements describe such situations as a woman being unfaithful, flirting, disobeying, drunk, nagging, and unwilling to have sex. The scale comprises nine items with a six point Likert scale response format ranging from strongly agree to strongly disagree. A high score indicates agreement that a particular situation justifies the use of physical violence. The Cronbach alpha for this sample was .89.

Experiences of violence was measured by one categorical question, "have you ever experienced physical violence since you started dating such as being hit, pushed, grabbed, etc., by a boyfriend/girlfriend/partner."

Questions posed in the focus group were both structured and unstructured. All responses were open-ended. Structured questions with open-ended responses included the following: (1) definitions of dating violence, (2) circumstances when violence might be justified, and (3) descriptions of a dating violence incident either they or someone they knew had experienced. All structured questions were asked to both male and female participants in the focus groups. Unstructured questions with open-ended responses were also used as probes for clarification and the examination of new unsolicited information revealed by students during the course of the focus group.

To compare dating violence experience and perceptions of dating violence for Filipino American students and to explore differences between males and females, t-tests and chi-square tests were performed. Logistic regression was conducted to examine the effects of definitions of violence and contextual justifications on dating violence experience. Content analyses for the focus groups were conducted to extract recurrent themes. This qualitative data was used to highlight and expand the quantitative data collected from the surveys.

FINDINGS

The average age of the Filipino students was about 20 years. Most (64%) were born in the U.S. The average length of time in the U.S. for non-native born students was 12 years. The sample consisted of more females (61%) than males. This is most likely a consequence of the sampling design that targeted ethnic minorities in social science and humanities courses. The sample tended to be in higher class standings: freshman and sophomore (41.5%), junior and senior (58.5%). Both Filipino men and women began dating at 15.8 years of age. T-tests and chi-squares did not show any statistically significant gender differences across any of the sample's characteristics.

About a fifth of males and a third of the females reported having experienced dating violence. Although not significant, females reported a higher rate of having experienced physical dating violence than males (refer to Table 1).

Definitions and justifications of violence subscale means are presented in Table 2. To gain a better understanding of the definitions and justifications of violence, items that comprised the subscales were also examined. The mean scale score indicated that psychological violence was defined more narrowly than the other two forms of violence. Although both Filipino males and females agreed that psychological aggression was dating violence, males did so to a significantly lesser degree. In reference to the items that comprised the

TABLE 1. Ever Experienced Physical Violence?

	Yes	No
Female	32 (31.4%)	70 (68.6%)
Male	13 (20.6%)	50 (79.4%)
Total	45 (27.3%)	120 (72.7%)

TABLE 2. Definitions of Violence and Contextual Justification Mean Scores by Gender

DEFINITIONS	Male		Female			
	Mean	SD	Mean	SD	df	t
Psychological Subscale	3.90	.96	4.23	.88	167	− 2.23*
Argue	2.31	1.10	2.34	1.20	169	− .12
Disregard opinion	3.70	1.46	4.08	1.33	169	− 1.73
Demand to know where at	3.24	1.24	3.42	1.28	169	− .92
Criticize in front of others	3.18	1.46	3.71	1.29	168	− 2.48*
Not allow decisions	3.51	1.45	4.06	1.36	169	− .92*
Physical Subscale	5.55	.45	5.55	.68	169	− .02
Punch face	5.96	.27	5.81	.93	128	1.52
Throw objects at	5.64	.62	5.68	.78	169	− .36
Push partner	5.06	.89	5.17	.95	169	− .78
Threaten to use knife	5.85	.44	5.86	.58	169	− .06
Sexual (Force sex)	5.88	.48	5.79	.88	169	.78
Justification Scale	1.87	.59	1.74	.76	167	1.16
She has an affair	2.48	1.46	2.02	1.30	169	2.14*
She is drunk	1.78	1.01	1.53	.90	169	1.67
He acted self-defense	3.79	1.51	3.75	1.45	169	.17
She screams hysterically	1.97	.93	1.80	1.18	168	1.00
She is unwilling to have sex	1.23	.76	1.29	1.05	168	− .41
She nags	1.51	.86	1.37	.83	169	1.08
He's in bad mood	1.34	.81	1.20	.81	169	1.11
She flirts	1.85	1.16	1.51	.93	169	2.11*
She disobeyed	1.39	.82	1.25	.81	169	1.08

*p = .05

Psychological Violence Subscale, Filipino females tended to agree at a significantly higher rate than males that being criticized in front of others and not being allowed to make their own decisions was dating violence. There was a trend toward significance (p = .08) for the item "demand to know where one's partner is all the time." Females tended to rate this question item as dating violence slightly more than Filipino males.

Given the limited opportunity to elaborate on the nuances of psychological abuse in the survey portion of the study, the focus groups revealed that both Filipino females and males were very attuned to the various aspects of psychological abuse. Participants referred to psychological abuse as "mind games."

> I consider mind games to be abusive because you're causing them (their partners) to think one way but then you are acting in another way. You're leading that person on . . . You're subjecting them to torture, or a type of suspense . . . if the person's wracking their brains over it, then definitely it could be considered abuse. (J–Male)

> I think that's emotional abuse to mess with someone's mind. It's so common that we overlook it . . . . (G–Female)

> . . . when you're at a party with a bunch of friends and a guy might put his girlfriend down in front of other people. It doesn't have to be isolated incidents . . . It could happen with a group of people, and it could go unnoticed. (R–Female)

Both male and female participants also indicated an understanding of the insidious and deleterious consequences of psychological abuse.

> . . . especially in relationships because you're so close to a person and they know so much about you. They could pull so much on you, and they could destroy you emotionally. (S–Male).

> . . . it (psychological abuse) also makes their self-esteem lower . . . if it makes them feel worse about themselves, or takes away from their confidence, to me, that's abuse, too. (R–Female)

Mean score findings indicated that Filipino male and female students tended to strongly agree that physical and sexual aggressive behaviors are dating violence. In regards to items that comprised the Physical Violence Subscale, no significant gender differences emerged. Focus group data concurred with the survey data. When asked to define dating violence, responses were initially descriptions of physical and sexual aggression.

> I think that when people say dating violence, they tend to think physical violence . . .' (K–Female).

> I'm a third year student here, and the first thing that comes to my mind is date rape–anyone forcing himself or herself upon another person

without his/her consent. Forcing themselves even when the person says no. (J–Male).

Overall, with the exception of defending oneself, respondents did not tend to justify violence under any context. The mean scale score for the Contextual Justification Scale showed no significant gender differences. However, there were significant gender differences found with two of the items comprising the scale: having an affair and flirting. Males tended to justify violence at a slightly higher level than females under these circumstances. Conversely, focus group findings suggested that some Filipino women may endorse the belief that flirting warrants violence. One female focus group participant, for example, stated that she was hit by her partner because she was flirting with another male at a party. She stated that her behavior provoked her partner's feelings of insecurity, and hitting was a demonstration of his caring for her.

Although not represented in the survey, participants in the Filipino female focus group recognized that alcohol is often used as an excuse to rationalize the violence.

> . . . it's kind of sad, because women tend to take it (alcohol) as an excuse. They let it (aggressive behavior) pass by when guys are drinking, smoking, or fighting. And, the day after, the girl will just let it go. I think that's really bad because they take it as an excuse and then do it over and over again. (K–Female)

The relationship between perceptions of and experiences of dating are presented in Table 3. Overall, both males and females generally agreed that physically and sexually aggressive acts were dating violence whether or not they had experienced violence. However, Filipino females who had experienced physical dating violence were in higher agreement significantly more than their male counterparts that psychological aggression was a form of dating violence.

Table 4 presents the logistic regression findings for the estimated effects of the three definitions of violence subscales, contextual justification, and gender on the likelihood of experiencing violence among Filipino Americans. The regression model satisfied the Hosmer and Lemeshow (1989) goodness-of-fit test of significance. The justification of violence subscale was the only factor that had a significant effect ($\chi^2 = 5.04$, df = 8, p = .753) on the odds of having experienced dating violence. Specifically, the odds of having experienced dating violence were 1.7 times greater for individuals who tended to justify violent behavior than for those who did not. Although not significant, the direction of the coefficient for definitions of psychological and sexual violence was negative. This suggests that the more the individual defines aggressive psychological and sexual acts as violent, the less likely they are to have experienced dating violence. Conversely, the direction of the coefficient for physical abuse was positive, suggesting that a greater awareness of what constitutes physical violence results in a higher probability of experiencing dating violence. The findings also indicated that Filipino males were at less risk for experiencing violence than females. However, it was not significant at the .05 level. Interaction terms with gender and definitions of violence and contextual justification were evaluated to examine the possible interaction effects. However, none of the interaction terms were significant, and, therefore, they were not included in the model.

TABLE 3. Relationship Between Experiences of Dating Violence and Perceptions of Dating Violence Controlling for Gender

	EVER EXPERIENCE DATING VIOLENCE?							
	No				Yes			
	Male	Female			Male	Female		
	Mean	Mean	df	t	Mean	Mean	df	t
Psychological	3.94	4.27	121	− 1.87	3.55	4.17	38	− 2.34*
Physical	5.56	5.50	122	− .565	5.47	5.67	39	− 1.19
Sexual	5.88	5.78	122	.74	5.83	5.79	39	.14
Justification	1.87	1.68	120	1.66	1.96	1.92	39	.12

$p = .05$

TABLE 4. Logistic Regression: The Effects of Definitions and Contextual Justifications of Violence on Experiences of Violence

(N = 167)	b	SE	e^B (odds-ratio)	p
Gender (1 = m, 0 = fe)	− .643	.413	.52	.11
Physical subscale	.616	.397	1.85	.12
Psychological subscale	− .409	.225	.66	.06
Sexual subscale	− .029	.246	.97	.91
Justification scale	.566	.271	1.76	.03*

− 2 Log Likelihood = 172.19

Limitations of the Study

One of the limitations of the findings revolves around its generalizability to the Filipino American community. First, it was conducted with a select group of Filipino college students who were different in important ways from people in the community. The majority of these students represents children of immigrants. Most Filipino Americans in the U.S. are immigrants who are less acculturated than the students sampled, and, thus, they may manifest important differences in perceptions and experiences of dating violence. Second, the sample was comprised of undergraduate students who were more liberal than others from their respective ethnic groups in the community. Spence and Helmriech (1978) found that individuals tend to be more liberal in attitudes toward women while in college. Moreover, as individuals move upward in social class, they tend to become more homogeneous (Zeff, 1982). Thus, findings from this study may be applicable and useful in understanding the perceptions of dating violence for Filipino American student groups. Future research should consider community samples that will show more variation by level of acculturation, gender, and other sociodemographic factors, such as education and socioeconomic status. One of the dilemmas in obtaining a community sample revolves around funding. To date, national studies have not included Asian Americans in sampling designs or findings. This lack of attention may be related to the Asian American model minority myth.

The focus group data suggested the need for culturally sensitive instruments. Survey data, for example, revealed a narrow understanding of behaviors that constitute psychological abuse. However, the focus group data indicated a sophisticated understanding of the myriad of definitions and consequences of psychological abuse. When conducting research with Filipino Americans or any other ethnic population where there is a paucity of knowledge, it is highly recommended that a blended methodological approach of qualitative and survey designs be employed. Qualitative research techniques allow the social context to be elaborated, particularly if instruments employed are Western-based. Although this study has inherent limitations, it offers new knowledge about Filipino Americans' perceptions of and experiences with dating violence.

DISCUSSION

Overall, Filipino females reported rates of dating violence that are consistent with other studies (Arias, Samios, & O'Leary, 1987). Conversely, Filipino males reported having experienced dating violence at a rate similar to Chinese American male students, but lower than White males (Yick & Agbayani-Siewert, in press; Thompson, 1991). These rates of Filipino American dating violence are notable, considering that that the respondents in this study had only been dating for approximately four years. Data analysis indicated that there were no significant differences between Filipino male and female experiences with dating violence. Most studies have revealed that rates of violence are similar across genders (Riggs et al., 1990). However, physical violence generally does not result in similar injuries when perpetrated by a male versus a female. Domestic and dating violence perpetrated against women results in more severe and life threatening injuries than that experienced by male victims (Langan & Innes, 1986; Brush, 1990). Female focus group participants described being slapped, hit with objects, and thrown in the air. On the other hand, when males described their experiences of dating violence, they recounted being slapped or pushed during play.

The non-significant gender differences in experiences of physical violence may be explained by an existing egalitarian sex role structure among Filipino Americans. Extant literature has suggested a relationship between patriarchal ideologies and intimate violence (Watson & Ebrey, 1991). Findings from Ho's (1990) qualitative study on Southeast Asian American domestic violence suggests that traditional patriarchal Asian values foster a degree of personal and social acceptance of physical violence towards women.

Filipino American rates of dating violence may also be explained by a reluctance to report violence. The cultural practices of *hiya* (shame) and *tayo-tayo* (just among us) may create barriers in reporting abuse and seeking available services. Filipino Americans tend to keep personal information within the family. The Tagalog term, *tayo-tayo* is used to express the sentiment that personal difficulties should not be made public.

Survey findings indicated that both Filipino males and females were more cognizant of physical and sexual acts of aggression as dating violence as opposed to psychological violence. Historically, physical abuse has gained more widespread attention in the media and in the justice system (Sigler, 1989). Consequently, there may be less concerted efforts on educating the public about psychological abuse and behaviors that fall under this category. An understanding of Asian cultural context may also assist in explaining this finding. Euro-American orientations tend to emphasize a dichotomy between body and mind, while Filipinos and other Asian groups place less emphasis on intrapsychic concerns (Kuo, 1984; Uba, 1994). This is reflected in empirical findings that suggest Filipino Americans tend to somatize emotional distress (Flaskerud & Soldevilla, 1986; Tompar-Tiu & Sustento-Seneriches, 1994).

Survey findings also indicated that Filipino females appear to view behaviors such as fault-finding and controlling as dating violence. In addition, females who have experienced physical violence during a dating relationship appear to be more likely to identify psychological behaviors as abusive compared to their male counterparts. Conversely, focus group findings suggest that both Filipino American males and females are highly aware of the range of behaviors that comprise psychological abuse. Both Filipino men and women conveyed the idea that the function of lying and misrepresenting the truth is to manipulate and control others. Focus group members also communicated a sophisticated understanding of the damaging consequences of psychological abuse. The discrepancy between the survey and focus group findings suggests that the survey instrument used to measure psychological abuse did not capture all of the subtleties and nuances involved in this type of abuse for Filipino Americans.

Contextual justifications was the only perception that significantly predicted a likelihood of experiencing dating violence. Since no significant gender interaction was found, it appears that the finding is applicable to both males and females. Justifications for the use of force are embedded in a culture that believes violence is acceptable if the reasons are valid (Sigler, 1989). Cultural norms prescribe rules of retributive justice, implying that if an individual believes he or she has sufficient cause for violence, then these rules can be invoked (Greenblat, 1985). Although males and females similarly did not justify violence under any circumstance except in situations of self-defense, gender differences were found with two of the items relating to the sexual behavior. Filipino males are more likely to endorse physical violence than females if the woman is flirting or having an affair. For Filipino American males, any perceived deviation from an expectation of female sexual fidelity may provide the retributive context for violence. Justifying violence in situations where sexual infidelity is believed to have occurred may be a reflection of the Asian cultural norm of "saving face" (Foo & Margolin, 1995). The Tagalog term *hiya* (shame) reflects a similar sentiment. *Hiya* functions to maintain harmony and smooth interpersonal relationships within the family and the larger collective (Agbayani-Siewert, 1994). Although extant literature suggests that Filipino Americans are characterized by an egalitarian sex role structure, expectations regarding women's sexual behavior reflect traditional patriarchal beliefs. Sex role expectations of Filipino women at times appear to be distributed between two opposing principles, egalitarian and patriarchal. Filipino women are expected to contribute to the social standing and economic well-being of the household similar to males while simultaneously portraying traditional feminine traits and roles. It is generally expected that males will engage in extra-marital affairs while females are expected to remain monogamous (Gilandas, 1982). The Philippine heroine, Maria Clara, represents an idealized image of the Filipino woman. Maria Clara participated in the war for independence against the United States during the early 1900s. She is described as epitomizing virtue, chastity, beauty, traditional femininity, and strength (Chant & McIlwaine, 1995). The idealized version of Filipino women as sexually chaste and yet equal to males did not exist prior to Spanish colonialism. Both men and women were free to engage in premarital sex, and trial marriages were encouraged. The expectation of traditional feminine behavior probably stems from vestiges of Catholicism and patriarchal Spanish culture. Consequently, the seemingly inconsistent and paradoxical expectations regarding Filipino women may be an admixture of Spanish colonialism and indigenous Filipino culture.

IMPLICATIONS FOR PRACTICE AND RESEARCH

Despite the image of Asian Americans as a model minority, findings from this study show that Filipino Americans do experience dating violence. Filipino American rates of dating violence may be underreported. The literature consistently reports that Asian American students seldom utilize student services, counseling, campus hot-lines, and support groups (Sue, 1988). Effective prevention of dating violence requires the partnership of a multitude of community systems extending beyond educational institutions, such as the justice system, police, policy makers, service providers, and neighborhood coalitions. Involvement in the Filipino American community is essential to generate support for policies and programs to stem the increasing rate of violence. Intimate violence in the Filipino American community has been referred to as "a community secret" (Actuga, 1992). Therefore, in order to generate community involvement and support, the Filipino American community must first be informed about the prevalence and personal and social consequences of dating violence.

Campus and community prevention programs are also essential. General topics can include information about what comprises dating violence and the risk factors associated with victimization. The content of the material should be culturally specific. For example, understanding that Filipino American students may not place great importance on intrapsychic orientations suggests narrower definitions of psychological abuse compared to definitions of physical and sexual violence. Thus, educational prevention programs should focus on what comprises psychological abuse. For Filipino Americans, an examination of the justifications for violence is essential, especially those concerning women's sexual behavior. In addition, an examination of historical factors may aid students in understanding cultural sanctions of violence against women (e.g., influences of Spanish colonialism on gender roles). An ethnic group's cultural strengths should also be incorporated into any prevention program, such as an overview of Filipino American collectivist roots and egalitarianism, both historical and current. Prevention programs should consider the benefits of gender specific groups that allow Filipino American males and females to separately examine their cultural beliefs and values concerning sexual behavior. The gender specific focus groups used in this study seemed to foster an open environment for discussion and disclosure.

The cultural practice of *tayo tayo* may also affect the practitioner-client relationship. Research on Filipino Americans indicates that professional and religious counseling is rarely sought for personal or family problems, although reading materials are often used as a means to problem-solve and educate (Agbayani-Siewert, 1993). Case studies describing actual accounts of Filipino American women caught in a cycle of domestic violence have been successfully used as part of an Asian American shelter program as a tool for education and outreach (Actuga, 1994). Culturally and socially relevant examples were integrated throughout the case studies. An example of a vignette incorporating cultural material for Filipino American students would be the depiction of a student who keeps the abuse secret for fear that her family would be shamed (*hiya*). Vignettes may also provide a non-threatening introduction or a stimulus for discussion on the topic of dating violence. In a counseling relationship or group session, vignettes can also be structured as problem solving exercises.

REFERENCES

Agbayani-Siewert, P. (1994). Filipino American culture and family: Guidelines for practitioners. *Families in Society: The Journal of Contemporary Human Services*, 75, 429-438.

Agbayani-Siewert, A., & Jones, L. (1997). Filipino American women, work, and family: An examination of factors affecting high labor force participation. *International Social Work, 40*, 407-423.

Agoncillo, T.A. (1990). *History of the Filipino people*. Quezon City, Philippines: Garotech Publising.

Bem, S.L. (1993). *The lens of gender*. New Haven, CT: Yale University Press.

Brush, L.D. (1990). Violent acts and injurious outcomes in married couples: Methodological issues in the National Survey of Families and Households. *Gender and Society, 4*, 56-67.

Castillo, T.B. (1942). *The changing social status of the Filipino Woman During the American Administration*. Unpublished Thesis, University of Southern California, Los Angeles, CA.

Chant, S.H. (1995). Women of a lesser cost: female labour, foreign exchange, and Philipinne development. In S.H. Chant & C. McIlwaine (Eds.). *Women of a lesser cost: Female labour, foreign exchange, and Philipinne development* (pp. 12-16). Boulder, CO: Pluto.

Clark, M.L., Beckett, J., Wells, M., & Dungee-Anderson, D. (1994). Courtship violence among African American college students. *Journal of Black Psychology, 20* (3), 264-281.

Flaskerud, J., & Soldevilla, E. (1986). Filipino and Vietnamese clients: Utilizing an

Asian mental health center. *Journal of Psychosocial Nursing and Mental Health, 24*, 32-36.

Gilandas, A. (1982). *Sex and the single Filipina: The Omega woman.* Manila, Philippines: Philippine Education Co., Inc.

Green, J.W. (1982). *Cultural awareness in the human services.* Englewood Cliffs, NJ: Prentice Hall.

Greenblat, C.S. (1985). "Don't hit you wife . . . unless . . . ": Preliminary findings on normative support for the use of physical force by husbands. *Victimology, 10,* 221-241.

Ho, C. (1990). An analysis of domestic violence in Asian American communities: A multicultural approach to counseling. *Women & Therapy, 9*(1-2), 129-150.

Ho, M. (1989). Applying family therapy to Asian/Pacific Americans. *Contemporary Family Therapy, 11*, 61-70.

Hosmer, D., & Lemeshow, S. (1989). *Applied Logistic Regression.* New York: John Wiley & Sons.

Koss, M.P., Gidycz, C.A., & Wisniewski, N. (1987). The scope of rape: Incidence and prevalence of sexual aggression and victimization in a national sample of higher education students. *Journal of Consulting and Clinical Psychology, 55,* 162-170.

Kuo, W. (1984). Prevalence of depression among Asian Americans. *Journal of Nervous and Mental Disease, 172,* 449-457.

Langan, P., & Innes, P. (August, 1986). Preventing domestic violence against women. *Bureau of Justice Statistics Special Report.* Washington, DC: US Department of Justice, p. 3.

Makepeace, J. (1981). Courtship violence among college students. *Family Relations, 30,* 97-102.

Mananzan, M. J., Sr. (1991). The Filipino women: Before and after the Spanish conquest of the Philippines. Sr. M.J. Mananzan (Ed.), *Essays on Women* (Vol. Series 1, pp. 6-35). Manila, Philippines: The Institute of Women's Studies, St. Scholastica's College.

Mangahas, F. (1987). From Babylans to suffragettes: The status of Filipino women from pre-colonial times to the early American period. P.S. Azarcon (Editor), *Kamalayan: Feminist writings in the Philippines* (pp. 8-20). Quezon City, Philippines.

Masaki, B., & Wong, L. (1997). Domestic violence in the Asian community. In E. Lee (Ed.), *Working with Asian Americans: A guide for clinicians* (pp. 439-451). New York: Guilford Press.

Neufeld, J., McNamara, J.R., & Ertl, M. (1999). Incidence and prevalence of dating partner abuse and its relationship to dating practices. *Journal of Interpersonal Violence, 14* (2), 125-136.

Rimonte, N. (1997). Colonialism's legacy: The inferiorizing of the Filipino. In Maria Root (Ed.), *Filipino Americans: Transformation and Identity* (39-62). Thousand Oaks, CA: Sage.

Santos, R. (1983). The social and emotional development of Filipino American children. In G. Powell (Ed.), *The psychological development of minority group children,* (pp. 131-146). New York: Brunner/Mazel.

Sigler, R. (1989). *Domestic Violence in Context: An Assessment of Community Attitudes*. Lexington, MA: D.C. Heath & Company.

Spence, J., & Helmreich, R. (1978). *Masculinity and femininity: Their psychological dimensions, correlates and antecedents*. Austin: University of Texas Press.

Suarez, K.E. (1994). Teenage dating violence: The need for expanded awareness and legislation. *California Law Review, 82*(2), 423-471.

Sue, S. (1988). Psychotherapeutic services for ethnic minorities. *American Psychologist, 43*, 301-308.

Tan, J., & Davidson, G. (1994). Filipina-Australian marriages: Further perspectives on spousal violence. *Australian Journal of Social Issues, 29*(3), 265-282.

Tompar-Tiu, A., & Sustento-Seneriches, J. (1994). *Depression and other mental health issues: The Filipino American Experience*. San Francisco: Jossey-Bass.

Triandis, H. (1993). Collectivism and individualism as cultural syndromes. *Cross-Cultural Research, 27*, 155-180.

Uba, L. (1994*). Asian Americans: Personality patterns, identity, and mental health*. New York: Guildford Press.

Watson, R., & Ebrey, P. (1992). *Marriage and inequality in Chinese Society*. Berkeley, CA: University of California Press.

White, J.W., & Koss, M.P. (1991). Courtship violence: Incidence in a national sample of higher education students. *Violence and Victims, 6*, 247-256.

Yap, J., (1986). Philippine ethnoculture and human sexuality. *Journal of Social Work and Human Sexuality, 4*(3), 121-134.

Yick, A., & Agbayani-Siewert, P. (2000). Chinese Americans and dating violence: A sociocultural context. *Journal of Multicultural Social Work*.

Zeff, S.B. (1982). A cross-cultural study of Mexican American, Black American, and White American women at a large urban university. *Hispanic Journal of Behavioral Sciences, 4*(2), 245-261.

"Being Indian," "Being American":
A Balancing Act or a Creative Blend?

Shobha Srinivasan

SUMMARY. This is a cross-cultural study that seeks to understand an aspect of Asian Indian women's realities by exploring concepts such as: attitudes toward gender roles, level of stress in their lives, and their ethnic identity. It compares Asian Indian women raised in the U.S. (n = 45), with women born and raised in India (n = 50) and with European American women in the U.S. (n = 50). Additionally, excerpts from in-depth interviews with Asian Indian women in the U.S. are included. Most Asian Indian women in this study feel that they are both Indian and American and feel the two can be very well combined. However, they have problems with their families for not being Indian enough, especially on issues regarding marriage, career choice, and dating. The study found that "being Indian" might be different for the first generation Indian immigrants and the Asian Indian women who were born and raised in the U.S. These Asian Indian women are striving to claim a new identity for themselves, one which is both Indian and American. *[Article copies available for a fee from The Haworth Document Delivery Service: 1-800-342-9678. E-mail address: <getinfo@haworthpressinc.com> Website: <http://www.HaworthPress.com> © 2001 by The Haworth Press, Inc. All rights reserved.]*

Shobha Srinivasan, PhD, is affiliated with the National Research Center on Asian American Mental Health, 1 Shields Avenue, University of California, Davis, Davis, CA 95616-8686 (E-mail: srinivasan@ucdavis.edu).

The author wishes to acknowledge the assistance and support of the Women's Resources and Research Center and the South Asian Women's Alliance, University of California, Davis.

This project was supported in part by NIMH Grant number R01 MH44331 and the Justice and Peace Commission, Mumbai, India.

[Haworth co-indexing entry note]: "Being Indian," "Being American": A Balancing Act or a Creative Blend?" Srinivasan, Shobha. Co-published simultaneously in *Journal of Human Behavior in the Social Environment* (The Haworth Press, Inc.) Vol. 3, No. 3/4, 2001, pp. 135-158; and: *Psychosocial Aspects of the Asian-American Experience: Diversity Within Diversity* (ed: Namkee G. Choi) The Haworth Press, Inc., 2001, pp. 135-158. Single or multiple copies of this article are available for a fee from The Haworth Document Delivery Service [1-800-342-9678, 9:00 a.m. - 5:00 p.m. (EST). E-mail address: getinfo@haworthpressinc.com].

135

KEYWORDS. Asian Indian, gender socialization, cross-cultural identity

INTRODUCTION

Nisha is a junior in college in the U.S. A European American classmate asked her where she was from. Accustomed as she was to this question, despite her having been born in the U.S. and lived here all of her life, she replied that she was "Indian." To which the student asked, "What tribe?"

> "This was a new one for me," said Nisha. "After I have said 'Indian,' people usually say 'you mean from the country India?' or 'I love Indian food!', But this time, I was so surprised . . . it took me a few minutes. Then I said [my tribe's name is] 'Punjabi'[1] . . . . It bothers me that people ask me where I am from. Now when people ask me 'the' question, I ask them back 'where are you from?' I think, they [the European Americans], just feel they belong and I don't! But, when I go to India, people in my parents' hometown say that I am from 'Umricka.' I know I am just visiting . . . but I guess I am not 'Indian' there . . . Actually, I feel I am both Indian and American."

Questions such as those asked of Nisha, "where are you from?" or "who are you?", are the reality for many immigrants, especially those of color, even for those that have lived in the U.S. for several generations (Takaki, 1989). These immigrants are constantly required to identify, define, and clarify "who they are" and whether they are "American" or "Indian" or "Japanese" or "Samoan" or "Latina" or "African American." Visweswaran (1993) points out that the question "where are you from?" is never innocent, since it implies a lack of origin, a lack of roots, a lack of grounding, and "provokes a sudden failure of confidence, the fear of never replying adequately."

Kishwar (1996) writes that the question of "who you are" is contextual. For example, the issue of being Punjabi arises when you live outside of the state of Punjab in India. The issue of being Indian arises when an Indian steps out of the boundaries of India. Kishwar argues that if a person is asked if she is Indian within the boundaries of India, then such questions have repercussions for the ethos of the country and consequently for its people. Kishwar's insight could refer very well to the people in the U.S. While the U.S. has been called a "melting pot" or "salad bowl," for Nisha, who was born and raised in the U.S. and who says she is both American and Indian, and for people like her, the repeated questioning of her identity and affiliation may lead her to question and/or redefine her status, her role, and her identity in the U.S.

This is a study that focuses on Asian Indian women,[2] many of whom consider themselves to be both American and Indian. On the one hand, these women feel questioned about their "being American" and on the other hand, in a subtle way, there are doubts about their "being Indian." These doubts are, in part, because of the conflicts they experience within their families. At the India Nite annual gathering in 1998, Asian Indian students at the University of California, Davis gave voice to these pressures, tensions, expectations, and burdens their families place on them. They read statements which started with "A Good Indian Girl is expected to. . . . " Some of the statements were, for example: "A good Indian girl is expected to marry only an Indian boy that her parents choose for her;" "A good Indian girl should never go out to parties;" "A good Indian girl is expected not to talk back to her parents." These messages are clear and reaffirmed by the Asian Indian women's contact with extended family members in India, travels between India and the U.S., and also by their contact with the Asian Indian community in the U.S. (DasGupta, 1997; Kakar, 1986). This study then explores more deeply the issue of how Asian Indian women feel about their ethnicity.

PREVIOUS STUDIES

For many Asian Indian and Indian families, women are expected to be the carriers of cultural traditions (Kishwar, 1996). Gendered socialization in India perpetuates traditional gender roles, which in extreme forms, have resulted in wife abuse, dowry deaths, sati ("self-immolation" on the husband's funeral pyre), female infanticide, and female feticide (Srinivasan, 1999; Femina, 1994). The latest Human Development Report ranks India 95th out of 102 nations on the measure of gender empowerment (India moves on human development, 1999). Although the women's movement in India has grown dramatically and although awareness of gender inequality has increased within the last two decades, the awareness of women's rights in India is far less than in the U.S.

Very often, immigrants come to the U.S. from India steeped in gendered values. As a result, they practice a pattern of socialization where the pressures to conform are more stringent for girls than for boys. Among many Asian Indian families in the U.S. there is a desire of parents to restrict and protect their children, both boys and girls, but more so the girls (DasGupta, 1997). The more the parents protect their daughters, the more they place rigorous restrictions on their daughters' movements and choices. Asian Indian women are socialized, or as Corpi (1995) terms it "civilized," not only in matters of etiquette, but also on issues regarding the so-called Indian tradition, such as dating practices, choice of marriage partner, and choice of career. Restrictive dating practices among women is not uncommon in the Asian Indian community. In fact, dating people from other ethnic groups is not acceptable (Paranjpe, 1986), and it would be expected of the young girl to compromise, and sacrifice for the sake of the family. Filteau (1980) argues that this is because the concept of love in Asian Indian families includes values such as respect, integrity, duty, responsibility, sacrifice, compromise, and marriage. Thus love takes a different form in Asian Indian than it does in European American families (Mattai, 1997). Given this, it would be expected of Asian Indian women to conform and compromise their desires for the sake of the family. Thus Asian Indian girls are expected to respect the wishes of their elders, pay obeisance to them, serve others (especially men) in the family, be soft-spoken, and never raise their voices–all of which are actions which are scarcely (or much less) exacted of Asian Indian boys.

On the other hand, Asian Indian women who were born and raised in the U.S. are constantly interacting with their peers in school and college and with the larger American society. In the process, they acquire the egalitarian values of U.S. society and find that these conflict with what they have learned in their families. Many Asian Indian women travel between India and the U.S., and many also were born in countries other than India and the U.S. In their travels to India, however, they experience the very strict and harsh rules of behavior for women. Travelling between these various cultural frames (Hegde, 1998), they are like the people of the borderlands, as described by Azaldua (1987), struggling to resolve the contradictions they see within themselves and outside. Between their contact with and visits to India, their living in Asian Indian homes, interacting with the Asian Indian community in the U.S., and with the larger U.S. society, they find themselves performing a balancing act. They are constantly comparing themselves, their attitudes, their social locations, their achievements, and their failures, in relation to their counterparts in India and in the U.S. (essentially the European American dominant society). Negotiating these different worlds and cultural frames, the young Asian Indian women see themselves as bicultural (endorsing both Indian and American values and norms) or as culturally pluralistic (Ghuman, 1997; Singhal, 1997). This biculturalism or pluralism can be problematic when the values and norms considered Indian are those that subordinate women (Dasgupta, 1998). The problematic values are manifested mostly in the areas of marriage, courtship, and career. In this context, understanding the concept of Indian or American is complex to the say the least.

The first generation Indian immigrants do not have as much of a problem. They have dichotomized (Agarwal, 1991; Dasgupta, 1989) or compartmentalized (Helweg & Helweg, 1990) their lives outside of the family and their lives within the family, thereby resolving the Indian and the American. Within the family, they are Indian to the core; outside the family, in the larger society, they are American. This duality (Shah, 1993) or dichotomy may be because, for many post-1965 immigrants, their main purpose in coming to the U.S. and staying in the U.S. was to better their economic opportunities

(Singhal, 1997). Since for them the U.S. was the land of economic opportunity, "home" for the immigrant Indians has always meant India. For the 1.5 and second generation Asian Indians, however, "home" is the U.S.

Generally, the process of acculturation is stressful when there is an incongruity between expectations and actuality. This discrepancy results in increased mental health problems (Krishnan & Berry, 1992; Berry & Kim, 1988). For the children of immigrants, the process of adjusting to the U.S. can be very stressful. They are expected by their parents to behave and act outwardly in Indian gendered ways while inwardly these young women espouse egalitarian values (Dasgupta, 1998). Intergenerational clashes among Asian Indian families are most severe in the area of marriage (Leonard, 1997) and choice of career (Gupta, 1997; Shah, 1993). Tension is further exacerbated by the limited English language skills of their parents. The children of immigrants are generally better equipped with language skills and many times become cultural brokers or mediators for their families with the larger U.S. society (Lee, 1997). This causes a role reversal in the family and increases the stress in the lives of these children.

According to Willis (1981), socializing institutions produce two kinds of people: (1) those who conform, abide by the rules, and are "supposedly" successful and (2) those who are alienated, resist, whose culture and mindset clash with the imposed values and norms. The latter group, called the "cultural resisters," may not openly reject the "molding" given to them, but, through an active decision of their own, attempt to shape their counter culture. This appears to be the situation of the Asian Indian women who, while not openly challenging the gendered practices of their families or their understanding of "Indianness," are probably negotiating for themselves a new meaning of "being Indian."

OBJECTIVES OF THE STUDY

Asian Indians assess their failures and successes in comparison to Indians in India and to European Americans in the U.S. (Hegde, 1998). Given this exigency for Asian Indian women to negotiate these worlds in their everyday lives, this study points to the need for cross-cultural comparative studies that compare Asian Indian women in the U.S. to their counterparts in India and to European Americans in the U.S. The study tries to focus on what it means to be Indian and American for the 1.5 and second generation Asian Indians in the U.S. It looks at the association between "being Indian" and "being American" on their attitudes toward women's roles and on the stress in their lives. The following are the objectives of the study:

- Since the literature has shown that there is a pattern of gendered socialization among Indian and Asian Indian families, this study, first of all, tries to test whether there are any significant differences among the three groups of women–Indian, Asian Indian and European American–in their perceptions of gender roles and gender equality;

- Further, since Asian Indians appear to be performing a balancing act, it is expected that conforming to Indian and American norms, meeting family and societal expectations might be very stressful to them. Thus, the second objective was to find out if there were any significant differences in the level of stress faced by these three groups of women;
- Third, the study explores the meaning of "being Indian" and "being American" and its relationship to their attitudes toward gender equality and stress in their lives.

SAMPLE

The sample of women (n = 145) was drawn from pilot data collected at two locations: first, from college students in Mumbai, India, and second, at a university in Northern California. The data in Mumbai, India, was collected through a two-stage quota method. In the first stage colleges were chosen at random from North and South Mumbai, and, within each area, at least 80% of the people from whom the data was gathered had to be Hindu.[3] A self-selected snowball method was used in each area to recruit respondents. In India, there was no monetary remuneration or course credit given to the participants (Srinivasan, 1999). While the data was collected in two languages, English and Marathi (the local language in Mumbai, India), only those that responded in English were selected for further analysis. This eliminated the confounding effect of language. The English speaking college sample consisted of 103 Indian women, of which 50 were chosen at random so as to arrive at a comparable sample size to the two samples in the U.S.

In the U.S., the study was advertised at the Department of Psychology's Subject Recruitment Board, and participants received course credit. Asian Indian students were also recruited through two Asian Indian student organizations. A total of 45, 1.5 and second-generation Asian Indian women responded to the survey in the U.S.

Additionally, five in-depth interviews with Asian Indian women were conducted to highlight and give voice to various aspects of their lives. These were selected at random from the sample of Asian Indians who responded to the survey. Three of the women did not consent to being audiotaped, so detailed notes were recorded while talking to these women. The other two women consented to being audiotaped though one of them expressed that she would prefer that no one else heard the tape. These five women have been given aliases: Nisha, Parneet, Aparna, Seema, and Mona.

A total of 133 European American women responded to the survey in the U.S., of which 50 were chosen at random to arrive at a comparable sample size to the Asian Indian women. So, the final analysis consisted of three groups of women:

1. Women in India (n = 50);
2. 1.5 and second generation Asian Indian women in the U.S. (n = 45); and
3. European American women in the U.S. (n = 50).

Profile of the Sample

Table 1 displays the demographic profile of the sample (n = 145) and compares the three groups of women on age, religion, degree of religiosity, father's and mother's occupations, and household size.

Age. The age of the sample ranges from 17 years to 25 years with a mean of 20.44 years. There were no significant age differences among the three groups [F(2,142) = 0.81, p = .45]. Hence, the three groups are comparable with regard to age.

Religion. With regard to religion, a majority of the Indian women (76%) identified themselves as Hindu. Of the Asian Indians, 40% identified themselves as Hindu and 24% as Sikh. The high Sikh proportion is because California has a substantial Sikh population, many of whom immigrated to the U.S. in the early part of the century (Leonard, 1997). While women in India tended to check Hindu even if they practiced Jainism (n = 3),[4] Asian Indian women in the U.S. were very specific about their religious affiliations. This pattern of identifying themselves within specific religio-ethnic boundaries is a result of the process of immigration and subsequent adjustment to U.S. society, which has encouraged the formation of ethnic enclaves (Portes & Jensen, 1989). These enclaves are closely-knit networks of social support among peoples of similar language, religion, or culture (Singhal, 1997). Of the European American women, 64% stated that they were Christian and 34% said that they had no religion.

Religiosity. There was a significant difference among the three groups of women in the degree of religiosity reported [F(2,142) = 6.69, p < .01]. On a five point scale ranging from (1 to 5), "Not at all religious" to "Very religious," the Asian Indian (*M* = 3.38, SD = 1.01) and the Indian (*M* = 3.36, SD = 0.94) women reported significantly higher levels of religiosity than the European American women (*M* = 2.68, SD = 1.25).

Father's Occupation. From the European American sample, 76% of the women's fathers were in "professional/white collar" positions as compared to 60% in the Asian Indian group and only 44% from the Indian group. With regard to "blue-collar" jobs, the proportions were just the reverse. Approximately 44% of the Indian women's fathers were in "blue-collar" jobs as

TABLE 1. Profile of the Population

	Women in India N = 50	Asian Indian in the U.S. N = 45	European American in the U.S. N = 50	F (2,142)
Age				
Mean (sd)	20.22 (1.76)	20.51 (1.44)	20.60 (1.44)	ns
Religion				
Hinduism	76%	40%		
Christianity	22%	2%	64%	
Islam	2%	18%		
Sikhism		24%		
Buddhism/Jainism		9%	2%	
Atheist		4%	34%	
Religiosity				
Mean (sd)	3.38 (1.01)	3.36 (0.94)	2.65 (1.25)	6.69*
Household size				
Mean (sd)	7.56 (4.95)	7.91 (3.48)	4.80 (1.14)	11.21*
Father's Occupation				
Professional	44%	60%	76%	
Blue Collar	44%	20%	12%	
Own business	10%	16%	8%	
Disabled/Not working	2%	4%	4%	
Mother's Occupation				
Professional	14%	53%	54%	
Blue Collar	14%	16%	8%	
Own Business	2%	4%	16%	
Homemaker	70%	24%	20%	
Disabled/Not working		2%	2%	

* p < 0.01; **p < 0.05

compared to 20% of the Asian Indians and only 12% of the European American fathers. About 16% of the Asian Indian women's fathers had their own business as compared to 10% of the Indian women's sample and 8% of the European American sample.

Mother's Occupation. Fifty-three percent of Asian Indian women's mothers, 54% of the European American women, and only 14% of the Indian women's mothers were in "professional/white-collar" occupations. On the other hand, 70% of the Indian women's mothers were "homemakers," while only 24% from the Asian Indian sample and 20% from the European American sample had mothers who were "homemakers." This indicates that a much higher proportion of Indian immigrant women tend to work outside of the home as compared to their counterparts in India (Nandan & Eames, 1980).

Generally, most Indian immigrants to the U.S. belong to the "professional/white collar" category followed by the "wholesale/retail trade" (Leonard, 1997). This is true of this sample, too; however, there are considerable percentages of fathers (40%) and mothers (48%) who are not employed in the "professional" category. In fact, four of the fathers and four of the mothers are farm laborers where the jobs are seasonal. This representation in farm work is due to the fact that there is a large Asian Indian (largely from Punjab) farming community in California (Leonard, 1992). These families have sponsored the immigration of their family members and have also provided them with employment which Roland (1986) describes as a pattern of symbiosis-reciprocity, which not only allows for the sponsoring of families to the U.S. but also for assuming responsibility for them long after the immigrants arrive.

Household size. There was a significant difference in the household sizes $[(F(2,142) = 11.21, p < 0.01)]$, with Asian Indian ($M = 7.91$, SD = 3.48), and Indian ($M = 7.56$, SD = 4.95) household sizes being larger than European American households ($M = 4.80$, SD = 1.14). It is not uncommon for Indian immigrant households in the U.S. to be large because they provide for jobs and sponsor the immigration of extended family members to the U.S. (Ashcraft, 1986). Subsequently these extended families become the mainstay of social support both for raising children and for easing the adjustment of new immigrants to U.S. society (Pillai, 1980).

MEASURES

Attitude Toward Women Scale

The women were assessed on the short version of Attitude Toward Women Scale (AWS; Spence, Helmreich, & Stapp, 1973), which consists of 25 items. The AWS measures perception of gender equality and women's roles in society. This scale has been validated on several populations, including Asian Indians in the U.S. (Dasgupta, 1998). On a four-point scale (0 to 3), ranging from "Strongly Agree" to "Strongly Disagree," the scale includes items such as "Intoxication among women is worse than intoxication among men," "Sons in the family should be given more encouragement to go to college than daughters," and "A woman should be as free as a man to propose marriage."

However, since this scale had not been previously validated in India, it was cognitively pre-tested (Harachi, 1997) on a college and community sample in India. Cognitive pre-testing involves administering the scale to respondents who are similar to the population in which the study is being conducted. Specifically, fifteen respondents, both male and female, were asked to participate in this process. Each of the items in the scale was read and the respondent was asked to explain the meaning of the item. The purpose was to determine the respondent's interpretation of the items and assess whether the items on the scale were relevant to the population. Based on the feedback, some of the wordings in the items were changed to increase the clarity and make some of the statements culturally relevant (Srinivasan, 1999). For example, the word "obscenity" was changed to "using bad language"; "women should assume their rightful place" was changed to "women should have as much of a role as men"; "darn socks" was changed to "wash dishes," since socks are seldom used in India. Some of the items were reverse coded so that a high score on the scale means that the respondent has more liberal views on women's roles. The highest possible score was 75.

Brief Symptom Inventory

The Brief Symptom Inventory (BSI; Derogatis, 1992) is a 53 item self-rating scale, which assesses psychopathology. It is comprised of nine sub-scales and a set of additional items from which a global score of general health severity index can be calculated. The global score is used here as a measure of stress in the lives of the women. Here, too, some of the phrasing was changed to make the instrument culturally relevant. As a consequence of the cognitive pre-testing, words such as "feel blue" were changed to "feel gloomy"; "feeling afraid to travel in trains or buses' was changed to "feeling more afraid than others to travel in trains or buses."[5] The modified version was administered in India and the U.S. The responses to the items were measured on a five-point scale (0 to 4), ranging from "Not at all" to "Always." The mean composite score or the index on general health severity was calculated by summing all the items and dividing by the number of items endorsed. The highest possible score was 4. A higher score on the BSI is indicative of greater levels of stress or lower levels of general well being.

General Ethnicity Questionnaire Asian Indian and American Versions

The third assessment scale used was the General Ethnicity Questionnaire (GEQ). Most acculturation models generally propose that as immigrants become more acculturated to the host culture, they also simultaneously become less enculturated to their own native culture. Thus, they suggest a unidimensional acculturation model (Phinney, 1990). However, recent models of acculturation have been bidimensional or multidimensional (Phinney, 1990; LaFromboise, Coleman, & Gerton, 1993). The GEQ was originally developed for the Chinese

American population by Tsai, Ying, and Lee (in press). By adapting their two versions to the Asian Indian population, the General Ethnicity Questionnaire Asian Indian version (GEQAI) and General Ethnicity Questionnaire American version (GEQA) were derived. The intention was to simultaneously assess women on their degree of "being Indian" and "being American." The two scales are not measured on a single continuum, so it is possible that a person can be simultaneously "highly Indian" and "highly American."

The GEQAI and GEQA have thirty-eight items each. The GEQAI contains items such as "I listen to Indian music" and "I am familiar with Indian cultural practices and customs." The GEQA contains items such as, "I listen to American music," and "I am familiar with American cultural practices and customs." The answers to the items ranged on a five-point scale (1 to 5) from "Strongly disagree/Not at all" to "Strongly agree/Very much." The scale was pre-tested on Asian Indian college students in the U.S. On their recommendation, the item "I believe that my children should read, write, and speak English," was deleted from the GEQA. This is because the knowledge of English is taken for granted in the urban areas in India and thus would not be a question that was pertinent to ask of Indian immigrants to the U.S. In all the statements, it was decided, that the word "Chinese" would be substituted with "Indian" rather than "Asian Indian," "South Asian," or "East Indian." The overall scores for GEQAI and GEQA were developed by summing all the items and dividing the sum by the number of items respondents endorsed. These overall scores were used to assess the degree of "being Indian," and "being American."[6] The highest possible score was 5. A high score on the GEQAI indicates that the person is "very Indian" and a high score on the GEQA is indicative of the person being "very American." The GEQAI and GEQA were administered only to the Asian Indian women in the U.S.

RESULTS AND DISCUSSION

The analysis consists of data gathered from quantitative and qualitative sources. The quantitative data lays out the broader framework for understanding the women's attitudes toward gender roles, the stress in their lives, and whether the Asian Indian women feel that they are Indian or American. The qualitative data here substantiates and further explores how these egalitarian gender attitudes, stress levels, and "being Indian" and "being American" are experienced and articulated by Asian Indian women. Through a triangulation of data sources, the intention is to capture the voices and nuances of the lives of Asian Indian women and not merely to support findings from the quantitative part of the study. Thus, the in-depth interviews reveal and explore a deeper level of the nature of the findings.

Attitude Toward Women's Roles and Gender Equality–The Conflict

Table 2 shows that the three groups of women differed significantly from each other on the Attitude Toward Women's scale (F(2,142) = 42.88, p < .01). Tukey's post-hoc tests revealed that Indian women scored the lowest (*M* = 55.50, SD = 5.49), followed by Asian Indian women (*M* = 64.09, SD = 7.15), and finally by the European American women (*M* = 66.38, 5.87). This means that Indian women were the least egalitarian on gender roles, whereas European American women were the most egalitarian. The Asian Indian women, though they were in between and differed significantly from both groups, were closer to the European American women than the Indian women.

The lowest score on the attitude toward women's scale among the Indian women was expected, since socialization in India is mainly along gender lines. Despite the fact that Asian Indian women are quite egalitarian in their attitudes to women's roles, there are severe limitations placed on them by their families and communities (Dasgupta, 1998). The 1.5 and second generation Asian Indian women, not unlike their counterparts in India, are also socialized along gender lines into values and norms that perpetuate the inequality against women (Shah, 1993; Saran, 1985). For example, in a panel discussion on Mixed Relationships in 1997 sponsored by the South Asian Women's Alliance at the University of California, Davis, a second-generation

TABLE 2. Means and Standard Deviations of the Scales

	Women in India N = 50	Asian Indian in the U.S. N = 45	European American in the U.S. N = 50	F (2,142)
AWS Mean (sd)	55.50 (4.49)	64.09 (7.15)	66.38 (5.87)	42.88*
Stress/Well-Being Mean (sd)	1.12 (0.57)	1.12 (0.70)	0.80 (0.58)	4.30**
GEO Asian Indian composite score Mean (sd)	---	3.46 (0.53)	---	---
American composite score Mean (sd)	---	3.38 (0.41)	---	---
Overall, Indian Mean (sd)	---	4.20 (1.06)	---	---
Overall, American Mean (sd)	---	3.51 (1.20)	---	---

* p < 0.01; ** p < 0.05

Asian Indian woman talked about the restrictions that her family imposed with regard to dating. She said that she had been dating a European American man. Though they were very much in love, they had recently decided to break off the relationship because of the tension that her relationship had caused within her family. Her aunts, uncles, even those in India called and wrote to express their concern. As the oldest daughter, she was told that this relationship would have a negative affect on her younger siblings' chances of marrying. The strain resulted in her slipping in her grades at school, causing her parents to attribute the low grades to "that boy." For these reasons, she decided to end the relationship. She felt that she had no other alternative, especially if she wanted to "get back into the family" and not feel guilty.

What Asian Indian women feel as particularly discordant are the double standards they experience. Family members have one set of restrictions for women and quite another set or no restrictions at all for men. Mani (1993) has pointed out that it is the women who are called on to hold up the ways of the old country and preserve the name, prestige, and honor of the family. Mona said, "My brother has a European American girlfriend, and people in the family are okay with it. But, if I had even considered bringing a male friend to family functions, whom my family did not know, they would go berserk. It happened to my cousin. She married a European American man and she was held up as a bad example. They felt she had destroyed the honor and pride of the family."

Seema reported the same kind of discriminatory regulations with regard to sexual intimacy. Her older sister had an abusive husband, whom she subsequently divorced. "When they got divorced, my brother-in-law accused my sister of not being a virgin when they got married. He did this in front of my parents and other elders in the family. This bothered my parents–I think they felt ashamed. I wish they had asked him [the brother-in-law] whether he was a virgin at the time of the marriage. I am sure my parents never even thought of that." Virginity is still prized for women which brings Mani (1993) to state that the "questions of modernity and tradition have been debated on the literal and figurative bodies of women." In fact, on the AWS scale, the lowest scoring item among the Asian Indians and Indian women was the item that stated "Women should not be encouraged to become sexually intimate with anyone before marriage, even with their fiancées or those they intend to marry." It would seem that the Asian Indian women publicly espouse similar values on premarital sex that the parents have, even though what they publicly avow might differ from their "inner" attitudes.

Nisha experienced the same gendered treatment with regard to her choice of career and the pressure to get married. "I am going to graduate in a year and my parents have already started talking about marriage. They want me to get married now and continue my studies after my marriage. But I want to study medicine now . . . but when I finish I will be in my late twenties and my parents think that I will be too old to get married then. But my older brother is currently in medical school, and he doesn't have these pressures [to marry] that I do. So already the arguments have started . . . So this summer I decided to stay at school and not go home." Eng (1999) calls this "ducking of expectations" as a method of self-preservation.

Asian Indian women are taught or "civilized" about special rules of feminine etiquette and are constantly chastised about their inappropriate behavior (Prathikanti, 1997; Das & Kemp, 1991). Parneet said, "If my brother and I did something that my parents thought was inappropriate we would get scolded. But I was always scolded much more . . . Like once, I did not properly greet the elders who visited our home. My father scolded me in front of all the people right there–whereas he did not say a word to my brother . . . and he is older than me. I was told that if this is the way I was going to behave, my in-laws would think lowly of me. I was just 12 years old then!"

In short, by a comparison of Asian Indian women with their counterparts in India and with European Americans in the U.S., our findings show that their real problem lies in the pattern of socialization. Partly they internalize the egalitarian attitudes of American society, but partly they internalize the gendered attitudes of their family with regard to marriage, dating, and appropriate behavior. This [conflictual pattern of socialization] results in severe consequences.

Stress/General Well Being–Consequences of the Conflict

There were significant differences among the three groups on their level of stress or general well being ($F(2,142) = 4.30$, $p < .02$). Overall, the Asian Indian ($M = 1.12$, $SD = 0.70$) and Indian ($M = 1.12$, $SD = 0.57$) women were similar with higher levels of stress. Both differed significantly from the European American women ($M = 0.80$, $SD = 0.58$) (see Table 2).

One of the areas of stress is marriage. For the Indian and Asian Indian women, the "marriageable" age is between 20-24 years, while for European Americans the marriageable age is much higher. Hence, there is a lot of pressure, family expectations, and subsequent stress that Asian Indian women experience during their final years of their college lives. Among Indians and Asian Indians, parents largely still arrange marriages (Liddle & Joshi, 1986), unlike in European American families.

Seema narrated that her parents feel that it may be difficult to procure a "good match" for her since there is a stigma attached to the family due to her older sister's divorce. Not unlike India, extended family members in Indian immigrant families in the U.S. feel the pressures of an unmarried girl in the family, and matchmaking is common. As Seema said, "My Aunt calls and wants me to come home to meet men who are 'good candidates.' They say things like 'he is from such a good family'; 'they [the prospective groom's family] will let you study even after you get married'; 'he is so respectful to the elders,' etc. This is a very embarrassing and uncomfortable experience."

Another area of stress is choice of career. Most studies (Gupta, 1997; Shah, 1993) have shown that parents prefer their children to become doctors, engineers, or lawyers and to maintain a high GPA. However, this study found that the pressure on Asian Indian women seems to be to major in a subject that will give them a "good" employment opportunity and allow them to be marketable not only for employment but also for marriage (Prathikanti, 1997). Since the preservation of culture falls on the shoulders of women, there is an emphasis, as Nisha stated earlier, on getting the daughters married as soon as they complete their bachelor's degree. Aparna also said, "I wanted to teach and wanted to study psychology in college, but then my father believed that only crazy people study it. So I compromised. My majors were both history and psychology but I never told my parents. I had to work very hard to maintain my GPA. My family never found out till my graduation day that I did both . . . they were happy that I did not drop history."

Among the Asian Indian women, there was a discrepancy between the public expression of their values and feeling and their "inner" attitudes. This discrepancy has encouraged secrecy, which increases the stress in their lives. Parneet said, "I don't think my parents know that I am sexually active. I would never tell my parents or my family. I am always afraid that they will find out [that I am sexually active]."

While marriage pressures and career choices pose a lot of conflict in the lives of many Asian Indian women, there are other stressors that are related to living in the U.S. Aparna's parents, for instance, do not speak, read, or write English. As the only daughter in the family (she has a younger and older brother), since the age of six, she has been the "mediator" with the outside world for her parents. "I learnt to balance a checkbook by the time I was eight. I would read legal documents, file immigration papers, pay the bills, everything. It was my responsibility. My brothers were around but I felt I had to help out . . . be the responsible one. I became very mature at a young age. Being a girl in the family I felt I had more to do than my brothers . . . it was expected of me." Studies have shown that being a mediator or "cultural broker" for the family with the outside world at a young age and adhering to gender expectations (Kar, Campbell, & Jimenez, 1996) results in increased stress and strain in the lives of immigrant children (Lee, 1997).

General Ethnicity Questionnaire–"Being Indian" and "Being American"

There were forty-five Asian Indian women who answered the General Ethnicity Questionnaire Asian Indian version (GEQAI) ($M = 3.22$, SD = 0.70) and the General Ethnicity Questionnaire American version (GEQA) ($M = 3.87$, SD = 0.43). It was decided not to use this scale in further analysis because 14 of the 38 items relate to language ease and fluency. In the GEQA, all the 14 items referred to the respondent's comfort level with English. The Asian Indians overwhelmingly answered that they were very familiar and comfortable with English. This response pattern can be explained by the fact that even in India, people in the urban areas who have access to the educational system are well versed in English. So, a skewed distribution is expected. Based on this rationale, it was decided not to use the overall GEQAI and GEQA.

However, there were two separate statements in the GEQAI and GEQA, "Overall I am Indian" and "Overall I am American" which were also asked. These two items were used as indicators of their "Indian" and "American" ethnicity. Table 2 shows that "overall Indian" ($M = 4.20$, SD = 1.06) and "overall American" ($M = 3.51$, SD = 1.20) are not significantly correlated (-0.08, p = 0.59), which indicates that the two constructs are independent of each other (Tsai, Ying, Lee, in press). So, the contexts in which Asian Indian women consider themselves Indian and the contexts in which they consider themselves American are different. In fact, Asian Indian women assert that they are both Indian and American. In the words of Nisha, "I feel I am very Indian and also very American! Some may think it is a balancing act (to live in both worlds), but to me it is not contradictory." Seema called it "Enjoying the best of both worlds!"

Most Asian Indian women in this study felt that they were bicultural and that the two cultures can be very well combined. This way of thinking, or being culturally pluralistic, is not unlike an Indian philosophical way of thinking, which does not accept an "either/or" (analytical) way of looking at reality, but believes in a "both/and" (synthetic) way of perceiving reality. This perspective refuses to see things in oppositional terms, in terms of black and white, but believes instead in a multi-faceted description of reality. This system of epistemology is typified by the ancient Jaina story of three blind men who went to see the elephant. One felt its trunk and said it was thin and long. Another felt its legs and said it was fat and solid like a pillar. A third sensed its skin and said it was rough and grainy. All of them, the story continues, were describing different facets of the elephant. No one describes reality in its completeness. All of U.S. can only give labels. The best perspective is one which combines all facets and all labels.

A new meaning of "being Indian." Investigating further into the relationship between "overall Indian" and the Attitude Toward Women's Scale (AWS), there was a low negative correlation, which was not significant (-0.14, p = 0.36). However, there was a positive and significant, though low, correlation (0.37, p < 0.01) between "overall American" and AWS. This indicates that the more the Asian Indian woman endorsed that she was "overall American," the more likely she was to espouse egalitarian gender attitudes.

With regard to the relationship between general well being and "overall Indian," there was a low negative correlation (-0.32, $p < 0.05$). General well being was not significantly correlated to "overall American" (-0.06, $p = 0.68$). Thus, the more an Asian Indian woman said she was "overall Indian," the less likely she was to experience stress. Essentially, those who state that they are Indian feel less stress.

Hence, those who stated that they were both Indian and American were the ones who were most egalitarian and the ones who felt the least stress. However, if the Asian Indian women did actually feel stress, as some of them reported that they did, then it would be because of the non-egalitarian practices that were imposed on them by their families and not because of them endorsing that they were "being Indian." It appears that Asian Indian women do not understand "being Indian" as related to the restrictive and discriminatory practices enjoined on them by their families.

It is apparent that Asian Indian women experience stress in their lives. Their parents expect them to "be Indian" and to follow the gendered practices with regard to marriage, dating, and career. Yet, the more the Asian Indian women identified themselves with "being Indian," the less likely they were to feel stress. This may come across as a discrepancy. However, this so-called or apparent discrepancy exists because the concept of "being Indian" means one thing to the immigrant parents and quite another to the Asian Indian women.

Asian Indian women associate "being Indian" with something other than the restrictive practices on marriage, dating, and choice of career. For the Asian Indian woman, "being Indian" does not mean agreeing to marry a person or accepting a career chosen for them by their elders. "Being Indian" does not mean having one set of rules for men and another set for women; nor does "being Indian" for them include getting married off at a young age. This might be the understanding of their immigrant parents, but it is definitely not of their daughters.

Asian Indian women are aware of problems of communication and conflict within their families. Unlike their parents, however, they are quite willing to seek help and assistance outside of traditional family structures without seeing this as a lack of pride in their families and a rejection of their "Indianness." As Seema said, "My parents fight a lot and I want to discuss it with a counselor so that we can understand and resolve these issues. I love my parents and I respect them . . . I understand their problems . . . but by talking about my family problems outside the family, I don't love them less."

Kishwar (1996) argues that the immigrant Indians fear of the loss of culture make them impose far more repressive values and norms on their children. That is why we can understand Mona, when she said, "I want to go to India and see for myself if women my age have the kind of marriage and career pressures like I do!"

It is beyond the scope of this study to be very sure of what the Asian Indian women mean by "being Indian." Perhaps they are creating a new meaning. However, there are some glimpses of what it means to them from some of their actions and statements. "Being Indian" appears to be connected to their sense of pride in their religion, their cultural heritage, and their history. The fact that they are deeply interested in studying Indian history, that they want to understand their history in the U.S., that they put on shows of Indian dance and classical music, the fact that they identified themselves according to a specific religious-ethnic tradition, and the fact that they consider themselves simultaneously Indian and American all point to the fact that while they accept the egalitarian American attitudes, they consider their "being Indian" as connected with their cultural and historical roots. In addition, most of the Asian Indian women take the larger view of Indian culture, not seeing it as fossilized or something that needs to be preserved. For instance, they want to blend their knowledge of Indian and American/European/African American dance and music. This is apparent from the performances at India Nite, where the shows blend their various cultures and experiences.

Asian Indian women are negotiating a concept of "being Indian," which is quite different from that in the mind of their first generation immigrant parents. For example, Asian Indian women are very much part of organizations that belong to the fabric of the U.S. society, and they also participate in organizations which are concerned with issues in India. Aparna said, "I am very active in the campus NOW (National Organization for Women) and hope that through my identity as a woman, I can contribute and change notions for and about immigrant women in *this* society. I am concerned with rights and legislation that affects women here in the U.S. . . . Yes, I am concerned about India as well as other countries in the world but the U.S. is my focus . . . I hope to join the Peace Corps and go to India after I graduate."

CONCLUSION

The main focus of this study was on the lives and aspirations of Asian Indian women. While they were similar in their attitudes toward gender roles with their counterparts in the U.S., they were similar to their Indian counterparts in their level of stress. The stress was largely because of the conflict they experienced. On the one hand, living in the larger U.S. society, these Asian Indian women have internalized egalitarian gender values. They are expected/driven to *go out* and be American, achieve, succeed, make a lot of money, be like others, both men and non-Indians, but *at home, within their families*, they are expected to conform to gender roles. Within the realm of the family, they are expected to give up or compromise their dreams and aspirations and become "good Indian girls" who will marry a man chosen for them, not complain if they are being abused, carry on the family tradition, and protect the family honor.

The values and norms imposed on the Asian Indian youth are not the same for women as for men. Parneet's case is typical. "They [the parents] expect a lot from me, but it is not the same for my brother who has now dropped out of high school," she said. "Though they are upset with him because he is messing up his future, in my case if I do anything wrong, I am messing up the family name!"

For the most part, immigrant parents are interested in maintaining their contact with India and seeing the Indian culture perpetuated in the U.S. (Saran, 1985). It becomes the women's burden to perpetuate the Indian culture. The "fossilized" and "frozen in time" (Gupta, 1997) immigrant parents' values and traditions do not enhance the quality of life for these Asian Indian women, but instead pressure them and create conflicts within them.

As a result of this pressure and conflict, Asian Indian women experience a lot of stress, which appears very clearly in the interviews. Like the "cultural resisters," they are negotiating a new meaning of "being Indian," a meaning very different from that of their parents. Asian Indian women born in the U.S., are striving to claim a new composite identity for themselves, one that is both American and Indian. Unlike their immigrant parents, the young Asian Indian women insist on social and political participation in the U.S. society. Shah (1993) has argued that immigrant Indians are not a political power because they are not citizens. However, Nisha remarked, "My parents are citizens but they are not even part of their union at work. They believe that we should just do our work and not cause any problems. They never join the strikes . . . My parents say we have to be grateful to the people who gave them the jobs." Parneet said, "My parents give money, but only to groups that work in India . . . which is fine . . . but I feel they should also do something for the homeless or the poor here [in the U.S.]."

Asian Indian women are also composing their own mix or creative blend of American and Indian, which is neither a simple acceptance of the one or denial of the other (Fanon, 1991). For instance, they give expression to this creative blend through dance, music, art, and the new wave of South Asian literature. Stansfield (1994) notes that the second generation Indians in Britain have formed their combination of Indian and British/European music that has given Asian Indian youth a new sense of cultural pride. Perhaps Asian Indian women are trying to do the same thing here in the U.S.

Eng (1999), in her *Warrior Lessons,* says "'expectations' is a key word in the Asian American coming-of-age lexicon" (p.18). Now probably the "expectation" should be reversed where the second generation should expect of their immigrant parents to cast away the shroud of tradition and share in the second generation's sense of pride in their mix of "being Indian" and "being American."

FUTURE DIRECTIONS

This was a cross-cultural pilot study that compared one group of ethnic peoples with their counterparts in the country of origin and in their adopted country. Cross-cultural studies of this nature are few, but they provide a wealth of information. One cannot simply adopt, adapt, or modify existing scales and instruments from one culture to understand another cultural group's aspirations and realities, whether it is within the U.S. or outside. That would be similar to looking at their experiences and realities in a vacuum. The vacuum exists because we have yet to understand the lives and realities of immigrants and their children in the context of their peers, their social milieu, and their various cultural frames. In other words, the comparative cross-cultural approach offers tremendous scope and would be one area where further exploration needs to be done. Additionally, this study was limited to women. Had it taken into consideration men as well, a much broader picture would be gained.

This study also used qualitative data and integrated it with quantitative data. Qualitative interviews are, by nature, richer in content. The very deep personal quality of the sharing reveals a lot more than can be garnered from closed-ended, Likert scale questions. Quite often, it manifests underlying aspirations and conflicts that may not be so easily grasped by merely quantitative techniques. A combined method, where the qualitative information is gathered as a precursor to developing the instruments and informs the development of the scales, is also necessary. This would immensely enhance the wealth of cross-cultural studies.

Finally, this study provides a starting point for understanding new facets of the problem of ethnicity for Asian Indian women born in the U.S. Many of them do not have a strictly Indian ethnicity. For instance, when respondents for the study were being recruited in the U.S., it was advertised as a study for anyone who was of Indian/East Indian/Asian Indian origin. On that occasion, many Asian Indian students hesitantly asked whether they were eligible to participate in the study since their parents were Gujaratis, Punjabis, Jains, or Sikhs. Some others were not sure of their eligibility on the grounds that they were born and raised in the U.S. Given the fact that in the coming millennium the number of non-European ethnic groups in the U.S. is going to grow geometrically, we need to understand what the younger immigrants understand by their ethnicity and culture. For one thing, we need to understand more deeply what the young Asian Indians mean by "being Indian and being American," since it apparently does not have the same connotation for them as for their parents and for the average person on the street.

A globalized world, on the one hand, brings different nations under one umbrella; on the other, it paradoxically spawns the rise of numerous identities. The concept of "Asian American" subsumes under one heading various cultures, social histories, and experiences of immigration and is, therefore, ambiguous, having consequences for health, mental health, legal and social services access, delivery, and development. So also the concept of "being Indian and being American" must be understood more thoroughly, just as much as the concept of "being Vietnamese and being American," or "being Korean and being American," since all these ethnic designations will have a critical impact on advocacy and social policy.

NOTES

1. Residents of the state of Punjab in India are called Punjabi.

2. Asian Indian in this paper refers to 1.5 and second-generation Asian Indian American women in the U.S. Though they preferred to be called Indian, the phrase Asian Indian is used here for the sake of clarity so as to distinguish this group of women from those who are born, raised, and live in India. In this paper, this latter group in India is referred to as Indian women.

3. The two areas were chosen because South Mumbai is less urbanized as compared to North Mumbai. Also, since 80% of the Indian population is Hindu, we wanted the sample to be representative of the Indian population.

4. In India, the census category of Hindu subsumes under it Jainism and Buddhism.

5. In Mumbai, India, travelling by bus or train is the general mode of travel, unlike in the U.S. where the regular mode of travel is the private car. Generally, people in India dislike travelling by train and bus, because they consider it a nuisance and an inconvenience. Hence, we are asking if this fear or nuisance syndrome is more than for everybody else.

6. Due to limitations in sample size, it was not possible to validate the factors developed by Tsai, Ying, and Lee (in press) or test whether there were significant differences between immigrant foreign born Asian Indians and the U.S. born Asian Indians.

REFERENCES

Agarwal, P. (1991). *A passage from India: Post-1965 Indian immigrants and their children*. Palos Verdes, CA: Yuvati.

Ashcraft, N. (1986). The clash of traditions: Asian India immigrants in crisis. In R.H. Bacon & G.V. Cleo (Eds.), *Tradition and Transformation: Asian Indians in America*. (pp. 53-70). Williamsburg, VA: Studies in Third World Societies.

Azaldua, G. (1995). From Boderlands/La Frontera: The new mestiza. In L. Castillo-Speed (Ed.), *Women's Voices from the borderlands.* (pp. 250-256). New York: Simon & Schuster.

Berry, J.W., & Kim, U. (1988). Acculturation and mental health. In P.R. Dasen, J.W. Berry, & N. Sartorius (Eds.), *Health and cross-cultural psychology.* (pp. 207-236). Newbury Park, CA: Sage.

Corpi, L. (1995). Epiphany: The third gift. In L. Castillo-Speed (Ed.), *Women's Voices from the borderlands.* (pp. 240-249). New York: Simon & Schuster.

Das, A.K., & Kemp, S. F. (1997). Between two worlds: Counseling South Asian Americans. *Journal of Multicultural Counseling and Development, 25*(1), 23-33.

DasGupta, K. (1997). Raising bi-cultural children. In B.B. Khare (Ed.), *Asian Indian immigrants: Motifs on ethnicity and gender* (pp. 57-69). Dubuque, Iowa: Kendall/ Hunt.

Dasgupta, S.D. (1998). Gender roles and cultural continuum in the Asian Indian immigrant community in the U.S. *Sex Roles, 38* (11/12), 953-974.

Dasgupta, S.S. (1989). *On the train of an uncertain dream: Indian immigrant experience.* New York: AMS.

Derogatis, L.R. (1992). *BSI: Brief Symptom Inventory, administration, scoring and procedures manual.* Baltimore, MD: Clinical Psychometric Research.

Eng, P. (1999). *Warrior lessons.* New York: Pocket Books.

Fanon, F. (1991). *The wretched of the earth.* (C. Farrington, Trans.). New York: Grove Weidenfeld.

Femina (1994, June). Violence against women. *Femina.* Bombay, India.

Filteau, C.H. (1980). The role and concept of love in the Hindu family acculturation process. In K.V. Ujimoto & G. Hirabayashi (Eds.), *Visible minorities and multiculturalism: Asians in Canada.* (pp. 289-298). Toronto: Butterworths.

Ghuman, S.P.A. (1997). Assimilation or integration? A Study of Asian adolescents. *Educational Research, 39*(1), 23-35.

Gupta, M.D. (1997). "What is Indian about you?": A gendered transitional approach to ethnicity. *Gender and Society, 11* (5), 572-597.

Harachi, T.W. (1997). "A model to examine the cross-cultural equivalence of measures: A study in progress." Paper presented at the meeting the University of California, Davis, CA.

Hegde, R.S. (1998). Swinging the trapeze. In D.V. Tanno & A. Gonzalez (Eds.), *Communication and identity across cultures.* (pp. 34-55). Thousand Oaks, CA: Sage.

Helweg, A.W., & Helweg, U.M. (1990). *An immigrant success story: East Asians in America.* Philadelphia: University of Pennsylvania.

Indian moves on human development. (1999, July 13). *Indian Express,* p. 3.

Kakar, S. (1986). Male and female in India: Identity formation and its effects on cultural adaptation. In R.H. Bacon & G.V. Coelho (Eds.), *Tradition and Transformation: Asian Indians in America.* (pp. 27-42). Williamsburg, VA: Studies in Third World Societies.

Kar, S.B., Campbell, K., Jimenez, A., & Gupta, S.R. (1996). Invisible Americans: An exploration of Indo-Americans equality of life. *Amerasia Journal, 21*(3), 25-52.

Kishwar, M. (1996). Who am I? *Manushi, 94,* 6-17.

Krishnan, A. & Berry, J.W. (1992). Acculturative stress and acculturation attitudes among Asian Indian immigrants to the United States. *Psychology of Developing Societies, 4,* 187-212.

LaFramborse, T., Coleman, H.L., & Gerten, J. (1993). Psychological Impact of biculturalism: Evidence and theory. *Psychological Bulletin, 114,* 395-412.

Lee, E. (1997). Overview: The assessment and treatment of Asian American families. In E. Lee (Ed.), *Working with Asian Americans: A guide for clinicians.* (pp. 3-36). New York: The Guilford.

Leonard, K.I. (1992). *Making ethnic choices: California's Punjabi Mexican Americans.* Philadelphia: Temple University.

Leonard, K.I. (1997). *The South Asian Americans.* Westport, CT: Greenwood.

Liddle, J, & Joshi, R. (1986). *Daughters of independence: Gender, caste and class in India.* London: Zed Books.

Mani, L. (1993) Gender, class, and cultural conflict: Indu Krishnan's knowing her place. In Women of South Asian Descent (Eds.) *Our feet walk the sky: Women of the South Asian Diaspora.* (pp. 31-43). San Francisco: Aunt Lute Books.

Mattai, P.R. (1997). Cultural constraints and psychological changes. In B.B. Khare (Ed.), *Asian Indian immigrants: Motifs on ethnicity and gender.* (pp. 71-83). Dubuque, Iowa: Kendall/Hunt.

Nandan, Y., & Eames, E. (1980). Typology and analysis of the Asian Indian family. In P. Saran & E. Eames (Eds.), *The new ethnics: Asian Indians in the United States.* (pp. 199-215). New York: Praeger.

Paranjpe, A.C. (1986). Identity issues among immigrants: Reflections on the experience of Indo-Canadians in British Columbia. In R.H. Bacon & G.V. Coelho (Eds.), *Tradition and Transformation: Asian Indians in America.* (pp. 71-94). Williamsburg, VA: Studies in Third World Societies.

Phinney, J.S. (1990). Ethnic Identity in adolescents and adults: Review of research. *Psychological Bulletin, 108,* 499-514.

Pillai, A.K.B. (1980). Problems of psychological and cultural adaptation. In K.V. Ujimoto & G. Hirabayashi (Eds.), *Visible minorities and multiculturalism: Asians in Canada.* (pp. 194-202). Toronto: Butterworths.

Portes, A., & Jensen, L. (1989). The enclave and the entrants: Patterns of ethnic enterprise in Miami before and after Mariel. *American Sociological Review, 54,* 929-949.

Prathikanthi, S. (1997). East Indian American families. In E. Lee (Ed.), *Working with Asian Americans: A guide for clinicians.* (pp. 79-100). New York: The Guilford.

Roland, A. (1986). The Indian self-reflections in the mirror of American life. In R.H. Bacon & G.V. Coelho (Eds.), *Tradition and Transformation: Asian Indians in America.* (pp. 43-52). Williamsburg, VA: Studies in Third World Societies.

Saran. P. (1985). *The Asian Indian experience in the United States.* Cambridge MA: Schenkman.

Shah, N. (1993). *The ethnic strife: A study of Asian Indian women in the United States.* New York: Pinkerton and Thomas.

Singhal, S. (1997). Psycho-social and historical profiles. In B.B. Khare (Ed.), *Asian Indian immigrants: Motifs on ethnicity and gender.* (pp. 85-115). Dubuque, Iowa: Kendall/ Hunt.

Spence, T., Helmreich, R., & Stapp, J. (1973). A short version of the attitudes toward women scale (AWS). *Bulletin of Psychometric Society, 2,* 219-220.

Srinivasan, S. (1999, April). Violence in the family: Implications for attitudes toward gender. Paper presented at the meeting of the Pacific Sociological Association Meeting, Portland, OR.

Stansfield, D. (1994). More labels bang drum for Euro-Asian bhangra beat. *Billboard, 106* (40), 1-3.

Takaki, R. (1989). *Strangers from different shores: A history of Asian Americans.* Boston: Little Brown.

Tsai, J., Ying, Y.W., & Lee, P. (in press). The meaning of "Being Chinese" and "Being American": Variation among Chinese American young adults. *Journal of Cross-Cultural Psychology.*

Visweswaran. K. (1993). Predicaments of the hyphen. In Women of South Asian Descent Collective (Eds.), *Our feet walk the sky: Women of the South Asian Diaspora.* (pp. 301-312). San Francisco: Aunt Lute Books.

Willis, P.E. (1981). *Learning to labor: How working class kids get working class jobs.* New York: Columbia University.

The Current State
of Mental Health Research
on Asian Americans

Jennifer Lee
Annie Lei
Stanley Sue

SUMMARY. A review of research reveals that the prevalence rates of depression, somatization, and posttraumatic stress disorder among Asian Americans are at least as high as those for White Americans, and, in many cases, higher rates are exhibited. Findings with respect to anxiety have been equivocal. The conclusion that is best supported by research at this time is that Asian Americans are not extraordinarily well adjusted, in contrast to their stereotype as a model ethnic minority group. What has hindered researchers in determining the rates and distributions of mental disorders among Asian Americans has been methodological and conceptual problems. These problems involve (a) making cross-cultural comparisons using assessment instruments that have been standardized on one group and applied to another and (b) phenomena unique to Asian Americans, including their population size, heterogeneity, and rapid demographic changes. Suggestions for research directions are given. *[Article copies available for a fee from The Haworth Document Delivery Service: 1-800-342-9678. E-mail address: <getinfo@*

Jennifer Lee, Annie Lei, and Stanley Sue are affiliated with the University of California, Davis.

Correspondence concerning this article should be addressed to Jennifer Lee, Department of Psychology, University of California, One Shields Ave., Davis, CA 95616-8686 (E-mail: jxlee@ucdavis.edu).

The paper was supported in part by a grant from the National Institute on Mental Health (R01-MH44331).

[Haworth co-indexing entry note]: "The Current State of Mental Health Research on Asian Americans." Lee, Jennifer, Annie Lei, and Stanley Sue. Co-published simultaneously in *Journal of Human Behavior in the Social Environment* (The Haworth Press, Inc.) Vol. 3, No. 3/4, 2001, pp. 159-178; and: *Psychosocial Aspects of the Asian-American Experience: Diversity Within Diversity* (ed: Namkee G. Choi) The Haworth Press, Inc., 2001, pp. 159-178. Single or multiple copies of this article are available for a fee from The Haworth Document Delivery Service [1-800-342-9678, 9:00 a.m. - 5:00 p.m. (EST). E-mail address: getinfo@haworthpressinc.com].

haworthpressinc.com> Website: <http://www.HaworthPress.com> © 2001 by The Haworth Press, Inc. All rights reserved.]

KEYWORDS. Asian American mental health, cross-cultural assessment, culture and psychopathology

Because of relatively high educational, occupational, and economic attainments and low criminal activity and divorce, the general public as well as many mental health professionals view Asian Americans as a well adjusted and adapted ethnic minority population (Sue, Sue, Sue, & Takeuchi, 1995). Such a view has important consequences. For example, the belief that Asian Americans have few mental health problems has justified the lack of attention and resources devoted to this population. Until recently, few professionals who saw the multitude of mental health problems and who worked with Asian Americans could successfully argue against a model or well adjusted minority group stereotype. There were simply not enough research findings that investigated the mental health of Asian Americans, and published findings were difficult to find.

The purpose of this article is to present the available research findings regarding the mental health of Asian Americans. Essentially, we address the question of what we know concerning Asian American mental health. Several points are made. First, some studies that examine the prevalence of mental disorders among Asian Americans differ in their conclusions. Second, most research shows that rates of mental disturbance, particularly for conditions such as depression, somatization, and posttraumatic stress disorder, are at least as high as those for other Americans. Third, methodological and conceptual problems involved in Asian American research have hindered the ability to draw more precise and stronger conclusions. These problems include those that are typically pertinent to cross-cultural research as well as those that are unique to Asian Americans. Fourth, we point to promising directions in mental health research with Asian Americans. Because of the availability of research findings on these disorders, in our discussion of mental disorders, we focus on depression, anxiety, somatization, and posttraumatic stress disorder.

It should be noted that Asian Americans are extremely heterogeneous. There are nearly 12 million Asian Americans, who include Asian Indians, Cambodians, Chinese, Filipinos, Japanese, Koreans, Vietnamese, Pacific Islander Americans, and a whole host of other groups. Researchers focusing on Asian Americans must try to deal with a very diverse population who exhibit differences in cultural backgrounds, native countries of origin, circumstances for coming to the United States, generational statuses, and native language spoken. In terms of percentage increase, they make up the fastest growing ethnic group in the United States. Asian Americans represent a sizable proportion of the population in several states–for example, approximately 60% in Hawaii and 10% in California (Tanaka, Ebreo, Linn, & Morera, 1998). The relative size and heterogeneity of the Asian American population have made it difficult to study specific Asian ethnic groups. Much of the research has used "Asian" samples that include different groups. Furthermore, the research has focused primarily on students and adults. Other groups, such as the elderly or children, have not been the target of much research.

This paper is divided into three sections. The first section highlights recent research in the field of Asian American mental health. We review the Asian American research with respect to depression, anxiety, somatization, and posttraumatic stress disorder. Findings from the Chinese American Psychiatric Epidemiological Study (CAPES), the most rigorous and large-scale investigation of any Asian American group, are presented. The second section identifies research and methodological problems that investigators face when studying Asian Americans. Finally, the third section suggests directions for further research in Asian American mental health to reveal a more accurate view of this population.

MENTAL HEALTH RESEARCH FINDINGS

Depression

The bulk of research findings has indicated that depression is at least as prevalent among Asian Americans as it is among White Americans. In fact, several studies reveal that Asian Americans exhibited higher levels of depressive symptoms than did Whites. For example, Aldwin and Greenberger (1987) found that Korean college students in the United States were more depressed than their White counterparts. They found that for the Koreans, perceived parental traditionalism was associated with higher depression, while parental modernism was associated with lower depression. More recent findings also showed that Asian American college students (predominantly foreign-born Chinese Americans, Korean Americans, and Japanese Americans) scored significantly higher than Whites on depression (Okazaki, 1997). Loo, Tong, and True (1989) conducted a study using a community sample, interviewing adult residents in a large Chinatown. They found that over one-third of their sample reported symptoms of emotional tension. Feelings of depression were common, with 40% of the sample complaining of a "sinking feeling like being depressed."

Using the Center for Epidemiology Studies of Depression scale (CES-D), several studies have attempted to ascertain the rates of depression among

Asian Americans. Kuo (1984) found that Chinese, Japanese, Filipino, and Korean Americans in Seattle (recruited through directories, organizations, and snowballing techniques) generally reported slightly more depressive symptoms than White respondents from other studies. In terms of interethnic differences, Kuo and Tsai (1986) found that among Asian immigrants, the Koreans, who were the most recently arrived immigrants, exhibited twice the rate of depression found among the Chinese, Japanese, and Filipino groups in their study. Immigrants having a wide social network of friends or relatives who could provide support exhibited fewer depressive symptoms than those having few social supports. In addition, Kuo and Tsai (1986) proposed that immigrants with "hardy" personalities (those who felt a sense of control over their life events, maintained a strong commitment to their life activities, and perceived change as an opportunity for personal development) were more likely to experience fewer symptoms of depression than those who lacked hardy traits.

Hurh and Kim's study (1988) supported Kuo and Tsai's research. Korean immigrants in Chicago (recruited from a Korean phone directory) scored higher in depression than did the Chinese, Japanese, and Filipinos in Kuo's study. Finally, in a community sample in San Francisco, Chinese Americans, especially those who were immigrants and from a lower socioeconomic background, were found to be significantly more depressed than the Chinese Americans in Kuo's study and than Whites (Ying, 1988). The convergent research on depression suggests that the prevalence of depression is relatively high among Asian Americans and that rates may differ according to ethnicity and other factors (e.g., social class).

Anxiety

A fair amount of research on anxiety has also been devoted to Asian Americans, particularly recent immigrants and refugees. Stressors associated with the process and experiences of immigration, such as leaving behind family members and poor living conditions upon arrival in the United States, make the most recent immigrants primary candidates for developing anxiety symptoms (Iwamasa, 1997). For example, in a study looking at three sub-groups of Vietnamese refugees, Felsman, Leong, Johnson, and Felsman (1990) found high anxiety levels among unaccompanied minors, adolescents, and young adults. Nightmares and decreased sense of personal efficacy (Tran, 1993), pain, demoralization, anger, and worry (Kroll et al., 1989) and an increased sense of marginality (Smither & Rodriguez-Giegling, 1979) are typical symptoms identified with anxiety disorders.

A significant amount of research on anxiety has also been conducted with college students. Researchers have documented the high anxiety levels of Asian American college students for more than two decades. Findings based on the Omnibus Personality Inventory (OPI) suggested that Asian American college students were more likely than Whites to experience anxiety as well as loneliness and isolation (see Sue & Frank, 1973; Sue & Kirk, 1973, 1975). Similar adjustment difficulties were found using the same measure among a sample of recently immigrated Chinese students (who had spent six years or less in the United States). The recent immigrants exhibited less autonomy and extroversion and more anxiety than did Chinese students who had lived longer in the United States (Sue & Zane, 1985). Cambra, Klopf, and Oka (1978) found that self-reported incidents of speech anxiety among University of Hawaii students (predominantly Asian Americans) were higher than would be expected according to national norms, while Lai and Linden (1993) noted that cognitive anxiety was reported with many of the Asian American undergraduate college students. Okazaki (1994) also found that Asian American students reported higher levels of anxiety compared to White American college students. Finally, Sue, Ino, and Sue (1983) found that Chinese American male college students reported greater anxiety in social situations.

There are many factors that affect the development of anxiety symptoms. It has been suggested that these results may indicate that Asian Americans, as a minority group, experience more difficulties, as well as acculturative stress, in their everyday lives (Sue et al., 1995). Asian American college students may be experiencing considerable stress and anxiety from parental pressures to achieve academically. As mentioned earlier, Sue and Zane (1985) reported that recently immigrated Chinese students were more anxious than Chinese students who had lived longer in the United States, suggesting that some of the anxiety as well as other psychopathological symptoms may abate over time. Hmong refugees who were examined 1.5 and 3.5 years post-migration improved their scores between assessments on somatization, obsessive-compulsiveness, interpersonal sensitivity, and phobic anxiety (Westermeyer, Neider, & Vang, 1984). The researchers found that ability to obtain employment, proficiency with English, and integration into the new community were correlated to a decrease in scores at the later assessment. Research also suggests that immigrants who move to the United States at an earlier, as opposed to later, age experience fewer adjustment difficulties (Kuo & Tsai, 1986) and that immigrants possessing hardy personality traits were more apt to display positive adjustment to American lifestyles (Kuo, 1984).

It has also been posited that certain elements in the Asian culture, such as the emphasis on family and community, may actually serve as protective factors or buffers against the development of some anxiety symptoms. In a Chinese American sample in Washington, D.C., Lin, Ensel, Simeone, and Kuo (1979) found a significant and negative correlation between social support and illness symptoms. However, aspects of the same culture may also increase the likelihood of the development of anxiety symptoms. Cultural values such as the emphasis on maintaining interpersonal and social harmony cause individuals to be more cautious and sensitive to others and the external environment, thus leading to an increase or exacerbation of anxiety symptoms for those who lack adequate coping skills (Iwamasa, 1997). Evidence of heightened anxiety symptoms can be seen in the culture-bound syndrome of *taijin kyofusho* (for a more in-depth discussion, see Kirmayer, 1991; Tseng, Asai, Kitanishi, McLaughlin, & Kyomen, 1992). Taijin kyofusho, originally thought to be a Japanese-specific set of symptoms, is now believed to occur in China and Korea as well (Iwamasa, 1997).

Somatic Problems

Cross-cultural psychiatric research suggest that somatization is more prevalent among people in non-Western cultures, including ethnic Asians living in Asia and in the United States (Chun, Enomoto, & Sue, 1996; Kirmayer, 1984). In a psychiatric clinic in Taiwan, Tseng (1975) found that nearly 70% of the psychiatric outpatients presented predominantly or exclusively somatic complaints on their initial visit. Gaw (1974) made similar observations across varying ages and socioeconomic statuses in Chinese Americans living in the Chinatown area in Boston. It has also been suggested that somatic symptoms occur in the presence of, or may be the predominant presentation of, a psychiatric disorder (Hsu & Folstein, 1997; Gaw, 1993; Kleinman, 1977; Leff, 1988; Tseng, 1975). Many Asians also exhibit symptoms of neurasthenia, a condition that is characterized by fatigue, weakness, poor concentration, diffuse aches and pains, sleep disturbances, and gastrointestinal problems.

In a study comparing Chinese in Taiwan and White psychiatric patients in the United States with depressive syndromes, Kleinman (1977) found that only 20% of the American patients, compared to 88% of the Chinese patients, initially reported somatic but no affective complaints. Somatic complaints were also found to be more common among Thai depressive patients and Vietnamese soldiers than among White depressive patients residing in Thailand and among American soldiers in Vietnam, respectively (Bourne & Nguyen, 1967; Tongyonk, 1972). More recently, among Chinese American and White psychiatric patients with mood disorder and somatic comorbidity, Hsu and Folstein (1997) found that Chinese Americans presented significantly more symptoms of "true somatization" than their White counterparts (for more in-depth discussion of "true somatizers," see Bridges & Goldberg, 1985). Although several findings may suggest that somatization is more prevalent among Asian Americans and ethnic Asians, the Epidemiological Catchment Area (ECA) study data, analyzed by Zhang and Snowden (1999), revealed that Asian Americans reported significantly lower rates of somatization compared to Whites. The ECA data on Asian Americans, however, involved only a very small sample whose representativeness is unknown.

Two issues are important to address concerning somatization in Asians. First is the issue of "why" and second is the issue of "how." Why do Asian Americans and ethnic Asians express more somatic symptoms than do Whites? And how are somatic symptoms manifested? Are the symptom profiles of Asians similar to that of Whites? First, explanatory hypotheses for higher rates of somatization among Asians are consistent with Western conceptions of somatization. However, cultural hypotheses that emphasize the influences of different cultural values and practices have been posited to encourage and facilitate the development of somatization in Asian societies. The teachings and philosophies of a Confucian, collectivistic tradition discourage open displays of emotions in order to maintain social and familial harmony or avoid exposing personal weakness. Thus, either consciously or unconsciously, Asians are thought to deny the experience and expression of emotions (Chun, Enomoto, & Sue, 1996; Kleinman, 1977; Nguyen, 1982; Tseng, 1975). Furthermore, societal factors such as the stigmatization of mental illness in Asian societies make it more acceptable for psychological distress to be more readily expressed through the body rather than the mind (Chun, Enomoto, & Sue, 1996; Gaw, 1993; Kleinman, 1977; Nguyen, 1982; Tseng, 1975). Hsu and Folstein (1997), along with Leff (1988), also suggested that psychological expression of distress is a relatively recent Western phenomenon and that physical expression of psychological distress is normal in many cultures.

Second, the question of whether or not Asians are manifesting similar symptoms as defined by the DSM-IV has not been adequately examined. In addition to the most common complaints of some sort of physical pain, gastrointestinal, pseudoneurological, and sexual symptoms in both Asian and White somatizers, other reported somatic symptoms are actually quite different (Hsu & Folstein, 1997). Chinese American somatizers also complained significantly about cardiopulmonary and vestibular somatic symptoms, including dizziness, vertigo, blurred vision, tinnitus, palpitation, fatigue, and shortness of breath, all of which are not symptoms listed in the DSM-IV. While White somatizers expressed some cardiopulmonary and vestibular complaints, those symptoms were never the chief complaint and were not as prominent as with the Chinese somatizers (Hsu & Folstein, 1997). Somatic symptoms of Asians do not fit DSM-IV's criteria of somatization but rather are similar to characteristics of neurasthenia.

Further evidence of somatization in Asians can be found in neurasthenia research (for further discussion on this topic, please refer to Kleinman, 1980, 1982; Lin, 1982, 1989; Ware & Kleinman, 1992; Zheng et al., 1997) and other culture-bound syndromes that are somatic in nature. It has been argued that culture-bound syndromes, such as neurasthenia, *hwabyung* (Lin, 1984; Lin et al., 1992), and *koro* (Edwards, 1984), are culturally recognized and sanctioned expressions of psychiatric disorder, mainly depression and anxiety (Chun, Enomoto, & Sue, 1996; Kleinman, 1980, 1982). Thus the greater likelihood of encountering somatic complaints among Asian American clients is supported by most of the research findings.

Post-Traumatic Stress Disorder (PTSD)

PTSD has been studied particularly among the Southeast Asian refugee populations. The refugee migrations of the 1970s and 80s were characterized by exposure to life-threatening traumatic events (Bemak, Chung, & Bornemann, 1996). Mollica, Wyshak, and Lavelle (1987) categorized the major categories of trauma as deprivation of food and shelter, physical injury and torture, incarceration and reeducation camps, and witnessing of torture and killing. Accordingly, it is not surprising that compared to the general population, refugees have been found to have not only higher rates of PTSD, but higher rates of depression and anxiety as well (Marsella, Friedman, & Spain, 1993). Kinzie, Leung, and Boehnlein (1997) found that depression and post-traumatic stress disorder (PTSD) are common among Southeast Asian refugees. They estimate that these disorders affect about 20% of the refugees in the community and 50% to 70% of refugees in a psychiatric clinic. When Kinzie et al. (1990) examined specific ethnic groups in a patient sample, an alarming 95% of the Mien sample and 92% of the Cambodian sample were diagnosed with PTSD.

In addition to these pre-migration traumatic experiences, post-migration problems include acculturation difficulties, culture shock, and separation from family members (Mollica, Wyshak, & Lavelle, 1987). In a study with Cambodian adolescents, refugee status was found to have a negative impact on youths' psychological adjustment (Kinzie, Sack, Angell, Manson, & Rath, 1986). These difficulties may persist for many years. Kinzie and colleagues (1989) found that among Cambodian adolescents who survived concentration camps, 48% suffered from PTSD and 41% experienced depression even ten years after traumatization.

More recently, Abe, Zane, and Chun (1994) reported that the experience and expression of anger and the loss of cultural ties were associated with PTSD in Southeast Asian refugees. Also, in interviews with Vietnamese, Cambodian, and Hmong refugees, two major cultural themes of kinship solidarity and the search for equilibrium emerged (Frye, 1995). Research has also indicated that Vietnamese refugees have the lowest prevalence rate of PTSD and are generally better adjusted when compared with other refugee groups (Abueg & Chun, 1998). With respect to PTSD and the Asian American population, it appears to be a significant problem, confined primarily to Southeast Asian refugees in general and Cambodians and Laotians in particular.

Chinese American Psychiatric Epidemiology Study

Our review so far points to the possibility that Asian Americans experience significant levels of depression, anxiety, somatization, and posttraumatic stress disorders. Indeed, several other studies also indicate that Asian Americans score higher than do Whites on obsessive-compulsiveness, interpersonal sensitivity, phobic anxiety, paranoid ideation, psychoticism, and hostility (Cheng, Leong, & Geist, 1993; Zane, Enomoto, & Chun, 1994) and on several clinical scales of the MMPI (Sue, Keefe, Enomoto, Durvasula, & Chao, 1996). Nevertheless, in one major study, rates of mental disorders were found to be low. An analysis of data from the Epidemiological Catchment Area (ECA) study collected in the 1980s yielded findings that Asian Americans were, in fact, less likely than Whites to have such disorders as anxiety disorders, somatization, manic episode, bipolar disorder, schizophreniform, panic, drug and alcohol abuse, and antisocial personality (Zhang & Snowden, 1999). As mentioned previously, however, the Asian American sample was relatively small and may not be representative of Asian Americans in general. While we comment on the apparent discrepancies in the findings in the section on methodological problems, it is clear that a large-scale epidemiological study of Asian Americans is required in order to establish more definitive conclusions. David Takeuchi conducted such a study from the National Research Center on Asian American Mental Health.

The Chinese American Psychiatric Epidemiological Study (CAPES) has been methodologically the most advanced psychological investigation of any Asian group in the United States. The five-year project attempted to: (1) estimate the prevalence rates of selected mental disorders among Chinese Americans, and (2) identify the factors associated with mental health problems among Chinese Americans. Respondents were administered household interviews lasting about 90 minutes. The target population for the study included Chinese immigrants and native-born residents living in the Los Angeles area. They were sampled using a strata cluster, three-stage probability sampling method. Follow-up interviews with the same respondents were conducted about one year later, which allowed the unprecedented opportunity to note changes in mental health and the factors associated with changes. The interviews were conducted in English, Mandarin, or Cantonese depending on the respondent's language preference. Of the eligible respondents, 1,747 interviews were completed, which resulted in an 82% response rate.

The University of Michigan's version of the Composite International Diagnostic Interview (UM-CIDI) was used as the major diagnostic instrument. Components of the instrument have been previously used with Chinese samples and care was taken to pilot test the measure, after the backtranslation method was used to translate the instrument into Chinese. Also included in the interview schedule were: (a) sociodemographic information, including age, gender, educational level, household income, number of household members, year of immigration, country of origin, marital status, education, and English-proficiency; (b) a 90-item, self-reported Symptoms Check List (SCL-90); (c) questions related to stressors, including major life events and daily hassles; (d) information on social support, personality, and hardiness; (e) queries concerning help-seeking behaviors and utilization of mental health services; and (f) acculturation questions. Because of the vast amount of data collected (see Sue et al., 1995; Takeuchi et al., 1998), only the results pertaining to depression, anxiety, and neurasthenia/somatization are presented here.

The lifetime prevalence of major depression for Chinese Americans was found to be 6.9%. This figure is lower than the 17.1% lifetime prevalence rate for Americans in the National Comorbidity study (NCS) (Kessler et al., 1994) but higher than the 4.9% lifetime rate found in the ECA study of Americans (Robins & Regier, 1991). Similarly, the lifetime prevalence rates for dysthymia (5.0%) fell between the rates in the NCS (6.4%) and ECA surveys (3.2%). While the depression prevalence rates for Chinese Americans were within the range of other Americans, this was not the case in anxiety disorders. The lifetime prevalence rates for Chinese Americans compared with other Americans from the NCS and ECA surveys were (CAPES vs. NCS and ECA, respectively): 1.7% vs. 5.1% and unknown (for generalized anxiety disorder), 1.6% vs. 5.3% and 5.6% (for agoraphobia), 1.1% vs. 11.3% and 11.3% (for simple phobia), 1.2% vs. 13.3% and 2.7% (for social phobia), 0.4% vs. 3.5% and 1.6% (for panic disorder), and 0.7% vs. unknown and 1.5% (for panic attack). These rates for anxiety disorders are considerably lower than the corresponding rates found in the NCS and ECA surveys.

The Chinese Psychiatric Epidemiology Study was also able to shed some light on the phenomenon of neurasthenia/somatization. The World Health Organization's ICD-10 lists neurasthenia as a mental disorder. Using ICD-10 criteria, a surprisingly large proportion of Chinese Americans (i.e., 6.4%) reported symptoms characteristic of neurasthenia during the past 12 months (Zheng et al., 1997). Moreover, about 78% of them did not exhibit symptoms of other disorders. These findings cast doubt on the view that this somatic syndrome or neurasthenia is simply a manifestation of some other disorder such as depression. What this means is that neurasthenia may be a distinct and important disorder which appears primarily among Chinese rather than White Americans.

In summary, CAPES has confirmed that Chinese Americans experience significant levels of depressive and neurasthenic (somatic) problems. However, in contrast to other studies, it found the prevalence of anxiety disorders to be relatively low. What can account for these discrepant findings?

RESEARCH AND METHODOLOGICAL PROBLEMS

Obviously, the findings from CAPES may be correct: Chinese Americans may simply have low rates of anxiety but rates of depression that are similar to other Americans. Nevertheless, given the numerous studies that reveal high levels of anxiety among Chinese and Asian Americans, it is possible that because of methodological and conceptual limitations in previous studies, discrepant findings are expected. Let us examine what these limitations and problems are.

Cross Cultural Assessment Issues

Cross-cultural researchers have been continuously challenged by cultural variations in the assessment of Asian Americans. It has been particularly problematic to conduct valid assessment research because of cultural differences in self-disclosure tendencies and value systems. Asians come from an orientation with strong family ties (Fong, 1973) and an emphasis to inhibit self-expression and exert control over strong emotional expression (Lai & Linden, 1993). These response set factors may affect the validity of self-report personality inventories, especially when these inventories are compared with different cultural populations.

The tendency for Asians and Asian Americans to hold back information or not report symptoms that may cause themselves or their families shame is a major drawback of self-report inventories. For example, evidence of marital conflict, academic or job failure, and psychological symptoms may bring shame and stigmatization to individuals and their families (Uba, 1994). The threat of dishonoring the family may cause study participants to selectively report only certain culturally endorsed symptoms (Chun, Enomoto, & Sue, 1996). Response sets or styles of reporting thus confound self-report inventories. Among types of common response sets are *acquiescence, social desirability, positional, evasiveness,* and *carelessness* (Lonner & Ibrahim, 1990). Acquiescence is generally referred to as the subjects' tendency to agree with extremes. For example, Asian Americans may have a tendency to confirm affirmative statements out of politeness, reflecting the norms of the society. The response set of social desirability is the tendency to respond in ways considered to be more socially favorable. The positional response style refers to aggressively saying no to everything or consistently responding to neutral items. The response sets of evasiveness and carelessness correspond to the unwillingness to commit oneself and to making inconsistent judgments, respectively. Lai and Linden (1993) also identified two other response styles: impression management (also known as other-deception) and self-deception on psychological and physical symptom reporting. Linden, Paulhus, and Dobson (1986) found that all symptom reporting was confounded by response sets, even under anonymous testing conditions. Therefore, response sets can invalidate scores or cause serious concerns about the validity of what is measured. The problem here is that we do not know what kind of response sets may be operating for Asian Americans. Differences in response sets may exits between different Asian Americans groups, between acculturated and unacculturated, etc. Thus findings from one study to another may differ.

Another major issue in the assessment of Asian Americans concerns the adaptation and translation of inventories. Several questions are particularly important to the validity of a measurement and need to be addressed. The foremost question is whether the content of the measure is relevant to Asian Americans; is content validity ensured? Does the test, when applied to a different ethnic group, tap into the construct intended to be measured; is construct validity preserved? Another question deals with predictive validity; does the test (or scales in a test) actually predict the expected behavior in the new target group? Do the original test norms apply in the new culture or will new specific norms have to be developed? Culture does not determine behavior but is one of the many factors that interact and influence an individual's or a group's own way of interpreting and experiencing everyday life events (Toukmanian & Brouwers, 1998). Therefore, besides proceeding cautiously when adapting or translating measures, it is also important to keep in mind that psychological symptoms may be defined and manifested differently in various cultures. Definitions of mental health and styles of symptom manifestations may vary considerably due to differences in value systems and cultural traditions. Therefore, cross-cultural researchers should be wary of the lack of agreement on the many operational definitions of constructs (Sue & Sundberg, 1990). How these factors affect Asian Americans and what potential differential validity of translated measures exist for different Asian American groups are unknown. There, ethnic specific response sets and differential validity are potentially important confounding variables that may account for differences in research findings.

Sample and Population Issues

Despite the fact that the Asian American population is growing, it remains relatively small, with Asian Americans representing only about 4% of the United States population. Therefore, it is sometimes difficult to find adequate sample sizes and representative samples of Asian Americans. Oftentimes, convenience samples are relied upon. For example, they may be drawn from lists of Asian ethnic organizations, names suggested by other respondents (the snowballing technique) and universities. These different sampling sources may result in conflicting prevalence rates of psychopathology (Sue et al., 1995).

As mentioned earlier, the Asian American population is also extremely diverse and heterogeneous. According to the Asian and Pacific Islander Center of Census Information and Services (1993), there are at least 48 distinct Asian and Pacific Islander American ethnic groups in the United States. Even if we focus on just one particular group for study, the heterogeneity is problematic. For example, the Chinese American population is composed of both native and foreign-born individuals who come from mainland China, Taiwan, Hong Kong, Singapore, Vietnam, etc. Moreover, if diversity exists among Chinese Americans, combining all Asian American groups (taking an aggregate group) limits our ability to draw conclusions or make generalizations.

Not only is the Asian American population diverse, but the composition is constantly changing as well. For example, the Asian American population today is primarily born overseas, in contrast to the situation three decades ago. Demographic changes such as this are likely to produce different prevalence rates. Furthermore, traumas faced by Southeast Asian refugees, including their relatively recent entry into the United States, have drastically changed the prevalence rates for mental disorders among Asian Americans (Sue et al., 1995). If, in a study of Asian Americans, Southeast Asian refugees are oversampled, then prevalence rates may be high compared to a study in which there are few of these refugees.

Therefore, it is important to keep in mind that although aggregate research is meaningful for policy considerations, for illustrating broad cultural influences, and for establishing baseline data, potential dangers lie within if overgeneralized. Aggregate research can serve well as a starting point for more refined, specific group research. Mini-theories, instead of broad and inclusive ones, can examine principles in a more detailed manner.

FUTURE DIRECTIONS FOR RESEARCH

We suggest that more qualitative, longitudinal, developmental, and community research be undertaken to help us to better understand the complexities of Asian American mental health. First, qualitative research emphasizes an emic, or culture-specific approach. Qualitative methods, including ethnography, are helpful in understanding the meanings, patterns, rules, and behaviors that are found in ethnic minority communities (Burton, 1997). Two common qualitative techniques are open-ended interviews and focus groups. These strategies can be especially useful when employed in conjunction with quantitative methods and can aid in developing theory, ensuring conceptual equivalence and interpreting quantitative results (Sue, Kurasaki, & Srinivasan, 1999). For example, quantitative responses may achieve greater clarity and meaning after qualitative data provide important contextual information. This combination of methodologies in the study of the same phenomena or programs, called *triangulation,* is one important way to strengthen research design (for further discussion, see Patton, 1990). In addition, a qualitative approach in clinical assessment has been heralded for being flexible and valuable because of its emphasis on the significance of first-hand knowledge (Lonner & Ibrahim, 1990).

Second, longitudinal research is vital for observing the long-term aspects of mental health. For example, there has been evidence that some anxiety symptoms experienced by Asian immigrants and refugees abate over time (Iwamasa, 1997). Some research findings indicate that as an immigrant begins to adapt to a new environment, mental health can improve (e.g., Westermeyer, Neider, & Vang, 1984). And yet, as mentioned earlier, the long-term effects of traumatization (e.g., in refugee groups) can last for many years. It is imperative that investigators not only undertake longitudinal studies that span five or ten years, but that they also develop and implement research programs that span across generations. Cross-sectional research can also play an important role in studying generational issues. Nagata (1998), who has examined Japanese American internment and intergenerational relations, has noted that because experiences of trauma can have consequences that persist beyond the life experiences of one generation, it is useful to consider intergenerational dynamics.

Third, cross-sectional and longitudinal studies can help researchers learn more about developmental issues among Asian Americans. Despite the increasing numbers of Asian American children attending school in the major urban areas across the United States, little research has been conducted to assess the mental health and well-being of these children (Chung, 1997; Lee & Zhan, 1998). Issues such as obligation to parents, parent-child relations, parental attitudes about schooling, and identity formation are just some examples of what Asian American children and adolescents face. Asian American young adults and Asian American elderly are also confronted with issues that are specific to their developmental contexts. For example, Asian American young adults involved in interracial relationships may have to contend with family conflict. With regard to the elderly, the number of ethnic minority elderly is expected to increase faster than the number of White elderly in the next half century (Angel & Hogan, 1991). Wong and Ujimoto (1998) point to the dearth of research on how cultural transitions affect the mental health of aging immigrants and how they adjust to American society. This segment of the population encounters both challenges of aging and acculturation. In addition, elderly Asian immigrants are acknowledged as a high-risk population, with increased mental health needs and limited resources to draw on when confronting major life stresses (Sue & Morishima, 1982). Therefore, it is obvious that more developmental research is required to better understand the mental health of Asian Americans across the life cycle.

Fourth, mental health research needs to be better linked with the specific communities of Asian American subgroups. Research conducted in clinics and universities, though important, often removes the individuals undergoing study or treatment from their community context. These contexts can vary widely, and this has implications not only for research (e.g., on social networking and mental health), but for the development of prevention and treatment programs as well. Similarly, we need to study subgroups (different Asian ethnicities and individuals with different demographic characteristics/ backgrounds within different Asian ethnicities) in order to understand how prevalence rates vary from subgroup to subgroup.

Finally, we should keep in mind the research problems mentioned in the previous section of this paper. For example, the Asian American population is diverse and ever changing, and study samples need to reflect this heterogeneity to provide a more informed understanding of Asian American mental health. There are gaps in research when considering ethnic subgroups, such as Asian Indians, Indonesians, and Thais (Uba, 1994). Based on what we know, it is safe to say that Asian Americans are not extraordinarily well adjusted. The prevalence of depression is similar to that of other Americans. Rates of neurasthenia and somatization, as well as PTSD, appear to be high. In the case of anxiety, some research has yielded high rates while other studies have found low rates of anxiety. We believe that methodological and conceptual problems underlie the discrepant research findings. Considering the fact that significant mental health problems exist among Asian Americans, it is imperative to begin more specific research to determine not only the extent of problems but also their correlates in order to promote mental health and provide effective treatment.

REFERENCES

Abe, J., Zane, N., & Chun, K. (1994). Differential responses to trauma: Migration discriminants of post-traumatic stress disorders among Southeast Asian refugees. *Journal of Community Psychology, 22*, 121-135.

Abueg, F. R., & Chun, K. M. (1998). Traumatization stress among Asians and Asian Americans. In P. B. Organista, K. M. Chun, & G. Marin (Eds.), *Readings in ethnic psychology.* (pp. 283-294). New York: Routledge.

Aldwin, C., & Greenberger, E. (1987). Cultural differences in the predictors of depression. *American Journal of Community Psychology, 15* (6), 789-813.

Angel, J. L., & Hogan, D. P. (1991). The demography of minority aging populations. In *Minority elders: Longevity, economics, and health: Building a public policy base.* (pp. 1-13). Washington, DC: Gerontological Society of America.

Asian and Pacific Islander Center of Census Information and Services. (1993). *A profile of Asian and Pacific Islander immigrant populations in California.* San Francisco: Asian/Pacific Islander Data Consortium.

Bemak, F., Chung, R. C., & Bornemann, T. H. (1996). Counseling and psychotherapy with refugees. In P. B. Pedersen, J. G. Draguns, W. J. Walter, & J. E. Trimble

(Eds.), *Counseling across cultures* (4th ed.). (pp. 243-265). Thousand Oaks, CA: Sage.

Bourne, P. G., & Nguyen, D. S. (1967). A comparative study of neuropsychiatric causalities in the United States Army and the Army of the Republic of Vietnam. *Military Medicine, 132,* 904-909.

Bridges, K., & Goldberg, D. P. (1985). Somatic presentation of DSM-III psychiatric disorders in primary care. *Journal of Psychosomatic Research, 29* (6), 563-569.

Burton, L. M. (1997). Ethnography and the meaning of adolescence in high-risk neighborhoods. *Ethos, 25,* 208-217.

Cambra, R. E., Klopf, D. W., & Oka, B. J. (1978). *Communication apprehension among University of Hawaii students.* Unpublished manuscript, University of Hawaii, Honolulu, Department of Speech.

Cheng, D., Leong, F. T., & Geist, R. (1993). Cultural differences in psychological distress between Asian and Caucasian American college students. *Journal of Multicultural Counseling and Development, 21* (3), 182-190.

Chun, C. A., Enomoto, K., & Sue, S. (1996). Health care issues among Asian Americans: Implications of somatization. In P. M. Kato & T. Mann (Eds.), *Handbook of diversity issues in health psychology.* (pp. 347-365). New York: Plenum Press.

Chung, W. (1997). Asian American children. In E. Lee (Ed.), *Working with Asian Americans: A guide for clinicians.* (pp. 165-174). New York: The Guildford Press.

Edwards, J. W. (1984). Indigenous Koro, a genital retraction syndrome of insular Southeast Asia: A critical review. *Culture, Medicine and Psychiatry, 8,* 1-24.

Felsman, J. K., Leong, F. T. L., Johnson, M. C., & Felsman, I. C. (1990). Estimates of psychological distress among Vietnamese refugees: Adolescents, unaccompanied minors and young adults. *Social Science & Medicine, 31,* 1251-1256.

Fong, S. L. (1973). Assimilation and changing social roles of Chinese Americans. *Journal of Social Issues, 29,* 115-128.

Frye, B. A. (1995). Use of cultural themes in promoting health among Southeast Asian refugees. *American Journal of Health Promotion, 9* (4), 269-280.

Gaw, A. C. (1974). An integrated approach in the delivery of health care to a Chinese community in America: The Boston experience. In A. Kleinman, P. Kunstadter, E. R. Alexander, & J. L. Gale (Eds.), *Medicine in Chinese cultures: Comparative studies of health care in Chinese and other societies.* (pp. 327-349). Bethesda, MD: Fogarty International Center, NIH.

Gaw, A. C. (1993). Psychiatric care of Chinese Americans. In A. C. Gaw (Ed.), *Culture, Ethnicity and Mental Illness.* (pp. 245-280). Washington, DC: American Psychiatric Press.

Hsu, L. K. G., & Folstein, M. F. (1997). Somatoform disorders in Caucasian and Chinese Americans. *Journal of Nervous and Mental Disease, 185* (6), 382-387.

Hurh, W. M., & Kim, K. C. (1988). *Uprooting and adjustment: A sociological study of Korean immigrants' mental health.* Final report to the National Institute of Mental Health. Macomb, IL: Department of Sociology and Anthropology, Western Illinois University.

Iwamasa, G. Y. (1997). Asian Americans. In S. Friedman (Ed.), *Cultural issues in the treatment of anxiety.* (pp. 99-129). New York: The Guilford Press.

Kessler, R. C., McGonagle, K. A., Zhao, S., Nelson, C. B., Hughes, M., Eshleman, S., Wittchen, H., & Kendler, K. S. (1994). Lifetime and 12-month prevalence of DSM-III-R psychiatric disorders in the United States. *Archives of General Psychiatry, 51*, 8-19.

Kinzie, J., Boehnlein, J. K., Leung, P. K., Moore, L. J., Riley, C., & Smith, D. (1990). The prevalence of posttraumatic stress disorder and its clinical significance among Southeast Asian refugees. *American Journal of Psychiatry, 147*, 913-917.

Kinzie, J. D., Leung, P. K., & Boehnlein, J. K. (1997). Treatment of depressive disorders in refugees. In E. Lee (Ed.), *Working with Asian Americans: A guide for clinicians* (pp. 265-294). New York: The Guildford Press.

Kinzie, J. D., Sack, W. H., Angell, R. H., Clarke, G., & Rath, B. (1989). A three-year follow-up on Cambodian young people traumatized as children. *Journal of American Academy of Child and Adolescent Psychiatry, 28*, 501-504.

Kirmayer, L. J. (1984). Culture, affect and somatization. *Transcultural Psychiatric Research Review, 21*, 159-217.

Kirmayer, L. J. (1991). The place of culture in psychiatric nosology: Taijin Kyofusho and DSM-III-R. *Journal of Nervous and Mental Disease, 179*, 19-28.

Kleinman, A. (1977). Depression, somatization and the "new cross-cultural psychiatry." *Social Science & Medicine, 11*, 3-10.

Kleinman, A. (1980). *Patients and healers in the context of culture.* Berkeley: University of California Press.

Kleinman, A. (1982). Neurasthenia and depression: A study of somatization and the culture in China. *Culture, Medicine and Psychiatry, 6*, 117-190.

Kroll, J., Habenicht, M., Mackenzie, T., Yang, M., Chan, S., Vang, T., Nguyen, T., Ly, M., Phommasouvanh, B., Nguyen, H., Vang, Y., Souvannasoth, L., & Cuagao, R. (1989). Depression and posttraumatic stress disorder in Southeast Asian refugees. *American Journal of Psychiatry, 146*, 1592-1597.

Kuo, W. H. (1984). Prevalence of depression among Asian-Americans. *Journal of Nervous and Mental Disease, 172*, 449-457.

Kuo, W. H., & Tsai, Y. M. (1986). Social networking, hardiness, and immigrant's mental health. *Journal of Health and Social Behavior, 27*, 133-149.

Lai, J., & Linden, W. (1993). The smile of Asia: Acculturation effects on symptom reporting. *Canadian Journal of Behavioural Science, 25* (2), 303-313.

Lee, L. C. (1998). An overview. In L. C. Lee & N. W. S. Zane (Eds.), *Handbook of Asian American psychology.* (pp. 1-19). Thousand Oaks, CA: Sage.

Lee, & Zhan, (1998). Psychosocial status of children and youths. In L. C. Lee & N. W. S. Zane (Eds.), *Handbook of Asian American psychology* (pp. 137-163). Thousand Oaks, CA: Sage.

Leff, J. (1988). *Psychiatry around the globe.* London: Gaskell/Royal College of Psychiatrists.

Lin, K. M. (1983). Hwa-byung: A Korean culture-bound syndrome? *American Journal of Psychiatry, 140*, 105-107.

Lin, K. M., Lau, J. K. C., Yamamoto, J., Zheng, Y. P., Kim, H. S., Cho, K. H., & Nagasaki, G. (1992). Hwa-byung: A community study of Korean Americans. *Journal of Nervous and Mental Disease, 180*, 386-391.

Lin, N., Ensel, W. M., Simeone, R. S., & Kuo, W. (1979). Social support, stressful life events, and illness: A model and empirical test. *Journal of Health and Social Behavior, 20*, 108-119.

Lin, T. Y. (1982). Culture and psychiatry: A Chinese perspective. *Australian and New Zealand Journal of Psychiatry, 16*, 313-336.

Lin, T. Y. (1989). Neurasthenia revisited: Its place in modern psychiatry. *Culture, Medicine and Psychiatry, 13*, 105-129.

Linden, W., Paulhus, D. L., & Dobson, K. S. (1986). Effects of response styles on the report of psychological and somatic distress. *Journal of Consulting and Clinical Psychology, 54*, 309-313.

Lonner, W. J., & Ibrahim, F. A. (1990). Appraisal and assessment in cross-cultural counseling. In P. B. Pederson, J. G. Draguns, W. J. Lonner, & J. E. Trimble (Eds.), *Counseling across cultures* (4th ed.). (pp. 293-322). Thousand Oaks, CA: Sage.

Loo, C., Tong, B., & True, R. (1989). A bitter bean: Mental health status and attitudes in Chinatown. *Journal of Community Psychology, 17*, 283-296.

Marsella, A. J, Friedman, M., & Spain, H. (1993). Ethnocultural aspects of PTSD. *Review of Psychiatry, 12*, 157-181.

Mollica, R. F., Wyshak, G., & Lavelle, J. (1987). The psychosocial impact of war trauma and torture on Southeast Asian refugees. *American Journal of Psychiatry, 144*, 1567-1572.

Nagata, D. K. (1998). Internment and intergenerational relations. In L. C. Lee & N. W. S. Zane (Eds.), *Handbook of Asian American psychology.* (pp. 433-456). Thousand Oaks, CA: Sage.

Nguyen, S. D. (1982). Psychiatric and psychosomatic problems among Southeast Asian refugees. *Psychiatric Journal of the University of Ottawa, 7*, 163-172.

Okazaki, S. (1994). *Cultural variations in the self and emotional distress.* Unpublished doctoral dissertation, University of California, Los Angeles.

Okazaki, S. (1997). Sources of ethnic differences between Asian American and White American college students on measures of depression and social anxiety. *Journal of Abnormal Psychology, 106*, 52-60.

Patton, M. Q. (1990). *Qualitative evaluation and research methods.* Newbury Park, CA: Sage.

Robins, L., & Regier, D. A. (1991). *Psychiatric disorders in America: The Epidemiological Catchment Area Study.* New York: The Free Press.

Smither, R., & Rodriguez-Giegling, M. (1979). Marginality, modernity, and anxiety in Indochinese refugees. *Journal of Cross-Cultural Psychology, 10*, 469-478.

Sue, D., Ino, S., & Sue, D. M. (1983). Nonassertiveness of Asian-Americans: An inaccurate assumption? *Journal of Counseling Psychology, 30*, 581-588.

Sue, D., & Sundberg, N. D. (1990). Research and research hypotheses about effectiveness in intercultural counseling. In P. B. Pederson, J. G. Draguns, W. J. Lonner, & J. E. Trimble (Eds.), *Counseling across cultures* (4th ed.). (pp. 323-352). Thousand Oaks, CA: Sage.

Sue, D.W., & Frank, A. (1973). A typological approach to the psychological study of Chinese and Japanese American college males. *Journal of Social Issues, 29*, 129-148.

Sue, D. W., & Kirk, B. A. (1973). Differential characteristics of Japanese-American

Lee, Lei, and Sue 177

and Chinese-American college students. *Journal of Counseling Psychology, 20,* 142-148.

Sue, D.W., & Kirk, B.A. (1975). Asian Americans: Uses of counseling and psychiatric services on a college campus. *Journal of Counseling Psychology, 22,* 84-86.

Sue, S. (1993). The changing Asian American population: Mental health policy. In LEAP Asian Pacific American Public Policy Institute and UCLA Asian American Studies Center (Eds.), *The state of Asian Pacific America.* (pp. 79-94). Los Angeles: LEAP Asian Pacific American Public Policy Institute and UCLA Asian American Studies Center.

Sue, S., Keefe, K., Enomoto, K., Durvasula, R., & Chao, R. (1996). Asian American and White college students' performance on the MMPI-2. In J. N. Butcher (Ed.), *International adaptations of the MMPI: Research and clincal applications* (pp. 206-20). Minneapolis, MN: University of Minnesota Press.

Sue, S., Kurasaki, K. S., & Srinivasan, S. (1999). Ethnicity, gender, and cross-cultural issues in clinical research. In P. C. Kendall, J. N. Butcher, & G. N. Holmbeck (Eds.). *Handbook of research methods in clinical psychology* (2nd ed.). (pp. 54-71). New York: Wiley.

Sue, S., & Morishima, J. (1982). *The mental health of Asian Americans.* San Francisco: Jossey-Bass.

Sue, S., Sue, D. W., Sue, L., & Takeuchi, D. T. (1995). Psychopathology among Asian Americans: A model minority? *Cultural Diversity and Mental Health, 1,* 39-54.

Sue, S., & Zane, N. (1985). Academic achievement and socioemotional adjustment among Chinese university students. *Journal of Counseling Psychology, 32,* 570-579.

Takeuchi, D. T., Chung, R. C., Lin, K. M., Shen, H., Kurasaki, K., Chun, C. A., & Sue, S. (1998). Lifetime and twelve-month prevalence rates of major depressive episodes and dysthymia among Chinese Americans in Los Angeles. *The American Journal of Psychiatry, 155,* 1407-1414.

Tanaka, J. S., Ebreo, A., Linn, N., & Morera, O. F. (1998). Research methods: The construct validity of self-identity and its psychological implications. In L. C. Lee & N. W. S. Zane (Eds.), *Handbook of Asian American psychology.* (pp. 21-79). Thousand Oaks, CA: Sage.

Tongyonk, J. (1972). Depressions in Thailand in the perspective of comparative-transcultural psychiatry. *Journal of Psychiatric Association of Thailand, 17,* 44-50.

Toukmanian, S. G., & Brouwers, M. C. (1998). Cultural aspects of self-disclosure and psychotherapy. In S. S. Kazarian & D. R. Evans (Eds.), *Cultural clinical psychology.* (pp.106-126). New York: Oxford University Press.

Tran, T. V. (1993). Psychological traumas and depression in a sample of Vietnamese people in the United States. *Health and Social Work, 18,* 184-194.

Tseng, W. (1975). The nature of somatic complaints among psychiatric patients: The Chinese case. *Comprehensive Psychiatry, 16,* 237-245.

Tseng, W., Asai, M., Kitanishi, K., McLaughlin, D. G., & Kyomen, H. (1992). Diagnostic patterns of social phobia: Comparison in Tokyo and Hawaii. *Journal of Nervous and Mental Disease, 180,* 380-385.

Uba, L. (1994). *Asian Americans: Personality patterns, identity, and mental health.* New York: Guilford Press.

Ware, N. C., & Kleinman, A. (1992). Culture and somatic experience: The social course of illness in neurasthenia and chronic fatigue syndrome. *Psychosomatic Medicine, 54*, 546-566.

Westermeyer, J., Neider, J., & Vang, T. F. (1984). Acculturation and mental health: A study of Hmong refugees at 1.5 and 3.5 years postmigration. *Social Science & Medicine, 18*, 87-91.

Wong, P. T. P., & Ujimoto, K. V. (1998). The elderly: Their stress, coping, and mental health. In L. C. Lee & N. W. S. Zane (Eds.), *Handbook of Asian American psychology.* (pp. 165-209). Thousand Oaks, CA: Sage.

Ying, Y. (1988). Depressive symptomatology among Chinese-Americans as measured by the CES-D. *Journal of Clinical Psychology, 44*, 739-746.

Zane, N., Enomoto, K., & Chun, C. (1994). Treatment outcomes of Asian- and White-American clients in outpatient therapy. *Journal of Community Psychology, 22* (2), 177-191.

Zhang, A. Y., & Snowden, L. R. (1999). Ethnic characteristics of mental disorders in five U.S. communities. *Cultural Diversity and Ethnic Minority Psychology, 5* (2), 134-146.

Zheng, Y-P., Lin, K. M., Takeuchi, D., Kurasaki, K. S., Wang, Y., Cheung, F. (1997). An epidemiological study of neurasthenia in Chinese-Americans in Los Angeles. *Comprehensive Psychiatry, 38* (5), 249-259.

Is an Independent Self a Requisite for Asian Immigrants' Psychological Well-Being in the U.S.? The Case of Korean Americans

Kyoung Ja Hyun

SUMMARY. This study examined the effect of both independent and interdependent self-construals on Asian immigrants' psychological well-being in the U.S., using a community sample of adult Koreans. Given that society rewards certain behaviors and attitudes that are consistent with the valued social norms, an independent view of self that matches the expectation of American society was hypothesized to promote Korean immigrants' psychological well-being. Hierarchical regression analyses revealed that Korean immigrants with a highly independent self-construal expressed significantly less depressive symptoms

Kyoung Ja Hyun is affiliated with Ewha Womans University, Seoul, Korea.

Correspondence concerning this article should be addressed to Kyoung Ja Hyun, Department of Social Work, Ewha Womans University, Seo-Dai-Moon Ku, Seoul, Korea.

The author is grateful to Hazel Markus and Sheila Feld for sage advice and assistance throughout the project. The author also wishes to thank Kristine Ajrouch, Hiroko Akiyama, Namkee Choi, and Deborah Jackson for their helpful comments on drafts of this article.

Portions of this article draw on a dissertation completed by the author under the guidance of Hazel Markus at Stanford University and Sheila Feld at the University of Michigan. This article was presented at the Conference on Cultural Psychology at Stanford University, August, 1998. This research was supported in part by a University of Michigan dissertation research grant and by NIA grant T32-AG0017.

[Haworth co-indexing entry note]: "Is an Independent Self a Requisite for Asian Immigrants' Psychological Well-Being in the U.S.? The Case of Korean Americans." Hyun, Kyoung Ja. Co-published simultaneously in *Journal of Human Behavior in the Social Environment* (The Haworth Press, Inc.) Vol. 3, No. 3/4, 2001, pp. 179-200; and: *Psychosocial Aspects of the Asian-American Experience: Diversity Within Diversity* (ed: Namkee G. Choi) The Haworth Press, Inc., 2001, pp. 179-200. Single or multiple copies of this article are available for a fee from The Haworth Document Delivery Service [1-800-342-9678, 9:00 a.m. - 5:00 p.m. (EST). E-mail address: getinfo@haworthpressinc.com].

and significantly more life satisfaction than those with a less independent self-construal. Furthermore, as was also expected, an interdependent view of self that is valued in many Asian cultures did not hinder
Korean immigrants' psychological well-being, controlling for the correlates of these immigrants' mental health and self-construals. The results underscore the importance of self-conceptions in cross-cultural
adaptation, and suggest the need of future research focusing on the potential benefits of both types of self-construal for Asian immigrants in
the U.S. *[Article copies available for a fee from The Haworth Document Delivery Service: 1-800-342-9678. E-mail address: <getinfo@haworthpressinc.com>
Website: <http://www.HaworthPress.com> © 2001 by The Haworth Press, Inc.
All rights reserved.]*

KEYWORDS. Culture, self, Korean Americans, mental health, immigration

Asian immigrants to the United States have come from various cultures,
many of which cultivate collectivism and a view of self that is characterized
as interdependent with others (Triandis, 1990). In North America, however,
the individualist ideal pervades social institutions and practices and promotes
an independent self-construal among people. Individuals who strive to
achieve independence from others and those who realize and express their
unique attributes are highly valued and rewarded in the U.S., particularly
within European-American contexts (Markus & Kitayama, 1991, 1994). In
daily life, Asian immigrants who do not understand or take on the American
self-conception and cultural imperatives may experience discomfort, a sense
of differentness, and even confusion at times, which may all work against
their psychological well-being. Indeed, most empirical research on immigration and mental health considers the acculturative process as stressful and
recognizes the disrupting effects of culture change (e.g., Hurh & Kim, 1990;
Golding & Burnam, 1990; Kuo, 1984). Yet surprisingly little research has
focused on the fit between immigrants' self-conceptions and their new cultural environments, which may have important implications for their well-being.

This study examines one of the Asian immigrant groups in the U.S.,
Koreans, to shed light on this issue.[1] According to the U.S. Census, there
were about 70,000 Koreans residing in the United States in 1970, about
800,000 in 1990, and the current Korean American population is roughly
estimated at over one million (Lee, 1995). As the majority of Korean Americans are Korean born, their self-construals vary a great deal, reflecting differences in their exposures to both traditional Korean and American ideas and
practices of the self (Hyun, 1999). This provides a valuable opportunity to
explore how and to what extent two contrasting views of self, such as *inde-*

pendent, common in the U.S., and *interdependent,* valued in Korea, are related to Korean immigrants' psychological well-being. Even though an emphasis on independent or interdependent self-definition distinguishes individualistic and collectivistic cultures of the world, a number of recent empirical studies in various cultural contexts suggest that these two images of the self coexist within individuals in an orthogonal relationship (e.g., Hyun, 1999; Misra & Giri, 1995; Okazaki, 1994; Singelis, 1994). The purpose of this study is to determine whether these two contrasting views of self promote or hinder Asian immigrants' psychological well-being in the U.S.

THEORETICAL FRAMEWORK

Culture and Construction of the Self

Although individuals living in most modern societies may develop an awareness of the self as an individuated person while simultaneously viewing the self as connected to others, culture does intervene in this process by highlighting and promoting a set of particular ideas and practices about how to be a person, or a "good" person. In East Asian societies, such as China, Japan, and Korea, the person is viewed as fundamentally connected with others, thus stressing empathy, reciprocity, belongingness, kinship, hierarchy, loyalty, politeness, and social obligation (Fiske, Kitayama, Markus, & Nisbett, 1998). As reflected in Confucian humanism, East Asian collectivistic assumptions of personhood and identity emphasize the interrelatedness of the person and society (Hofstede, 1991). Hence, "the focus of life is the self in relation to others, so people experience themselves as mutually *interdependent*" (Fiske et al., p. 922). This East Asian model of the self values harmonious social relations, roles, norms, and group solidarity more than self-expression and individuality. In the United States, however, particularly within European-American contexts, the person is viewed as an autonomous, self-contained, "free" entity. Tied to the ideology of individualism, Western assumptions of personhood and identity emphasize the independence and autonomy of a self that is separate from other selves and from social contexts. In this model, the self "(a) comprises a unique configuration of internal attributes (e.g., traits, emotions, motives, values, and rights) and (b) behaves primarily as a consequence of these internal attributes" (Markus & Kitayama, 1994, p. 96). Individual achievement, happiness, and rights are more fundamental than group solidarity (Bellah, Madsen, Sullivan, Swidler, & Tipton, 1985).

These East Asian and European-American models of the self reveal striking differences in ontological emphasis and provide a window on the interdependence between culture and the self. It is important to recognize, however, that individuals' construction of the self can contain elements of both. Within the psychological literature, possible coexistence of contrasting self-definitions within the same individual has been broadly documented (Baumeister, 1998; Brewer & Gardner, 1996; Triandis, 1989). It is likely that most Korean Americans' self-conceptions involve some organization of these two contrasting cultural influences, even though there may be considerable variability in the ways in which their images and ideas of the independent and interdependent selves are configured. It thus seems important to consider how these two types of self-construal influence the nature of Korean immigrants' experiences and, in turn, their psychological well-being in the U.S.

Implications of Self-Construals for Korean Immigrants' Psychological Well-Being

The self of any given individual is "an organized locus of the various, sometimes competing, understandings of how to be a person," and functions as an interpretive, mediating, and orienting framework for individual behavior (Markus & Kitayama, 1994, p. 92). One's self-conceptions influence and in many cases determine what is perceived and how it is processed (Bargh, 1982; Kuiper & Rogers, 1979), and it also renders meaning and coherence to one's life (Baumeister, 1998; Markus & Wurf, 1987). Hence, whether an individual has a self that is shaped primarily by a European-American ontological tradition or by an East Asian one has the potential to make an enormous difference in how he or she thinks, feels, and behaves. For example, Markus and Kitayama (1991) argue that an independent construal of the self directs individuals to attend to themselves and to discover and express their unique attributes, feelings, and thoughts, whereas an interdependent construal of the self directs individuals to attend to others, control their feelings, and fit in with others so as to maintain harmonious social relations. The coding of social behavior as "positive" or "negative," the labeling of an experience as "good" or "bad," and the accompanying emotions also vary with the type of self-construal emphasized in a given culture (see Markus & Kitayama, 1994 for details). Accordingly, Korean immigrants' thought processes and emotional and behavioral characteristics are more likely to deviate from those of typical Americans if they do not hold or take on the characteristics of an independent self. Such a discrepancy may, in turn, leave the immigrants vulnerable to stress and confusion.

In the U.S., for example, Americans with an independent self-construal are likely to code self-assertion and expression of unique individual attributes as "positive" and to feel good about them, because following cultural directives is intrinsically rewarding (D'Andrade, 1984). These same behaviors, however, may not produce good feelings and may also be overlooked or even negatively viewed among Korean immigrants who do not hold an independent self-construal. When intercultural interaction occurs, these immigrants may thus sometimes fail to recognize and produce the appropriate social behaviors that allow them to fit in and to elicit approval or reward from others. Such failure to respond appropriately and naturally to situations in daily life may become a source of stress for them.

Within the social science literatures, a good fit between the person and the environment has been generally recognized as a source of well-being (Caplan, 1983; Germaine, 1991; Lawton, 1983; Niedenthal, Cantor, & Kihlstrom, 1985; Schmitz, 1990; Searle & Ward, 1990). As Merton (1968) contended, society rewards certain behaviors and attitudes that are consistent with the valued social norms. Therefore, a construal of the self that matches the expectations of the surrounding society would provide the individual with a sense of psychological comfort and reward as it directs the individual's psychological processes in a culturally mandated way. Korean immigrants with a highly independent self-construal are more likely to possess personal qualities that American society expects and rewards, such as being assertive, self-reliant, expressive, sociable, and confident (Seipel, 1988). These immigrants may thus find the American sociocultural environment more self-fulfilling and satisfactory than those immigrants with a less independent self-construal.

Immigration is a stressful life transition for Koreans, no matter how they construe themselves. Indeed, a perusal of the literature on Korean Americans' mental health reveals that the levels of depressive symptoms or discontentment reported by Korean subjects tend to be higher than those of their other Asian ethnic counterparts in the given studies or according to the community norms of American samples (e.g., Aldwin & Greenberger, 1987; Kim & Rew, 1994; Kincaid & Yum, 1987; Kuo, 1984; Shin, 1994). In a study of prevalence of depression among Asian Americans in Seattle, Kuo (1984) has identified three major factors as associated with Koreans' higher levels of depressive symptoms: (1) shorter length of residence in the U.S. than other Asian Americans, such as Chinese and Japanese; (2) higher experience of status incongruence (decrease in occupational status); and (3) limited ability in English. Higher occupational status, higher education, and being married were also found to be significantly associated with Korean immigrants' life satisfaction (Hurh & Kim, 1990). But few studies have identified any intrapersonal factors that may be associated with Korean Americans' psychological well-being. Although Shin (1994) found in a more recent study that self-esteem was negatively associated with Korean immigrant women's depressive symptoms, it is not clear whether self-esteem is a predictor of mental health or a component of it (Lawton, 1983). The foregoing assumptions about self-construals suggest, however, that having an independent self-construal will also be important.

The hypothesized importance of an independent self-construal for Korean immigrants' psychological well-being in the U.S. raises the issue of the role of an interdependent self-view in their mental heath. The literature on acculturation, although not directly focusing on self-construals, provides some insight into this issue. Living within two cultures can result in four different modes of adaptation: biculturalism, in which individuals maintain active and effective relationships with both cultures; assimilation, in which members of one culture seek a new identity in a second culture and lose (or do not maintain) their original culture; separation, in which individuals hold on to their original culture and do not seek participation in a second culture; and finally, marginalization, in which individuals fail to maintain active relationships with either culture (Berry & Sam, 1997). Among these four modes, biculturalism has been found to be positively related to well-being (Greene, 1997; see LaFromboise, Coleman, & Gerton, 1993 for a review). This suggests that an interdependent self-construal may very well help Korean immigrants as it enables them to perform socially sanctioned behaviors within their own ethnic cultural contexts, and thereby may not necessarily hinder their psychological well-being in the U.S. Moreover, an interdependent self-construal may contribute to these Koreans' sense of cultural identity, which has been found to buffer immigrants' stress (Lopez, 1996).

Although the foregoing analysis suggests potential benefits of both independent and interdependent self-views for Korean immigrants in the U.S., two empirical studies that have examined the role of self-construals in cross-cultural adaptation and mental health indicate that an interdependent self-construal may have a detrimental effect on American or Asian students in the U.S. In one study, East Asian students with a highly interdependent self-view reported higher levels of perceived stress in American graduate schools, whereas those with a highly independent self-view experienced lower levels of perceived stress (Cross, 1995). Similarly, Okazaki's (1997) research showed that higher interdependent self-construal and lower independent self-construal were significantly associated with greater social distress among Asian American and White American college students. It is not clear, however, whether the results of these studies were the function of self-construals, because both studies did not attempt to control for the factors that might be associated with these students' self-views. In a study of Koreans' self-construals in two sociocultural contexts, Seoul and Detroit, Hyun (1999) found that endorsement of traditional values and certain aspects of immigration experiences (i.e., poor English proficiency, perception of more personal limits and of less discrimination) were significantly associated with Korean immigrants' interdependent self-construals, whereas older age, greater exposure to Western ideas, perception of fewer personal limits, and experience of financial difficulty were significantly related to these immigrants' independent self-construals. It seems important to control for these factors so as to clarify how these two contrasting self-views are related to psychological well-being among immigrants adapting to a new culture.

Based on the foregoing assumptions about the role of self-construals in Korean immigrants' well-being in the U.S., this study examines the following hypotheses while controlling for the correlates of Korean immigrants' mental health and self-construals:

Hypothesis 1. Given the importance of the fit between immigrants' self-conceptions and the cultural frame of their adopted country, an independent self-construal is expected to contribute to Korean immigrants' psychological well-being in the U.S. Hence, Korean immigrants with a highly independent self-view will experience a greater sense of psychological well-being than those with a less independent self-view.

Hypothesis 2. Given the potential of an interdependent self-construal to help Korean immigrants maintain a sense of ethnic identity and cultural competence, which have been found to buffer immigrants' stress, an interdependent self-construal is not expected to hinder their psychological well-being in the U.S. Hence, Korean immigrants with a highly interdependent self-view will not experience a lower sense of psychological well-being than those with a less interdependent self-view.

METHOD

Sample

A total of 158 adult Korean immigrants (79 males and 79 females) in the Detroit area participated in this mail questionnaire study. The Detroit metropolitan area was chosen primarily because the lack of a Korean enclave in the area meant that Korean immigrants living in Detroit are relatively dispersed and may have more direct contact with American culture in daily life than those living in a Korean enclave in cities like Los Angeles. A systematic probability sampling method was used. The sampling frame included only Korean immigrants who were born in Korea, intended to live in the U.S. permanently, and were at least 24 years of age. Two sources of lists, the directory of the Korean community in Michigan and the local telephone directories published by Ameritech, were used to draw a representative sample that fit these criteria. Computer generated Kish tables were used to randomly select one eligible adult member from each of the eligible households (Kish, 1965). The data were collected between May and September 1994. Respondents received no financial compensation.[2]

Participants. The respondents were quite evenly distributed in terms of sex and three age categories (24-36, 37-48, and 49-63). Asian Americans are known to be extremely heterogeneous and bipolar in socioeconomic status between ethnic groups as well as within each ethnic group (Lin-Fu, 1988). The Korean immigrants in this sample were not the exception. Although Korean Americans are known to be highly educated, only two thirds of the respondents (66%) had at least 4 years of college education. The data revealed that a group of less educated Korean immigrants exists. The majority of the sample (82%) had a household income above $35,000. However, the distribution of the Detroit sample's income revealed the bipolar pattern: Some respondents' household incomes were less than $15,000-$20,000, whereas some other respondents' household incomes were above $120,000. Over 80% of the sample were married. The length of residence in the U.S. ranged from less than a year to 34 years, and the average length of residence was 16 years ($SD = 7.47$).

Response rate. The initial agreement rates of the Korean immigrant households listed only in the local telephone directories and of those listed in the Korean community directory were 88% and 91%, respectively. Of the 216 who agreed to participate, 158 people (73%) returned their questionnaires. Thus, the overall response rate was 66%.

Measures

The measures described below derive from a structured questionnaire that was constructed specifically for a larger study of Koreans in Seoul and Korean immigrants in Detroit.[3] The questionnaire was developed in English and then translated into Korean. The respondents were given a choice of the English or Korean version: 27 out of the 158 respondents (17%) chose the English version.

Psychological Well-Being Measures

Depressive symptoms were measured by the Center for Epidemiologic Studies-Depression Scale (CES-D). This is a self-report, 20-item scale intended "to elicit symptoms associated with depression and to identify high-risk groups for research and screening purposes" (Radloff & Locke, 1986, p. 177).[4] A Korean version of the CES-D, translated by Hurh and Kim (1988), was adopted with minor modifications. Respondents indicated how often during the past week they felt the way each item described on a 4-point scale (0 = rarely or none of the time, 3 = most or all of the time). Replies to these items were summed to form a single scale score ranging from 0 to 60. The alpha was .88.

Life satisfaction was assessed by one question: "Taking everything into consideration, how well are you satisfied with your current life?" The response categories ranged from 1 (very dissatisfied) to 5 (very satisfied).

Background Measures

The sociodemographic factors identified by prior research as associated with Korean immigrants' mental health were controlled. These include gender, education, health status, occupational status, and length of stay in the U.S.[5] Level of education was measured by the number of school years completed. Respondents rated seriousness of their health problems on a 4-point scale (1 = no problem or not serious at all, 4 = very serious). Respondents' occupations were recoded into a dummy variable with professional occupations (1) and all others (0). Length of stay in the U.S. was computed in years.

Correlates of Korean Immigrants' Self-Construals

Age was measured in years.

Traditional values were measured by agreement with 18 statements that describe Confucian prescripts, which emphasize harmonious social relations and proper social behavior based on age, gender, and status. The items reflect the Confucian code of conduct and interpersonal relations between: ruler and minister, parent and child, older brother and younger brother, and husband and wife. The former are prescribed to be wise, benevolent, and responsible for the latter, and the latter to be obedient, loyal, and respectful to the former. Replies to these items were averaged to form a single scale score from 1 (strongly disagree) to 6 (strongly agree). The alpha was .86.

Exposure to Western ideas was measured by the extent to which respondents were involved in Western (or American) culture. Respondents indicated how often they listened to Western music, watched a Western movie, played Western sports, read books and magazines written by Western people, and read English newspapers. Also measured were the number of times they have traveled to (or lived in) Western countries, their self-reported fluency in speaking a Western language (e.g., English, French, German, and Spanish), and their tendency to read Western books and magazines in their original language. Replies to these items were added to form a single scale score ranging from 0 to 34. The alpha was .76.

English proficiency. Respondents indicated their ability to do each of the following three activities in English on a scale from 1 (not at all) to 5 (fluently): (1) expressing feelings and thoughts; (2) reading materials; and (3) writing a letter. Replies were averaged to form the measure of perceived English proficiency. The alpha was .92.

Perception of personal limits. Respondents' perceptions of personal limits were measured by agreement with 4 statements about perceived personal limits because of race, limited ability in English, and relational limits with other ethnic groups in the U.S. For example, one item reads, "No matter how long I live in the U.S., I will never be able to completely assimilate into American society because I am an Asian." Replies to these items were averaged to form a single scale score ranging from 1 (strongly disagree) to 6 (strongly agree). The alpha was .72.

Perception of discrimination. The perception of discrimination scale included 4 statements about perceived structural and institutional discrimination in the U.S.: biased coverage of Korean immigrants by American mass media, discrimination in economic opportunities, unfair treatment by the U.S. government, and difficulty in succeeding in the U.S. Respondents' agreement with these items were averaged to form a single scale score ranging from 1 (strongly disagree) to 6 (strongly agree). The alpha was .63.

Experience of financial difficulty. Respondents' experience of financial difficulty was assessed by one question: "Looking back upon your life in America, how much do you think you have had economic difficulty?" The response categories ranged from 1 (not at all) to 5 (a great deal).

Self-Construal Measures

Interdependent self-construal was measured by agreement with 17 statements that describe the respondents as having knowledge of the self as connected to others, being motivated to maintain bonds and harmonious relationships with others, and showing concern over others' evaluations of them. Replies were averaged to form a single scale score ranging from 1 (completely disagree) to 8 (completely agree). The alpha was .86. (For items see the Appendix.)

Independent self-construal was assessed by agreement with 12 statements that describe the respondents as having self-knowledge as a distinct person as well as being motivated to express internal needs freely and to maintain a boundary between the self and others. Replies were averaged to form a single scale score ranging from 1 (completely disagree) to 8 (completely agree). The alpha was .79. (For items see the Appendix.)

Data Analyses

Hierarchical multiple regression was used to test the study hypotheses concerning the relationship between self-construals and Korean immigrants' psychological well-being in the U.S. In step 1, the background variables identified as associated with Korean immigrants' mental health were included (i.e., education, gender, occupational status, health status, and length of stay in the U.S.).[6] The variables associated with Korean immigrants' self-construals were entered in step 2 (i.e., age, traditional values, exposure to Western ideas, English proficiency, experience of financial difficulty, perception of personal limits, and perception of discrimination). In step 3, interdependent self-construal was included. Independent self-construal was entered in step 4 to determine the amount of additional variance it explained in Korean immigrants' depressive symptoms and life satisfaction after controlling for all the other factors considered for the study.

RESULTS

Descriptive Analyses

The scores of the CES-Depression scale for the Korean immigrant sample in Detroit ranged from 0 to 48, and the mean score was 12 (SD = .84). Consistent with the findings of prior research on Korean Americans' mental health, this mean was higher than the mean of white American and other Asian American samples, which ranged from 7.96 to 9.72 (cited in Kuo, 1984), but was comparable to that of other Korean American samples (e.g., Hurh & Kim, 1990). The mean score of life satisfaction for the sample was 3.77 (SD = .88) on a 5-point scale, which was between 3 (neither satisfied nor dissatisfied) and 4 (somewhat satisfied). On average, Detroit Koreans appeared to be relatively satisfied with their lives in the U.S. The correlation between the independent and interdependent self-construal scales was $-.15$ (p = .07). As predicted, independent self-construal was related to psychological well-being. Korean immigrants with a highly independent self-view had lower depressive symptoms ($r = -.22, p < .01$) and higher life satisfaction ($r = .33, p < .001$). Interdependent self-construal was also related to depressive symptoms. Korean immigrants with a highly interdependent self-view had greater depressive symptoms ($r = .25, p < .01$). As expected, however, interdependent self-construal was not related to life satisfaction ($r = -.06, p = ns$).

Depressive Symptoms

Table 1 presents the results of the regressions on depressive symptoms. The full model accounted for 38% of the variance in depressive symptoms. At step 1, poorer health was significantly associated with greater depressive symptoms. At the second step, depressive symptoms were also higher for younger Korean immigrants and for those immigrants who had limited ability

TABLE 1. Summary of Hierarchical Regression Analysis for Variables Predicting Korean Immigrants' Psychological Well-Being

Variables	Depressive Symptoms (n = 140)				Life Satisfaction (n = 136)			
	b	b (SE)	Beta	Increment R^2	b	b (SE)	Beta	Increment R^2
Step 1				.23***				.09*
Education	.06	.03	.15		−.12	.09	−.14	
Sex[a]	.03	.07	.04		.04	.16	.02	
Professional job[b]	−.13	.08	−.14		.32	.19	.16+	
Health problem[c]	.12	.03	.32***		−.09	.07	−.11	
Length of stay in the U.S.	.01	.01	.14		−.02	.01	−.14	
Step 2				.12**				.09+
Age	.01	.00	−.20+		.01	.01	.15	
Traditional values	−.03	.05	−.06		−.03	.11	−.03	
Exposure to Western ideas	.00	.01	.06		.01	.02	.06	
English proficiency	−.15	.05	−.37**		.18	.12	.21	
Financial difficulty	.05	.03	.14*		−.09	.07	−.12	
Perception of personal limits	.05	.03	.15+		−.10	.07	−.14	
Perception of discrimination	−.01	.04	−.02		−.01	.08	−.02	
Step 3				.01				.00
Interdependent self	.04	.04	.09		.07	.09	.07	
Step 4				.02*				.07***
Independent self	−.07	.03	−.17*		.25	.07	.29***	
Total R-squared				.38***				.25***

Note. The sample size varies due to missing values. [a]1 = male; 2 = female. [b]1 = Yes; 0 = No. [c]1 = no problem; 4 = very serious problem. + $p < .10$. * $p < .05$. ** $p < .01$. *** $p < .001$.

in English, experienced more financial difficulty in the U.S., and perceived more personal limits. As hypothesized, interdependent self-construal was not significantly associated with depressive symptoms at step 3 after controlling for the correlates of Korean immigrants' mental health and self-construals. At the final step, independent self-construal was, as expected, a significant predictor of Korean immigrants' depressive symptoms. It explained an additional 2% of the variance in depressive symptoms [F (1, 125) = 4.62, $p < .05$]. Korean immigrants who hold a highly independent self-construal expressed significantly less depressive symptoms than those with a less independent self-construal.

To clarify which correlates of Korean immigrants' self-construals accounted for the positive correlation between higher interdependent self-view and greater depressive symptoms, hierarchical regression analysis was repeated, including the self-construal variables in the equation prior to the entry of the individual correlates of self-construals in a stepwise manner (results not presented). When the self-construal variables were entered in step 2, after controlling for the correlates of Korean immigrants' mental health, both were significantly associated with depressive symptoms. However, the significant effect of interdependent self-construal on depressive symptoms disappeared after English proficiency and perception of personal limits were included in the equation, respectively. It appeared that Korean immigrants with a highly interdependent self-view had higher depressive symptoms than those with a less interdependent self-view, mostly because they had greater difficulty in English and perceived more personal limits in the U.S.

Life Satisfaction

The results of the regressions on life satisfaction are also shown in Table 1. The full model did not account for as much variance in life satisfaction as it did in depressive symptoms (25% as compared to 38%).[7] At step 1, having a professional job was significantly associated with greater life satisfaction, but its effect on life satisfaction was marginally significant. As hypothesized, interdependent self-construal was not associated with life satisfaction at step 3, and highly independent self-construal was significantly associated with greater life satisfaction for Korean immigrants at the final step. It was striking that this single variable explained an additional 7 percent of the variance in life satisfaction [$F (1, 121) = 10.83, p < .001$]. Korean immigrants who hold a highly independent self-construal were significantly more satisfied with their lives in the U.S. than those with a less independent self-construal.

Additional analyses were also conducted to ensure that the positive relationship between higher independent self-construal and greater psychological well-being was not a function of an item overlap between the measure of independent self-construal and the measures of psychological well-being (results not shown). Hence, two items in the independent self-construal scale (i.e., feeling proud of myself and having good social skills) were excluded in forming a single scale score. When hierarchical regression analyses were repeated with this revised measure of independent self-construal, the results were the same as those of the original analyses, thus providing further support for the importance of independent self-construal in Korean immigrants' psychological well-being. In sum, the results provided full support for the study hypotheses.

DISCUSSION

This study sought to illuminate the ways in which both independent and interdependent self-views are related to Korean immigrants' well-being in the U.S. As predicted, an independent self-construal that matches the expectation of American society significantly contributed to Korean immigrants' psychological well-being. The data indicate that a clear sense of an independent self not only deters depressive symptoms, but also promotes life satisfaction for Korean immigrants in the U.S. They also provided support for the hypothesis that an interdependent self-construal would not necessarily hinder Korean immigrants' psychological well-being, controlling for the correlates of these immigrants' mental health and self-construals. These findings begin to specify the role of self-construals in Korean immigrants' well-being and highlight the importance of self-conceptions in cross-cultural adaptation.

One major interest of this study was to demonstrate the extent to which holding an independent self-construal contributes to Korean immigrants' well-being in the U.S. Hence, little attention was paid to the specific factors that may mediate the relationship between independent self-view and these immigrants' psychological well-being. For example, preferred problem solving techniques and coping strategies may vary with the nature of self-construal, and may, in turn, affect well-being. In individualist cultures, taking direct action, confronting others, or speaking up in one's own behalf are the socially sanctioned, preferred means of addressing a problem or difficulty (Wiesz, Rothbaum, & Blackburn, 1984). In dealing with problems in daily life, Korean immigrants with a highly independent self-view are more likely to employ these direct coping strategies that are functional in the U.S. Thus, they may be able to elicit approval or reward from the members of mainstream society more easily than other Koreans, and may, in turn, experience a greater sense of well-being. In Cross's (1995) study of East Asian graduate students in the U.S., she noted that those students with a highly independent self-view used more direct coping strategies that were significantly associated with lower levels of perceived stress. Another possible mediator may be a sense of mastery, which has been found to deter depressive symptoms among Koreans in Canada (Noh & Avison, 1996). Korean immigrants who strongly endorse independent self-construals are more likely to view life as being under their own control as opposed to being externally determined, and such a sense of mastery may have a salutary effect on their mental health. Further specification of the ways in which an independent self-view promotes Korean immigrants' well-being would be valuable to fully appreciate the role of self-construals in cross-cultural adaptation.

In this study, as expected, Korean immigrants who strongly endorsed interdependent self-views did not report more depressive symptoms nor less life satisfaction than did other Koreans. By contrast, poor English proficiency and perception of more personal limits–two of the predictors of Korean immigrants' interdependent self-construals–were significantly associated with higher depressive symptoms. These findings suggest that possible stressors for Korean immigrants are language barriers and a perception of personal limits rather than the interdependent self-construal. In general, however, there is a possibility of reverse causation of the factors associated with Korean immigrants' interdependent self-views and depressive symptoms. For example, this study could not determine whether limited ability in English and a perception of personal limits insulate Korean immigrants from American challenges to interdependent self-construals and promote symptoms of depression, or whether those immigrants who strongly hold interdependent self-construals perceive more difficulty in English and more personal limits in the U.S., and, in turn, develop depressive symptoms. Longitudinal research is necessary to clarify the causal direction of the relationships among interdependent self-construal, English proficiency, perception of personal limits, and psychological distress.

In sum, this study demonstrates that Korean immigrants who hold the important characteristics of an independent self experience a greater sense of overall well-being in the U.S. As argued by some researchers (Kleinman & Kleinman, 1985), the results indicate that psychological distress can have a sociocultural origin and underscore the importance of the fit between immigrants' self-conceptions and the cultural frame of their adopted country. To live successfully and effectively in the U.S., Korean immigrants need to understand American cultural meanings and practices. This study tells us that holding or taking on the American self-conception and cultural imperatives will ease these immigrants' adaptation to the U.S. and enhance their well-being. This should not obscure, however, the important meaning Korean immigrants may derive from the interdependent self-view that is valued in a Korean culture. This study also shows that holding an interdependent self-view does not hinder Korean immigrants' psychological well-being. This finding increases the possibility that interdependent self-construal may serve a positive function for them. Some researchers suggest that among individuals living in two cultures, those with a strong sense of a self, whether it is independent or interdependent, would be able to acquire more easily bicultural competence that is positively related to well-being (LaFromboise et al., 1993). To understand the potential benefits of both types of self-construal for Korean immigrants, future research needs to examine how and to what extent the interdependent self-view contributes to their well-being in the U.S.

Although the findings of this study are helpful in specifying the role of self-construals in Korean immigrants' well-being, there are some limitations to this study. First, this study was based on a regional sample, and the sample size was small. Second, the validity and reliability of the measures constructed specifically for the study need to be tested further. Third, the cross-sectional design of this study limits causal interpretations about the factors associated with Korean immigrants' psychological well-being. Finally, because this study was based on a single cultural context, it is difficult to know if the effect of independent self-construal is indeed moderated by cultural environment, even though the assumptions and interpretations provided here imply such interaction.

Implications for Social Work Practice

One of the social work profession's major goals in working with Asian immigrants or refugees is to facilitate their adaptation to the U.S. This study strongly suggests that an independent self-construal has the potential to promote these individuals' successful adaptation to American society. The results also provide support for culture learning–social skills training that helps newer Asian immigrants (or refugees) understand and incorporate American cultural meanings and practices into their self-systems (see Hyun, 1995 for discussion on culture learning training). Furthermore, an assessment of these individuals' needs must include an evaluation of their command of English. As discussed earlier, English proficiency is influential on Korean immigrants' self-construals and mental health. Limited ability in English has also been identified as a major source of distress for Asians in the U.S. (Kuo, 1984; Nicassio, Solomon, Guest, & McCullough, 1986). This study indicates that systematic, rigorous efforts to make English education service available and accessible to Asian immigrant populations are needed. Finally and most importantly, in working with individuals from Asian cultural contexts, social workers need to recognize that an interdependent self-view does not hinder their successful adaptation to the U.S. Moreover, they need to attend to and validate the positive role that an interdependent self-view may play in their American lives, as suggested by the acculturation literature.

Some findings of this study are also suggestive for the development of an effective English education curriculum for Asian immigrants and refugees. This study revealed that an independent self-construal has a beneficial effect on Korean immigrants' well-being, whereas these immigrants' perception of more personal limits, which is significantly associated with a less independent self-view (Hyun, 1999), is strongly related to higher depressive symptoms. A perusal of the items in the independent self-construal and perception of personal limit scales sheds more light on these findings. It indicates that Korean immigrants who hold a less independent self-construal and perceive more personal limits may experience difficulty in expressing and asserting themselves and may also lack culturally appropriate social skills that can promote smooth interethnic relationships. The curriculum of English education for the Asian immigrant populations can be tailored not only to teach English language, but also to teach various kinds of social skills that can facilitate their adaptation to the U.S. Some helpful social skills might include making friends, appropriate greetings, self-presentation in a job interview, making or refusing a request, expressing disagreement, and being assertive.

CONCLUSION

This study is among the first to use a community sample of adult Koreans to examine the ways in which both independent and interdependent self-views are related to Asian immigrants' psychological well-being in the U.S. The results suggest that the independent self may be a requisite to successfully living in the U.S., whereas the interdependent self may be a source for preserving cultural identity among many Asian immigrant groups that value interdependence. Future research needs to clarify further the potential benefits of both types of self-construal for Asian immigrants, and explore the ways in which to facilitate these immigrants' construction of an independent self, while at the same time nurturing the interdependent self-views they may hold.

NOTES

1. Korea has been officially divided into North Korea and South Korea since 1948. Korean immigrants mentioned in this article refer to those Koreans from South Korea.

2. Details of the sampling are available upon request.

3. Details of the questionnaire and scale construction can be obtained from the author.

4. The reliability and validity of the CES-D have been demonstrated as a screening tool for detecting depressive symptoms among various populations, including Black, Hispanic, and Asian Americans (Kuo, 1984; Golding & Burman, 1990; Noh, Avison, & Kaspar, 1992; Roberts, 1980).

5. See Kuo (1984), Hurh & Kim (1990), and Kim & Rew (1994) for details.

6. Some research has identified marital status and income as correlates of Korean immigrants' mental health (e.g., Hurh & Kim, 1990; Noh, Speechley, Kaspar, & Wu, 1992; Sasao & Chun, 1994). When these relationships were tested in the current study, however, they were not significant and were, therefore, not included in the final models.

7. Because of the problems that correlated independent variables can create with the estimation of regression coefficients, steps were taken to identify problems with multicollinearity. In case of the regressions on depressive symptoms, none was severe enough to render the regression coefficients unstable. However, variance of English proficiency and that of exposure to Western ideas in predicting life satisfaction appeared to overlap, resulting in the regression coefficients of these variables being unstable. When separate regression analyses on life satisfaction were conducted after removing one of these two in the equation, English proficiency emerged as a significant predictor of life satisfaction, whereas the effect of exposure to Western ideas remained as non-significant. However, this did not affect the magnitude of the significance of independent self-construal in explaining life satisfaction. Therefore, both variables were kept in the final models to maintain comparability of the results of the regressions on depressive symptoms and life satisfaction.

REFERENCES

Aldwin, C., & Greenberger, E. (1987). Cultural differences in the predictors of depression. *American Journal of Community Psychology, 15* (6), 789-813.

Bargh, J. A. (1982). Attention and automaticity in the processing of self-relevant information. *Journal of Personality and Social Psychology, 43*, 425-436.

Baumeister, R. (1998). The self. In D. Gilbert, S. Fiske, & G. Lindzey (Eds.), *Handbook of social psychology, Vol. 1* (pp. 680-740). New York: McGraw-Hill.

Bellah, R., Madsen, R., Sullivan, W., Swidler, A., & Tipton, S. (1985). *Habits of the heart.* New York: Harper & Row.

Berry, J. W., & Sam, D. (1997). Acculturation and adaptation. In J. W. Berry, M. H. Segall, & C. Kagitçibasi (Eds.), *Handbook of cross-cultural psychology, Vol. 3* (pp. 291-326). Needham Heights, MA: Allyn & Bacon.

Brewer, M. B., & Gardner, W. (1996). Who is this "We"? Levels of collective identity and self representations. *Journal of Personality and Social Psychology, 71* (1), 83-93.

Caplan, R. D. (1983). Person-environment fit: Past, present, and future. In C. L. Cooper (Ed.), *Stress research* (pp. 35-78). New York: Wiley.

Cross, S. (1995). Self-construals, coping, and stress in cross-cultural adaptation. *Journal of Cross-Cultural Psychology, 26* (6), 673-697.

D'Andrade, R. G. (1984). Cultural meaning systems. In R. A. Shweder & R. A. LeVine (Eds.), *Culture theory: Essays on mind, self, and emotion* (pp. 88-119). Cambridge, England: Cambridge University Press.

Fiske, A., Kitayama, S., Markus, H., & Nisbett, R. (1998). The cultural matrix of social psychology. In D. Gilbert, S. Fiske, & G. Lindzey (Eds.), *Handbook of social psychology, Vol. 2* (pp. 915-981). New York: McGraw-Hill.

Germaine, C. B. (1991). *Human behavior in the social environment.* New York: Columbia University Press.

Golding, J., & Burnam, M. A. (1990). Immigration, stress, and depressive symptoms in a Mexican-American community. *The Journal of Nervous and Mental Disease, 178* (3), 161-171.

Greene, M. A. (1997). Biculturalism and mental health among Mexican-American adolescents. Unpublished doctoral dissertation. Temple University.

Hofstede, G. (1991). *Cultures and organizations: Software of the mind.* London: McGraw-Hill.

Hurh, W. M., & Kim, K. C. (1988). Uprooting and adjustment: A sociological study of Korean immigrants' mental health. Final report to National Institute of Mental Health. Macomb, IL: Department of Sociology and Anthropology. Western Illinois University.

Hurh, W. M., & Kim, K. C. (1990). Correlates of Korean immigrants' mental health. *The Journal of Nervous and Mental Disease, 178* (11), 703-711.

Hyun, K. J. (1995). A primary prevention training model for the unmet needs of newly arrived Korean immigrants. *Prevention in Human Services, 12* (1), 25-41.

Hyun, K. J. (1999). The evolving Korean self in two sociocultural contexts: Seoul, Korea and Detroit, U.S. Unpublished manuscript. University of Chicago.

Kim, S., & Rew, L. (1994). Ethnic identity, role integration, quality of life, and depression in Korean-American women. *Archives of Psychiatric Nursing, 8* (6), 348-356.

Kincaid, D. L., & Yum, J. O. (1987). A comparative study of Korean, Filipino and Samoan immigrants to Hawaii: Socioeconomic consequences. *Human Organization, 46* (1), 70-77.

Kish, L. (1965). *Survey sampling.* New York: John Wiley & Sons.

Kleinman, A., & Kleinman, J. (1985). Somatization: The interconnections in Chinese society among culture, depressive experiences, and the meanings of pain. In A. Kleinman & B. Good (Eds.). *Culture and depression* (pp. 429-490). Berkeley, CA: University of California Press.

Kuiper, N. A., & Rogers, T. B. (1979). Encoding of personal information: Self-other differences. *Journal of Personality and Social Psychology, 37,* 499-514.

Kuo, W. H. (1984). Prevalence of depression among Asian-Americans. *The Journal of Nervous and Mental Disease, 172* (8), 449-457.

LaFromboise, T., Coleman, L. K., & Gerton, J. (1993). Psychological impact of biculturalism: Evidence and theory. *Psychological Bulletin, 114,* 395-412.

Lawton, M. P. (1983). The varieties of wellbeing. *Experimental Aging Research, 9* (2), 65-72.

Lee, Y. M. (1995). Demographic characteristics of Korean Americans. *WE, Summer,* 43-44.

Lin-Fu, J. (1988). Population characteristics and health care needs of Asian Pacific Americans. *Public Health Reports, 103* (1), 18-27.

Lopez, E. M. (1996). The immigrant experience of Latin Americans in the United States: Is self-affirmation paving the way to a successful adaptation? Unpublished doctoral dissertation. State University New York at Buffalo.

Markus, H., & Kitayama, S. (1991). Culture and the self: Implications for cognition, emotion, and motivation. *Psychological Review, 98* (2), 224-253.

Markus, H., & Kitayama, S. (1994). The cultural construction of self and emotion: Implications for social behavior. In S. Kitayama & H. Markus (Eds.), *Emotion and culture: Empirical studies of mutual influence* (pp. 89-130). Washington, DC: American Psychological Association.

Markus, H., & Wurf, E. (1987). The dynamic self-concept: A social psychological perspective. *Annual Review of Psychology, 38,* 29-337.

Merton, R. M. (1968). *Social theory and social structure.* New York: Free Press.

Misra, G., & Giri, R. (1995). Is Indian self predominantly interdependent? *Journal of Indian Psychology, 13* (1), 16-29.

Nicassio, P., Solomon, G., Guest, S., & McCullough, J. (1986). Emigration stress and language proficiency as correlates of depression in a sample of Southeast Asian refugees. *International Journal of Social Psychiatry, 32* (1), 22-28.

Niedenthal, P. M., Cantor, N., & Kihlstrom, J. (1985). Prototype-matching: A strategy for social decision-making. *Journal of Personality and Social Psychology, 48,* 575-584.

Noh, S., & Avison, W. (1996). Asian immigrants and the stress process: A study of Koreans in Canada. *Journal of Health and Social Behavior, 37,* 192-206.

Noh, S., Avison, W., & Kaspar, V. (1992). Depressive symptoms among Korean immigrants: Assessment of a translation of the Center for Epidemiologic Studies-Depression scale. *Psychological Assessment, 4* (1), 84-91.

Noh, S., Speechley, M., Kaspar, V., & Wu, Z. (1992). Depression in Korean immigrants in Canada: I. Method of the study and prevalence of depression. *The Journal of Nervous and Mental Disease, 180* (9), 573-577.

Okazaki, S. (1994). Cultural variations in the self and emotional distress. Unpublished doctoral dissertation. University of California, Los Angeles.

Okazaki, S. (1997). Sources of ethnic differences between Asian American and White American college students on measures of depression and social anxiety. *Journal of Abnormal Psychology, 106* (1), 52-60.

Radloff, L. S., & Locke, B. (1986). The community mental health survey and the CES-D scale. In M. Weissman, J. Myers, & C. Ross (Eds.), *Community surveys of psychiatric disorders* (pp. 177-189). New Brunswick, NJ: Rutgers University Press.

Roberts, R. E. (1980). Reliability of the CES-D scale in different ethnic contexts. *Psychiatry Research, 2,* 125-134.

Sasao, T., & Chun, C. (1994). After the *Sa-i-gu* (April 29) Los Angeles riots: Correlates of subjective well-being in the Korean-American community. *Journal of Community Psychology, 22* (4), 136-152.

Schmitz, P. G. (1990). Individualism-collectivism and acculturation modes. Paper presented at the International Conference on the Individualism and Collectivism, Seoul, July.

Searle, W., & Ward, C. (1990). The prediction of psychological and sociocultural adjustment during cross-cultural transitions. *International Journal of Intercultural Relations, 14,* 449-464.

Seipel, M. (1988). Locus of control as related to life experiences of Korean immigrants. *International Journal of Intercultural Relations, 12* (1), 61-71.

Shin, K. R. (1994). Psychosocial predictors of depressive symptoms in Korean-American women in New York city. *Women & Health, 21* (1), 73-84.

Singelis, T. M. (1994). The measurement of independent and interdependent self-construals. *Personality and Social Psychology Bulletin, 20* (5), 580-591.

Triandis, H. C. (1989). The self and social behavior in differing cultural contexts. *Psychological Review, 96,* 506-520.

Triandis, H. C. (1990). Cross-cultural studies of individualism and collectivism.

Nebraska Symposium on Motivation (pp. 41-133). Lincoln, NB: University of Nebraska Press.

Weisz, J. R., Rothbaum, F., & Blackburn, T. C. (1984). Standing out and standing in: The Psychology of control in America and Japan. *American Psychologist, 39,* 955-969.

APPENDIX

I. *Interdependent Self-Construal Scale*

1. I will sacrifice my self interest for the benefit of those people who are important to me.
2. I always try to put myself in the other person's shoes.
3. I always try to maintain harmony with those around me.
4. I feel guilty when I say "No" to someone who asks me a favor or for help.
5. In making decisions, I always consider how my decision will affect others before I consider how it will affect me.
6. If it will make things easier for the people I care about, I don't mind changing my own decision.
7. It is difficult for me to say "No" to someone who asks me a favor or for help.
8. I often have the feeling that my relationship with my family and close friends are more important than my own accomplishments.
9. If I fail to behave well as a parent or a son/daughter or both, I feel guilty.
10. If I think I have failed to behave or perform appropriately in accordance with my social status as expected by others, I feel shame.
11. When I watch a sad movie, I feel sad easily and even shed tears sometimes.
12. I think I am an ordinary person.
13. I feel affection and intimacy in the we-ness feeling I get from the people with whom I can identify.
14. Whenever others pay attention to me, I feel shy.
15. I think the various roles I perform as a member of my family constitute the most important part of myself.
16. If other people do not like my idea, I tend to change it, even though I like it.
17. If what I believe is right hurts other people's feelings, I usually do not insist on it.

II. *Independent Self-Construal Scale*

1. I am usually assertive about my own rights.
2. Even though people around me may hold a different opinion, I stick to what I believe in.
3. I strive to achieve my life goals not for anybody else, but for my own sake.
4. I usually express my thoughts and feelings openly.
5. Nothing can keep me from doing something if I want to do it.
6. I prefer to be direct and straightforward when dealing with people I have just met.
7. I think I am an independent human being.
8. I always try to pursue my own happiness.
9. In any situation, I don't do what I don't want to do.
10. Even when I strongly disagree with my boss or my professor, I tend to go along with them.[a]
11. I often feel proud of myself.
12. I have good social skills necessary to meet people and make friends.

[a]Item 10 was reversed in calculating the mean.

Model Minority Demystified:
Emotional Costs
of Multiple Victimizations
in the Lives of Women of Japanese Descent

Mieko Yoshihama

SUMMARY. This population-based study investigated the prevalence of domestic violence and other types of interpersonal victimization among a random sample of women of Japanese descent (immigrants from Japan and Japanese Americans) in Los Angeles. This study found a high prevalence of domestic violence, as well as other types of violence, perpetrated by non-intimates. Differences by country of birth were found in some, but not all, types of victimization; a larger proportion of Japan-born respondents reported experiencing contact and no-contact sexual violence perpetrated by non-intimates and witnessing their fathers' violence against their mothers. The severity of domestic violence experienced during the respondents' lifetimes was significantly

Mieko Yoshihama, MSW, ACSW, PhD, is affiliated with School of Social Work, University of Michigan, 1080 S. University, Ann Arbor, MI 48109-1106 (E-mail: miekoy@umich.edu).

The author would like to thank the interviewers, as well as Kiyoko Fukushima and Noriko Tsukada, who assisted in the translation of the research instruments and data entry. Special thanks to Arno K. Kumagai and Carol Mowbray for their thoughtful review of the manuscript and many valuable discussions and to Jan Anderson and Kimberly Clum for their skillful editorial assistance. The author wishes to express special gratitude to the 211 women who participated in the study and who spoke candidly about their experiences with domestic violence.

This study was partially funded by the National Institute of Mental Health (RO3 MH54351-01) with additional funding from the University of Michigan Office of Vice President for Research and School of Social Work.

[Haworth co-indexing entry note]: "Model Minority Demystified: Emotinal Costs of Multiple Victimizations in the Lives of Women of Japanese Descent." Yoshihama, Mieko. Co-published simultaneously in *Journal of Human Behavior in the Social Environment* (The Haworth Press, Inc.) Vol. 3, No. 3/4, 2001, pp. 201-224; and: *Psychosocial Aspects of the Asian American Experience: Diversity Within Diversity* (ed: Namkee G. Choi) The Haworth Press, Inc., 2001, pp. 201-224. Single or multiple copies of this article are available for a fee from The Haworth Document Delivery Service [1-800-342-9678, 9:00 a.m. - 5:00 p.m. (EST). E-mail address: getinfo@haworthpressinc.com].

201

associated with a higher degree of psychological distress. Findings question the commonly presumed image of the model minority and call for increased efforts to assess the history of domestic violence and other types of interpersonal victimization when working with women of Japanese descent. *[Article copies available for a fee from The Haworth Document Delivery Service: 1-800-342-9678. E-mail address: <getinfo@haworthpressinc. com> Website: <http://www.HaworthPress.com> © 2001 by The Haworth Press, Inc. All rights reserved.]*

KEYWORDS. Domestic violence, sexual violence, women abuse, mental health, Japanese American

The National Violence Against Women Survey (NVAWS), a large-scale nationwide study, found women of Asian Pacific descent to have the lowest rate of physical and sexual assault victimization of any major racial or ethnic group (Tjaden & Thoennes, 1998). This finding of the NVAWS, the largest survey of its kind, appears to be consistent with the image of the model minority. What the NVAWS does not tell us, however, are the rates of victimization among the various ethnic groups of Asian Pacific descent in the U.S., such as Japanese American and Chinese American, nor variations by immigration status within a single ethnic group.

The Asian Pacific population in the U.S. is not a monolithic population. Enormous diversity exists among its ethnic subgroups with respect to socio-economic characteristics, reflecting in part different socio-historical contexts within which they themselves or their ancestors immigrated to the U.S. or arrived as refugees. Such diversity warns against aggregation of subgroups (Uehara, Takeuchi, & Smukler, 1994). In an attempt to fill this gap in empirical research on domestic violence among Asian Pacific Americans, the present study employed a different approach from that of the NVAWS. Instead of aggregating women of any Asian Pacific descent, this study focused on women of a single ethnic background, the Japanese, one of the largest subgroups of the population in the U.S. Nationwide, there are approximately 850,000 individuals of Japanese descent, 15% of whom reside in Los Angeles County (U.S. Census Bureau, 1994), where this study was conducted. The inclusion of women who share a single cultural background but were born in two different countries (the U.S. and Japan) allowed for the investigation of the experience of domestic violence victimization by immigration status.

Using an expanded and more culturally relevant measure of domestic violence, this study investigated women's experience of domestic violence and other types of interpersonal victimization among a community-based random sample of women. Based on the stress-distress model, the relationship between the experience of domestic violence and the level of psychological distress was also examined, while taking into consideration various other types of victimization. Specifically, this study investigated the following hypotheses: (1) Women's immigration status is not associated with domestic violence victimization; and (2) The level of psychological distress experienced by women is associated with the severity of domestic violence victimization and that of other types of victimization perpetrated by non-intimates. In addition, this study also investigated whether specific types of partners' violence (e.g., physical violence, emotional violence, and sexual violence) were more likely to contribute to negative mental health.

DOMESTIC VIOLENCE AGAINST ASIAN PACIFIC AMERICAN WOMEN

In the U.S., it is estimated that at a minimum 22-31% of women experience physical violence at the hands of a male intimate partner sometime during their lives (Neff, Holamon, & Schluter, 1995; Tjaden & Thoennes, 1998). Although research on domestic violence has proliferated in the U.S. over the last two decades, domestic violence in Asian Pacific American communities has received little attention. Recently, however, studies of domestic violence are slowly emerging in several areas in these diverse communities. Attitudinal studies have documented a relatively high degree of tolerance for domestic violence among Asian Pacific Americans (Family Violence Prevention Fund, 1993; Yick & Agbayani-Siewert, 1997). Qualitative and descriptive studies have elucidated values and attitudes shared in Asian Pacific cultures that condone women's subordinate status in the family and men's use of violence against women, thereby contributing to the vulnerability of women of Asian Pacific descent (Agtuca, 1992; Dasgupta & Warrier, 1996; Ho, 1990; Song-Kim, 1992; Yoshihama, 2000). Most of these studies have focused on specific ethnic subgroups, due in large part to the enormous cultural and linguistic diversity among Asian Pacific American populations.

Despite the increase in research on domestic violence against Asian Pacific American women, population-based studies remain scarce. In the absence of this type of study, the prevalence of domestic violence victimization among Asian Pacific American women is estimated based on agency-based data, such as the number of cases reported to law enforcement, the criminal justice system, shelters, and social service agencies (e.g., U.S. Commission on Civil Rights, 1992). The number of Asian Pacific American battered women known to legal or social service agencies, however, represents only the tip of the iceberg because there are many barriers to seeking and accessing services, such as financial constraints and a lack of transportation. Like other women of color, Asian Pacific American women may face additional barriers, such as a lack of culturally competent services and cultural norms discouraging use of outside assistance services (Lai, 1986; Richie & Kanuha, 1993; Yoshihama, 2000). For immigrants and refugee women, limited familiarity with the U.S. social system and a lack of bilingual services may create additional obstacles. Reliable prevalence estimates of domestic violence are indispensable to developing services for Asian Pacific American battered women, some of whom may have special needs.

In various Asian Pacific countries, population-based studies found rates of domestic violence victimization that are comparable to the rates in the U.S. (Hoffman, Demo, & Edwards, 1994; Kim & Cho, 1992; Nelson & Zimmerman, 1996; Tokyo-to, 1998). These findings suggest that immigrant women from Asian Pacific countries experience domestic violence. Whether the rates of domestic violence vary by immigration status among Asian Pacific Americans, however, remains unexamined. Studies of persons of Mexican descent in the U.S. have found a significantly lower rate of domestic violence among immigrants born in Mexico than that among U.S.-born Mexican Americans (Kaufman Kantor, Jasinski, & Aldarondo, 1994; Sorenson & Telles, 1991). These findings underscore the importance of considering within-group differences by country of birth.

Mental Health Effects of Domestic Violence

Over the last several decades, research has examined the psychosocial etiology of mental health problems and has implicated a wide range of life events and ongoing strains as significant risk factors for psychological distress (Avison & Turner, 1988; Kessler & Wethington, 1991). This stress-distress framework has been applied to studies of the relationship between domestic violence victimization and mental health in women. Studies have consistently found a strong and significant relationship between the experience of domestic violence and various symptoms of distress, such as depressive symptoms, heightened anxiety, and post-traumatic stress symptoms (Astin, Lawrence, & Foy, 1993; Houskamp & Foy, 1991; Kemp, Green, Hovanitz, & Rawlings, 1995; Kemp, Rawlings, & Green, 1991; also see Campbell & Lewandowski, 1997 and Golding, 1996 for a comprehensive review). Among those women who have experienced partners' violence, the severer the victimization, the severer the level of distress. Domestic violence takes various forms, such as physical, sexual, and emotional violence, and often is perpetrated repeatedly over a period of time. Although most previous studies have focused on physical violence, a number of recent studies have found partners' emotional violence to be significantly associated with psychological distress (Dutton, Goodman, & Bennett, 1999; Sackett & Saunders, 1999; Tolman & Bhosley, 1991). These findings call for increased attention to this previously neglected form of partners' violence.

The relationship between experiences of domestic violence and women's psychological well-being may be confounded by other victimizations experienced by women. Recent or concurrent stressors, such as negative life events and strains, are likely to affect the environment within which women attempt to cope with domestic violence. Studies have found a higher level of distress among battered women who experienced child abuse or recent stressors than among those who did not (Astin et al., 1993; Campbell, Kub, Belknap, Templin, & Thomas, 1997; Kemp et al., 1995). Victimization by someone other than a male partner, such as child abuse, physical assault, property crime, and sexual assault, is common in the lives of women (Finkelhor, Hotaling, Lewin, & Smith, 1990; Norris, 1992; Resnick, Kilpatrick, Dansky, Saunders, & Best, 1993; Russell, 1983a, 1983b; Sheffield, 1993). Examinations of the relationship between the experience of domestic violence experiences and mental health must account for multiple victimizations women may have experienced and the impact of recent stressors.

Women's victimization has received little attention in mental health research on Asian Pacific Americans. As is the case with domestic violence, population-based research on child abuse, sexual violence, and other types of victimization among Asian Pacific American women is scarce. One notable exception is a recent study of Chinese Americans in Los Angeles, which found a strong association between the lifetime experience of depression and dysthymia and the lifetime experience of traumatic life events (Takeuchi, Chung, Lin et al., 1998). Although this study examined the respondents' experience of rape, sexual molestation, child abuse, and neglect, the specific relationship between these types of victimization and affective disorders was not reported (Takeuchi et al., 1998). Other existing studies are primarily descriptive studies of child abuse cases (Ima & Hohm, 1991; Rao, Di Clemente, & Ponton, 1992) or incidents of hate crimes (National Asian Pacific American Legal Consortium, 1996). The present study expands research on Asian Pacific Americans' mental health by focusing specifically on domestic violence and other types of interpersonal victimization experienced by a community-based random sample of women.

METHODS

Sampling Method and Interview Procedures

The respondents were 211 women randomly selected from a list of households containing persons with a Japanese surname in Los Angeles County. Following the introductory letter, a screening telephone call was made to the household to identify any woman who met the following criteria: Japanese descent, born in the U.S. or Japan, age between 18 and 49, and having had an intimate heterosexual relationship. Only one woman per household was selected using a random procedure, the next birthday method. At this time, a detailed explanation about the purpose and procedures of the study, potential risks, the participant's rights, and the limitations of confidentiality (e.g., the need to report suspected child abuse) was provided verbally. Face-to-face interviews were conducted by trained interviewers who were matched to the respondent's preferred language (English or Japanese); the interviewers were of Japanese or other Asian Pacific descent. A written consent was obtained at the beginning of the interview. In addition to approval from the Institutional Review Board, a Certificate of Confidentiality was obtained from the National Institute of Mental Health, Department of Health and Human Services. The interview was audiotaped if the respondent consented (67% of the cases). On average, the interview lasted 90 minutes. At the end of the interview, the respondent received $20 and a list of available assistance programs, including those services provided in Japanese. All respondents were also asked whether they wished to speak to a counselor, and a referral for counseling was made if needed. Of the 407 households that were determined to have at least one eligible woman, a total of 211 women completed the interview–a response rate of 52%. Demographically, the respondents were not significantly different from non-participants, except that the respondents (mean age 37.2) were younger than non-participants (mean age 40.6).

MEASURES

Domestic Violence Victimization

Using behavior-specific questions, the respondent was asked whether she had ever experienced, at the hands of her current or former partners, each of 31 forms of physical violence, ranging from pushing to use of lethal weapons; 21 forms of emotional violence, ranging from verbal debasement and restriction of social activities to threat of physical violence, and 11 forms of sexual violence, ranging from unwanted touching to forced intercourse. These items were drawn from various studies in the United States and Japan (Marshall, 1992; Straus & Gelles, 1986; Tolman, 1989; Yoshihama & Sorenson, 1994) and included forms of domestic violence reported by Japanese women in previous studies in Japan (e.g., overturning a dining table, refusing to use contraceptives) (Yoshihama & Sorenson, 1994). Specific forms of violence examined were described in Yoshihama (1999). The age at which the respondent first experienced each type of violence was also obtained.

Additional questions asked included whether the respondent had ever sustained injuries due to a partner's violence, whether she had sought counseling, whether the partner's violence was reported to the police, and whether the partner also abused her and/or his children. If there were multiple perpetrators, the information was obtained regarding the one who the respondent considered to have perpetrated the most serious incident.

Other Types of Victimization

Two types of victimization in the family were examined: the respondent was asked whether she had been physically abused by her parents during childhood and whether, to her knowledge, her father had physically abused her mother.

A series of behavior-specific questions examined four types of victimization perpetrated by non-intimates during the respondents' lifetimes: (1) contact sexual violence (2 items), which included unwanted touching of breasts and genital areas and sexual assault; (2) no-contact sexual violence (4 items), which included stalking, exhibitionism, obscene phone calls, and voyeurism; (3) physical assault (3 items), which included mugging, race-based assault, and other types of physical assault; and (4) property crimes (4 items), including car theft, household burglary, theft of personal items from a car, and purse snatching or pick-pocketing.

Immigration Status

Although many previous studies of domestic violence have used country of birth as a crude indicator of immigration status (or generation position), the life experience of those who immigrated to the U.S. during pre-teen years (sometimes referred to as the 1.5 generation) may be more similar to the experience of those who were born in the U.S. than to that of those who immigrated as an adolescent or as an adult (Allensworth, 1997; Myers & Cranford, 1998). Thus, in this study, comparisons were made between those born in the U.S. or those who immigrated to the U.S. before age 13 (the 1.5 and higher generation, hereinafter, n = 167) and those who immigrated to the U.S. at age 13 and older (the first generation, hereinafter, n = 44).

Psychological Distress

The current level of psychological distress was measured using the Symptoms Check List-90R (SCL-90R); the SCL-90R was self-administered by the respondents during the face-to-face interview according to the instructions of the scale author (Derogatis, 1994). This measure was chosen based on its validity and reliability with the Japanese American population (Takeuchi, Kuo, Kim, & Leaf, 1990) and also, in part, due to the availability of a version translated into Japanese. The Global Severity Index of the SCL-90R (SCL-90R GSI), calculated by dividing the sum score of all 90 symptoms by the total number of responses (Derogatis, 1994), was used as an indicator of the current level of overall psychological distress. This score, which ranges from 0 to 4, combines information concerning the range of psychological distress (e.g., the number of symptoms experienced) with that of the intensity of distress. A higher GSI score indicates a higher level of distress during the previous week. The internal consistencies for the nine specific dimensions for 1.5 and higher generation respondents (Cronbach's α = .82 to .91) and those for first generation Japan-born respondents (Cronbach's α = .74 to .93) were comparable to that reported by the scale author (Cronbach's α = .77 to .90, Derogatis, Richels, & Rock, 1976).

Recent Stressors

The respondent was asked whether she experienced specific types of stressful life events or ongoing strains during the previous 12 months. Drawing from previous studies (Aneshensel, Rutter, & Lachenbruch, 1991; Golding & Burnam, 1990), stressors in the following eight domains were investigated: serious illness or injury of the respondents; serious illness or injury of family members or friends; events or strains in the workplace or school; transition in life (e.g., children leaving home); financial difficulties; stressful events occurring to people in the social network; accidents and natural disasters; and other. As was done in Aneshensel and colleagues, the experience of stressors in each domain was scored dichotomously, either present (1) or absent (0), and a composite score of the level of recent stressors was computed by summing the scores of each of the nine categories, resulting in a score of 0 to 8.

Control Variables

In the analysis of the relationship between victimization experiences and psychological distress, the respondent's age was included as a control variables based on previous research that documents a significant relationship between age and psychological distress (Kessler, McGonagle, Zhao, Nelson, Hughes, Eshleman et al., 1994; Robins, Locke, & Regier, 1991). An age adjustment was also necessary because an increase in age is associated with increased exposure to risks for victimization (Yoshihama & Gillespie, under review).

Analysis

In addition to the proportion of respondents who reported experiencing various types of partners' violence (physical, emotional, sexual, and any violence), the severity of specific types of victimization was assessed by computing the number of specific forms of violence experienced for each type of partners' violence (physical, emotional, and sexual). Because the exposure to risk for domestic violence is positively associated with age, age-adjusted estimates of the probability of experiencing partners' physical, emotional, and sexual violence were obtained using a method of survival analysis, the Kaplan-Meier estimator (KM estimator). This analysis takes the possibility that women who have not been abused at the time of the interview may be abused at a later date into account in estimating the probability of experiencing violence. The KM estimator provides the estimated cumulative probability of experiencing partners' violence by a certain age. Thus, the KM estimate at age 49 (the maximum value in the respondents' age distribution) was calculated for partners' physical, emotional, and sexual violence as a proxy estimate of the lifetime prevalence, assuming that the probability of experiencing partners' violence for the first time after age 50 is slim. Differences in the probability of experiencing partners' violence in connection with immigration status (1.5 or above vs. first generation) were assessed using the logrank test.

Similarly, the proportion of women who had witnessed a father's violence towards a mother, as well as the proportions of women who had experienced childhood physical abuse, contact sexual violence, no-contact sexual violence, physical assault, and property crimes, were computed. In addition, for the latter four types of victimization, which were assessed using multiple items, the number of items endorsed was computed as an indicator of the severity. Differences by immigration status were examined by chi-square statistics or t-tests.

One-tailed t-tests were used to compare the mean SCL-GSI scores between women who had experienced any domestic violence and those who had not. To test whether the experience of domestic violence and other interpersonal victimization contributes to a higher level of current psychological distress, multiple regression analysis was performed using the ordinary least square (OLS) method with SCL-90R GSI as an outcome variable.

RESULTS

Respondents

The majority of respondents were married or in a committed relationship (76%) and employed (78%) at the time of the interview (Table 1). Approximately half had graduated from college and had an annual household income of more than $60,000. Nearly half had an annual personal income of less than $15,000. The respondents were comparable to the general population of

TABLE 1. The Respondents' Socio-Demographic Characteristics by Immigration Status

	Total n = 211	1.5 and higher generation n = 167	First generation n = 44	Significance test
Mean age (SD)	37.2 (10.2)	36.0 (10.7)	41.7 (5.8)	$t = 4.76, p < .001$
Mean years of schooling (SD)	15.3 (2.0)	15.4 (2.0)	14.6 (1.8)	$t = 2.48, p = .014$
% employed	77.7	78.4	75.0	$\chi^2 = .24, ns$
% married or in committed relationship	76.3	71.9	93.2	$\chi^2 = 8.76 \, p = .003$
% with household income <$60,000	63.2	67.5	47.7	$\chi^2 = 5.79, p = .016$
% with personal income <$15,000	55.2	58.1	44.2	$\chi^2 = 2.67, ns$
Level of psychological distress [SCL-90R GSI] (SD)	.46 (.50)	.48 (.50)	.37 (.48)	$t = 1.28, ns$
Recent stressors (SD)	2.08 (1.13)	2.01(1.10)	2.32 (1.22)	$t = 1.61, ns$

women of Japanese descent aged 18 to 49 (at the 1990 census) in Los Angeles County born in the United States or Japan, with respect to marital status, employment status, and education. However, women with higher personal and household incomes were overrepresented in this study.

One fourth of the respondents (27%, n = 57) were born in Japan, a proportion comparable to that in the general population of Japanese descent in Los Angeles County. The length of stay in the United States among Japan-born respondents varied considerably (range 3-42), with the mean being 19 years (SD = 10.9). Thirteen respondents immigrated to the U.S. before age 13, whereas 44 did so at age 13 and older. The former lived in the U.S. for a significantly longer period (M = 34.1, SD = 7.2) than the latter (M = 14.5, SD = 7.2), $t = 8.62, p < .001$. Those two groups were also different with respect to their English proficiency and ethnic identity, with the former more likely to be interviewed in English ($\chi^2 = 40.9, p < .001$) and to identify themselves as Japanese Americans as opposed to Japanese ($\chi^2 = 31.2, p < .001$).

As indicated previously, comparisons were made between the 1.5 or higher generation (i.e., respondents who immigrated to the U.S. before age 13 and those who were born in the U.S.) and the first generation (those who immigrated to the U.S. at age 13 and older). The former tended to be older, $t = 4.76, p < .001$, to have had more schooling, $\chi^2 = 2.48, p = .014$, and to have higher household incomes, $\chi^2 = 5.79, p = .016$. No differences by immigration status were found with respect to employment status, personal income, current stressors, or current distress.

Experiences of Domestic Violence

Of the total respondents, 80% (n = 169) reported experiencing some type of partners' violence during their lifetimes. Using two-sample t-test and Chi-square analysis, respondents' demographic characteristics were compared between women who had experienced partners' violence and those who had not. There were no significant group differences with respect to age, education, employment status, relationship status, household income, or personal income.

With respect to the specific type of partners' violence, 52% of the respondents (n = 109) experienced physical violence, 76% emotional violence (n = 160), and 30% sexual violence (n = 63) (see Table 2). Seventeen respondents (8%) had been injured at least once due to a partner's violence, eight of whom were injured multiple times; three respondents had been injured during the previous year. Of the 169 respondents who experienced partners' violence, 27 (16%) had sought assistance from counselors. Only two cases were known to the police. Thirteen (6%) of the total respondents (20% of those respondents with children) stated that their partners abused the children as well.

The Kaplan-Meier estimate of the cumulative probability of experiencing partners' violence at age 49, the estimate of the lifetime prevalence, was 57% for physical violence, 79% for emotional violence, and 35% for sexual violence. No differences by immigration status were found for the probability of experiencing partners' physical or sexual violence. However, 1.5 and higher generation respondents were more likely to experience partners' emotional violence than the first generation respondents (logrank = 12.68, $df = 1$, $p = .0004$). (Cox regression analysis controlling for the respondents' education, relationship status, and household income yielded results consistent with those using the KM estimator.)

OTHER TYPES OF VICTIMIZATION

Respondents reported experiencing various other types of victimization (see Table 2). One in eight (13%) reported having been physically abused as a child by parents. Thirty-eight women (18%) indicated that they had witnessed, or known through other means, their fathers' abuse toward their mothers. A significantly higher proportion of first generation respondents reported their fathers' violence towards their mothers than did 1.5 and higher generation respondents, $\chi^2 = 12.68$, $p < .001$. One third reported contact sexual violence, and three fourths reported at least one form of no-contact sexual violence, such as obscene phone calls, flashing, and voyeurism. The

TABLE 2. The Respondents' Experiences with Victimization by Immigration Status

		Total n = 211	1.5 and higher generation n = 167	First generation n = 44	Significance test
Experiences of Domestic Violence					
Any Domestic Violence:	% Experienced	80.1	82.0	72.7	$\chi^2 = 1.89$, *ns*
	Mean severity (*SD*)	1.95 (1.36)	1.96 (1.34)	1.89 (1.43)	*t* = .34, *ns*
Physical Violence:	% Experienced	51.7	51.5	52.3	
	KM estimate at age 49	57.4	58.0	54.5	Logrank 1.19, *ns*
	Mean severity (*SD*)	1.54 (2.52)	1.53 (2.52)	1.59 (2.54)	*t* = .14, *ns*
Emotional Violence:	% Experienced	75.8	78.4	65.9	
	KM estimate at age 49	79.4	82.2	69.3	Logrank 12.68, *p* = .0004
	Mean severity (*SD*)	3.25 (3.28)	3.32 (3.22)	2.98 (3.51)	*t* = .62, *ns*
Sexual Violence:	% Experienced	29.9	30.5	27.3	
	KM estimate at age 49	35.2	35.5	32.0	Logrank 1.34, *ns*
	Mean severity (*SD*)	.59 (1.14)	.62 (1.19)	.48 (.93)	*t* = .75, *ns*
Other Types of Victimization					
Parental Physical Abuse:	% Experienced	13.3	12.6	15.9	$\chi^2 = .34$, *ns*
Father's Domestic Violence:	% Witnessed	18.0	13.2	36.4	$\chi^2 = 12.68$, *p* <.001
Contact Sexual Violence:	% Experienced	33.6	29.9	47.7	$\chi^2 = 4.94$, *p* = .026
	Mean severity (*SD*)	.36 (.52)	.32 (.52)	.48 (.51)	*t* = 1.76, *p* = .08
No–Contact Sexual Violence:	% Experienced	74.9	71.9	86.4	$\chi^2 = 3.90$, *p* = .048
	Mean severity (*SD*)	1.30 (1.03)	1.16 (.97)	1.84 (1.10)	*t* = 4.01, *p* < .001
Physical Assault:	% Experienced	18.5	19.2	15.9	$\chi^2 = .25$, *ns*
	Mean severity (*SD*)	.21 (.46)	.21 (.45)	.20 (.51)	*t* = .06, *ns*
Property Crimes:	% Experienced	80.1	82.6	70.5	$\chi^2 = 3.24$, *p* = .07
	Mean severity (*SD*)	1.37 (.95)	1.42 (.93)	1.18 (1.04)	*t* = 1.47, *ns*

majority (80%) reported having experienced some form of property crime, and 19% had been physically assaulted by someone other than their male intimate partners. There was a significant association between immigration status and both forms of sexual violence, with a higher proportion of the first generation respondents reporting contact sexual violence, $\chi^2 = 4.94$, $p = .026$ and no-contact sexual violence, $\chi^2 = 3.90$, $p = .048$. The severity of these

types of victimization was also significantly higher among the first generation respondents than the 1.5 and higher generation. Post-hoc analyses found
that the first generation respondents were more likely to report unwanted
touching and exhibitionism than were the 1.5 and higher generation respondents. The age at which the first generation respondents experienced unwanted
touching ranged from 4 to 39 and that for exhibitionism ranged from 5 to 49;
the vast majority of them had first experienced an incident in Japan prior to
relocating to the U.S. (83%, 84%, respectively).

PSYCHOLOGICAL DISTRESS AND ITS RELATIONSHIP
TO DOMESTIC VIOLENCE

The mean SCL-GSI score for the total respondents in the present study
was .46 (SD = .50, Range = 0-2.69). This mean was slightly higher than that
of a non-patient female adult normative sample provided by the scale author
(M = .36, SD = .35, Derogatis, 1994). No difference by immigration status
was found, t = 1.28, p = .20. The degree of psychological distress was
significantly higher among those women who had experienced partners'
violence of any kind than those who had not, M = .50 (SD = .52) vs. M = .29
(SD = .34), t = 3.28, p = .001. The difference was in the hypothesized
direction.

Table 3 presents the results of OLS multiple regression analysis predicting
the level of psychological distress. Using the block entry method, age and
immigration status were first entered, which explained 9% of the variance.
[Although the first generation and the 1.5 and higher generation respondents
were significantly different with respect to current relationship status and
education, including those variables in the model which resulted in little
change, and therefore a more parsimonious model is presented here.] Childhood physical abuse, witnessing the father's violence against the mother, and
four types of lifetime victimization by non-intimates were entered next,
which explained an additional 14% of the variance. The experiences of childhood physical abuse and property crimes were significantly positively associated with the severity of psychological distress. Partners' physical violence
was entered next, and it explained an additional 2% of the variance and was
significantly associated with the level of psychological distress. When the
severity of emotional violence and sexual violence were entered, the severity
of partners' physical violence was no longer significant. Instead, the severity
of partners' emotional violence was significantly associated with the level of
psychological distress. The level of recent stressors was entered last, and it
was not associated with the level of psychological distress. Overall, the
model explained 29% of the total variance in current psychological distress
(adjusted R^2 = .25). The interaction between partners' physical violence and

TABLE 3. Results of Multiple Regression Analysis: Standardized Betas and Unstandardized Betas (SE) for Current Psychological Distress ($N = 211$)

Block	I β	I b (se)	II β	II b (se)	III β	III b (se)	IV β	IV b (se)	V β	V b (se)
1 Age (years)	−.29	−.01 (.003)****	−.35	−.02 (.003)****	−.35	−.02 (.003)****	−.36	−.02 (.003)****	−.36	−.02 (.003)****
Immigration status (1.5+ generation)	−.02	−.03 (.08)	−.06	−.07 (.08)	−.05	−.06 (.08)	−.02	−.03 (.08)	−.03	−.04 (.08)
2 Child physical abuse			.24	.35 (.10)***	.20	.30 (.10)***	.20	.29 (.10)***	.20	.29 (.10)***
Witnessing father's DV			.11	.14 (.09)	.12	.15 (.09)*	.11	.14 (.09)	.10	.13 (.09)
Contact sexual violence			−.03	−.03 (.06)	−.04	−.04 (.06)	−.06	−.05 (.06)	−.05	−.05 (.06)
No-contact sexual violence			.12	.06 (.03)*	.08	.04 (.03)	.07	.03 (.03)	.07	.03 (.03)
Physical assault			−.10	−.10 (.07)	−.09	−.10 (.07)	−.10	−.11 (.07)	−.10	−.10 (.07)
Property crimes			.17	.09 (.03)**	.16	.08 (.03)**	.14	.07 (.03)**	.14	.07 (.03)**
3 Severity of partners' PV					.16	.03 (.01)**	−.02	−.003 (.02)	−.02	−.004 (.02)
4 Severity of partners' EV							.23	.03 (.01)***	.22	.03 (.01)***
Severity of partners' SV							.08	.04 (.03)	.08	.03 (.03)
5 Recent stressors									.09	.04 (.03)
Change in R^2				.14		.02		.04		.007
F test for R^2 change				$F_{(6,202)} = 5.89$****		$F_{(1,201)} = 5.69$**		$F_{(2,199)} = 7.18$		$F_{(1,198)} = 1.93$
R^2 (Adjusted R^2)		.09 (.08)		.22 (.19)		.24 (.21)		.28 (.24)		.29 (.25)
Overall F test		$F_{(2,208)} = 9.79$****		$F_{(8,202)} = 721$****		$F_{(9,201)} = 7.19$***		$F_{(11,199)} = 718$****		$F_{(12,198)} = 6.77$****

DV = domestic violence; PV = physical violence; EV = emotional violence; SV = sexual violence
* < .10   ** < .05   *** < .01   **** < .001

emotional violence, or any other interaction between types of partners' violence, was not significant (not shown).

DISCUSSION

Multiple Victimizations

This study is the first to document the prevalence of domestic violence in an Asian Pacific American population in the United States. The study respondents had relatively high levels of education and household income. These characteristics may contribute to the image of the successful, model minority which does not suffer from the social ills that afflict other racial groups of color. However, this study questions the image of the successful minority by revealing a higher level of psychological distress among women of Japanese descent than that found among a normative female sample. The probability of domestic violence victimization among women of Japanese descent was high. Many types of sexual violence victimization, such as stalking, exhibitionism, and unwanted touching, were also prevalent. So were property and violent crimes, such as household burglary, car theft, physical assault, and mugging, mirroring experiences of other residents of Los Angeles and other large urban cities. The experience of domestic violence and several other forms of victimization were positively associated with the level of psychological distress. As far as violence against women is concerned, this presumably model minority group was not shielded from its negative effect.

The probability of experiencing partners' physical and sexual violence was similarly high for the first generation immigrant women and for 1.5 and higher generation women. The first generation immigrant women were, however, less likely to experience partners' emotional violence. At least two explanations are plausible. First, this finding may reflect the true difference in the experience of partners' emotional violence by immigration status in that a smaller proportion of the first generation respondents actually experienced partners' emotional violence. An alternative explanation would be that the first generation respondents were less likely to recognize partners' violence as "abuse" and/or less likely to disclose such an experience. Although both explanations are plausible (and they are not mutually exclusive), findings of previous studies are fairly consistent in that men who abuse their partners physically and/or sexually also resort to a wide range of emotional violence (Follingstad, Rutledge, Berg, Hause, & Polek, 1990; Walker, 1984). Considering that similar proportions of the first generation and the 1.5 and higher generation respondents in this study reported partners' physical and sexual violence, the observed difference in the rates of emotional violence is likely to reflect the difference in recognition and disclosure as opposed to the difference in actual experience.

The observed rate of childhood physical abuse (13%) is likely an underestimation, a methodological artifact, because the respondents' experience of child abuse was asked through a broad screening-type question, "Have you ever been abused by your parents?" Underreporting is likely when a screening-type question is used due largely to the individuals' tendency to narrowly define what constitutes abuse or violence (Koss, 1992; Wyatt & Peters, 1986). In the present study, similar proportions of first generation and 1.5 and higher generation respondents reported parental physical abuse. This finding contradicts the far smaller number of child abuse cases reported to child welfare agencies annually in Japan (1,961 cases, Koseisho, 1995) compared to that in the U.S. (over 3 million cases, Sedlack, 1991). This study's finding suggests that child physical abuse in Japan may be much more prevalent than that suggested by the number of reported cases. In fact, a recent study in

Tokyo found that 9% of the respondents, a sample of 500 mothers of pre-schoolers, had physically abused their children, and an additional 30% were at high risk for abusing their children (Kodomono Gyakutai Boshi Senta, 1999). Further research is needed in this area.

Notable differences by immigration status were observed in several types of victimization. A higher proportion of first generation respondents reported that their fathers had physically abused their mothers than their 1.5 and higher generation counterparts. While this observed difference may indicate a higher prevalence of domestic violence among women in Japan compared to that among women of Japanese descent in the U.S., no prevalence data are currently available that would allow for such comparison. Future studies of women in Japan, the first generation immigrant Japanese women in the U.S., and Japanese American women, using comparable sampling methods and the definition and measure of domestic violence, should shed light on the sub-group variations and commonalities in the prevalence and patterns of domestic violence victimization.

A higher proportion of first generation respondents reported experiencing contact and no-contact sexual violence than 1.5 and higher generation respondents. The distribution of the age at which the respondents first experienced these types of sexual violence indicated that the incidents had taken place in Japan prior to their immigration to the U.S. The difference in the socio-cultural contexts in the two countries may account for the observed differences. For example, trains, subways, and buses are a primary mode of transportation in Japan, where people share a small, often extremely crowded, space. This physical proximity may increase the risk of experiencing certain types of sexual violence. In fact, unwanted touching of women's bodies is so prevalent in Japan that a public campaign has been initiated, which includes posters and announcements on the trains and subways encouraging riders to intervene if they witness an incident or to report the incident if victimized. One recent study in Japan found that the majority of women surveyed had experienced unwanted touching at least once while riding on public transportation (Seiboryokuwo Yurusanai Onnanokai, 1995). Public transportation and crowded streets also contribute to the risk of victimization by exhibitionists. Although neither contact nor no-contact sexual violence was significantly associated with current psychological distress in this study, the observed difference in the rates of sexual violence victimization by immigration status warrants further study.

PSYCHOLOGICAL DISTRESS AND THE ROLE OF VICTIMIZATION

As hypothesized, the severity of domestic violence significantly contributed to a higher degree of current psychological distress. This finding is consistent with the relationship between the intensity of recent domestic violence experiences and the severity of psychological distress found in studies of convenience samples of battered women who were recruited at shelter programs (Astin et al., 1993; Kemp et al., 1991, 1995). A notable finding was that the experience of partners' emotional violence was a stronger predictor of psychological distress than the experience of physical violence. This finding is consistent with several recent studies with convenience samples of battered women (Dutton et al., 1999; Sackett & Saunders, 1999; Tolman & Bhosley, 1991). The present study, which used a community-based random sample of a previously under-studied population, provides additional empirical support for the negative effects of emotional violence, a form of partners' violence often not measured by researchers and/or dismissed as "minor" or "not severe" by policymakers and lay persons. In certain states, the experience of partners' emotional violence alone does not satisfy criteria for obtaining a restraining order against an intimate partner. Thus, more systematic examination of the prevalence, severity, and mental health consequences of partners' emotional violence is needed in order to develop more effective policies and services.

Even in the presence of a strong association between the experience of domestic violence and psychological distress, the experience of childhood physical abuse was significantly associated with elevated current psychological distress. It appears that experiencing this type of victimization during childhood has long lasting negative effects on women's mental health. This finding should prompt practitioners to inquire about childhood abuse history when working with battered women or any women. The experience of property crimes was also associated with higher levels of psychological distress. These findings collectively underscore the importance of considering multiple forms of victimization in examining the relationship between domestic violence and psychological distress in women.

METHODOLOGICAL ISSUES

Methodologically, this study has a number of strengths. It investigated the women's experience with a range of interpersonal victimization during their lifetimes using a community-based random sample. Because only a small fraction of battered women use domestic violence programs, the use of a community-based random sample helped examine the experience of domestic violence and the mental health of those women who may never contact assistance programs. An additional strength of the study involves investigation of within group differences, especially comparisons of the probability of victimization by immigration status. The observed differences in the reported rates of certain types of victimization (e.g., partners' emotional violence, witnessing parental domestic violence, contact and no-contact sexual violence), albeit subject to further studies, warn against aggregating individuals regardless of their immigration status, corroborating the results of other researchers (Uehara et al., 1994).

The age-adjusted estimates of the lifetime prevalence of partners' violence, measured by the Kaplan-Meier estimates at age 49 (57% for physical violence; 79% for emotional violence, and 35% for sexual violence), were slightly higher than the proportion of respondents who reported experiencing partners' violence (52%, 76%, 30%, respectively). These differences were due to the fact that the Kaplan-Meier estimator adjusts for the possibility that women who have not been abused at the time of the interview may be abused at a later date. The use of survival analysis represents a substantial methodological improvement. Nonetheless, the age-adjusted probability of domestic violence is believed to be an underestimation because respondents were likely to have forgotten or to have failed to report victimization experienced in their remote past (Yoshihama & Gillespie, under review). Because retrospective studies involve vague, faulty, or incomplete recall on the part of the respondents, the present study used behavior-specific questions to promote an accurate and more complete recollection of the respondents' experiences with victimization. The retrospective design is, however, limited in determining a causal relationship between domestic violence and psychological distress. The use of SCL-90R, a measure of the past-week's psychological distress, helped establish the time sequence in which respondents experienced symptoms of distress following, or concurrently with, domestic violence, other types of victimization, and stressors. However, a respondent's current psychological distress may confound the recall of past and current victimization (Eich, Macaulay, & Ryan, 1994). A study design that allows the assessment of the onset of mental health problems in relation to the timing of various types of victimization and stressors is necessary in order to more accurately estimate the extent to which these events contribute to individuals' mental health problems.

The response rate of 52%, albeit comparable to that in studies of similar design using long, face-to-face interviews with a community-based random sample of women (50%, Russell & Howell, 1983; 55%, Wyatt, 1985), limits the generalizability of study findings. Respondents, however, did not differ significantly from non-participants sociodemographically. In addition, the extent to which the respondents were representative of women of Japanese descent aged 18 to 49 in Los Angeles County appears to support the generalizability of the findings to the experiences of domestic violence among this group, at least within Los Angeles County itself.

IMPLICATIONS FOR PRACTICE

The image of model minority may hamper practitioners' readiness or willingness to assess experiences of violent victimization when working with women of Japanese descent. Women of Japanese descent in this study, however, reported experiencing multiple types of interpersonal victimization, both inside and outside the home, some of which had a significant negative effect on their well-being. Nevertheless, only a small fraction of them (approximately one in six) had sought counseling. Although a high level of distress does not necessarily translate into a disorder that requires clinical attention, the unmet needs for mental health services are suspected to be high among women of Japanese descent in general, and among those who have experienced partners' violence in particular. Prevention programs, as well as assessment and intervention, targeted at this previously under-served population are urgently needed. The high rate of multiple victimizations highlights the importance of assessing the history of not only domestic violence, but also other types of interpersonal violence in working with women of Japanese descent. In light of the recent increase in the number of hate crimes against persons of Asian Pacific descent (Los Angeles County Commission on Human Relations, 1998; National Asian Pacific American Legal Consortium, 1996), it is important to inquire about the experience of race-based assault (hate crimes) as well.

The first generation immigrant women experienced rates of partners' physical and sexual violence similar to those of the 1.5 and higher generation women. Many immigrant women lack English proficiency and/or are not familiar with U.S. social systems. Special efforts are required to reach out to this population, such as services provided in immigrants' native languages (Jang, Lee, & Morello-Frosch, 1990). Because such services are labor-intensive and costly, additional resources, such as funding from the federal, state, and local governments, should be allocated.

Additional population-based studies of the prevalence, nature, and mental health effects of victimization among previously under-studied Asian Pacific American women are needed to develop more inclusive and effective social policy and services. This study represents an important step in filling the current gap in population-based data on the prevalence and mental health consequences of domestic violence among Asian Pacific American women.

REFERENCES

Agtuca, J. R. (1992). *A community secret: For the Filipina in an abusive relationship*. Seattle: Seal Press.

Allensworth, E. M. (1997). Earnings mobility of first and "1.5" generation Mexican-origin women and men: A comparison with US-born Mexican Americans and non-Hispanic whites. *International Migration Review, 31*(2), 386-410.

Aneshensel, C. S., Rutter, C. M., & Lachenbruch, P. A. (1991). Social structure, stress, and mental health: Competing conceptual and analytic models. *American Sociological Review, 56*(2), 166-178.

Astin, M. C., Lawrence, K. J., & Foy, D. W. (1993). Posttraumatic stress disorder among battered women: Risk and resiliency factors. *Violence and Victims, 8*(1), 17-28.

Avison, W. R., & Turner, R. J. (1988). Stressful life events and depressive symptoms: Disaggregating the effects of acute stressors and chronic strains. *Journal of Health and Social Behavior, 29*(3), 253-264.

Campbell, J. C., Kub, J., Belknap, R. A., Templin, T., & Thomas, N. (1997). Predictors of depression in battered women. *Violence Against Women, 3*(3), 271-293.

Campbell, J. C., & Lewandowski, L. (1997). Mental and physical health effects of intimate partner violence on women and children. *Psychiatric Clinics of North America, 20*(2), 353-374.

Dasgupta, S. D., & Warrier, S. (1996). In the footsteps of "Arundhati": Asian Indian women's experience of domestic violence in the United States. *Violence Against Women, 2*(3), 238-259.

Derogatis, L. R. (1994). *SCL-90-R: Administration, scoring, and procedures manual* (3rd ed.). Minneapolis, MN: National Computer Systems, Inc.

Derogatis, L. R., Richels, K., & Rock, A. F. (1976). The SCL-90 and the MMPI: A step in the validation of a new self-report scale. *British Journal of Psychiatry, 128*, 280-289.

Dutton, M. A., Goodman, L. A., & Bennett, L. (1999). Court-involved battered women's responses to violence: The role of psychological, physical, and sexual abuse. *Violence and Victims, 14*(1), 89-104.

Eich, E., Macaulay, D., & Ryan, L. (1994). Mood dependent memory for events of the personal past. *Journal of Experimental Psychology, General, 123*, 201-215.

Family Violence Prevention Fund. (1993). *Men beating women: Ending domestic violence–A qualitative and quantitative study of public attitudes on violence against women*. Author.

Finkelhor, D., Hotaling, G., Lewin, I. A., & Smith, C. (1990). Sexual abuse in a national survey of adult men and women: Prevalence, characteristics, and risk factors. *Child Abuse & Neglect, 14*(1), 19-28.

Follingstad, D. R., Rutledge, L. L., Berg, B. J., Hause, E. S., & Polek, D. S. (1990). The role of emotional abuse in physically abusive relationships. *Journal of Family Violence, 5*, 107-120.

Golding, J. M. (1996). Exploratory paper on mental health consequences. *The cost of domestic violence to the health care system. Final Report Part II*. Report prepared for the Office of the Assistant Secretary for Planning and Evaluation, U.S. Dept. of Health and Human Services.

Golding, J. M., & Burnam, M. A. (1990). Immigration, stress, and depressive symptoms in a Mexican-American community. *Journal of Nervous and Mental Disease, 178*(3), 161-171.

Ho, C. K. (1990). An analysis of domestic violence in Asian American communities: A multicultural approach to counseling. *Women & Therapy, 9*(1/2), 129-150.

Hoffman, K. L., Demo, D. H., & Edwards, J. N. (1994). Physical wife abuse in a non-Western society: An integrated theoretical approach. *Journal of Marriage and the Family, 56,* 131-146.

Houskamp, B. M., & Foy, D. W. (1991). The assessment of posttraumatic stress disorder in battered women. *Journal of Interpersonal Violence, 6*(3), 367-375.

Ima, K., & Hohm, C. F. (1991). Child maltreatment among Asian and Pacific Islander refugees and immigrants: The San Diego case. *Journal of Interpersonal Violence, 6*(3), 267-285.

Jang, D., Lee, D., & Morello-Frosch, R. (1990). Domestic violence in the immigrant and refugee community: Responding to the needs of immigrant women. *Response, 13*(4), 2-6.

Kaufman Kantor, G., Jasinski, J. L., & Aldarondo, E. (1994). Sociocultural status and incidence of marital violence in Hispanic families. *Violence & Victims, 9*(3), 207-222.

Kemp, A., Green, B., Hovanitz, C., & Rawlings, E. (1995). Incidence and correlates of posttraumatic stress disorder in battered women: Shelter and community samples. *Journal of Interpersonal Violence, 10*(1), 43-55.

Kemp, A., Rawlings, E. I., & Green, B. L. (1991). Post-traumatic stress disorder (PTSD) in battered women: A shelter sample. *Journal of Traumatic Stress, 4*(1), 137-148.

Kessler, R. C., McGonagle, K. A., Zhao, S., Nelson, C. B., Hughes, M., Eshleman, S., Wittchen, H-U., & Kendler, K. S. (1994). Lifetime and 12-month prevalence of DSM-III-R psychiatric disorders in the United States: Results from the National Commodity Survey. *Archives of General Psychiatry, 51,* 8-19.

Kessler, R. C., & Wethington, E. (1991). The reliability of life event reports in a community survey. *Psychological Medicine, 21*(3), 723-738.

Kim, K. I., & Cho, Y. G. (1992). Epidemiological survey of spousal abuse in Korea. In E. C. Viano (Ed.), *Intimate violence: Interdisciplinary perspectives.* Washington, DC: Hemisphere.

Kodomono Gyakutai Boshi Senta [Child Abuse Prevention Center]. (1999, March). *Shutoken ippanjinko niokeru jidogyakutai no chosahokokusho.* Tokyo: Author.

Koseisho Daijin Kanbo Tokei Johobukyoku [Ministry of Health and Welfare, Statistics and Information Bureau]. (1995). *Shakaifukushi gyosei gyomu hokoku: Heisei 6 nendo ban* [Report on social welfare administration 1994]. Tokyo: Koseisho Tokeikyokai.

Koss, M. P. (1992). The underdetection of rape: Methodological choices influence incidence estimates. *Journal of Social Issues, 48*(1), 61-75.

Lai, T. A. (1986). Asian women: Resisting the violence. In M. C. Burns (Ed.), *The speaking profits us: Violence in the lives of women of color* (pp. 8-11). Seattle: Center for the Prevention of Sexual and Domestic Violence.

Los Angeles County Commission on Human Relations. (1998). *Hate crime in Los Angeles County in 1997.* Los Angeles: Author.

Marshall, L. L. (1992). Development of the severity of violence against women scales. *Journal of Family Violence, 7*(2), 103-121.

Myers, D., & Cranford, C. J. (1998). Temporal differentiation in the occupational mobility of immigrant and native-born Latina workers. *American Sociological Review, 63*(1), 68-93.

National Asian Pacific American Legal Consortium (1996). *Audit of violence against Asian Pacific Americans: The violent impact on the growing community* (4th annual report). Washington, DC: Author.

Neff, J., Holamon, B., & Schluter, T. (1995). Spousal violence among Anglos, Blacks, and Mexican Americans: The role of demographic variables, psychosocial predictors, and alcohol consumption. *Journal of Family Violence, 10*(1), 1-21.

Nelson, E., & Zimmerman, C. (1996). *Household survey on domestic violence in Cambodia.* Phnom Penh, Cambodia: Ministry of Women's Affairs and Project Against Domestic Violence.

Norris, F. H. (1992). Epidemiology of trauma: Frequency and impact of different potentially traumatic events on different demographic groups. *Journal of Consulting and Clinical Psychology, 60*(3), 409-418.

Rao, K., Di Clemente, R. J., & Ponton, L. D. (1992). Child sexual abuse of Asian compared with other populations. *Journal of the American Academy of Child & Adolescent Psychiatry, 31*, 880-886.

Resnick, H. S., Kilpatrick, D. G., Dansky, B. S., Saunders, B. E., & Best, C. L. (1993). Prevalence of civilian trauma and posttraumatic stress disorder in a representative national sample of women. *Journal of Consulting and Clinical Psychology, 61*(6), 984-991.

Richie, B. E., & Kanuha, V. (1993). Battered women of color in public health care systems: Racism, sexism and violence. In B. Blair & S. E. Cayleff (Eds.), *Wings of gauze: Women of color and the experience of health and illness* (pp. 288-299). Detroit, MI: Wayne State University Press.

Robins, L. N., Locke, B., & Regier, D. A. (1991). An overview of psychiatric disorders in America. In L. N. Robins & D. A. Regier (Eds.), *Psychiatric disorders in America: The Epidemiologic Catchment Area Study* (Chap. 13, pp. 328-386). New York: Free Press.

Russell, D. E. H. (1983a). The incidence and prevalence of intrafamilial and extrafamilial sexual abuse of female children. *Child Abuse & Neglect, 7*, 133-146.

Russell, D. E. H. (1983b). The prevalence and incidence of forcible rape and attempted rape of females. *Victimology: An International Journal, 7*(1/4), 81-93.

Russell, D. E., & Howell, N. (1983). The prevalence of rape in the United States revised. *Signs, 8*(4), 688-695.

Sackett, L. A., & Saunders, D. G. (1999). The impact of different forms of psychological abuse on battered women. *Violence and victims, 14*(1), 1-13.

Sedlack, A. J. (1991). *National incidence and prevalence of child abuse and neglect: 1988. Revised report.* Rockville, MD: Westat.

Seiboryokuwo Yurusanai Onnanokai. (1995). *Chikan no inai denshani noritai! STOP chikan anketo hokokushu.* Osaka: Author.

Sheffield, C. J. (1993). The invisible intruder: Women's experiences of obscene phone calls. In P. B. Bart & E. G. Moran (Eds.), *Violence against women: The bloody footprints* (pp. 73-78). Newbury Park, CA: Sage.

Sorenson, S. B., & Telles, C. A., (1991). Self-reports of spousal violence in a Mexican-American and non-Hispanic white population. *Violence and Victims, 6*(1), 3-15.

Song-Kim, Y. I. (1992). Battered Korean women in urban United States. In S. M.

Furuto, B. Renuka, D. K. Chung, K. Murase, & F. Ross-Sheriff (Eds.), *Social work practice with Asian Americans* (pp. 213-226). Newbury Park, CA: Sage.

Straus, M. A., & Gelles, R. J. (1986). Societal change and change in family violence from 1975 to 1985 as revealed by two national surveys. *Journal of Marriage and the Family, 48,* 465-479.

Takeuchi, D. T., Kuo, H-S., Kim, K., & Leaf, P. J. (1990). Psychiatric symptom dimensions among Asian Americans and Native Hawaiians: An analysis of the Symptom Checklist. *Journal of Community Psychology, 17,* 319-329.

Takeuchi, D. T., Chung, R. C. Y., Lin, K. M., Shen, H. K., Kurasaki, K., Chun, C. A., & Sue, S. (1998). Lifetime and twelve-month prevalence rates of major depressive episodes and dysthmia among Chinese Americans in Los Angeles. *American Journal of Psychiatry, 155*(10), 1407-1414.

Tjaden, P., & Thoennes, N. (1998, November). *Prevalence, incidence, and consequences of violence against women: Findings from the National Violence Against Women Survey.* National Institute of Justice Centers for Disease Control and Prevention, Research in Brief. Washington, DC: U.S. Department of Justice.

Tolman, R. M. (1989). The development of a measure of psychological maltreatment of women by their male partners. *Violence and Victims, 4*(3), 159-177.

Tolman, R. M., & Bhosley, G. (1991). The outcome of participation in shelter-sponsored program for men who batter. In D. Knudsen & J. Miller (Eds.), *Abused and battered: Social and legal responses* (pp. 113-122). New York: Aldine de Gruyter.

Tokyo-to. (1998, March). *Josei ni taisuru boryoku chosa hokokusho* [A report of the study of violence against women]. Tokyo: Author.

Uehara, E. S., Takeuchi, D. T., & Smukler, M. (1994). Effects of combining disparate groups in the analysis of ethnic differences: Variations among Asian American mental health service consumers in level of community functioning. *American Journal of Community Psychology, 22*(1), 83-99.

U.S. Census Bureau (1994). *Los Angeles County: Major Asian and Pacific Islander groups.*

U.S. Commission on Civil Rights (1992, February). The plight of battered Asian American women. In *Civil rights issues facing Asian Americans in the 1990s* (pp. 174-180). Washington, DC: Author.

Walker, L. E. (1984). *The battered woman syndrome.* New York: Springer.

Wyatt, G. E. (1985). The sexual abuse of Afro-American and white American women in childhood. *Child Abuse & Neglect, 9,* 507-519.

Wyatt, G. E., & Peters, S. D. (1986). Methodological considerations in research on the prevalence of child sexual abuse. *Child Abuse & Neglect, 10*(2), 241-251.

Yick, A. G., & Agbayani-Siewert, P. (1997). Perceptions of domestic violence in a Chinese American community. *Journal of Interpersonal Violence, 12*(6), 832-846.

Yoshihama, M. (1999). Domestic violence against women of Japanese descent in Los Angeles: Two methods of estimating prevalence. *Violence Against Women, 5*(8), 869-897.

Yoshihama, M. (2000). Reinterpreting strength and safety in socio-cultural context: Dynamics of domestic violence and experiences of women of Japanese descent. *Children and Youth Services Review, 22*(3), 205-227.

Yoshihama, M., & Gillespie, B. (under review). Age adjustment and recall bias in the analysis of domestic violence data: Methodological improvement through the application of survival analysis methods.

Yoshihama, M., & Sorenson, S. B. (1994). Physical, sexual, and emotional abuse by male intimates: Experiences of women in Japan. *Violence and Victims*, 9(1), 63-77.

Acculturation, Premigration Traumatic Experiences, and Depression Among Vietnamese Americans

Dung Ngo
Thanh V. Tran
Judith L. Gibbons
Joan M. Oliver

SUMMARY. This study investigated the role of acculturation as a potential mediator or moderator for premigration traumatic experiences (PTE) and depression. The mediator effect refers to an effect in which acculturation mediates the negative impact of PTE on depression. On the other hand, the moderator effect signifies an interaction effect in which acculturation buffers the impact of PTE on depression. In other words, the negative impact of PTE on depression is hypothesized to vary according to different levels of acculturation. These two competing hypotheses were tested in a community-based sample of 261 adult Vietnamese Americans aged 25 and over. The sample consisted of 48% males and 64% of the sample were married. The average length of residence in the U.S. was 7 years. Multiple regression analyses did not support the mediator effect of acculturation, but did support its moderator effect as a buffer of PTE. Specifically, PTE had a much stronger effect on depression among those with lower levels of acculturation than those

Dung Ngo, Judith L. Gibbons, and Joan M. Oliver are affiliated with Saint Louis University, Department of Psychology, 221 N. Grand Blvd., St. Louis, MO 63103.

Thanh V. Tran is affiliated with Boston College, Graduate School of Social Work, 140 Commonwealth Ave., Chestnut Hill, MA 02467.

This research is supported in part by grant AM49462 from the National Institute on Mental Health awarded to Thanh V. Tran.

[Haworth co-indexing entry note]: "Acculturation, Premigration Traumatic Experience, and Depression Among Vietnamese Americans." Ngo et al. Co-published simultaneously in *Journal of Human Behavior in the Social Environment* (The Haworth Press, Inc.) Vol. 3, No. 3/4, 2001, pp. 225-242; and: *Psychosocial Aspects of the Asian-American Experience: Diversity Within Diversity* (ed: Namkee G. Choi) The Haworth Press, Inc., 2001, pp. 225-242. Single or multiple copies of this article are available for a fee from The Haworth Document Delivery Service [1-800-342-9678, 9:00 a.m. - 5:00 p.m. (EST). E-mail address: getinfo@haworthpressinc.com].

225

with higher levels of acculturation. Implications for future research and clinical practices are discussed. *[Article copies available for a fee from The Haworth Document Delivery Service: 1-800-342-9678. E-mail address: <getinfo@haworthpressinc.com> Website: <http://www.HaworthPress.com> © 2001 by The Haworth Press, Inc. All rights reserved.]*

KEYWORDS. Acculturation, premigration, trauma, depression, Vietnamese

INTRODUCTION

Previous studies have not investigated the role of acculturation as a mechanism for coping with stress. However, it appears that immigrants who have successfully acculturated to the host society tend to report a more positive mental health status than those who are not so successful in their acculturation process (Tran, 1993; Vega, Warheit, Buhl-Auth, & Meinhardt, 1984). Thus, if acculturation is viewed from the context of coping, it may have profound clinical implications for mental health prevention among immigrants and refugees, especially those who have been exposed to mass traumatic experiences prior to coming into a host country. The purpose of this study is to evaluate two conceptual models concerning the role of acculturation as a potential mediator or moderator of premigration traumatic experiences (PTE) on depression among Vietnamese Americans. The mediator role of acculturation suggests that it mediates the effect of PTE on depression. More specifically, PTE leads to higher feelings of depression but its effect would be weaker when controlling for acculturation. The moderator role of acculturation suggests that, given the effect of PTE on depression, its effect will be weaker for those individuals with higher levels of acculturation. In other words, high acculturation will moderate the negative impact of PTE on depression.

Acculturation was originally described by anthropologists as a group-level process in which there are profound cultural changes when individuals from two different cultures interact or have regular contact (Redfield, Linton, & Herskovits, 1936). While it is assumed that mutual changes occur during this process, significant changes are expected to occur in the "non-dominant" group as opposed to the "dominant" group. Although understanding the process of acculturation at the group-level remains an important area of research in cross-cultural psychology, considerable attention has been given to changes at the individual-level as well. It has been noted that individuals undergoing the process of acculturation frequently experience many important changes. Among these are physical changes (e.g., having a new living environment); biological changes (e.g., contracting new diseases); political changes; economic changes; cultural changes; social/interpersonal changes, as well as psychological changes (Berry & Kim, 1988). These physical and behavioral changes and their impact on the individuals' mental health and social adjustment have been well documented among refugees and immigrants

Understanding acculturation of immigrants or refugees in a host society is an important matter at both the policy and intervention levels. It has generally been assumed that immigrants can make successful transition between cultures and that their acculturation can be managed, by both the individuals and social agencies of the host culture, to enhance successful adaptation and to reduce or prevent emotional distress (Berry, 1990). Thus, the ability of newly arrived refugees or immigrants to make a smooth transition into their host society indicates the success of both social policy and clinical interventions. Further, successful acculturation can be viewed as an indicator of positive mental health status (Berry & Kim, 1988).

However, previous research on acculturation and mental health has generated inconclusive results. For example, Fabrega (1969) reported that less acculturated immigrants tend to suffer from more psychological distress than those who are more acculturated (see also Vega, Warheit, Buhl-auth, & Meinhardt, 1984). Other studies found that immigrants who are more acculturated in the host society are often alienated from their own ethnic community (Burnam, Hough, Karno, Escobar, & Telles, 1987). These findings can be interpreted to imply that individuals who are more acculturated tend to alienate themselves from the support network of their own ethnic community and are, therefore, vulnerable to psychological disorders (Krause, Bennett, & Tran, 1989). Previous studies also support the hypothesis that immigrants who can maintain a balance between their two cultures experience fewer psychological disorders than those who are either less or highly acculturated (Buriel, 1984; Ramirez, 1984). Specific acculturation strategies have also been linked to a more positive mental health status (Berry & Sam, 1997).

Immigrants and refugees from war-torn countries or from regions with great political upheavals and economic hardships have often experienced numerous traumatic experiences before emigration. Moreover, the traumatic events often encountered by most political refugees (e.g., from Southeast Asia) during their flight for freedom have also been consistently reported. Premigration traumatic experiences, such as war, torture, death, and starvation can put immigrants and refugees at a considerable risk for social and mental health problems in a host culture. Unfortunately, many of these risk factors are beyond the preventive reach of mental health professionals or social service agencies because they often occurred in the immigrants' native homeland or during the migration period.

PSYCHOLOGICAL CONSEQUENCE OF TRAUMA EXPERIENCES

The relationship between trauma and its psychological consequences has been well established in research literature. Numerous studies of prisoners of war (POWs), combat veterans, natural disaster survivors, as well as rape and torture victims have revealed that posttraumatic stress symptoms are remarkably common among these victims (e.g., Goldfeld, Mollica, Pesavento, & Faraone, 1988). One of the most common psychiatric disorders often found among trauma survivors is posttraumatic stress disorder (PTSD) (Wilson & Keane, 1997). PTSD is characterized by a set of symptoms (or syndromes) that an individual may develop following exposure to an extremely traumatic stressor; the exposure to the traumatic events could be either direct personal experience (e.g., being raped) or vicarious, such as witnessing or hearing about the events. These symptoms often include both psychological and behavioral components (Goldfeld et al., 1988). The fourth edition of the Diagnostic and Statistical Manual of Mental Disorders (APA, DSM-IV, 1994) lists a host of PTSD symptoms or behaviors a person may develop after being exposed to a traumatic event (or events) that involved intense fear, helplessness, or horror.

In addition to symptoms of PTSD, other studies have also reported that traumatic experiences frequently lead to a host of other psychological and behavioral symptoms, such as depression, anxiety, and alcoholism (Breslau, Davis, Andreski, & Peterson, 1991; Norris, 1992; Ursano & Rundell, 1990). Moreover, high rates of psychiatric comorbidity have been observed quite frequently among trauma survivors, particularly among individuals with PTSD (e.g., Helzer, Robins, & McEvoy, 1987). These researchers analyzed data using a community sample assessed in the Epidemiologic Catchment Area Study and found that individuals with PTSD were twice as likely as those without PTSD to suffer from some other psychological disorder. Another study using a community sample of Vietnam veterans reported that nearly 99% of those who met diagnostic criteria for PTSD qualified for one other diagnosis, including depression, dysthymia, anxiety, or substance abuse/dependency (Kulka, Schlenger, Fairbank, Hough, Jordan, Marmar, & Weiss, 1988). However, the psychological effects of traumatic events vary greatly among trauma victims. Furthermore, the intensity of impact on a person's functioning depends on many factors, including but not limited to cultural beliefs, religious beliefs, socialization experiences, available coping strategies, and available social and psychological support resources.

MENTAL HEALTH STATUS OF VIETNAMESE REFUGEES

Vietnamese refugees in the U.S. have been identified as the largest subgroup among the Southeast Asians (Office of Refugee Resettlement, 1993). As the Vietnamese-American community continues to evolve, more systematic research designs that examine mental health issues of this population are greatly in need. Previous studies on Vietnamese refugees typically examined three main areas, including psychological adaptation (e.g., Lin, Tazuma, & Masuda, 1979; Lin, Masuda & Tazuma, 1982); social and language adaptation (Nicassio, Solomon, Guest, & McCullough, 1992; Tran, 1988; 1990); and economic adjustment (Caplan, Whitmore, & Choy, 1989; Tran, 1992). Substantial mental health problems, such as chronic PTSD and depression, among the Vietnamese population have been reported in the United States, Canada, Norway, and Japan (Beiser, 1990; Kinzie, Boehnlein, Leung, Moore, Riley, & Smith, 1990; Kleinman, 1990; Vaglum, 1993). As with other ethnic groups of Southeast Asian refugees, mental health problems among the Vietnamese refugees were found to include anxiety, depression, intergenerational conflict, psychosomatic illness, and adjustment problems (Nguyen, 1982). Compared to other subgroups of Southeast Asian refugees, Vietnamese refugees encounter similar mental health and adjustment problems.

Vietnamese refugees who escaped from their Communist controlled country by boats between the late 1970s and the early 1980s and those newcomers who were detained in reeducation camps are the most vulnerable to psychiatric disorders. These individuals have experienced a multitude of traumas, including rape, being lost, hunger, witnessing death and/or murder of loved ones, and torture (Mollica, Wyshak, & Lavelle, 1987; U.S. Committee for Refugees, 1984). The psychiatric disorders which have been diagnosed most frequently among this specific subgroup of Vietnamese population include, but are not limited to, depression and PTSD (Kroll, Habenicht, Mackenzie, et al., 1989; Mollica, Caspi-Yavin, Bollini, Truong, Tor, & Lavelle, 1992).

RESEARCH HYPOTHESES

To understand the role of acculturation as a potential mediator or moderator of PTE on depression, two conceptual models are presented. Models A in Figure 1 suggest that acculturation mediates the effect of PTE on depression. In other words, PTE leads to higher feelings of depression (see Model A1), but its effect would be weaker (see Model A2) when controlling for acculturation. Model B in Figure 1 suggests that, given the effect of PTE on depression, its effect will be weaker for those individuals with higher levels of acculturation. In other words, high acculturation will moderate the negative impact of PTE on depression.

METHOD

Participants

The original sample consisted of 349 Vietnamese adults residing in a North Eastern State at the time of recruitment (summer 1996). The following selection criteria were used for participant selection: (1) 18 years of age or

FIGURE 1. Conceptual Models for Mediator and Moderator Effects.

Mediator Model

Model A1: Unadjusted Effect ($Y = a + b_1X_1$)

Model A2: Adjusted Effect ($Y = a + b_1X_1 + b_2X_2 + $ Control Variables)[a]

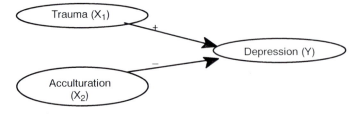

Moderator Model

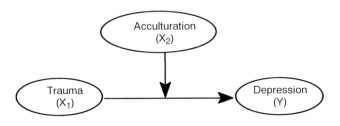

$$Y = a + b_1X_1 + b_2X_2 + b_3(X_1 * X_2) + \text{Control Variables}$$

Note. [a]Control Variables = Age, Gender, Marital Status, Education, Family Income, and Length of Residence in the U.S.

older; (2) having been resettled in the U.S. for at least one year; and (3) being proficient in the Vietnamese language. Participants were asked during the initial screening process to verify whether they met these criteria; if so, they were asked to participate. Each participant was asked during the screening phase whether she or he could read and understand written as well as spoken Vietnamese. Proficiency of Vietnamese language was determined by participants' self-acknowledgement. Both females and males were recruited using the same procedure.

In this study, a sample of 261 respondents aged 25 and older were selected for the analyses. This decision regarding age was based on the criterion that a respondent must be at least 4 years old by the end of the Vietnam War (i.e., 1975) in order to remember or feel the impact of past traumatic events. Among this selected sample, the average age was 42 years; 48% were males, and 64% were married at the time of data collection. The average number of years they had been living in the U.S. was 7 years.

Procedure

Participants were recruited primarily through Vietnamese social service agencies, outpatient health care clinics, health education programs, and from residential areas. At each of these sites, a Vietnamese liaison was recruited to assist in identifying potential participants. The inclusion criteria and other relevant information were carefully explained to the liaison at each site. Each participant was also informed about the issue of confidentiality, potential risks/benefits, and asked if they would volunteer to participate.

For those who had agreed to participate, a questionnaire in Vietnamese was either hand delivered to their home address or s/he picked one up at a recruiting site in proximity to his or her home. The questionnaire took approximately 30-45 minutes to complete. Participants were encouraged to contact the liaison or the researchers for any questions that may arise. Each participant received an incentive of $15 for his or her participation. Generally, the questionnaire was completed and returned within one to two days.

Measures

Depression. Level of depression was measured by the Vietnamese translated version of the Center for Epidemiologic Studies-Depression Scale (CES-D). The cross-cultural translation procedure requires forward and backward translation, focus groups, and expert evaluation. More importantly, this translation procedure involved an equal number of bilingual female and male translators to avoid gender-specific problems in the use of language and expression.

The CES-D is a 20-item, self-report, Likert-type rating scale. It was designed to measure the occurrence and persistence of depressive symptoms in the past week among non-clinical samples, specifically, the CES-D scale aimed at assessing "affective component and depressed mood" (Radloff, 1977). The CES-D scale has been translated into a number of languages and has been widely used to assess the prevalence of depressive symptomatology among non-clinical populations of different racial and ethnic groups (Roberts, 1980), including American Indian adolescents, Korean immigrants

(Noh, Avison, & Kaspar, 1992), Chinese Americans (Ying, 1988), and Caucasians and African-Americans (Radloff, 1977). The item "I felt as good as other people" was omitted from the present analyses because the research team felt that its translation did not reflect the construct of depression in the Vietnamese culture. Cronbach's alpha coefficient for the Vietnamese version used in this study was .91. Higher scores on this scale refer to higher levels of depression. Scores could range from 0 to 60.

Premigration traumatic events. Premigration traumatic experiences were measured by using a subscale of the Harvard Trauma Questionnaire (HTQ-Vietnamese version), developed by the Indochinese Psychiatry Clinic (IPC) located in Boston, Massachusetts (Mollica, Caspi-Yavin, Bollini, Truong, Tor, & Lavelle, 1991). Sixteen items assessing various traumatic experiences, from "lack of food or water" through "torture," and "rape or sexual assault" to "murder of family or friends," were used in this study. Participants were asked to indicate whether or not they had "experienced" the listed events. Each response was dichotomized as 0 (no) to 1 (yes). The index PTE has a Cronbach's alpha coefficient at .84. Higher scores in this index refer to a higher number of traumatic experiences

Acculturation. This variable is measured by six items assessing the degree to which respondents used Vietnamese or English in various social (talk to friends) and intellectual situations (thinking). Higher scores in this scale refer to higher levels of acculturation. The scale has a Cronbach's alpha at .87 (see Tran, 1993).

Control variables. The age of the participants ranged from 25 to 73 years. Gender was coded 1 for males and 0 for females. Marital status was coded 1 for currently married and 0 for all other categories. Education was measured by the total number of years respondents spent in school in Vietnam and in the U.S. Family income was coded 1 (no earned income) to 12 ($55,000 or more a year). Length of residence in the U.S. ranged from 1 year to 26 years. Table 1 presents descriptive statistics for all variables used in the analyses. Means and standard deviations are reported for all variables. However, the means of the dummy variables should be interpreted as the percent of the category coded as 1. For example, the mean of gender is .487. This value should be read as 48% of the sample were males.

RESULTS

Evaluation of the Mediator Effect

The results of the regression analysis for the mediator model are presented in Table 2. It appears that premigration traumatic experiences had a statisti-

TABLE 1. Description of Variables Used in the Analysis.

Variables	Mean	SD
Age	42.05	12.40
Gender (1 = male, 0 = female)	.49	.50
Marital Status (1 = married, 0 = other)	.64	.48
Education: Years in school (Vietnam + U.S.)	14.09	4.24
Family Income	7.34	3.38
Length of Residence in U.S. (years)	7.31	5.45
Premigration Traumatic Experiences (PTE)	4.53	4.11
Acculturation	14.28	4.58
Depression	12.23	8.12

Notes. For dummy variables (0/1), the means are percent of categories coded as 1. The range of family income is from 1 for no earned income to 12 for $55,000 and higher.

cally significant effect on depression. That is, respondents who had more traumatic experiences were more likely to suffer from higher degrees of depression (beta = .357, $p < .001$). However, acculturation did not have a statistically significant relationship with depression. In addition, acculturation improves the magnitude of the regression coefficient of PTE from .624 (see Table 2) in the unadjusted analysis to .706 in the adjusted analysis. This finding is entirely unexpected. It was expected that the adjusted regression coefficient of PTE should be smaller than its unadjusted coefficient for the mediator effect to be operating. However, given the meaningful direction of the relationship between acculturation and depression (beta = $-.107$, $p > .05$), one should not rule out the probability of a statistically significant relationship between these variables.

In the present study, it is concluded that the data do not support the mediator model of acculturation, PTE, and depression. Other control variables found to have statistically significant relationships with depression include gender, marital status, education, and family income. The findings under the mediator model in Table 2 indicate that male respondents were less depressed than their female counterparts (beta = $-.125$, $p < .05$), that married respondents were less depressed than non-married respondents (beta = $-.145$, $p < .05$), that respondents with a higher level of education were less depressed (beta = $-.124$, $p < .05$, one tailed test), and that respondents with higher family income were also less likely to be depressed (beta = $-.125$, $p < .05$, one-tailed test).

TABLE 2. Regression Analysis of Depression Under Different Conceptual Models (N = 261).

Models	Mediator Model		Moderator Model	
Coefficients	b (SE)	Beta	b (SE)	Beta
Variables				
Unadjusted				
PTE[a]	.624 (.116)***	.316		
Adjusted				
PTE[a]	.706 (.137)***	.357	1.535 (.346)***	.776
Acculturation	−.191 (.125)	−.107	.070 (.159)	.039
Age	2E-04 (.047)	3E-04	−.002 (.047)	−.004
Gender	−2.028 (.992)*	−.125	−1.928 (.981)[#]	−.118
Marital Status	−2.449 (1.090)*	−.145	−2.356 (1.078)*	−.139
Education	−.239 (.135)[#]	−.124	−.243 (.133)[#]	−.126
Family Income	−.300 (.173)[#]	−.125	−.275 (.171)	−.114
Length in US	.067 (.097)	.045	.066 (.096)	.044
PTE × Acculturation			−.057 (.022)***	−.460
R^2	.195		.216	

Notes. * $p < .05$; ** $p < .01$; *** $p < 001$; [#]$p < .05$ for one tailed test.
PTE[a] = Premigration Traumatic Events

Evaluation of the Moderator Effect

The primary purpose of the moderator model is the testing of the interaction effect between PTE and acculturation on depression. An interaction term between PTE and acculturation was constructed by the multiplication of these two variables. The results presented under the moderator model of Table 2 confirm a statistically significant interaction effect of PTE and acculturation on depression (beta = −.460, $p < .001$). This statistically significant interaction effect suggests that acculturation can moderate the effect of PTE on depression. The meaning of this relationship is that although PTE tends to induce higher feelings of depression, its effect is weaker among respondents with higher levels of acculturation, and stronger among less acculturated respondents.

To further illustrate the interaction effect between PTE and acculturation, the sample was divided into two groups: low and high levels of acculturation. The same regression equation examining the effect of PTE on depression was applied for both samples. The results presented in Table 3 clearly support the moderator effect of acculturation. Both the adjusted and unadjusted regression coefficients of PTE on depression between low and high acculturated respondents indicate that the impact of PTE on depression was twice greater among less acculturated respondents than among more acculturated respondents.

DISCUSSION

The main objective of this study was to understand the role of acculturation as a mechanism for coping with emotional distress. In this study, only PTE was examined in the context of acculturation and depression. Results obtained from this study suggest that acculturation does indeed moderate the degree of negative impact of PTE on levels of emotional distress among Vietnamese refugees. In other words, refugees who have higher levels of acculturation in the host society tend to experience lower levels of depression than less acculturated individuals.

A fundamental research question that remains to be examined is what motivates an immigrant or refugee to acculturate (or not acculturate) into a host society? It seems that the extent to which immigrants and refugees acculturate may be determined by various factors (Berry & Kim, 1988), including mode of acculturation (e.g., integration, assimilation, or marginalization), phase of acculturation, nature of the host society (e.g., multicultural, discrimination, social support), and characteristics of the acculturating individual (e.g., age, status, appraisal, coping, attitudes, contact, length of resi-

TABLE 3. Regression Analysis of Depression Under Low and High Acculturation Levels: Further Illustration of the Moderator Effect of Acculturation for PTE and Depression.

	Low Acculturation (n = 84)	High Acculturation (n = 177)
PTE	b (SE)	b (SE)
Unadjusted	.888 (.193)***	.452 (.142)***
Adjusted	1.076 (.219)**	.443 (.174)**

Notes. * $p < .05$;** $p < .01$; *** $p < .001$. Adjusted coefficients were controlled for age, gender, marital status, education, family income, and length in U.S.

dence). Understanding this question and the relationship among these factors may be important for social agencies and mental health professionals who have direct contact with these individuals. This effort related to facilitating acculturation can serve as a preventive measure against the negative impact of trauma on the psychological well being of these immigrants or refugees. Refugee groups are appropriate targets for prevention programs, since they come to a host country often with a massive trauma history and are at greater risk for psychopathology than the non-refugee population.

For Vietnamese refugees, interventions at the primary prevention level (group-oriented) may have a better outcome with respect to better adjustment and psychological well being than secondary (early treatment) or tertiary (rehabilitation) levels. Although Vietnamese refugees may respond more positively to primary prevention, interventions at the individual level should not be neglected. Mental health treatment of refugees presents a tremendous challenge to Western mental health professionals. There are a vast number of obstacles that could affect the quality of treatment with refugees; most notable are language barriers and cultural differences. While many refugees are not familiar with mental health services, there is a serious lack of trained indigenous mental health professionals. Furthermore, it is not yet known which treatment modalities might best fit with refugees' perceptions and attitudes toward treatment and psychopathology. Nonetheless, clinicians who work with refugees must be patient, supportive, and culturally sensitive to their religious beliefs and cultural values. For example, Buddhists believe that one's current life is a reflection of one's past life. Therefore, current adversities are believed to be the result of "bad karma," suggesting that one did not live virtuously in previous life. This religious or philosophical belief may deter the effort of an immigrant to acculturate into his/her host society. Therefore, one must accept the consequences willingly and strive to improve one's current life by performing good deeds in hope for a better life. The concept of "karma" can be summed up as follows, "if you sowed bad seeds, you will harvest bad fruits." When treating Asian-American clients, including Vietnamese, clinicians should not take such views about life as a sign of mental feebleness or pessimism. Successful treatment requires clinicians to listen empathetically and to respect the belief systems of their clients.

The understanding of refugees' past traumatic histories is important for both social services agencies and mental health professionals in helping these individuals achieve a smooth transition into mainstream society. Several considerations should be noted in the assessment of refugees' trauma. Lee and Lu (1989) suggested a framework for a thorough assessment of traumatic experiences among refugees, which includes significant events and stressors at two major stages of emigration. First, during the pre-emigration period the client should be asked about various catastrophic experiences in the country of origin. The various types of traumatic events should include, among others, war, torture, imprisonment, assaults, famine, death, and loss of loved ones. Since the psychological effect of trauma varies from one individual to another, it is also important to ask the clients for their perceptions about the degree of life threat of the events to their personal safety. In addition, it is also critical to explore the refugees' decisions or reasons for their flight, as well as their refugee camp experiences and the nature of the legal immigration process. It should also be added that many political refugees encountered experienced horrific events (e.g., rape by sea pirates or poor sanitary condition in refugee camps) during their flight for freedom. Thus, it is critical to assess for traumatic experiences during this period.

Second, assessment of stressors among immigrants and refugees should also include stressors in the post-emigration stage, the period after resettlement in a host country. The post-emigration stressors may be related to economic, employment, sociocultural, language, family, and acculturation. As noted earlier, when assessing for trauma stressors, it would also be most helpful to assess the degree of impact the traumatic experiences have on the daily functioning of these individuals. Although this study only examined pre-migration traumatic experiences in the context of acculturation and depression, it is also important to study the role of acculturation as a mechanism for coping with post-migration stress.

This study contains several limitations, which should be mentioned. First, issues of reliability and validity are more complex in cross-cultural studies (van de Vijert & Leung, 1997). Correspondingly, such shortcomings are inevitable in this study. One item on the CES-D scale was omitted from the analyses due to the imprecise translation of that item. The Vietnamese version of the item, "I felt that I was just as good as other people" was translated too literally. This item appeared to suggest the overt endorsement of high self-worth, a behavior that is socially disapproved in Vietnamese culture. Accordingly, it was omitted from all analyses, leaving the CES-D scale with 19 items. While this decision may not affect the study at the conceptual level, the scale lacked the original structure. Nonetheless, the CES-D scale, with one item deleted, still served the purpose of this study. Its internal consistency reliability remained adequate.

Second, the Harvard Trauma Questionnaire (HTQ) seems to be biased against females with respect to the types of trauma events. The trauma event scale appeared to capture the life experiences of Vietnamese men more so than that of women. Many items seemed to target war trauma and reeducation camp experiences with which women lacked direct encounters. Furthermore, although the HTQ was originally designed to capture the typical traumatic experiences of Southeast-Asian refugees who presented to the Indochinese Psychiatry Clinic (Boston, MA) (Mollica et al., 1992), its cultural validation among large community-based samples has yet to be tested. Additionally, the acculturation scale used in this study emphasized mainly language accultura-tion, as opposed to other behavioral components of acculturation. Future studies should employ a more comprehensive acculturation scale.

Furthermore, this study did not have the capacity to measure the duration, intensity, and severity of the impact of the trauma events. Simply asking participants to indicate whether they have experienced the listed traumatic events does not allow us to fully capture the unique life experiences of these individuals. For example, virtually all Vietnamese refugees who escaped illegally (either by land or by boat) during the late 1970s would be most likely to encounter one or more of the following events: "being close to death," "lack of shelter," "becoming lost or being kidnapped," "illness without medical care," or "death/separation from loved ones." However, the lack of information regarding the duration and the intensity of the events limits our ability to understand the impact of these traumatic experiences. For instance, what is the nature of the event "being close to death or being tortured?" With regard to the experience of "combat situations," for exam-ple, it would be helpful to know whether participants had direct experience fighting in the battle field or simply had lived through the event of war. This information will help us to better understand the nature and impact of the traumatic events experienced by the Vietnamese refugees.

The problem that is inherent in all correlational studies is the inability to determine causal relationships. Since this study is a correlational study, it cannot escape from this problem. For instance, the results did not identify the variables that directly caused depression. In addition, the possible biases resulting from the use of self-report measures should also be taken into consideration. In a self-report study, participants may over- or under-report psychological symptoms or painful experiences. Data from this study re-vealed that among the 16 traumatic event categories, participants endorsed the item pertaining to "rape or sexual assault" at lowest frequency. It has been reported previously that Vietnamese women who escaped during the 1970s, either by land or by sea, were at high risk for being raped by sea pirates or by land-border patrols. Perhaps such experiences were too painful to revisit or admit. Moreover, the acknowledgment of being raped would be extremely shameful in Asian cultures. For this reason, many men and women were discouraged from talking about it, thus, keeping the painful experience forever suppressed. Finally, although the sample size of this study was ade-quate, it may not be representative of the Vietnamese population in the U.S. The Vietnamese population in the U.S. varies tremendously in important ways, such as emigration experiences, age, and level of acculturation and education. Thus, generalization would have to be made very carefully.

Future studies should aim at improving the appropriateness of assessment techniques with Vietnamese refugees who may have different attitudes toward the experience and acknowledgment of depressive symptoms. Since the Vietnamese population living in the U.S. varies immensely in terms of life and emigration experiences, future research should attempt to identify these subgroups for the purpose of comparison. It is crucially important not to treat the Vietnamese Americans as a homogenous group. These goals may illuminate our understanding of the unique life experiences and the effects of their life vicissitudes.

CONCLUSION

In summary, findings from this study indicate that acculturation moderates the impact of traumatic experiences on psychological well being of refugees. These findings suggest important implications for both social services agencies and mental health professionals. If successful adjustment in a host society reduces the negative impact of past trauma history on mental health, then primary prevention programs should receive priority to assist refugees in achieving smooth transition into a host country and in coping with past traumatic experiences. Although it is important to examine the direct effect of acculturation on depression, it is more theoretically and clinically meaningful to examine acculturation in the context of being a coping mechanism. The evaluation of two competing conceptual models of acculturation, PTE and depression, in this study suggest that researchers, human service agencies, and mental health professionals should reexamine the role of acculturation in the process of adjustment and adaptation among newly arrived immigrants and refugees. Moreover, acculturation should be examined using more comprehensive theoretical models for both research and intervention purposes.

REFERENCES

American Psychiatric Association (1994). *Diagnostic and statistical manual of mental disorders*, (4th ed.). Washington, DC: American Psychiatric Press.

Beiser, M. (1990). Mental health of refugees in resettlement countries. In W. Holtzman & T. H. Bornemann (Eds.). *Mental health of immigrants and refugees* (pp. 51-65). Austin, TX: Hogg Foundation for Mental Health.

Berry, J. W. (1990). Cultural and adaptation. In W. H. Holtzman & T. H. Bornemann (Eds.). *Mental health of immigrants and refugees* (pp. 90-102). Austin, TX: Hogg Foundation for Mental Health.

Berry, J. W., & Kim, U. (1988). Acculturation and mental health. In P. Dasen, J. W. Berry, & N. Sartorius (Eds.). *Health and cross-cultural psychology*: Towards applications (pp. 207-236). London: Sage.

Berry, J. W., & Sam, D. L. (1997). Acculturation and adaptation. In J. W. Berry, M. H. Segall, & C. Kagitcibasi (Eds.). *The Handbook of Cross-Cultural Psychology (2nd Ed., Vol 3). Social Behavioral and Application*, pp. 291-326. Boston Allyn & Bacon.

Breslau, N., Davis, G. C., Andreski, P., & Peterson, E. (1991). Traumatic events and posttraumatic stress disorder in and urban population of young adults. *Archives of General Psychiatry, 48*, 216-222.

Brown, G. S., Bifulco, A., & Harris, T. (1987). Life events, vulnerability, and onset of depression: Some refinements. *British Journal of Psychiatry, 150*, 30-42.

Buriel, R. (1984). Integration with traditional Mexican American culture and socio-cultural adjustment. In J. L. Martinez, & R. H. Mendoza (Eds.). *Chicano Psychology* (2nd ed.) (pp. 95-130). New York: Academic Press.

Burnam, M., Hough, R., Karno, M., Escobar, J., & Telles, C. (1987). Acculturation and life time prevalence of psychiatric disorders among Mexican Americans in Los Angeles. *Journal of Health and Social Behavior, 28*, 89-102.

Caplan, N., Whitmore, J. K., & Choy, M. H. (1989). *The boat people and achievement in America*. Ann Arbor, MI: University of Michigan Press.

Fabrega, H. (1969). Social psychiatric aspects of acculturation and migration: A general statement. *Comprehensive Psychiatry, 140*, 1103-1105.

Goldfeld, A. E., Mollica, R. F., Pesavento, B. H., & Faraone, S. V. (1988). The physical and psychological consequence of torture. *Journal of American Medical Association, 259*, 2725-2729.

Helzer, J. E., Robins, L. N., & McEvoy, L. (1987). Post-traumatic stress disorder in the general population: Findings of the Epidemiological Catchment Area Survey. *The New England Journal of Medicine, 317*, 1630-1634.

Keane, T. M., & Wolfe, J. (1990). Comorbidity in post-traumatic stress disorder: An analysis of community and clinical studies. *Journal of Applied Social Psychology, 20*, 1776-1788.

Kinzie, J. D., Boehnlein, K. J., Leung, K. P., Moore, J. L., Riley, C., & Smith, D. (1990). The prevalence of post-traumatic stress disorder and its clinical significance among Southeast Asian refugees. *American Journal of Psychiatry, 147*, 913-917.

Krause, N., Bennett, J., & Tran, T. V. (1989). Age differences in the acculturation process. *Psychology and Aging, 4*, 321–332.

Kroll, J., Habenicht, M., Mackenzie, T., Yang, M., Chan, S., Vang, T., Nguyen, T., Ly, M., Phommasouvanh, B., Nguyen, H., Vang, Y., Souvannasoth, L., & Cabugao, R. (1989). Depression and post-traumatic stress disorder in Southeast Asian refugees. *American Journal of Psychiatry, 146*, 1592-1597.

Kulka, R. A., Schlenger, W. E., Fairbank, J. A., Hough, R. L., Jordan, B. K., Marmar, C. R., & Weiss, D. S. (1988). *National Vietnam veterans readjustment study (NVVRS): Description, current status, and initial PTSD prevalence estimates.* Washington, DC: Veterans Administration.

Lee, E., & Lu, F. (1989). Assessment and treatment of Asian-American survivors of mass violence. *Journal of Traumatic Stress, 2*, 93-119.

Lin, K. M., Tazuma, L., & Masuda, M. (1979). Adaptational problems of Vietnamese refugees-part I: Health and mental health status. *Archives of General Psychiatry, 36,* 955-961.

Mollica, R. F., Wyshak, G., Lavelle, J. (1987). The psychosocial impact of war trauma and torture on Southeast Asian refugees. *American Journal of Psychiatry, 144,* 1567-1572.

Mollica, R. F., Caspi-Yavin, Y., Bollini, P., Truong, T., Tor, S., & Lavelle, J. (1991). The Harvard Trauma Questionnaire: Validating a cross-cultural instrument for measuring torture, trauma and post-traumatic stress disorder in indochinese refugees. *Journal of Nervous and Mental Disease, 180* (2), 111-116.

Mollica, R. F., Caspi-Yavin, Y., Bollini, P., Truong, T., Tor, S., & Lavelle, J. (1992). Validating a cross-cultural instrument for measuring torture, trauma, and post-traumatic stress disorder in Indochinese refugees. *Journal of Nervous and Mental Disease, 180,* 110-115.

Nicassio, P. M., Solomon, M., Guest, S. S., & McCullough, J. E. (1992). Migration stress and language proficiency as correlates of depression in a sample of Southeast Asian refugees. *International Migration Review, 26,* 23-29.

Nguyen, S. D. (1982). The psycho-social adjustment and mental health needs and Southeast Asian refugees. *Psychiatric Journal of the University of Ottawa, 7,* 26-36.

Noh, S., Avison, W. R., & Kaspar, V. (1992). Depressive symptoms among Korean immigrants: Assessment of a translation of the Center for Epidemiologic Studies Depression Scale. *Psychological Assessment, 4,* 84-91.

Office of Refugee Resettlement. (1993). *Refugee Resettlement Program. Report to the Congress.* Washington, DC: U.S. Department of Health and Human Services.

Radloff, L. S. (1977). The CES-D scale: A self-report depression scale for research in the general population. *Applied Psychological Measurement, 3,* 385-401.

Ramirez, M. (1984). Assessing and understanding biculturalism-multicuralism in Mexican American adults. In J. L. Martinez & R. H. Mendoza (Eds.). *Chicano Psychology* (2nd edition) (pp. 77-94). New York: Academic Press.

Redfield, R., Linton, R., & Herskovits, M. J. (1936). Memorandum on the study of acculturation. *American Anthropologist, 38,* 149-152.

Roberts, R. E. (1980a). Reliability of the CES-D in different ethnic contexts. *Psychological Research, 2,* 125-134.

Tran, T. V. (1988). Sex differences in English language acculturation and learning strategies among Vietnamese adults aged 40 and over in the United States. *Sex Roles: A Journal of Research, 19,* 747-758.

Tran, T. V. (1990). Language acculturation among older Vietnamese refugee adults. *The Gerontologist, 30,* 94-98.

Tran, T. V. (1992). Adjustment among different age and ethnic groups of Indochinese in the United States. *The Gerontologist, 32,* 508-518.

Tran, T.V. (1993). Psychological traumas and depression in a sample of Vietnamese people in the United States. *Health and Social Work, 18,* 184-194.

U.S. Committee for Refugees (1984). *Vietnamese boat people: Pirates' vulnerable prey.* Washington, DC: American Council for Nationalities Service.

Vaglum, H. P. (1993). Vietnamese boat refugees: The influence of war and flight traumatization on mental health on arrival in the country of resettlement. *Acta Psychiatrica Scandinavia, 88*, 162-168.

Van de Vijert, F., & Leung, K. (1997). *Methods and data analysis for cross-cultural research*. Thousand Oaks, CA: Sage.

Vega, W., Warheit, G., Buhl-Auth, J., & Meinhardt, K. (1984). The prevalence of depressive symptoms among Mexican Americans and Anglos. *American Journal of Epidemiology, 120*, 592-607.

Wilson, J. P., & Keane, T. M. (1997). *Assessing psychological trauma and PTSD*. New York: The Guilford Press

Ying, Y. (1988). Depressive symptomatology among Chinese-Americans as measured by the CES-D. *Journal of Clinical Psychology, 44*, 739-746.

Somatic Complaint and Social Suffering Among Survivors· of the Cambodian Killing Fields

Edwina S. Uehara
Paula T. Morelli
Jennifer Abe-Kim

SUMMARY. Illness narratives from two Cambodian Killing Fields survivors are used to explore conflicts between professional and lay perspectives on somatic complaints. Professionals see somatic complaints as *psychopathology*, while Cambodian survivors see it as *authentic embodied* pain. Survivor perspectives implicate professionals and care systems as causes of suffering. More inquiry is needed to understand survivor perspectives and the role of care systems in exacerbating/alleviating survivor suffering. *[Article copies available for a fee from The Haworth Document Delivery Service: 1-800-342-9678. E-mail address: <getinfo@haworthpressinc.com> Website: <http://www.HaworthPress.com> © 2001 by The Haworth Press, Inc. All rights reserved.]*

Edwina S. Uehara is affiliated with the School of Social Work, University of Washington, 4101 Fifteenth Avenue NE, Seattle, WA 98105-6299 (E-mail: eddi@u.washington.edu).

Paula T. Morelli is affiliated with the School of Social Work, University of Hawaii, Honolulu, Hawaii.

Jennifer Abe-Kim is affiliated with the Department of Psychology, Loyola Marymont University, Los Angeles, CA 90045.

Address correspondence to Edwina S. Uehara.

The authors gratefully acknowledge support from the National Research Center on Asian American Mental Health at the University of California, NIMH grant R01MH4433. The authors wish to thank Michael Smukler for his careful review of the paper in draft form.

[Haworth co-indexing entry note]: "Somatic Complaint and Social Suffering Among Cambodian Survivors of the Killling Fields." Uehara, Edwina S., Paula T. Morelli, and Jennifer Abe-Kim. Co-published simultaneously in *Journal of Human Behavior in the Social Environment* (The Haworth Press, Inc.) Vol. 3, No. 3/4, 2001, pp. 243-262; and: *Psychosocial Aspects of the Asian-American Experience: Diversity Within Diversity* (ed: Namkee G. Choi) The Haworth Press, Inc., 2001, pp. 243-262. Single or multiple copies of this article are available for a fee from The Haworth Document Delivery Service [1-800-342-9678, 9:00 a.m. - 5:00 p.m. (EST). E-mail address: getinfo@haworthpressinc.com].

KEYWORDS. Cambodians, somatization, mental health, social suffering

In the mid-1970s, following decades of economic and political destabilization and internal strife, Cambodians suffered one of the most brutal attacks by a government against its citizens that the world has ever witnessed (Kiernan, 1997). Upon seizing power in 1975, the Khmer Rouge leader, Pol Pot, ordered the closing off of the country from all contact with the world, the forced commitment of its urban population to work camps in the countryside, and the "re-education" of citizens considered dangerous or disloyal to the new regime (Kiernan, 1996; Chandler, 1991). A vast cross-section of the population was viewed as suspect, and the terror waged by the Khmer Rouge against the Cambodian citizenry was stunning in cruelty and scale. Conservatively, analysts estimate that in the 1975-1979 period of the "Killing Fields," over 1.5 million Cambodian men, women and children died at the hands of the Khmer Rouge (Kiernan, 1996). Many who survived suffered starvation, torture, the destruction of homes and towns, the witnessing of mass executions, and the loss of loved ones. The conditions awaiting those who escaped to refugee camps too often repeated and extended the suffering (Lin, 1986).

Two decades later, many Cambodians who fled the country continue to experience disturbing and disabling symptoms, including depression, anxiety, post-traumatic stress, and chronic somatic complaints (Levav, 1998; Mollica, Poole, & Tor, 1998; Kinzie, 1989, 1993; Rumbaut, 1985; Carlson & Rosser-Hogan, 1991, 1994). Not surprisingly, many studies have found that Cambodian refugees are among the Asian American ethnic groups at highest risk for psychological and physical distress (Mienhardt et al., 1984, cited in D'Avanzo, Frye, & Froman, 1994).

Clinical studies conducted over the past twenty years provide, at best, mixed evidence for the long term effectiveness of treatments aimed at symptom reduction (Beemak & Timm, 1994; Kinzie et al., 1987; Boehnlin & Kinzie, 1992; Kroll et al., 1990). This equivocal track record has led some to question the efficacy of conventional treatments and the appropriateness of the etiologic/interpretive frameworks that we in the helping professions bring to our work with survivors (e.g., see Eisenbruch, 1991; Frye, 1990; also Kleinman, Das, & Lock, 1997; Langer, 1991, 1997). Most cogent for social workers, given our commitment to understanding the person in sociocultural environment, is the criticism that helping professionals have failed to take a sufficiently contextualized view of the suffering of atrocity survivors (Kleinman, Das, & Lock, 1997; Langer 1991, 1997). How we as social workers view the agony of those who have survived atrocities such as the Killing Fields is far from academic, since professional viewpoints and practices critically shape the course of care and well-being of survivors. Too often our professional response has "clinicalized" suffering, turning it into a psychological or medical and, therefore, an individual problem. In reducing suffering to clinically and bureaucratically manageable "symptoms," we too often violate the experience of sufferers and risk contributing to the suffering we seek to remedy (see Kleinman, Das, & Lock, 1997, p. x).

To remedy this situation requires making the survivor's perspectives, desires and explanatory models more central to the professional's construal of survivor needs. As Kleinman suggests, these perspectives and models are inchoate; they flow from an *interpretation*, rather than "just a direct rendering" of the survivor's personal narrative (Kleinman, 1989, p. 240). The professional's first task in creating an appropriate model of care is thus to understand survivor perspectives on their own experiences and to identify points of conflict between survivor and professional explanatory models (see Kleinman, 1989, pp. 121-136).

In this paper, we explore these conflicts and their ramifications through a comparison of survivor and prevailing professional perspectives on somatization. Somatic complaints, or the expressions of "personal and social distress in an idiom of bodily complaints and medical help seeking" (Kleinman & Good, 1985, p. 430), are among the most commonly presented in medical and mental health settings (Rief & Hiller, 1998) and are acknowledged as a source of great tension between professionals and lay persons (e.g., see Kleinman & Kleinman, 1985). We begin our analysis with a review and critique of the prevailing professional view on somatic complaint. We note that, despite the strong professional tendency to view somatic complaints as individual and psychological in origin, there has been and continues to be great uncertainty surrounding the etiology of somatic symptoms. For various reasons, professionals have chosen to resolve this "medical doubt" in such a manner that implicates the character of the complainant as the major problem that professional practice must confront and manage (May, Doyle, & Chew-Graham, 1999, p. 523). We next describe patterns of somatic complaint as depicted in the detailed personal illness narratives of two Cambodian survivors of the Killing Fields. Specifically, we summarize from these narratives survivor perspectives on their interactions with professionals around somatic complaints and the nature, consequences, and causes of their somatic suffering. Our interpretation of these narratives suggests that, like professionals, survivors' view somatic pain as etiologically enigmatic. However, survivors' narratives reflect a perspective on somatic complaints that is more socially contextual and clearly implicates the role of prevailing professional views in survivor suffering. Based on our analysis, we suggest the need both for more systematic inquiry into Cambodian survivor models of somatic complaint and suffering and for exploration of how prevailing professional culture and organization contributes to "social suffering." By this term, we refer to the "devastating injuries" that political, economic, and institutional forces can inflict on people, and, reciprocally, injuries caused by how these forces shape societal responses to social problems (Kleinman, Das, & Lock, 1997, p. ix). We close with some suggestions for strengthening social work and mental health practice with Cambodian survivors of the Killing Fields.

BACKGROUND: PROFESSIONAL PERSPECTIVES ON "SOMATIC COMPLAINTS"

The term, "somatization" is typically used within Western medical and mental health systems to refer to both: (1) a family of psychiatric ("somato-form") disorders in the DSM-IV or ICD-10 which do not fall neatly into the categories of "mental" or "physical" disease and (2) a pattern of clinical presentation and help-seeking behavior in which bodily symptoms are presented to the exclusion/eclipse of emotional distress (Kirmayer & Young, 1997, p. 420). Somatization is tied to a psychodynamic theory of illness causation in which psychological conflict or distress is thought to be converted into the experience of pain, fatigue, or other forms of bodily distress (May, Doyle, & Chew-Graham, 1999, p. 530). The prevailing professional interpretation of somatic complaints is thus based on an etiologic model of individual dysfunction or psychopathology, the classic marker for which is the absence of observable signs of organic disease adequate to "explain" the patient's level and chronicity of complaint. "Observable" is the key word here, reflecting the sharp distinction made in biomedicine between "objective" evidence of disease demonstrated via "physical signs and laboratory testing" and the person's subjective report of distress (Kirmayer & Young, 1997, p. 427). In general terms, the clinician's conceptualization of the patient's complaint can be formulated as follows:

> "Real" intrapsychic or psychosocial distress -> Patient's "experienced" bodily pain -> Patient immobilization -> Presentation of somatic complaints in clinical encounter (adapted from May, Doyle, & Chew-Graham, 1999, p. 530)

Within the prevailing framework, those who complain of somatic symptoms in the absence of physiological confirmation are regarded with suspicion; and those who repeatedly present with somatic complaints ("chronic somatizers") are looked upon as "problem patients," since they fail to get better with treatment, perdure in seeking professional attention, and make demands on professional care systems that cannot be fulfilled (Kleinman & Kleinman, 1987, p. 448). The tendency to "negativize" somatic patients has been strengthened by the evolution of the socio-legal role of clinicians within the welfare state, viz., as society's "experts" whose diagnoses separate the "truly sick" from "malingerers" for purposes of awarding public assistance and related medical benefits. Thus, as May, Doyle, and Chew-Graham (1999) point out, the label "somatization" subtly implicates the moral character of the complainant and highlights the "management" problem they pose for medical and welfare systems.

It is commonly presumed that somatization is more prevalent within those populations less skilled at accurately apprehending and expressing the nature of their psychological experiences–e.g., low-income and certain minority group populations, including those historically subject to oppression and trauma. The therapeutic implication here is that patients should be taught to replace their somatic expressions of distress with acceptance of and talk about psychological or emotional causes, because this psychological idiom is a more accurate representation of their situations (Cheung, 1993; see Kirmayer & Young, 1997, p. 426). In work with Cambodian refugees, for example, many helping professionals believe that a goal is to help clients learn to accept psychiatric diagnoses and treatments for such conditions. Client refusal to accept the psychological origins of their somatic symptoms is attributed to various cultural factors. For example, some speculate that the "loss of face" associated with mental illness makes somatization "instead of admission of problems" a "culturally acceptable way" of communicating need for help (Catalico, 1997, p. 79; also Frye & D'Avanzo, 1994). Others suggest that Cambodians may be less skilled at expressing affective states directly (i.e., in psychologistic terms) (Cheung, 1993) and that Cambodian women may be especially unassertive and reluctant to express affective distress to mainstream care professionals (Frye & D'Avanzo, 1994, pp. 74-75).

While acknowledging the benefits of psychiatric treatments to some individuals, including individual Cambodian refugees, critics increasingly question the presumptions of individual pathology and medical certainty associated with professional perspectives on somatization. The assumption that somatic expressions emanate from psychological/emotional causes (and thus indicate some form of specific pathology or dysfunction in the individual) is suspect on several grounds. First, the assumption that somatic pain is essentially "psychological" rather than "physical" in nature is only one possible construction of the relationship between affect, psyche, and soma. As Kleinman and Kleinman (1987) point out, alternative assumptions are not only possible, but also prevalent in other cultures. Thus, the dualistic conception of somatic symptoms as occurring "in place" of emotional expression is more an indication of prevalent professional constructions than of "real" pathology. Second, the assumption that somatization is characteristic of specific ethnocultural groups is disputed by recent evidence showing that somatization is common across a wide variety of privileged and less-privileged cultural groups and societies. This wide prevalence challenges the notion that somatization is indicative of a special form of psychopathology (Kirmayer & Young, 1997, p. 420). Indeed, from a cross-cultural perspective, Kleinman and Kleinman suggest that it is not somatization but rather "psychologiza-tion" that appears unusual and in need of explanation (1987, p. 435; also Good, 1994). And finally, as Kirmayer and Young (1997) point out, the corollary assumption that the expression of distress in somatic terms is some-how more "unsophisticated," primitive, or regressed is based on several doubtful premises:

> . . . that greater psychological insight necessarily results in fewer somatic symptoms; that psychological idioms are inherently more "advanced" than somatic idioms; that somatic idioms are "less differentiated and inarticulate; and finally that psychological (and by analogy, cultural) development moves along a one-dimensional continuum from primi-tive to advanced (Kirmayer & Young, 1997; also, Kirmayer, 1986).

Professional perspectives on somatic complaint are grounded in psychiat-ric models that cannot *directly* explain the causal mechanisms that produce the symptoms that lead the patient to present. The fundamental indeterminacy of diagnosis means that a "correct" interpretation of somatic complaints is "a rhetorical achievement rather than an empirical discovery" (Kirmayer & Young, 1997, p. 425). The professional's "interpretation" is not simply a matter of truth, but of strategic choice. That choice, some suggest, should reflect the professional's best efforts to understand "what will be of the most benefit to the patient" (Kirmayer & Young, 1997, p. 425). As Kleinman (1989) insists, "beneficial" professional interpretations are those that honor the ways in which Cambodian survivors themselves perceive their symptoms and suffering.

How do survivor perspectives on bodily pain and suffering differ from those of professionals, and what do these differences tell us about profession in the etiology of pain and suffering? In the following sections, we explore these questions through an analysis and interpretation of data from illness and help-seeking narratives. We begin by summarizing the larger study from which these narratives are drawn and the methods used in the current analysis.

METHODS

The narrative data used in this analysis derive from a pilot study of the social networks and health-seeking efforts of 31 Cambodian Americans who experienced severe psychological and somatic distress following their first hand experiences of the Cambodian Killing Fields (1975-1979). Participants range between the ages of 30 and 60. Nineteen of 31 are women. Two-thirds of participants have children, and two-thirds receive some form of federal income subsidy (e.g., SSI, SSDI or AFDC). At the time of the study, all lived in a large, metropolitan area in the Pacific Northwest.

Modified versions of the traumatic events list from the Cambodian version of the Harvard Trauma Questionnaire (Mollica et al., 1992) and a post-traumatic stress disorder screening protocol (DSM-IV APA 1994) were used to determine history of distress. To be eligible for the study, participants had to report having experienced at least 5 traumatic events during the 1975-1979 period, and 5 PTSD symptoms for at least six months at some point since 1975. Participants were obtained through both a community mental health center serving approximately 95% of Cambodians who receive publicly-funded mental health services in the city, and a large Khmer Buddhist society (temple) serving the Cambodian community. All participants screened through the mental health agency were active clients at the time of the study; all screened through the Buddhist society were receiving no professional mental health services at the time of the study.

Each interview was conducted by an interviewer with assistance from a translator when needed. All interviewers had extensive prior clinical experience with traumatized populations, and all translators received prior training in how to effectively interpret in clinical mental health settings. Interviewers and translators received intensive training on how to conduct ethnographic interviews (Leigh & Green, 1989) prior to and during the course of fieldwork (see Uehara, 1996, for details on training content and processes). Interviews were conducted at participant homes and took place over a period of between three to six two-hour sessions. The study's interview guide was designed to help the interviewer/translator team elicit participant narratives with minimum probing and interjections from interviewers. Study participants were encouraged to talk freely about a wide range of topics, including family life history, experiences during the Pol Pot regime and the meaning of those experiences, any and all physical and emotional symptoms they have experienced since Cambodia, and the role of family and social networks in health-promotion.

With permission of participants, interview sessions were taped and subsequently transcribed by individuals fluent in both Cambodian and English. Approximately three-quarters of all interviews required translation from Cambodian to English. In these cases, transcribers were instructed to translate all recorded survivor discourse as "faithfully" as possible–e.g., without synopsizing or editing. Transcriptions were carefully checked against tapes to enhance comprehensiveness and fidelity.

For the current analysis, we selected narrative segments from the transcripts of two survivors ("Sophiap" and "Phala"). Both were 30 year old women and mental health clients with PTSD diagnoses at the time of the study, and both reported presenting "medically unexplained" somatic symptoms to internists, psychiatrists, mental health counselors/social workers, or other care professionals. Both women provided detailed narrative descriptions of these encounters. Most importantly, the patterns of somatic complaint and professional responses described by these women were also reported by many participants in our study. Although we include direct transcript segments for illustration, for the sake of brevity, we will present much of Sophiap's and Phala's illness narratives in summary form. Transcript citations are presented in brackets; interview number is listed first, followed by transcript page number(s). Thus, in the summary of Sophiap's illness narrative below, the citation, "[2,4]" refers to the transcript of her second interview, page 4.

FINDINGS

Patterns of Somatic Complaints

Sophiap's Illness Narrative: "My physical body hurts more than just those . . . ailments":

Childhood during the time of the Killing Fields: Sophiap was nine years old when the Khmer Rouge forcibly evacuated her farming village in Northwest Cambodia. She was quickly separated from her mother and six siblings; her mother became ill during the evacuation and died. Sophiap was sent to a "krom komaa" or children's work camp. She fled from the krom komaa several times, often in a desperate attempt to find and rejoin her oldest sister. Each time she fled she was caught; each time she was caught she was beaten "close to death" [1,8-9]. Once, she was shot in the foot by soldiers. In 1979, shortly after Sophiap finally reunited with her oldest sister and niece, the three were attempting to flee with others when they were caught in the crossfire between Khmer Rouge and Vietnamese troops. Trapped in a bunker, Sophiap recalls dead bodies were piled above and below her:

> . . . And then I came out to the top of the bunker and I sat there thinking that when we went in, there were three of us, my sister held my hand and she held her child's on her side, running into the shelter. . . . So when I gained my self awareness, I jumped to dig through. Not too deep, only several people buried on top of her, her hands embracing her child. I turned her around to see that her back was totally hit everywhere. I looked at her stomach, the intestines came out, the feet were amputated, and the fingers were cut. [2,4]

Two Cambodians passing by "took pity" upon them, and helped carry Sophiap's sister to a field hospital run by an international organization. As they arrived, the field hospital was shelled and burned to the ground. Sophiap's sister died, as did many medical personnel. Sophiap "snatched the baby and ran for three days and nights," without food or water:

> . . . people were dead everywhere. Sometimes while running, the bullets hit people and they would just drop dead. So I ran into Thailand, about three days and three nights later . . . some Thai soldiers . . . said, "Why are you carrying a corpse? It's dead; throw it away." She didn't cry for three days and three nights.

Sophiap's somatic complaints: In 1985, after six years in Thai refugee camps, Sophiap, one brother, her niece (who survived). and a few remaining family members were resettled in the U.S. She was twenty years old. She spoke no English and soon began ESL classes and vocational training. But in 1987, she says, "I fell ill and I haven't been able to do anything since." Sophiap describes her initial suffering:

> I could not pinpoint it, like headaches and dizziness. And inside, my physical body was not well, my hands and my legs started shaking. So my sponsor advised me to go to the doctor. They checked my blood and everything else but could not find anything. So in June 1987, they looked and said I had a bladder infection. I no longer had the energy that I used to have . . . Like walking around, I could hardly do that. I got thinner and thinner, not knowing the reason why. I kept going to the doctor, they said I wasn't sick, but I kept losing pounds. They gave me TB tests and stuff like that. [2,9]

> . . . So I kept getting sick until 1990. One day in 1990, I was not able to get out of bed. I could no longer walk. I kept on having pain, starting in 1987. Whatever I ate hurt me, I could not eat a lot. So the doctor said I had an ulcer, the doctor in Beaverton. So in a week I was put to sleep twice, they gave me shots then they inserted a tube down my throat to my stomach. [3,1]

After continuing to experience extreme pain in her stomach area, she went to the emergency room for an x-ray. Sophiap says she was diagnosed with gallstones and underwent an operation to remove the stones in December, 1990. Although the operation relieved the acute pain, she continued to experience bodily pain and other physical symptoms. "Ever since the time of the operation until now," she says, "the inside of my body is not well."

Sophiap reports currently experiencing a wide range of physical complaints: she has excruciating headaches, stomach pains, and dizzy spells. She reports having recurring bladder infections and chronic physical exhaustion. Her heart races, her hands and feet shake, she cannot sleep, and she experiences pain "all over" her body:

> It's like I'm being stabbed by a knife . . . the pain spreads to my chest . . . The pain lasts throughout the night, then it exhausted itself out. It broke me to the point that I could not walk . . . Sometimes if it's not the severe sharp pain, it would be a mild pain like cramps . . . Sometimes if I had the Tylenol Three, I would fall asleep, but when the medicine potency runs out, the pain starts again . . . Sometimes, I go to the emergency [room] [3, 5-6].

Since resettling in the U.S., Sophiap has received acupuncture, spot-burning, traditional Khmer herbs, absolution from Buddhist monks and Kru Khmer. But the major sources of treatment have been from medical and mental health systems. Over the past 10 years, physicians have prescribed more than 50 different kinds of medication for Sophiap's pain. Their effects have not been long-lasting, and she continuously struggles to manage her pain: "Those medications, you can't say they don't help, when I take them they help, when I stop, it hurts again and that's how it's been." A psychiatrist diagnosed Sophiap as having post-traumatic stress disorder; her exchanges with him still allow her to "have hope," since he acknowledges her pain and attempts to explain how medications might help. However, she says, her internist's responses negate and thus exacerbate her suffering:

> I ask my doctor [internist] why am I so sick, I'm sick constantly. The doctor then answered that he cannot detect it, but my ailment cannot kill me, it cannot kill me like cancer and stuff. That's how he answered me! And so I responded that the ailment cannot kill me, that may be true, but they can hurt me and make it hard for me to live . . . He has thrown quite a bit of [unpleasant] words at me. He said you're sick, but you're not sick every day and I should be able to work.
> . . . the doctor keeps on saying that because I keep thinking that I'm sick, that's why I'm sick. And then I said, I don't believe that. It's because I'm in so much pain that's why I say I'm in pain. [4,2-3]

She says that doctors cannot find the source of her bodily pain; and that despite tapping a vast number and range of caregivers, she is still "the same."

Sophiap's construction of causes and consequences of her body's pain: Sophiap's construction of the causes of her pain is quite eclectic. She makes reference to her failure to cultivate good merit in a previous life as a possible cause of her contemporary suffering [5,5]. However, like many other survivors we interviewed, she also resists this explanation. Thus she describes an exchange with a monk, which took place in a Thai refugee camp:

The monk said that everything came about because, well, like–because of our bad karma. . . . The monk said that our karma, we're receiving our own karma (the effects of our own actions), like what we had committed from previous life. I asked the monk what I did in last life. Why didn't it take its toll immediately then in that life. Last life I committed sin but this life I haven't done anything. Why am I the only one receiving the bad karma, I asked him that. The monk said that's the belief in our religion. . . . But in this life I haven't done anything to anybody, I haven't done anything. I haven't stolen, I haven't robbed. I haven't inflicted physical wounds nor killed others. I haven't done anything. . . . [5, 9-10]

She sometimes speculates that "eating filthy things" [4,3] has caused her pain. More often she attributes her pain to the severe torture she experienced during the Pol Pot era [4,5], the traumatic loss of her sister and other family, and being left to "drift alone" [4,3]. Ultimately, however, she asserts that her illness is something she cannot get to the bottom of; a mystery that cannot be solved or comprehended. Her pain, she says, exists everywhere, in every part of her body, and is greater than the sum of all diagnosable diseases: "My physical body hurts more than just those . . . ailments, it hurts all over." [4,2]

Her body's illness prevents her from working and socializing. "My obstruction," Sophiap tells our interviewer, "is my illness" [3,8]. All other obstacles are removable except for her bodily pain: "the only problem is my physical body being sick; anything else is not a problem" [3,7]. Sophiap also feels that her sickness makes her "different" from other Cambodian survivors: "During that era, some people had lived just like I did. Why are they all right when they got here? They're not sick." [4,3] "I don't see young people my age ever having these kinds of illnesses. Other folks have suffered but are not sick now." [5,8] And like other survivors, she feels profoundly apart from the rest of the world. "Even on the regular days [when] I am not sick," she says, "I still don't have the energy that the normal people do . . . It's never completely cured like you folks" [4,3].

At one point, the interviewer presses an "heroic" interpretation upon Sophiap's illness discourse, but Sophiap rejects it:

[*Interviewer: . . . you have this incredible spirit inside of you that, when . . . you still crawled through those woods for days and–*] [interrupts, laughing]: Strong mind–but my body cannot go forward. Right now my feelings are like this: "If others can do so and so, why am I so weak? I'm going to keep doing it until I succeed." I can't make it. My mouth keeps speaking in vain, my feelings say so, but my physical strength doesn't measure up with others, and that's how it is. [6,2]

Phala's Illness Narrative: "I am not crazy! I am in pain."

Childhood before and during the time of the Killing Fields: Phala recalls little of her childhood prior to the time of the Killing Fields, except for one thing: her father, she reports, was always physically brutal toward her. The oldest of several children ("I can't recall how many," she says), she was a disappointment to her father, who had hoped for a son. "And he reminded me of it often":

> . . . I remember when he hit me with a bamboo stick, very big, and he hit me until the bamboo stick was all broken. And I was really hurt for many years, so that my mother wasn't able to farm. She had to stay to take care of me. . . . My mother was afraid to leave me alone, because she said that my father hit me until I was sick, almost to death . . . [2,4-5]

Like Sophiap, Phala was also nine years old when the Khmer Rouge invaded her small farming village. And like Sophiap, Phala's family was quickly separated in age-graded work camps. Phala was nearly starved, working and living under brutal conditions ("I had to sleep with dogs, with chicken poop, dog poop, pig poop, cow poop and everything" [2,8]). In her village of approximately 400, many were shot by Khmer Rouge soldiers during the evacuation. She said, "maybe only 30 to 40 survived." Several times, Phala's family attempted to flee to Thailand with other families, but was fired upon by Khmer Rouge soldiers. In one such attempt Phala's mother was shot and her sister and baby brother killed ["they . . . ran a knife through him" she says, "and I had nightmares about him"]. In another, she recounts, her young cousin was shot to death:

> We stopped for picking fruit and my cousin, she climbed up the tree and picked up some fruit and ate it. I was too tired to climb, so I just stayed down there and sat. They shot her and she fell over me . . . everybody just ran. [1,4]

By the time she made it to the Thai border, most members of Phala's family–and the members of her village–were dead.

Phala cannot now recall how much time she spent in Thai refugee camps prior to resettling in the U.S., nor who sponsored her. She remembers that she came to the U.S. in the mid-1980s in a group without her father, and then joined her father shortly afterwards in California. Although she tried to attend ESL classes, Phala found it very difficult to concentrate and to be around "crowds" for more than a couple of hours at a time (she would develop headaches and dizziness). Her father continued to physically and emotionally abuse her:

. . . he would say, "this stubborn female won't die. All the ones I loved have died. And the one that I hate, has come to cause me suffering." [2,8]

Phala's somatic complaints: Phala's chronic pain began in 1987 when she was pregnant with her first child and her father became very sick. She was his only caretaker. Her headaches and dizziness became excruciating ("it hurt so bad like it was going to explode" [2,2]). Her ears began to ache:

> . . . sometimes [my] ear hurt by itself, sometimes it hurt all together. . . it hurt like [she makes pounding noise and shrieking noise]. It hurt really bad, until I was in tears. [2,11]

Like Sophiap, Phala tried out a wide variety of Khmer and mainstream Western care options and caregivers, including Chinese and Cambodian herbs, prayer, acupuncturists, physical therapists, and counselors. Like Sophiap, her main help-seeking resource was "American doctors." Phala saw American doctors first for her headaches, earaches, and dizziness. However, she says, "they couldn't find anything wrong with me. They said there was nothing" [2,3]. Phala soon developed excruciating pain in her legs, hip, and back:

> . . . anytime I do anything, it rubs up against it and hurts bad. It's like that. Sometimes even when I bend a little bit, it gets stuck. You know, my back, I cannot move . . . I scream like something. It's like a sharp pain and I can't move.

The doctor takes an x-ray, but cannot find the cause of her pain:

> . . . they said it wasn't any type of serious injury. They said that it wasn't anything serious. But it still hurts like that. I still hurt like that. [1,13]

She developed chest pains, arm pains, stiffness, extreme weakness, and shakes:

> . . . when its during cold seasons, I'm not able to wash dishes. I wash one or two dishes, it [her arm] gets stuck like that. . . . sometimes when I clean the wall, you know, I hold the sponge, and I do like that, and I couldn't move. It's stiff, you know, it's stiff. When I scrub the wall, sometimes I can't move. And I can't grip it. Sometimes when I wear pants with a zipper, I can't zip it up. . . . it's like I have no strength . . . [2,12] . . . when I talk, I shake. If I held a spoon to eat with it, it would fall out.

Again, she seeks help from an American doctor:

> . . . But the doctor [uses disparaging Cambodian adjective for him] said that there's nothing wrong with me. I keep cursing at the doctor: "crazy doctor! I'm not crazy! I'm in pain. I'm not crazy." He would say, "you're not sick or in pain, you think too much." I keep going, but . . . American doctors don't believe me. they don't believe that I'm in pain. [2,17]

Repeated attempts to get relief from "American doctors" failed, and her condition "stayed the same." Doctors continually dismiss her pain, Phala reports, and they eventually play a major role in taking away her welfare benefits in the late 1980s:

> They said that, from my ability to talk and things, they said I could work. So, they stopped giving it to us. . . . They say I can do it [work], and I can't do it. My body and my mind, I can't do it [2,18]. Americans, they don't believe it. And when you tell them about it, they say that you're lying. . . . But I wouldn't lie. . . they say, "you can talk, you can move your arms and legs." Of course I can do it, I'm not paralyzed . . . I can still breathe. [1,19]

About two or three years prior to our interview, Phala stopped going to the "American doctors" who don't believe her:

> . . . because they said that there was nothing wrong with me . . . And I keep having pain, pain, pain. And they: "oh, nothing's wrong." [4,4]

She now goes to an East Indian doctor, who listens and talks to her about how to manage her pain. Phala also goes to a counselor at an Asian American mental health center, who also talks to her and tries to explain "how to deal with some of the pain, some of the problems" [3,10]. These help in some sense, Phala suggests, but "not really. I still have . . . all those pains. . . . There doesn't seem to be anything that's helpful."

Phala's construction of causes and consequences of her body's pain: Like Sophiap, Phala describes a number of possible explanations for her body's illnesses. At one point, she suggests that her failure to receive *chhuoh plung* (a fire set to "warm" a woman who has just given birth and thus restore cold-heat balance) after her first child's birth may be partly responsible for her current problems with walking and her general weakness. She also attributes her back problems to her father's severe physical abuse (both when she was younger and when she was pregnant with her first child). Like Sophiap, she is somewhat skeptical of karmic and other theological explanations for her contemporary suffering ("I believe and I don't believe," she says). She sometimes suggests that her leg and hip pain may be due to the fact that she was forced to sleep in animal feces by the Khmer Rouge (" . . . all the time, in mud and cow poop," she recalls, "that's why I think that, right now, my legs hurt" [1,2]). Like Sophiap, she associates the trauma of her Killing Field experiences as the major cause of her embodied pain and states, "I do not recall experiencing any of these pains until after the Killing Fields." But ultimately, she asserts the specific causes of her pain and suffering as unknown. Repeatedly throughout her interviews, she tells us, "I don't know. It just comes. I don't know. Just all the pains and stuff like that. It just comes when it comes. So I don't know" [2,12].

An Interpretation of Sophiap's and Phala's Somatization Narratives

Clearly, to Sophiap and Phala, somatic complaint is not an indirect or dysfunctional expression of psychiatric distress, but rather *authentic and embodied pain*. Their illness narratives suggest complex and eclectic explanations for this pain. Central to this explanation are the atrocities or traumas experienced by each during the Killing Fields. For Sophiap, these atrocities include the repeated physical beatings she endured, seeing the tortuous death of her beloved sister and the mass murder of strangers, the "disappearance" of her brothers, the death of her mother and most of her extended family, and the terror of being abandoned as a child to "drift alone." For Phala, the etiology of her contemporary pain includes near-starvation, physical degradation (sleeping in animal feces), witnessing of murders (including her cousin, shot to death in a treetop), and massive family losses suffered during the Killing Fields. In Phala's case, however, chronic abuse from her father, predating and subsequent to the Killing Fields, is also seen as etiologically important. After resettlement in the United States, these two forces intersect in exquisitely painful ways–recall, for example, her father's condemnation of her for being "still here," while "all those he loved" have died, and her report of increasingly severe headaches and dizziness when she was pregnant with her first child and sole caretaker for her sick father (since she is now the only family member left). Both Sophiap and Phala also acknowledge a cosmologically diverse range of possible explanations. For example, they both consider (though somewhat skeptically) the explanations for suffering and pain proffered by Buddhist theology and Khmer spiritism. Phala also considers the possibility that failure to achieve proper *chi* balance subsequent to child birth may have contributed to her current back pain and general bodily weakness; Sophiap speculates that her body has been polluted by the "filthy things" she was forced to eat during the time of the Killing Fields.

Ultimately, however, neither Sophiap nor Phala can theorize about the specific ways in which the trauma of the Killing Fields and other social factors directly cause somatic pain. Thus, as in prevailing professional explanatory models, the etiology of somatization remains essentially in doubt. Phala expresses this in a simple and straightforward way–i.e., throughout her interviews she repeatedly asserts, "I just don't know" what really causes her body's many forms of pain. Sophiap goes one step further: the cause of her pain is not known, cannot be known, and is "more so than these [diagnosed] diseases." To Sophiap, somatic pain and suffering is essentially unfathomable.

Interestingly, and in contrast to some previous reports in the literature, our analysis of illness narratives did not suggest that Sophiap and Phala either avoid or are incapable of expressing negative affect or feelings. In fact, the majority of the 31 participants in the larger study quite readily and easily describe psychological states and affective complaints: sadness, hopelessness, frustration, emotional numbness, anger, "feeling like giving up," and so on.

Ironically, reports of affective distress often arise around encounters with care professionals. These encounters figure largely into survivor explanatory frameworks of pain and suffering. For example, a professional's acceptance of bodily pain and suffering as "legitimate" and authentic provides a certain measure of relief. When in response to Phala's description of her somatic pain, the Indian doctor and the counselor focus on talking about ways to manage pain, she feels "helped, but not helped." In other words, while the methods of pain relief discussed provide little or only temporary relief at the best, being believed is dignifying and "helpful" in itself. On the other hand, when the presentation of bodily pain is dismissed, discredited, or "translated" into psychological distress by care professionals, Sophiap and Phala report feeling affective distress–especially anger, hurt, discouragement, and frustration.

In clear contrast to the explanatory framework prevalent among professionals, the implicit model in Sophiap's and Phala's somatization narratives can be understood as follows:

"Real" embodied pain -> Loss of function -> Clinical encounter and somatic presentation -> Psychological distress (anger, frustration, etc.) (adapted from May, Doyle, & Chew-Graham, 1999: 530).

Within this perspective, the major forces behind suffering are social (traumas associated with the war; childhood abuse; clinical encounters) rather than psychodynamic (dysfunction or pathology of the individual). Suffering begins with the etiologically enigmatic embodiment of traumas experienced during the Killing Fields, often intertwined in complex ways with other traumas and events in the survivor's life trajectory. Subsequent interactions with care professionals can serve to exacerbate the individual's experience of distress and suffering (see Kleinman, Das, & Lock, 1997).

SUMMARY AND IMPLICATIONS:
THE PROFESSIONAL'S ROLE
IN CHANGING THE CULTURE AND ORGANIZATION
OF CARE FOR CAMBODIAN SURVIVORS

The limited scope of the present analysis precludes drawing firm conclusions. Clearly, more research on larger samples is needed to understand the similarities and differences among Cambodian survivor experiences of somatization. Comparison of professional and survivor narratives are also needed to understand somatic transactions in care settings. At the same time, we note that the findings from this analysis support other published critiques of professional care systems and raise issues that warrant future analysis. These issues include the professional's tendency to disparage survivor reports of pain, to pathologize somatic complaints and complainants, and to exacerbate (however unwittingly) the survivor's experience of distress and suffering. Underlying these issues is the presumption within care systems that prevailing professional beliefs about somatic complaint are "real" and "truthful," while those of survivors are "constructed" and "untrue," despite the paucity of evidence supporting this distinction. This "biomedical ethnocentrism" (see Unshuld, 1981; Pescosolido, 1991) is reinforced by other factors, including the evolution of the socio-legal "gatekeeper" role played by care professionals within the medical and welfare systems and the intractability of the survivor's pain.

Care systems are currently organized in such a way that attaches much more power and influence to professional than to patient viewpoints. Nevertheless, as Sophiap's and Phala's narratives suggest, survivors are capable of resisting the dominant (professional) viewpoint. In doing so, as May, Doyle, and Chew-Graham (1999) point out, they exercise the power of self-definition ("I am not crazy!" Phala insists to her doctor, "I am in pain."). In their insistence that their pain is both organic and intractable, Sophiap and Phala maintain a complex relationship with professionals and care systems. On one hand, the survivors construct and present their complaints very much within the terms of the prevailing biomedical model (which confers primacy and legitimacy to organic disease). On the other hand, by insisting that their suffering is unfathomable and incurable, Sophiap and Phala, in essence, assert that they cannot be helped by the prevailing perspectives and practices in care systems. This is precisely the case, Shay (1994) and Langer (1991) suggest, because the essential injuries brought about by atrocities such as the Cambodian Killing Fields are moral and social–and so the central treatments must be moral and social (Shay, 1994).

Appropriate intervention on behalf of atrocity survivors, as Shay (1994) suggests, requires a fundamental reorganization of the culture and structure of care. We must create new models of healing that restore the power of self-definition and control to the survivor and emphasize what Shay calls the communilization of trauma (see also Boehnlein, 1987). Communilization entails both allowing the survivor to present her narrative in her own terms and providing "trustworthy listening" on the part of care professionals. To be trustworthy listeners, professionals must be strong enough to hear narratives of atrocity, pain, and suffering without denying the reality of experience or disparaging the victim, and must be willing to do their best to imagine themselves in the unimaginable scenes described by survivors. This, in turn, requires a very personal and emotional level of involvement with survivors that is, in many respects, at odds with the distance we have been taught to maintain as professionals (Uehara et al., 1998, p. 55). Without emotion in the listener, Shay asserts, there can be no communilization of the trauma. Respectful and personally-committed listening must in turn lead to patient- or client-centered practices that make it much more difficult for professionals to pathologize somatic complaints and other survivor responses to atrocity. These responses should instead be seen, as Eisenbruch suggests, as "normal . . . existential responses" to the massive social, cultural, and personal losses they have suffered (Eisenbruch, 1991). Conventional treatments clearly have a place in a communalized approach to care, as do alternative caregivers such as Kru Khmer, Buddhist monks, and Chinese herbalists. However, professionals must acknowledge the questionable efficacy of such treatments for curing the uncurable. As Langer asserts, after experiencing atrocities of the sort experienced by Sophiap and Phala, a return to "normal" is unlikely (Langer, 1991; also Shay, 1994). How much healing and recovery a survivor can obtain from mainstream or alternative therapies during his lifetime is unknown (Shay, 1994: 186). Thus a communalized model must offer caring as well as cure; refuge as well as rehabilitation. Ultimately, as Shay suggests, our approach to care must encompass a political and preventive orientation as well. As an integral part of care, we must advocate for the eradiction of "that which causes traumatic symptoms" for which there is no medical cure–i.e., for the end to geopolitical atrocities such as the Killing Fields (Shay, 1994: Uehara et al., 1998).

REFERENCES

Bemak, F. & Timm, J. (1994). Case study of an adolescent Cambodian Refugee: A clinical, developmental, and cultural perspective. *International Journal for the Advancement of Counseling 17*, 47-56.

Boehnlein, J. (1987). Clinical relevance of grief and mourning among Cambodian refugees. *Social Science and Medicine 25*, 765-772.

Boehnlein, J. & Kinzie, J.D. (1992). DSM diagnosis of posttraumatic stress disorder and cultural sensitivity: A response. *Journal of Nervous and Mental Disease 1870*, 597-599.

Carlson, E. & Rosser-Hogan. R. (1991). Trauma experiences, posttraumatic stress, dissociation and depression in Cambodian refugees. *American Journal of Psychiatry 148*, 1548-1551.

Carlson, E. & Rosser-Hogan, R. (1994). Cross-cultural response to trauma: A study of traumatic experiences and posttraumatic symptoms in Cambodian refugees. *Journal of Traumatic Stress 7*, 43-58.

Chandler, D. (1991). *The Tragedy of Cambodian History: Politics, War, and Revolution Since 1945.* New Haven, CT: Yale University Press.

D'Avanzo, C. E., Frye, B., & Froman, R. (1984). Stress in Cambodian refugee families. *Journal of Nursing Scholarship 26*, 101-105.

Eisenbruch, M. (1991). From posttraumatic stress disorder to cultural bereavement: Diagnosis of Southeast Asian refugees. *Social Science & Medicine 33*, 673-680.

Frye, B. (1990). The process of health care decision making among Cambodian immigrant women. *International Quarterly of Community Health Education 10*, 113-124.

Frye, B. & D'Avanzo, C. (1994). Cultural themes in family stress and violence among Cambodian refugee women in the inner city. *Advances in Nursing Science 16*, 64-77.

Good, B. (1994). *Medicine, Rationality, and Experience.* Cambridge: Cambridge University Press.

Kinzie, J.D. (1989). Therapeutic approaches to traumatized Cambodian refugees. *Journal of Traumatic Stress 2*, 75-91.

Kinzie, J.D. (1993). Posttraumatic effects and their treatment among Southeast Asian Refugees. In J. P. Wilson & B. Raphael (Eds.), *International Handbook of Traumatic Stress* (pp. 311-320). New York: Plenum Press.

Kinzie, J.D., Leung, P., Boehnlein, J.K., & Fleck, J. (1987). Antidepresseant Blood Levels in Southeast Asians: Clinical and cultural implications. *Journal of Nervous and Mental Disease 175*, 480-485.

Kleinman, A., Das, V., & Lock, M. (Eds). (1997). *Social Suffering.* Berkeley, CA: University of California Press.

Kleinman, A. & Good, B. (Eds). (1985). *Culture and Depression: Studies in the Anthropology and Cross-Cultural Psychiatry of Affect and Disorder.* Berkeley, CA: University of California Press.

Kleinman, A. & Kleinman, J. (1985). Somatization: The interconnections in Chinese Society among culture, depressive experiences, and the meanings of pain. In A. Kleinman and B. Good (Eds.), *Culture and Depression: Studies in the Anthropology and Cross-Cultural Psychiatry of Affect and Disorder* (pp. 429-490). Berkeley, CA: University of California Press.

Kleinman, A. (1988). *The Illness Narratives: Suffering, Healing & the Human Condition.* New York: Basic Books.

Kiernan, B. (1996). *The Pol Pot Regime: Race, Power, and Genocide in Cambodia under the Khmer Rouge, 1975-1979.* New Haven, CT: Yale University Press.

Kiernan, B. (1997). A World Turned Upside Down. In D. Pran (Compiler), *Children of Cambodia's Killing Fields: Memoirs by Survivors* (pp. xi-xvii,). New Haven, CT: Yale University Press.

Kirmayer, L. J. & Young, A. (1998). Culture and somatization: Clinical, epidemiological, and ethnographic perspectives. *Psychosomatic Medicine 60*, 420-430.

Kirmayer, L.J. (1986). Somatization and the social construction of illness experience.

In McHugh, S. & Vallis, T.M. (Eds.), *Illness Behavior: A Multidisciplinary Perspective* (pp. 111-133). New York: Plenum Press.

Kroll, J., Habenicht, M., MacKenzie, T., Yang, M., Chan, S., Vang, T., Nguyen, T., Ly, M., Phommasouvanh, B., Nguyen, H., Van, V., Souvannasoth, L., & Cabugao, R. (1989). Depression and posttraumatic stress disorder in Southeast Asian refugees. *American Journal of Psychiatry 146,* 1592-1597.

Kroll, J., Habenicht, M., MacKenzie, T., Yang, M., Chan, S., Vang, T., Nguyen, T., Ly, M., Phommasouvanh, B., Nguyen, H., Van, V., Souvannasoth, L., & Cabugao, R. (1990). Medication compliance, antidepressant blood levels, and side effects in Southeast Asian patients. *Journal of Clinical Psychopharmacology 10,* 279-283.

Langer, Lawrence. (1991). *Holocaust Testimonies: The Ruins of Memory.* New Haven, CT: Yale University Press.

Langer, L. (1997). The alarmed vision: Social suffering and holocaust atrocity. In A. Kleinman, V. Das, & M Lock (Eds.), *Social Suffering* (pp. 47-66). Berkeley, CA: University of California Press.

Leigh, J. & Green, J. (1989). Teaching ethnographic methods to social service workers. *Practicing Anthropology 11,* 8-10.

Levav, I. (1998). Individuals under conditions of maximum adversity: The holocaust. In B. P. Dohrenwend (ed.), *Adversity, Stress and Psychopathology* (pp. 13-33). New York: Oxford University Press.

Lin, K. (1986). Psychopathology and social disruption in refugees. In C. L. Williams & J. Westermeyeter (Eds.), *Refugee Mental Health in Resettlement Countries* (pp. 61-73). Washington: Hemisphere Publishing Corporation.

May, C., Doyle, H., & Chew-Graham, C. (1999). Medical knowledge and the intractable patient: The case of chronic low back pain. *Social Science & Medicine 48,* 523-534.

Meinhardt, K., Tom, S., Tse, P., & Yu, C. (1984). *Santa Clara County Health Department Asian Health Assessment Project.* San Jose: Santa Clara County Health Department Division of Mental Health Services, 1-45.

Mollica, R., Poole, C., & Tor, S. The legacy of the Cambodian tragedy. In B. P. Dohrenwend (ed.), *Adversity, Stress and Psychopathology* (pp. 34-5). New York: Oxford University Press.

Mollica, R., Caspi-Yavin, Y., Truong, T., Tor, S., & Lavelle, J. (1992). The Harvard Trauma Questionnaire. *The Journal of Nervous and Mental Disease 180,* 111-116.

Rief, W. & Hiller, W. (1998). Somatization–future perspectives on a common phenomenon. *Journal of Psychosomatic Research 44,* 529-536.

Shay, J. (1994). *Achilles in Vietnam: Combat Trauma and the Undoing of Character.* New York: Atheneum.

Unschuld, Paul. (1981). Cross-cultural relations. Medical ethno-masochism. *Social Science and Medicine 15,* 1-2.

Uehara, E., Farris, M., Morelli, P., & Ishisaka, A. (1998). "Eloquent chaos" in the oral discourses of Killing Fields survivors: An exploration of atrocity and narrativization. Unpublished manuscript.

Culturally Competent Substance Abuse Treatment for Asian/Pacific Islander Women

Paula T. Morelli
Rowena Fong
Julie Oliveira

SUMMARY. In response to the urgent need for substance abuse treatment among pregnant and postpartum Asian/Pacific Islander (A/PI) women, heath care and social service providers in a rural community of Hawaii established a culturally based, women-centered residential treatment program. The program was designed to address barriers that often prevent A/PI women from engaging and completing treatment. Treatment included Hawaiian healing practices or deep cultural therapy, provision for newborns to live with their mothers, infant health-care services, parent education, and infant-mother bonding guided by *kupuna* (elders) of the community.

Analysis of twenty-one in-depth interviews revealed factors that A/PI women participants found vital to their treatment process: having their children with them in a non-punitive, mutually respectful treatment milieu; working with consistent, competent residential staff and

---

Paula T. Morelli, PhD, Rowena Fong, EdD, and Julie Oliveira, MSW, are affiliated with the University of Hawaii at Manoa, School of Social Work, 2500 Campus Road, Hawaii Hall 213, Honolulu, HI 96822 (E-mail: morelli@hawaii.edu).

The authors want to thank the staff and participants in the Na Wahine Makalapua Project, the State of Hawaii, Department of Health, Alcohol and Drug Abuse Division, and the Center for Substance Abuse Prevention for funding this study.

A version of this paper was presented at the Council on Social Work Education, Annual Program Meeting in San Francisco, March 1999.

[Haworth co-indexing entry note]: "Culturally Competent Substance Abuse Treatment for Asian/Pacific Islander Women." Morelli, Paula T., Rowena Fong, and Julie Oliveira. Co-published simultaneously in *Journal of Human Behavior in the Social Environment* (The Haworth Press, Inc.) Vol. 3, No. 3/4, 2001, pp. 263-280; and: *Psychosocial Aspects of the Asian-American Experience: Diversity Within Diversity* (ed: Namkee G. Choi) The Haworth Press, Inc., 2001, pp. 263-280. Single or multiple copies of this article are available for a fee from The Haworth Document Delivery Service [1-800-342-9678, 9:00 a.m. - 5:00 p.m. (EST). E-mail address: getinfo@haworthpressinc.com].

263

culturally-sensitive interdisciplinary professionals; and involvement in a range of substance abuse interventions, including cultural healing practices.

Findings underscore the importance of learning about and affirming women's lived-experiences and cultural contexts in the development of culturally competent practice models, interventions, research procedures, and policies that focus on the complex needs of chemically dependent pregnant and parenting women (Brindis & Theidon, 1997). *[Article copies available for a fee from The Haworth Document Delivery Service: 1-800-342-9678. E-mail address: <getinfo@haworthpressinc.com> Website: <http://www.HaworthPress.com> © 2001 by The Haworth Press, Inc. All rights reserved.]*

KEYWORDS. Cultural competence, substance abuse, Asian/Pacific Islander women

Culturally competent social work practice is a growing concern for the 21st century. It is predicted that by the year 2000 one out of four people in the United States will be a person of color (Lecca, Quervalu, Nunes, & Gonzales, 1998). Western health-science practices and interventions, which are based on white, male-dominant paradigms, have been criticized for being culturally and gender insensitive. Social workers and other professionals are faced, therefore, with the challenge of utilizing practices founded on the cultural beliefs and values of clients who come from diverse socio-cultural backgrounds.

New definitions, frameworks, and practice models aimed at developing cultural competency among those serving ethnic minority clients with problems such as substance abuse, depression and cancer are in the process of evolving (Lecca, Quervalu, Nunes, & Gonzales, 1998; Philleo & Brisbane, 1998; Vargas & Koss-Chioino, 1992). Current definitions of culturally competent practice focus on understanding the impact of the varying social environments at the micro, mezzo, and macro levels. Chung (1992), for example, defines cultural competency as "a set of congruent behaviors, attitudes, and policies that come together in a system, agency, or profession that enables that system, agency, profession to work effectively in cross cultural settings." Miley, O'Melia, and Dubois (1998) view community as a necessary component for a culturally competent framework, which includes the practitioner and agency. Fong, Boyd, and Browne (1999) conceptualize culturally competent practice as a practice model focused on the biculturalization of interventions. The process of biculturalizing interventions involves utilization of both indigenous healing and western treatment methods, integrating cultural values, beliefs, and techniques that are respected by the client, thereby increasing the potential for improved levels of functioning. The inclusion of various natural support systems is also an essential part of culturally competent practice. For example, in Hispanic/Latino cultures botanical (herb) shops and grocers from the same community often offer support to families with problems (Delgado, 1995). In the Pacific Islander culture of Hawaiians, *kupuna,* elders or grandparents can provide guidance and support for mothers who abuse alcohol or other substances (Mokuau, 1998; Fong & Morelli, 1998).

Innovative culture-specific interventions that use traditional healing practices and natural social support systems are becoming increasingly important for treating the expanding substance abuse problem among ethnic minorities. A growing body of literature affirms the relevance and efficacy of specific cultural perspectives and practices in the development of drug abuse prevention and intervention strategies (DeCambra, Marshall, & Ono, 1999; Mokuau, 1999; Fong & Morelli, 1998; Jileck, 1994; Maypole & Anderson, 1987; Wing, Crow, & Thompson, 1995).

In order to advance our knowledge about potential ways to develop culturally competent substance abuse treatment, this article examines the perspectives of pregnant and postpartum A/PI women regarding the processes and factors which were critical to facilitating their healing, abstinence, and personal growth during their participation in a women-centered, culturally-based substance abuse treatment program.

SUBSTANCE ABUSE AND ASIAN/PACIFIC ISLANDER WOMEN

Substance abuse among females now nearly equals that of males in the United States. The ratio for illegal drug use among adult males to adult females is 1.5 to 1, and for 12- to 18-year-olds the ratio is 1 to 1 (National Center on Addiction and Substance Abuse at Columbia University [CASA], 1996). Women of childbearing age (15-44 years of age) who use illicit drugs currently number 4.1 million (Substance Abuse and Mental Health Services Administration [SAMHSA], 1997; National Institute on Drug Abuse [NIDA], 1998). More than 1.5 million (38%) of these women reported having children living with them, and 400,000 (11%) had at least one child under 2 years of age (SAMHSA, 1997). The 1995 National Household Survey on Drug Abuse determined that 2.3% of the estimated 2.7 million women who are pregnant each year are current drug users.

Asian/Pacific Islanders (A/PI) are defined by the U.S. Department of Health and Human Services (1995) as persons "having origins in any of the original peoples of the Far East, Southeast Asia, the Indian subcontinent or the Pacific Islands." Asians and Pacific Islanders include more than 60 separate racial/ethnic groups and subgroups that are heterogeneous. Despite the fact that A/PI are one of the fastest growing populations in the United

States, having increased by 155% between 1980 and 1993, very little is known about prevalence of substance abuse within this group.

The Department of Health and Human Services pooling data from 1991, 1992, and 1993 found that substance abuse among A/PI was less frequent than other Americans (SAMHSA, 1998). However, much less is known about Asian/Pacific Islander women's substance abuse and health needs, as they are seldom the focus of research. The national women's health agenda assumes A/PI women's health needs are minimal or nonexistent (Yi, 1996). However, a study conducted by the Hawaii State Department of Health (1996) on substance abuse among 603 childbearing-age women (12-47 years of age) found that 15.6 % of the A/PI women (Filipino, Hawaiian, Japanese, Korean, Samoan and other Asians) reported using alcohol at least once a week over a year, 4.8% used drugs only, and 6% used both alcohol and drugs at least once a week. Relative to national statistics, percentages from the Hawaii study suggest that substance abuse among A/PI women is increasing.

PARADIGM SHIFTS IN SUBSTANCE ABUSE TREATMENT

Substance abuse treatment for women, clearly, is a priority; however, programs designed with men as the target population have not given recognition to women's treatment needs, such as child care and relational therapy. Meeting the need for "women-centered" substance abuse treatment (Brindis & Theidon, 1997) requires continual awareness of multiple barriers, which may prevent women from obtaining treatment. Barriers to treatment include: the pariah-like stigmatization of women who use alcohol or other drugs (Metsch et al., 1995; Broom & Stevens, 1991), which is increased if a woman is pregnant (Brindis & Theidon, 1997); severe problems in other areas of their lives, such as, abuse as a child, domestic violence, sexual assault, incest, and violence (Brindis & Theidon, 1997); fear of losing children to the welfare system; child care needs; family responsibilities; family treatment needs (Abbott, 1994; Schliebner, 1994; Wald, Harvey, & Hibbard, 1995); a substance abusing partner; and lack of culturally compatible treatment modalities.

The origins of male-focused treatment paradigms can be traced to early developmental theories that continue to dominate educational and practice settings. The male-biased theories of psychological development cast women as inadequate, inferior, masochistic, incomplete, an aside, or non-existent (Freud, 1924, 1925, 1931, 1932; Piaget, 1965; Kohlberg, 1958, 1981). Freudian theory, in particular, has been a powerful force in shaping societal views about the meaning and purpose of women's lives in the twentieth century. According to Gayle Rubin, Freud's essays on women should be read "as description of how a group is prepared, psychologically, at a tender age, to live with its oppression" (Donovan, 1994). For almost three quarters of a century, the practice of brainwashing women about male supremacy and defining women as psychologically and physically impaired remained at the core of psychiatric treatment efforts.

In opposition to gender-oppressive constructions of women's lives, subsequent theories of women's psychological development emphasize the centrality of relationships for women (Belensky et al., 1986; Gilligan, 1982; Miller, 1976 in Covington & Surrey, 1997). The relational model of women's development, based on the work of Jean Baker Miller (1976), utilizes the perspectives, language, and concepts that originate from women's experiences and explores the strengths and problems arising for women from this relational orientation (Covington & Surrey, 1997). According to Baker, women's primary motivation throughout life is establishing a basic sense of connection to others. Women's sense of self and self-worth is established through connections, a feeling of mutual presence and joining in relational process, and is based on empathy and mutuality in relationships. Unfortunately, when viewed from a male oriented developmental perspective, the centrality of relationship for women's psychological health has been pathologized as dependence, codependency, fixation, and passivity (Covington & Surrey, 1997).

From a women-centered development perspective, there are five patterns of relational disconnection that may foster substance abuse and increase risks of relapse in women: (1) nonmutual relationships: historically male-female relationships in our culture have been rooted in non-mutuality, and power-over the other leading over time to compulsive caretaking, idealized notions of the "good" mother, or withdrawal from real relationships; (2) effects of isolation and shaming: failure of the relational context to validate a woman's experience or her attempts at connection may leave her feeling condemned to isolation and shamed; (3) limiting relational images: cultural images that limit or distort a woman's sense of what it means to be healthy, worthwhile, physically attractive, and successful in order to be worthy of connection can lead to the use of substances to alter the self to fit cultural images; (4) abuse, violation, and systemic violence: all women are at risk of being abused, but the risk of childhood abuse is increased for women raised in an alcoholic family and, as an adult, higher for women with an alcoholic male partner, all of which needs to be understood within the context of societal violence; and (5) distortion of sexuality: substance abuse is often the result of attempts to numb the emotional pain of sexual abuse experiences, and, in turn, reduce sexual inhibition (Covington & Surrey, 1997). Thus, women may use drugs: (1) to make or maintain connections, (2) to dissociate from or deal with emotional pain, (3) because a partner is using, (4) to change herself in order to feel worthy of a relationship or a combination of the factors mentioned previously.

Although mainstream drug and alcohol treatment programs have often ignored the political, economic, and socio-cultural context in which substance abuse occurs, several indigenous organizations in North America, Australia, and New Zealand have begun developing innovative culture-specific interventions for addictions (Brady, 1995). One example of such a study seeking to identify barriers and obstacles to obtaining care for alcoholism among Muskogee Indians in Oklahoma found that the Muskogee viewed health as a unity of mind, body, and spirit, admitted to feeling shamed in Western alcohol treatment programs, and believed that treatment should incorporate the entire family (Wing et al., 1995). Duran and Duran (1995) have argued that answers to the problem of substance addiction continue to exist within Native communities and that "practitioners must search within the traditional teaching and processes in order to address the problem in a more relevant manner."

A CULTURALLY BASED, WOMEN-CENTERED, COMMUNITY RESIDENTIAL TREATMENT PROGRAM

Faced with increasing numbers of A/PI women in need of substance abuse treatment in the Hawaii State Department of Health, Alcohol and Drug Abuse Division, via a demonstration grant, the Center for Substance Abuse Prevention (CSAP) funded a women-centered, culturally based treatment program for pregnant and postpartum women in the Wai'anae community called Na Wahine Makalapua (NWM; Beautiful Women or Women to Blossom Forth).

NWM consisted of two major components, a supervised, safe residence for mother and child and a substance abuse treatment program, which utilized Hawaiian deep healing processes and community-based supports which included over 115 agencies and such as Kapiolani Medical Center Special Care Clinic, the Parent Child Development Center, Kaiser Baby S.A.F.E. Public Health Nursing from the State of Hawaii Department of Health, Head Start programs, and many others. The residential setting provided the services and education aimed at supporting the mother and infant bonding process, maintaining an environment where the women would treat themselves and others in ways that promoted positive self-esteem, and providing childcare while mothers attended a culturally based substance abuse treatment program. The average residential stay was 3.5 months.

The heart of the substance abuse treatment was Hawaiian deep cultural therapy, which incorporated Hawaiian values and traditional healing practices. NWM Hawaiian deep cultural therapy consisted of *ho'oponopono* (conflict resolution), deep culture (storytelling); *Lo'i* (taro patch), and *Lomilomi* (massage therapy). The underlying principles and processes of these traditional Hawaiian healing practices are in harmony with women's relational needs and provide a beginning point for their healing processes.

Ho'oponopono (conflict resolution). *Ho'oponopono* was an integral part of the treatment provided. *Ho'oponopono* literally means "to set to right." *Ho'o* is to "make, cause, or bring about, pono is to make correct, right, and in perfect order," while *ponopono* (reduplicated) is "to put in order, care for, attend to that which is socially morally approved and desirable" (Pukui, 1972, 1979). *Ho'oponopono* is a method of conflict resolution and problem solving, (Mokuau, 1990; Paglinawan, 1972; Shook, 1985).

The values and concepts inherent in the *ho'oponopono* process are *aloha*, *lokahi*, *'ohana*, and *mana* (Mokuau, 1990). *Ho'oponopono* is conducted in the spirit of *aloha* or love, which emphasizes the importance of soothing and preventing conflict, shame, and other interpersonal disruption. If the harmony is disrupted, conducting one's self in the spirit of *aloha* implies that the individuals involved should have the courage to ask for and give forgiveness (Shook, 1985).

Lokahi means eliminating the negatives in one's life and replacing them with positive energy of love and understanding. *Lokahi* reunites the *'aumakua* (family ancestor god) with the family so that the whole becomes greater than its individual parts. The *'ohana* (family) in Hawaiian culture is the center of life, referring to the family unit, nuclear or extended. It can also refer to a group of people who are not related by blood, but who share a common goal, vision, or purpose (Pukui et al, 1972)–people committed to people who share fully in order to resolve problems or meet tasks.

Mana refers to "supernatural or divine power." In describing *mana*, Pukui (1979) suggested that "a Hawaiian's openness with the spirits and gods was just a part of natural consciousness . . . it was a second sense." Spiritual awareness guided the Native Hawaiians in their relationship with things of nature, such as the mountains, oceans, trees, birds, and in their recognition that nature also embodies spiritual power. Native Hawaiians sought to maintain a relationship between the individual, the community, nature, and the spiritual realm (Mokuau, 1990) through prayer and reliance on guidance from higher powers.

Ho'oponopono may take hours, days, or longer. Each person is given an opportunity to speak without others interrupting and to release all negatives that initiated *ho'oponopono*. After the *wehewehe* (discussion), the *mihi* (forgiveness) stage begins in which participants request forgiveness from each other and the higher powers. If participants are unable to forgive each other, the *haku* (leader) may request *ho'omalu* (time out) to allow for a cooling off period, so that the participants have time to think through the problems and decide if they want to proceed or *mo ka piko* (sever the ties). This happens when a person refuses to accept responsibility for his or her actions or words.

If the participants agree to proceed and not hold a grudge (*ho'omauhala*), the next phase is *kala* (untying the knot of the problem). In this phase, participants agree to release the problem and any negative energy from their lives. *Ho'ponopono* must begin and end with prayer and a closing ritual, usually involving food (Mokuau, 1990; Paglinawan, 1972; Shook, 1985; Pukui et al., 1979).

Deep culture (storytelling). The use of oral exchange of genealogies, history, traditions, values, and legends was passed from one generation to the next to perpetuate the culture. Deep culture, storytelling, is used as a therapeutic method of teaching and healing. A *kapu* (restriction) to discourage participants from leaving the session when the emotional pain becomes unbearable is set forth at the beginning. The *kupuna* (elder) facilitating the session requires the participants to role-play parts of well-known Hawaiian legends. The story lines resemble the struggles of the participants to overcome current challenges, such as substance abuse, depression, spiritual loss, or physical abuse. The reenactments can lead to participants' catharsis and healing.

Lo'i (irrigated terrace for taro). The legend of *kalo* explains the rationale for working in the *lo'i*. Although many versions of this legend exists, the common belief is that taro is the first-born child of Papa (mother-earth) and Wakea (father-sky). In the *kumulipo*, a chant describing the creation of the Hawaiian people, this first child is the beginning of the animate and inanimate. His younger brother, Haloa, is the father of all mankind. Because of this spiritual connection, Hawaiians believe that *lo'i* as a food source has special *mana* (Shintani, 1991). *Oha*, the root or core of the taro plant, is not only the "staff of life" in the Hawaiian diet, but is also the first part of the word family, and combined with the plural form, na, completes the word *'ohana*.

Besides the spiritual, food, and family connections, the *lo'i* also serves as a place for change and education. For some of the participants, it is believed that over time the long hard days will encourage values of *laulima* (working together), *lokahi* (harmony), and *ho'omaluhia* (patience) so that difficult challenges are faced with positive Hawaiian values. It is hoped that the values of the *lo'i* will permeate their lives. The *lo'i* requires the intensive manual labor of bending and getting into "knee-deep" water to weed and harvest the taro. Depending on the size of the *lo'i* patch, it may require daily maintenance. As part of the substance abuse treatment program, the participants spent one day per week in the *lo'i*.

Lomilomi (massage therapy). Lomilomi is a spiritually based ancient Hawaiian healing art designed to produce a gentle, graceful, rhythmic, light or deep massage to parts of the external body's pressure points, nerve centers, muscle tissue, and internal organs. It removes toxic waste, tension, pain, and fatigue and replaces them with positive energy, increases circulation, and improves muscle tone. *Lomilomi* requires an attitude on the part of the person, who must be clean and positive in mind, body, and spirit and who must trust that *lomilomi* will help, coming as it does from the higher power.

The use of prayer is the foundation of Hawaiian healing practices; it is said before, during, and after a session. Communication at this spiritual level creates trust, and when two spirits or souls meet, healing takes place. These Hawaiian healing practices, which are supported by the residential family services, life skills training, family and individual counseling including fathers or significant others, parenting education, and *kupuna* (elder) counseling, were expected to increase women's ability to make relational connections and to bring them closer to their cultural values, which would enable them to enhance their self-esteems and would increase the likelihood of their completing the treatment program.

RESEARCH METHOD

Data Collection

Using a semi-structured interview guide facilitated by ethnographic interviewing methods a sample of twenty-one A/PI program participants shared their substance abuse treatment narratives in two to four hour interviews. The interview guide was designed to examine a participant's: (1) status at the time of entry into the program, (2) experiences in the residential and treatment programs, (3) expectations, perceptions and evaluation of the services received, (4) perceptions of the program's effectiveness in diminishing substance abuse, (5) perceptions of the program's effectiveness in aiding in mother-infant bonding, (6) the effectiveness of *kupuna* and cultural forms of treatment, (7) current life situation, and (8) recommendations.

Sample

A total of forty-nine women participated in NWM for varying periods of time between October 1992 and June 1995. Thirty-two of the original participants were located. Twenty-five of the 32 women consented to be interviewed for the 1998 evaluation conducted 2 years after the demonstration project closed. Twenty-one A/PI women's narratives were analyzed for this study, 4 non-A/PI were not included. Women in the sample had an average of three children and ranged in age from 20 to 37 years old.

Eighty-one percent or 17 women reported Hawaiian/Part-Hawaiian as their primary ethnicity, followed by 19% (4) Asian and Southeast Asians.

Nearly three-fourths (15) of the women were single, and a little more than half (12) of the women had graduated from high school. Less than half (8) of the women reported an unstable employment history. Eighty-six percent (18) of the women were court ordered into treatment or referred by Child Protective Services (CPS). Methamphetamine/ice was the substance used by the majority of women (17), followed by cocaine, alcohol, and marijuana.

Analysis and Coding

Women's narratives were analyzed utilizing the relational theory of women's psychological development and grounded theory coding techniques in data analysis. The researchers sought to reveal and represent the women's experiences while in the recovery program. In this way, feminist perspectives provided the lens through which A/PI women's narratives were acknowledged and validated as essential to understanding treatment-facilitating processes (Harding, 1987; Reinhartz, 1992). The focus was to learn about the women's process of involvement in the program and to better understand what was important in enabling them to remain in the program.

The semi-structured interview guide provided the initial direction for open coding and questions used to develop conceptual categories (Strauss & Corbin, 1990). Twelve major conceptual categories, each with several subcategories, emerged. For the purposes of this discussion, these categories were further consolidated into five major finding-areas.

FINDINGS

In their detailed and often compelling interviews, A/PI women elucidated their experiences in the areas of: (1) residential treatment, (2) substance abuse treatment, (3) parent skill building, (4) transitional and after-care, and (5) personal growth. Factors and experiences that A/PI women identified as important in their healing and the combined group responses are summarized in this section.

Residential Treatment

The interviews revealed that the following factors of the residential program were a significant part of the women's commitment to remain in the program (not in order of importance):

- A flexible but clearly structured residential treatment program;
- A manageable daily routine of life-sustaining family activities: cooking, cleaning, personal care, child-care, and periods to socialize;

- Being in a safe, secure residence enabled women to focus on their treatment with decreased fear of outside distractions;
- Having their infant child in residence with them;
- Positive emotional support enabled women to raise their self-esteem and change negative attitudes;
- Trained, qualified child-care and residential staff that understand the dynamics and effects of substance abuse, and are sensitive to A/PI women's needs enabled them to have confidence in the program.

Fifty-two percent of the women felt the NWM staff were emotionally supportive and competent in their work. From the women's perspectives, being able to trust that staff would not use their past behavior against them or act in punitive ways toward them was most important in enabling them to remain committed to the program and recovery. As the program improved over time through training, better staffing, and treatment coordination, women reported greater satisfaction with the services and their progress.

Substance Abuse Treatment

Sixty-eight percent of the women who participated in Hawaiian deep cultural therapy reported that the healing practices were instrumental in their recovery process. These practices aided A/PI women in reconnecting with their spirituality, facing their emotional pain, confronting the effects of their substance abuse, and beginning the healing process. Two study participants share the impact of *ho'oponopono* on them.

> Participant Pua:
> *At Ho'omau Ke Ola [community treatment center] we would have ho'oponopono and you'd go and let out all your bad vibes . . . where you just leave all the crap that you went through behind us. Just throw it away, wash it away, throw it out in the ocean and let it just let go. You know? and that was spiritual . . . it was good.*

> Participant Kehau:
> *All that hurt and hate that I had inside . . . after that [ho'oponopono], wow, it's awesome, just like one whole burden left out of me. I had a problem stuffing things . . . then you just build up, build up, build up, an before you know it, you're one big time bomb.*

The majority of the women in this study, 17 of the 21 (80%), were substance free at the time of this study and had remained substance-free for 1 1/2 to 5 years: Five participants who completed the program in 1993 had been substance free for 5 years, one woman who completed the program in 1994 was substance free for approximately 3 1/2 years, 8 women were substance free for approximately 2 to 2 1/2 years, and 3 women for approximately 1 1/2 years. Four individuals are currently participating in further substance abuse treatment. Although the NWM residential program appeared to be a major contributing factor in A/PI women's healing and recovery, over time other unaccounted for factors may have influenced post treatment sobriety.

Parent Skill-Building

Fourteen out of the 21 women (66%) stated that the Hawaiian parenting classes were helpful in developing: positive parenting skills (bathing, feeding, discipline, positive talk to children, time management, schedule, structuring routines); positive attitudes (developing patience, responsibility, attention-giving); and knowledge (child development, attachment and bonding, child safety, nutrition). Five out of 21 (23%) reported no impact or dissatisfaction with the parenting classes. Kanai and Kea discuss the difference the Hawaiian parenting classes made in their skills.

Participant Kanani:
They taught me to be a little more responsible. Like with appointments, because I was always using [drugs] I couldn't do any of that stuff [parenting]. They taught me how to take care of my body [because] whatever I was eating was going to my baby when I was nursing.

Participant Kea:
I was really bad before, very mean as a person. And the classes made me be more patient. I guess, I give my daughter more attention. So, that's what I guess helped me.

As part of their parent skill-building the women learned to *lomilomi* (massage) their babies each morning. Through gentle *lomilomi*, their mother's touch, the soothing tones of a chanting maternal voice the babies would be lovingly nurtured. Participant Kanani shares her experiences with *lomilomi* teachings and its value.

We spent about 30 minutes to an hour a day doing lomilomi . . . we take off baby's clothing and keep the diaper on so that they don't wet the floor. You use baby oil . . . I remember this being done to me when I was a child . . . that's the lomilomi process . . . because the baby has this stiffening of muscle and you lomi the muscle to straighten the legs to stretch the muscle so that baby can move properly . . . full body physical contact with the baby and talking to them and making them feel good and letting them know this is mommy and mommy is doing this. Just having the child to mother contact was good.

For Kanani, the ability to provide *lomilomi* to her child brought back the positive feelings associated with the human touch and her childhood. She was reminded that she was able to give this to her baby, which in turn brought back a strong sense of self-confidence, pride in her cultural heritage and hope for the future.

Transitional and After-Care

In this sample, 43% (n = 9) of the participants met the criteria for graduation from NWM and received post-residential support and services for one year. These women continued to be drug free from the time they left the program, a period of at least 2 1/2 to 3 years. Although NWM stopped providing services in June 1996 and aftercare was no longer officially available, women continued to contact the executive director and program manager of NWM, who are currently operating a respite care program for Children's Protective Services-involving women and also working for *Ho 'omau Ke Ola*, the agency that provided Hawaiian deep cultural therapy.

Participant Kaui discusses the continuing connection she feels with those that have helped her in recovery.

> *I learned the staff cared because of their consistency and through lowering my own pride. I couldn't lower my pride when I was first in Na Wahine [NWM]. Pride was my worst enemy. I just didn't know how [to lower my pride]. It was protecting me. Ho'omau Ke Ola and Na Wahine together have been my foundation in recovery. No matter what I've done, during the program time or out of the program time, relapsing or whatever it was, they still held me, nurtured me. They still love me. They still call me, "come to participate in this . . . when we are having an anger management class, do you wanna come? It will be good for you." They get me involved. Today they're my foundation. I'm allowed to come in. When I'm happy, when I'm sad, when I'm confused, I'm allowed to come . . . That's a whole lot of difference from when I first started off. I wasn't gonna tell them anything about me because I thought they would hurt me with it.*

Personal Growth

The course of women's personal growth varied widely among the 21 women; however, the following themes emerged as turning points in their perceptions of and movement toward positive change: (1) ability to understand alcoholism or substance abuse as a disease not a personal flaw, (2) recognizing, admitting, and accepting the ongoing nature of addiction, (3) living through relapse and recognizing their own readiness to accept help, (4) accepting responsibility for behavior that would cause them to lose their children to Child Protective Services authorities, (5) becoming aware of the need to regain an identity lost in non-mutual relationships, (6) awareness of deepening spirituality, (7) developing as a responsible, loving-lovable adult and parent, and (8) reaching out to help others. Participant Pua talks about her struggle toward personal growth:

> *I was in an abusive relationship. He used to beat me up and stuff like that. I still went back, because he told me he was going to change. He didn't. And I kept going back. For 15 years I was in an abusive relationship, because he stripped all my identity and stuff. So, I felt like I couldn't go on my own. I needed him. So, I was codependent, you know. Through Na Wahine [NWM], I gained back my identity and me and I don't have that feeling any more.*

As with all of the women who were able to come to find a path, the reasoning, resources, and relational support, Pua's story is an example of the multilayered issues that must be worked through to gain back a sense of self in relation to the world she lives in.

DISCUSSION AND CONCLUSION

Implications for Practice

A/PI women emphasized the importance of non-judgmental, trust building in establishing a relationship with residential staff or treatment professionals. The consistent expression of genuine care, concern, and support from staff was a cornerstone of positive relationships. For those women who were able to establish mutually enhancing relationships, the process became a model, which continued to be a source of empowerment for them.

Women, who successfully completed this multi-dimensional treatment program found the women-centered, family systems approach enabled them to establish and maintain relationships during treatment and aftercare that were critical to their recovery. The mutual respect and caring between staff and the women enabled the complex individual processes of healing to occur. Supporting and enhancing client strengths, while being sensitive to previous abuse issues were important dynamics in enabling women to remain in the program.

Implications for Policy

The findings of this study strongly suggest that effective treatment and recovery requires that policies support multi-dimensional treatment frameworks for substance abuse and include the biculturalization of Hawaiian and western treatment interventions. For A/PI women who are substance abusers, programs that include strong family systems treatment and services components are critical to treatment effectiveness. Planned, purposeful aftercare and follow-up services must be part of their treatment program. A/PI women were aware of and valued staff who were knowledgeable about and implemented a range of substance abuse treatment modalities; ongoing training at all levels of service provision would increase the effectiveness of treatment services.

Both Hawaiian and non-Hawaiian A/PI women credited Hawaiian cultural practices with aiding in their abstinence and healing. An equally interesting finding was the small number of Hawaiian women (3) who did not find deep cultural therapy of benefit to them because it did not seem relevant to their process. These findings suggest that culturally based substance abuse treatment can be effective for individuals from different cultures, depending on their readiness and willingness to participate. It is recommended that individual assessment be utilized to determine predisposition for culture-based treatment.

Programs for women who abuse substances need to be structured in ways that promote relational bonds and stimulate and challenge them toward growth and recovery. The personnel who provide care to A/PI women with substance abuse problems must have knowledge about the dynamics of substance abuse among women and a developing understanding of health beliefs within cultures, traditional healing practices, current theories of women's development, and relational treatment modalities. The willingness to biculturalize interventions to accommodate the treatment needs of A/PI women and those from other cultures is a step toward cultural competence.

Finally, continued studies are necessary to determine the extent to which culturally based residential treatment efforts affect A/PI women's long term functioning and ability to remain off drugs. Future research should also address the effectiveness of specific cultural practices in aiding A/PI women to remain substance free, explore how A/PI women with substance abuse problems might design their own treatment, and examine how A/PI communities can support substance abuse education, prevention, and treatment.

REFERENCES

Abbott, A. A. (1993). A Feminist Approach to Substance Abuse Treatment and Service Delivery. *Social Work in Health Care, 19* (3-4), 67-83.

Belenky, M. F., Clinchy, B. M., Goldberger, N. R., & Tarule, J. M. (1986). *Women's Ways of Knowing: The Development of Self, Voice and Mind.* New York: Basic Books.

Brady, M. (1995). Culture in Treatment, Culture as Treatment: A critical appraisal of developments in addictions programs for indigenous North Americans and Australians. *Social Science & Medicine, 41*(11), 1487-1498.

Brindis, C. D., & Theidon, K. S. (1997). The Role of Case Management in Substance Abuse Treatment Services for Women and Their Children. *Journal of Psychoactive Drugs, 29*(1), 79-88.

Broom, D., & Stevens, A. (1981). Doubly Deviant: Women using alcohol and other drugs. *The International Journal of Drug Policy, 2*(4), 25-27.

Chung, D. (1992). Asian Cultural Communities. In S. M. Furuto, D. K. Biswas, K. Chung, K. Murase, & F. Ross-Sherriff (Eds.), *Social Work Practice with Asian Americans* (pp. 274-275). Newbury Park, CA: Sage.

Covington, S. S., & Surrey, J. L. (1997). The Relational Model of Women's Psychological Development: Implications for Substance Abuse. In R. W. Wilsnack & S. C. Wilsnack (Eds.), *Gender and Alcohol: Individual and Social Perspectives* (pp. 335-354). New Brunswick, NJ: Rutgers Center of Alcohol Studies.

DeCambra, H., Marshall, W. E., & Ono, M. (1999). Ho`omau Ke Ola: To perpetuate life as it was meant to be. In N. Mokuau (Ed.), *Responding to Pacific Islanders: Competent perspectives for substance abuse prevention* (DHHS Publication NO. SMA 98-3193, pp. 73-96). Washington, DC: Government Printing Office.

Delgado, M. (1995). Natural Support Systems and the AOD Services: Challenges and rewards for practice. *Alcoholism Treatment Quarterly, 12,* 17-31.

Department of Health. (1996). *Blind Study of Substance Abuse and Need for Treatment Among Women of Childbearing Age in Hawaii.* Honolulu: Alcohol and Drug Abuse Division.

Donovan, J. (1994). *Feminist Theory: The Intellectual Traditions of American Feminism.* New York: Continuum.

Duran, E., & Duran, B. (1995). *Native American Postcolonial Psychology.* Albany: State University of New York.

Fong, R., & Morelli, P. (1998). *Fifth Year Evaluation of the Na Wahine Makalapua: Pregnant and Postpartum Women and their Infants in Hawai`i.* Honolulu: University of Hawai`i.

Fong, R., Boyd, C., & Browne, C. (1999). The Gandhi Technique: A bicultural approach for empowering Asian and Pacific Islander families. *Journal of Multicultural Social Work, 7*(1/2), 95-110.

Freud, S. (1924). The Passing of the Oedipus Complex, *Sexuality and the Psychology of Love.* New York: Collier.

Freud, S. (1925). Some Psychological Consequences of the Anatomical Distinction Between the Sexes, *Sexuality and the Psychology of Love.* New York: Collier.

Freud, S. (1931). Female Sexuality, *Sexuality and the Psychology of Love*. New York: Collier.

Freud, S. (1932). Femininity. In J. Strachey (Ed.), *The Standard Edition of the Complete Works of Sigmund Freud*. London: Hogarth.

Gilligan, C. (1982). *In a Different Voice: Psychological Theory and Women's Development*. Cambridge, MA: Harvard University Press.

Harding, S. (1987). Introduction: Is there a feminist method? In S. Harding (Ed.), *Feminism and Methodology* (pp. 1-14). Bloomington, IN: Indiana University Press.

Jilek, W. G. (1994). Traditional Healing in the prevention and treatment of alcohol and drug abuse. *Transcultural Psychiatric Research Review*, 31(3), 219-256.

Kohlberg, L. (1958). *The Development of Modes of Thinking and Choices in Years 10 to 16*. Chicago: University of Chicago.

Kohlberg, L. (1981). *The Philosophy of Moral Development*. San Francisco: Harper and Row.

Lecca, P., Quervalu, I., Nunes, J., & Gonzales, H. (1998). *Cultural Competency in Health, Social & Human Services*. New York: Garland.

Maypole, D. E., & Anderson, R. B. (1987). Culture Specific Substance Abuse Prevention for Blacks. *Community Mental Health Journal*, 23(2), 135-139.

Metsch, L. R., Rivers, J. E., Miller, M., Bohs, R., McCoy, C. B., Morrow, C. J., Bandstra, E. S., Jackson, V., & Glassen, M. (1995). Implementation of a Family-Centered Treatment Program for Substance-Abusing Women and their Children: Barriers and resolutions. *Journal of Psychoactive Drugs*, 27(1), 73-83.

Miley, K., O'Melia, M., & Dubois, B. (1998). *General Social Work Practice: An Empowering Approach*. Boston: Allyn and Bacon.

Miller, J. B. (1986). *Toward a New Psychology of Women*. Boston: Beacon Press.

Mokuau, N. (1990). The Impoverishment of Native Hawaiians and the Social Work Challenge. *Health and Social Work*, 15(3), 235-242.

Mokuau, N. (1998). Pacific Islanders. In J. Philleo & F. Brisbane (Eds.), *Cultural Competence in Substance Abuse Prevention* (pp. 127-152). Washington, DC: National Association of Social Workers and Center for Substance Abuse Prevention.

Mokuau, N. (1999). Substance abuse among Pacific Islanders: Cultural context and implications for prevention programs. In B. W. K. Yee, N. Makuau, & S. Kim (Eds.), *Developing cultural competence in Asian-American and Pacific Islander Communities: Opportunities in primary health care and substance abuse prevention* (DHHS Publication No. SMA 98-3193, pp. 221-248). Washington, DC: US Government Printing Office.

National Center on Addiction and Substance Abuse. (1996). *Substance Abuse and the American Woman*. New York: Columbia University.

National Institute on Drug Abuse. (1998). *Women and Drug Abuse*: <www.health.org/wda.htm>.

Paglinawan, L. (1972). *Ho'oponopono Project II*. Honolulu: Queen Liliuokalani Children's Center.

Philleo, J., & Brisbane, F. (1998). *Cultural Competence in Substance Abuse Prevention.* Washington, DC: National Association of Social Workers and the Center for Substance Abuse Prevention.

Piaget, J. (1965). *The Moral Judgement of the Child.* New York: The Free Press.

Pukui, M., Haertig, E. W., & Lee, C. (1972). *Nana I Ke Kumu: Look to the source.* (Vol. I). Honolulu: Hui Hanai.

Pukui, M., Haertig, E. W., Lee, C., & McDermott, J. (1979). *Nana I Ke Kumu: Look to the source.* (Vol. II). Honolulu: Hui Hanai.

Reinharz, S. (1992). Feminist Interview Research. In S. Reinharz (Ed.), *Feminist Methods in Social Research* (pp. 18-45). New York: Oxford University Press.

Schliebner, C. T. (1994). Gender-Sensitive Therapy: An alternative for women in substance abuse treatment. *Journal of Substance Abuse Treatment, 11*(6), 511-515.

Shintani, T., & Hughes, C. (1991). *The Wai`anae Book of Hawaiian Health: The Wai`anae Diet Program Manual.* Honolulu: Wai`anae Coast Comprehensive Center.

Shook, E. V. (1985). *Ho`oponopono.* Honolulu: University of Hawai`i Press.

Strauss, S., & Corbin, J. (1990). *Basics of Qualitative Research: Grounded Theory Procedures and Techniques.* Newbury Park, CA: Sage.

Substance Abuse and Mental Health Services Administration. (SAMHSA) (1996). *Preliminary Estimates from the 1995 National Household Survey of Drug Abuse.* Advanced Report Number 18. Rockville, MD: Department of Health and Human Services.

Substance Abuse and Mental Health Services Administration. (SAMHSA) (1997). *Substance Use Among Women in the United States.* Rockville, MD: Department of Health and Human Services.

Substance Abuse and Mental Health Services Administration. (SAMHSA) (1998). *Prevalence of Substance Use Among Racial and Ethnic Subgroups in the United States, 1991-1993.* Rockville, MD: Department of Health and Human Services.

US Department of Health and Human Services. (1995). *Drug Use Among Racial/ Ethnic Minorities.* Rockville, MD: National Institutes of Health.

Vargas, L., & Koss-Chioino, J. (1992). *Working with Culture: Psychotherapeutic Interventions with Ethnic Minority Children and Adolescents.* San Francisco: Jossey-Bass.

Wald, R., Harvey, S. M., & Hibbard, J. (1995). A Treatment Model for Women Substance Users. *The International Journal of Addictions, 30*(7), 881-888.

Wing, D. M., Crow, S. S., & Thompson, T. (1995). An Ethnonursing Study of Muscogee (Cree) Indians and Effective Health Care Practices for Treating Alcohol Abuse. *Family and Community Health, 18*(2), 52-64.

Yi, J. K. (1996). Are Asian/Pacific Islander American Women Represented in Women's Health Research? *Women's Health Issues, 6*(4), 237-238.

Stress, Coping, and Depression Among Elderly Korean Immigrants

Ada C. Mui

SUMMARY. The effects of life stresses and social support on depressive symptoms in older Korean Americans (n = 67), recruited at senior centers and meal sites, were examined. Those who reported poorer health, who had more stressful life events, who were dissatisfied with help received from family members, and who reported few good friends were more likely to be depressed than those who did not. The impact of these factors on the quality of life of elderly Korean immigrants can be understood in the context of their immigration experience and Korean cultural values. *[Article copies available for a fee from The Haworth Document Delivery Service: 1-800-342-9678. E-mail address: <getinfo@haworthpressinc.com> Website: <http://www.HaworthPress.com> © 2001 by The Haworth Press, Inc. All rights reserved.]*

KEYWORDS. Korean, immigrant, depression, elderly, mental health

The Asian and Pacific Islander (API) population in the United States grew by 141% between the censuses of 1970 and 1980 while the total U.S. population increased by only 11%. The population growth rate in the 1980-1990 decade was 10% for the total U.S. population and almost 100% for APIs

Ada C. Mui, PhD, ACSW, is Associate Professor, Columbia University School of Social Work, 622 West 113th Street, New York, NY 10025 (E-mail: acm5@columbia.edu).

This study was supported by the 1996-1997 Columbia University School of Social Work Faculty Innovative Research Award.

[Haworth co-indexing entry note]: "Stress, Coping, and Depression Among Elderly Korean Immigrants." Mui, Ada C. Co-published simultaneously in *Journal of Human Behavior in the Social Environment* (The Haworth Press, Inc.) Vol. 3, No. 3/4, 2001, pp. 281-299; and: *Psychosocial Aspects of the Asian-American Experience: Diversity Within Diversity* (ed: Namkee G. Choi) The Haworth Press, Inc., 2001, pp. 281-299. Single or multiple copies of this article are available for a fee from The Haworth Document Delivery Service [1-800-342-9678, 9:00 a.m. - 5:00 p.m. (EST). E-mail address: getinfo@haworthpressinc.com].

(U.S. Bureau of Census, 1991). Researchers project that the API populations will rise to almost 10 million in the next decade and to almost 20 million by the year 2030. The API population is composed of at least 26 census-defined ethnic subgroups, some of which have been in the United States since the 1850s, while substantial numbers of them immigrated to this country only in the past three decades. The API elderly population constitutes the fastest growing racial group aged 65 and older in the United States, but it has been neglected in many national studies (Mui, 1996b). When the data on API are collected, API subgroups are often not broken down and the sample size is often too small for meaningful analysis (Mui 1996b; Tanjasiri, Wallace, & Shibata, 1995). Therefore, there are substantial knowledge gaps regarding the state of API elders due to a lack of empirical data (LaVeist, 1995). Numerous medical, psychological, social, and biological research questions remain unanswered because data on these populations are scarce (Gibson, 1989; Jackson, 1989; Mui 1996a).

The API population is extremely diverse, and there are a lot of within-group cultural variations in family values, beliefs, norms, language, health-seeking behaviors, and many other areas. Among the Asian-American groups, the population size of Chinese, Japanese, and Koreans is relatively large compared to other Asian groups. These three groups share some similar cultural roots, and the majority of them were voluntary immigrants (as opposed to Vietnamese or Laotians, who came for political asylum) (Ishii-Kuntz, 1997). They also differ in many ways. For example, in terms of immigration history, Chinese men who came to the United States as railroad workers in the mid- to late 19th century were likely to have come alone, leaving their families behind in China (Ishii-Kuntz, 1997). In contrast, Japanese immigrants who came here in the early 20th century either brought their families or started their families in this country. The Korean elderly immigrants, however, most likely came to the United States after the passage of the 1965 Immigration Act. This law allowed these Korean immigrants to reunite with their families because they were granted visas under the family reunification category. Because of this immigration history, Korean elderly people are more likely than their counterparts in the other API groups to be recent immigrants, and they may need support in the adaptation and acculturation process. In Ishii-Kuntz's study (1997), compared to Chinese-American and Japanese-American families, Korean-American families had significantly lower average income; Korean elderly parents were strongly embedded in family support networks, as shown by their frequent interaction with relatives and friends; and Korean elderly parents received more support from their children. Ishii-Kuntz's data (1997) also suggested that Korean adult children had a stronger sense of filial obligation to their parents than their Chinese or Japanese counterparts. In addition, Korean adult children who had this stronger sense of filial obligation were more likely to provide both emotional and financial support to their elderly parents. Among the three Asian groups, those who were first born (an indication of a lower level of acculturation) were more likely than the others to provide financial assistance to their elderly parents. Youn and Song (1992) suggested that elderly Korean parents experienced conflicts in their family relationships as they grew older. Based on the literature, the author, in this study, attempts to explore the mental health status of the Korean elderly immigrant population using a stress and coping framework. Specifically, the research question is: what factors are associated with the mental health status of Korean elders?

LITERATURE REVIEW

Researchers (Kiefer et al., 1985; Lee, Crittenden, & Yu, 1996) who examined the quality-of-life issues found that Korean elders who had less social support had difficulty in psychosocial adaptation. Very few of those studies examined depression specifically (see Table 1 for a summary of recent quality-of-life studies on Korean elderly populations). Depression may occur frequently in elderly immigrants because they have limited resources but must deal with physical losses and stressful life events (Gelfand & Yee, 1991; Lee et al., 1996). Despite substantial prevalence rates, symptoms of depression often go unrecognized, undiagnosed, and untreated due to patient- and health-care-related barriers and problems in the organization and financing of mental health services for older adults, especially minority elders (Gottlieb, 1991). Studies (Loo, Tong, & True, 1989; Snowden & Cheung, 1990) also suggest that minority elders and immigrants tend to underutilize mental health services, even though the prevalence and types of reported psychological disorders were similar to those in the white population. Depressive symptoms do not tend to remit spontaneously in older adults (Allen & Blazer, 1991), and undiagnosed and untreated depression in late life usually cause tremendous distress for older adults, their families, and society. Research suggests that older Korean-Americans and older whites are at a similar risk for depression (Yamamoto, Rhee, & Chang, 1994). Factors associated with depression among older Korean immigrants have been lower levels of social contact and fewer close friends (Lee et al., 1996). Other studies have found that elderly Korean immigrants' relationships with family was a significant factor in their psychological well-being (Sung, 1991; Youn & Song, 1992). The stresses of immigration and acculturation have also been found to pose additional risks for situational stress and somatic symptoms, often occurring when family supports are weakened or unavailable (Gelfand & Yee, 1991; Koh & Bell, 1987). However, depressed elderly immigrants are less likely than white elders to be identified by service providers, and they are less likely

TABLE 1. Summary of Recent Quality-of-Life Studies on Korean Elderly People

Authors	Sample	Research Questions	Multivariate Method	Major Findings
Ferraro & Su, 1999	865 Elderly Koreans in Korea	Predictors of depression (CES-D[a])	Yes	Predictors for depression were fewer household members, poor health, higher IADLs, flnancial strain, fewer family contacts, and receiving family financial support.
Kiefer et al., 1985	50 Elderly Korean immigrants	Adjustment problems of Korean American elders	No	Persons who had difficulty in psycho social adaptation had little education, had shorter stays, and lived alone. Men adjusted better than women.
Koh & Bell, 1987	151 Elderly Korean immigrants	Intergenerational relations and living arrangements	No	Compared to Korean elders in Korea, Korean immigrants were more likely to live alone and not wish to live with their children.
Lee et al., 1996	200 Elderly Korean immigrants	Social support and depression, measured by the CES-D[a]	Yes	Korean immigrants who had more close friends and more social contacts were less likely to be depressed.
Lee et al., 1993	50 Elderly Korean immigrants	Heart disease risk factors and attitude toward prevention	No	Compared to white elders, Korean elders had a lower frequency of heart disease and all risk factors, except diabetes.
Moon & Pearl, 1991	36 Elderly Koreans in Los Angeles and 51 in Oklahoma	Psychological adjustment., measured by Deans Alienation Scale (DAS)	Yes	Compared to Korean elders in Oklahoma, Korean elders in Los Angeles were younger, had shorter lengths of stay in the U.S., lived with their spouse, and had better psychological adjustment in terms of sense of powerlessness, isolation, and alienation.
Slung, 1991	450 Elderly Koreans In Korea	Informal support networks	Yes	94% of the sample cited family support as the source of help they turned to most often. Intimate family relationships predicted total well-being (physical and financial).
Pang, 1995	69 Elderly Korean immigrants	Prevalence of depression, measured by the Diagnostic Interview Schedule (DIS-III)	No	Lifetime prevalence rate for the Korean immigrants was 7.1%. Both the depressed and nondepressed groups expressed loneliness, sadness, and somatic symptoms.
Wallace et al.,1996	231 Elderly Korean immigrants	Health practices	Yes	Compared to non-Hispanic white elders, Korean elders practiced a somewhat higher number of healthy behaviors. Older Korean men had problems with smoking cessation.
Yamamoto et al., 1994	100 Elderly Korean immigrants	Psychiatric disorders, measured by the Diagnostic Interview Schedule (DIS-III)	No	Compared to the U.S. elders, Korean elders were not different in the prevalence of DSM-III disorders, with the exception of alcohol abuse and dependence. Korean men had a higher rate of alcoholism.
Youn & Song, 1992	623 Elderly Koreans in Korea	Perceived conflict with family	No	Older Koreans in Korea experienced more conflicts in their relationships as they grew older.

[a]CES-D represents the Center for Epidemiological Studies of Depression Scale.

to receive treatment because of language barriers (Chi & Boey, 1993; Mui, 1996b).

In the United States, epidemiological studies have examined the prevalence of depressive symptoms in communities, using a variety of self-rating scales and interviews. Depending on the selected instruments and cutoff points, the reported prevalence of depression among those over 65 ranged from 2% to 5% for major depressive disorders to as high as 44% to 50% for depressive symptoms (Blazer et al., 1988). Of all the psychological problems that affect elderly people, depression is the risk factor most frequently associated with suicide (Lapierre et al., 1992). One fifth of all late-life suicides are due to depression (APA, 1988). The mental health status of elderly Korean immigrants deserves careful evaluation because previous research on Korean elderly immigrants is scant. As a function of immigration policies such as family reunification laws and the cultural norms of filial piety, the number of Korean and other Asian elderly immigrants will continue to grow in the years to come (Mui, 1996b).

Previous research on the mental health of the U. S. elderly population as a whole has shown that older people are more likely to be depressed if they are female, have poor self-rated health, live alone, and have a poor quality of social support (Burnette & Mui, 1994; Mui, 1993; 1996b; 1996c). A preponderance of studies on white and other ethnic elderly has shown that elderly females are more often depressed than elderly males (Mui, 1993, 1996b). Other researchers (Husaini et al., 1990; Krause, 1986) have found that family and social support was associated with less depression because social support can mediate the impact of stress among the elderly. Furthermore, lower rate of depression was associated more with perceived satisfaction with family help than with the size of the support network (Borden, 1991; Mui, 1996b; Wethington & Kessler, 1986). There is also evidence of cultural and ethnic differences in family support. For example, Cantor (1979) found that Hispanic elders consistently had higher levels of support from their children than either black or white elders did. Compared to white elders, both black and Hispanic elders were disproportionately poor and underserved by mental health systems (Butler, Lewis, & Sunderland, 1991; Mui & Burnette, 1994). In addition, some differences in family support between ethnic groups can be attributed to culture, socioeconomic status, and immigration patterns (Linn, Hunter, & Perry, 1979; Markides & Mindel, 1987).

Previous studies (Burnette & Mui, 1994; Kemp, Staples, & Lopes-Aqueres, 1987; Mahard, 1988; Mui, 1993; 1996c) on both white and ethnic elders have also found that older persons who rated their health as poor were more likely to be depressed. The issue of the coexistence of depression with physical illness is important and complex (Ouslander, 1982). Depressive symptoms are natural responses to physical illness. Furthermore, some of the depressive symptoms, such as sleep disturbance and fatigue, can result from physical illnesses or from drug treatments for those illnesses. A wide variety of physical illnesses can be accompanied by depressive symptoms in the elderly (Ouslander, 1982; Reifler, 1991). In this study, a stress and coping framework (Aldwin, 1994; Lazarus & Folkman, 1984) was used to conceptualize and examine the relation among stresses, coping resources, and depression outcome for Korean elders. The stress and coping framework acknowledges the importance of personal and environmental stresses, such as family conflicts, acculturation, adaptation, and their effects on elders' overall well-being (Aldwin, 1994; Mui, 1993). Methods for coping with stress are determined by cognitive appraisal and include both cognitive and behavioral efforts to manage stresses that are appraised as taxing. Coping resources usually include physical, psychological, and social supports that are available to an individual (Burnette & Mui, 1994; Lazarus & Folkman, 1984; Mui, 1993). To test whether the traditional stress and coping paradigm for explaining depression is applicable to the Asian elderly immigrants, this study examined the role of stress and coping resources (social support system) in predicting depression of the Korean elderly immigrants living in the community.

METHOD

Respondents were 67 elderly Korean immigrants who live in a major U.S. metropolitan region and who volunteered to participate in the study. Possible subjects were approached and interviewed by Korean social work student volunteers at senior centers and congregate meal sites in a Northeast metropolitan area in December 1996. Korean elders were included in the study when judged to be without psychiatric or memory problems, as determined by the Short Portable Mental Status Questionnaire (SPMSQ) (Chi & Boey, 1993). The SPMSQ is a 10-item test of mental functioning. No or mild impairment is indicated by 9 to 10 correct answers, moderate impairment by 6 to 8 correct answers, and severe impairment by 0 to 5 correct answers. No one was screened out by this procedure because they had scored 9 or 10 in the scale. All respondents who volunteered for the study were administered the Korean questionnaire by the Korean social work students through face-to-face interviews, to assess their sociodemographics, informal support system, self-rated health status, stressful life events, and depression. The response rate was 100%.

Measures

The dependent variable, depression, was measured by the Geriatric Depression Scale (GDS). The GDS was chosen because it is one of the most widely used and highly recommended screening measures for depression in older adults (Olin et al., 1992; Thompson, Futterman, & Gallagher, 1988). This scale has also been used with elderly Chinese immigrants, and good reliability was evidenced in those studies (Mui, 1996a; 1996b). It is a 30-item inventory that takes 10 to 15 minutes to administer. Previous study populations have included psychiatric and medical patients and healthy normal elders. The GDS has excellent reliability and validity (test-retest reliability = .85; internal consistency = .94). The GDS has been validated against the Research Diagnostic Criteria (RDC) (Spitzer et al., 1978) and is able to discriminate among healthy normals and mildly and severely depressed. It performs as well as the DSM-III-R symptom checklist in predicting clinical diagnoses (Parmelee, Lawton, & Katz, 1989). The assessment of depression in an elderly population is more difficult than in a younger population because of the higher prevalence of somatic complaints, genuine physical problems, and use of medication. One of the strengths of the GDS is that it contains no somatic items, which tend to inflate the total scores of an elderly population and introduce age bias into the depression-screening scale (Berry, Storandt, & Coyne, 1984; Kessler et al., 1992). Another strength of the GDS is its simple yes/no response format for symptom endorsement; this is preferable for subjects with limited formal education (Olin et al., 1992).

Independent variables, including stress factors, coping resources, and other demographic factors, are discussed in the following. Measures of stress factors were perceived health status (rated by the respondents on a 4-point scale ranging from excellent to poor), numbers of stressful life events, and living arrangements. Stressful life events were measured by asking respondents to answer yes or no to the following question: "In the past year, did you experience the following events?" These events were children moved out, serious illness or injury of family member, family discord, unemployment, and financial difficulty. These stressful life events were selected because previous studies found that numbers of stressful events were correlated with higher depression (Chi & Boey, 1993; Mui, 1996b). Living arrangement was measured by asking the Korean respondents whether or not they lived alone. Coping resources were operationally defined by five areas: size of social network, help provided by family members, satisfaction with the quality of family help, existence of a close friend, and contact with friends. Sociodemographic variables (age, sex, marital status, income, language spoken, education, and length of stay in the United States) were also measured to ascertain background characteristics of the sample.

RESULTS

Respondents' Characteristics

Table 2 shows that the mean age of the respondents was 69.2 years with a standard deviation of 6.1. Almost half of the respondents were age 70 or

TABLE 2. Profile of the Elderly Korean Immigrant Sample by Gender

	Women (n = 34)	Men (n = 33)	Total (n = 67)
Age			
60-69	51.5%	52.6%	51.6%
70-79	42.4	32.3	37.5
80 and above	6.1	16.1	10.9
Mean age (SD)	68.6 (6.5)	70.3 (8.2)	69.2 (6.1)
Marital status****			
Married	38.2%	87.9%	62.7%
Widowed	61.8	12.1	37.3
Language spoken			
Korean	100.0%	100.0%	100.0%
Educational attainment			
No education	14.7%	9.1%	11.9%
Elementary school	35.3	12.1	23.8
High school	35.3	57.6	46.4
College or higher	14.7	21.2	17.9
Religion**			
No religion	2.9%	12.1%	7.5%
Buddhist	11.8	0.0	5.9
Catholic	23.5	3.0	13.4
Protestant	58.8	84.9	71.6
Other	2.9	0.0	1.5
Income			
Less than $500/month	45.5%	39.4%	42.4%
$501 to $1,000/month	42.4	33.3	37.9
$1,001 or more	12.1	27.3	19.7
No. of years in the U.S. (mean)	12.1	11.4	11.8
Born overseas	100.0%	100.0%	100.0%

Note: Chi-square statistics were used.
** $p < .01$. **** $p < .0001$.

older. All were participants in senior centers and congregate meal sites, and the majority had at least an elementary school education. Sixty-three percent were married, and 37.3% were widowed. The average length of stay in the United States was about 12 years (range from 3 to 15 years), and all respondents were born in Asian countries. There were no major gender differences except that the men were more likely to be married and more likely to be Protestants.

Coping Resources and Stressful Life Events

Table 3 describes the respondents' social network size, help provided by family members, satisfaction with the quality of family help, and living arrangements. About 13% of the respondents lived alone, fewer than the white elderly population in general (Burnette & Mui, 1994). The remaining respondents lived with spouses and/or children. There were no gender differences in social network characteristics in this sample. The average number of family members of the respondents was 7.5 (including adult children, grand-

TABLE 3. Family Support and Perceived Health Status of the Elderly Korean Immigrant Sample, by Gender

	Women (n = 34)		Men (n = 33)		Total (n = 67)	
Family Network	*M*	*SD*	*M*	*SD*	*M*	*SD*
No. of sons	1.5	0.9	1.5	0.8	1.5	0.9
No. of daughters	1.6	1.0	1.4	0.7	1.5	0.8
No. of daughters-in-law	1.4	1.0	1.3	0.9	1.3	1.0
No. of sons-in-law	1.5	0.9	1.2	0.4	1.3	0.7
No. of brothers	1.3	1.5	0.7	0.5	1.1	1.2
No. of sisters	1.1	1.4	0.6	0.5	0.9	1.2
No. of grandchildren	2.8	2.4	2.5	2.3	2.6	2.3
Average no. of family members	7.9	6.6	7.1	4.7	7.5	5.7
Living arrangement*						
Living alone	17.7%		9.1%		13.4%	
With spouse	2.9		45.5		35.8	
With spouse and children	26.5		42.4		33.3	
With children	44.1		0.0		11.5	
With other relatives	8.8		3.0		6.0	
Assistance provided by family members						
Emotional support	61.8%		75.8%		68.7%	
Financial support*	23.5		45.5		34.3	
Help with decision making	70.6		66.7		68.7	
Help with daily activities***	20.6		60.6		40.3	
Help with medical care*	47.1		72.7		59.7	
Entertainment in leisure**	47.1		72.7		59.7	
No. of assistance (mean)**	2.7		3.9		3.3	
Perceived dissatisfaction with family help*						
Very dissatisfied	5.9%		3.0%		4.5%	
Dissatisfied	41.1		12.1		26.8	
Satisfied	17.7		33.3		25.4	
Very Satisfied	35.3		51.5		43.3	
Self-rated health*						
Excellent	2.9%		21.2%		11.9%	
Good	38.2		33.3		35.8	
Fair	29.4		30.3		29.9	
Poor	29.4		15.2		22.4	

Note: Chi-square statistics were used.
* $p < .05$. ** $p < .01$. *** $p < .001$.

children, in-laws, and siblings). The men seemed to receive more assistance from families than did the women. About one third of the families provided financial support to their elderly relatives. More of the male respondents (72.9%) had family members spending leisure time with them than did their female counterparts (47.1%). About two thirds of the respondents received help in decision making and medical care. Male respondents seemed to be more satisfied with the help they received from family members than did the female respondents. However, for the whole sample, almost one third of the respondents expressed some dissatisfaction with the quality of help they received.

Table 4 presents other coping resources and the stressful life events that respondents had experienced in the year immediately preceding the interview. In terms of friendship network and quantity of social contacts, no

TABLE 4. Coping Resources and Stressful Life Events of the Elderly Korean Immigrant Sample, by Gender (%)

	Women (n = 34)	Men (n = 33)	Total (n = 67)
Do you have any close friends?			
Yes	76.5	75.8	76.1
No	23.5	24.2	23.9
How many friends do you know well enough to visit in their homes?			
None	35.3	25.0	30.3
One or two	11.8	21.9	16.7
Three or four	11.8	15.6	13.6
Five or more	41.1	37.5	39.4
In the past week, about how many times did you talk to someone (friend/relative) on the phone?			
Not at all	11.8	27.3	19.4
Once or twice	14.7	9.0	11.9
Three or four times	44.1	36.4	40.3
Five or more times	29.4	27.3	28.4
During past week, how many times did you spend time with someone who does not live with you?			
Not at all	29.4	39.4	34.3
Once or twice	32.4	18.2	25.4
Three or four times	29.4	30.3	29.9
Five or more times	8.8	12.1	10.4
Is there someone who would give you help if you needed it?			
Yes	61.8	72.7	67.2
No	38.2	27.3	32.8
Stressful life events			
Children moved out	23.5	15.2	19.4
Illness/injury of family member	26.5	12.1	19.4
Serious illness/injury	23.5	9.1	16.4
Family discord	8.8	9.1	9.0
Unemployment in the family	17.7	15.2	16.4
Financial difficulty	44.1	24.2	34.3
Total number of events (mean)*	1.4	0.8	1.1

Note: Chi-square statistics were used.
* $p < .05$.

gender differences between the women and the men were noted. Female respondents seemed to experience significantly more stressful life events than did their male counterparts (1.4 vs. 0.8 events). Overall, a significant portion of respondents experienced difficult times, with 19% having children move out, 19% having serious illness or injury, and 34% having financial problems at home. The data suggest that a significant portion of the respondents had had to make a lot of adjustments in the previous year due to the occurrence of these life events.

Depressive Symptomatology

The GDS measures depression, with scores ranging from 0 to 30 representing the total number of depressive symptoms. According to Brink and his colleagues (1982), those who reported 10 or fewer symptoms were considered as normal, 11-20 symptoms as mildly depressed, and 21 or more symptoms as moderately to severely depressed. Using data from this sample, the alpha coefficient of the Korean-language GDS was .88, which indicates a good internal consistency reliability for this scale, and the split-half reliability was .84. Overall, there were some gender differences in the GDS depression scores (Table 5). The mean score of the female respondents was significantly higher (11.6) than that of the male respondents (9.5), which is considered normal. This finding seems to be consistent with the literature, which found that older Korean men have adjusted better to life in the United States than older Korean women (Kiefer et al., 1985). Using the Brink et al. (1982) cutoff points, 9% of the total sample were found to be severely depressed. Although these data are not intended as population estimates, the rate of depression in this community sample was higher than that found in other community samples of elderly people (Mui, 1996b; Rankin, Galbraith, & Johnson, 1993)

To examine factors associated with depression in elderly Korean immigrants, a regression analysis was conducted. Three stress factors (perceived health, living alone, total number of stressful life events), two coping resource factors (number of good friends and satisfaction with family help), and two demographic factors (gender and age) were included because these variables were found to be important predictors in other studies (Mui, 1993; 1996b). Results indicated that the model explained 40% of the variance in depression (Table 6). Five variables were significant in predicting depressive symptoms: poor self-rated health (Beta = .20), living alone (Beta = .21), number of stressful life events (Beta = .24), number of good friends (Beta = −.31), and perceived dissatisfaction with family help (Beta = .22). The predictive power of poor perceived health and living alone is consistent with the findings of earlier studies using white and other ethnic elderly populations (Burnette & Mui, 1994; Mui, 1993; 1996b; 1996c).

DISCUSSION

Elderly Korean respondents in the present study admitted to depressive symptoms (as measured by Geriatric Depression Scale) at a rate (mean = 10.3) that is much higher than that found in an elderly Chinese immigrant sample (mean = 7.2) (Mui, 1996b). Based on this finding, one might speculate that older Korean immigrants feel more frustrated or disappointed about

TABLE 5. Percentage of Respondents Agreeing with Geriatric Depression Scale (GDS) Items

	Women (n = 34)	Men (n = 33)	Total (n = 67)
Geriatric Depression Scale			
1. Satisfied with life*	66.7	84.9	75.8
2. Dropped activities/interests	41.2	45.5	43.3
3. Life is empty	52.9	45.5	49.3
4. Often get bored	20.6	27.3	23.9
5. Hopeful about the future	47.1	48.5	47.8
6. Obsessive thoughts*	47.1	21.2	34.3
7. In good spirits	79.4	87.9	83.6
8. Fear bad things	41.2	42.4	41.8
9. Happy most of the time	75.8	75.8	75.8
10. Often feel helpless	35.3	33.3	34.3
11. Often get restless	38.2	30.3	34.3
12. Prefer to stay home	29.4	48.5	38.8
13. Worry about the future	35.3	27.3	31.3
14. Problem with memory	45.5	27.3	36.4
15. Wonderful to be alive	84.9	87.9	86.4
16. Feel downhearted and blue	29.4	27.3	28.4
17. Feel worthless	26.5	39.4	32.8
18. Worry about the past*	26.5	6.1	16.4
19. Life is exciting	70.6	59.4	65.2
20. Hard to start new projects*	64.7	37.5	51.5
21. Full of energy	39.4	46.9	43.1
22. Situation hopeless*	36.4	46.9	41.5
23. Others are better off	41.2	37.5	39.4
24. Upset over little things	30.3	30.3	30.3
25. Feel like crying*	35.3	15.6	25.8
26. Trouble concentrating	44.1	40.6	42.4
27. Enjoy getting up in morning	79.4	81.1	80.6
28. Avoid social gatherings	32.4	33.4	32.8
29. Easy to make decisions*	52.9	81.8	67.2
30. Mind as clear as used to be	44.1	45.4	44.8
Mean of GDS Long Form (*SD*)**	11.6 (7.2)	9.5 (6.9)	10.3 (7.0)
Normal (0-10)	52.9	57.6	55.2
Mildly depressed (11- 20)	35.3	36.4	35.8
Moderately to severely depressed (21-30)	11.8	6.1	9.0

Note: Chi-square statistics were used.
* $p < .05$.

TABLE 6. Regression Model: Correlates of Depressive Symptoms Among Elderly Korean Immigrant Sample (*n* = 67)

Variable	*b*	*SE*	*Beta*
Demographic factors			
Gender	1.07	1.54	0.08
Age	−0.06	0.10	−0.06
Stress factors			
Self-rated health [a]	1.49	0.82	0.20*
Living alone	1.31	0.85	0.21*
Number of stressful events	1.50	0.75	0.24*
Coping resources			
Dissatisfaction with family help [a]	1.29	0.74	0.22*
Number of good friends	−1.70	0.60	0.31**
R-square	.40		
Adjusted *R*-square	.34		
F	6.41****		

[a] In terms of the coding of the variables, the higher the score, the more unfavorable the rating.
* $p < .05$. ** $p < .01$. **** $p < .0001$.

their lives than their Chinese counterparts. It is not clear whether this is due to Korean elders' high expectation for their lives and/or their families or whether they had more unmet needs than their families can meet. Furthermore, it appears that older Korean women are particularly vulnerable to symptoms of depression than are older Korean men. This finding is consistent with literature that suggested that older Korean men adjust better than older Korean women (Kiefer et al., 1985). Older Korean men may adjust better in a foreign land because many of them are still married. On the other hand, older Korean women are less likely to be married and more likely to live alone. This also may reflect differences in the way depressed symptoms are interpreted or expressed by men and women, or it may reflect differences in life expectations between the two gender groups.

Depression in elderly Korean immigrants may be due to the stresses associated with immigration, language barriers, acculturation, financial hardship, poor health/illness, social isolation, and splitting of the household (Tables 2 and 4). Indeed, the data indicate that Korean elders in this study reported more changes within their family systems and with financial difficulties than with other life events. Almost 20% reported having had children move out of the home. Children moving out and splitting of households may be an indication of intergenerational conflicts and/or less family support by adult children (Mui, 1996b; Wong & Reker, 1986). This may be a difficult emotional issue for elderly Korean immigrants because this cohort of Korean elders grew up in a traditional Korean culture in which family loyalty and filial piety were central values (Moon & Pearl, 1991; Sung, 1990). For Korean elders, old age was usually associated with increasing authority in the family and respect from the children and grandchildren in their homeland. However, their children may have adapted well to American culture, in which older parents and adult children relate to each other more as peers, each group living apart and independently. For Korean elders who may still have high expectations about multigenerational living arrangements and a strong sense of family solidarity, the acculturation gap between the aging parents and the adult children may be upsetting for the elders.

The findings of this study in terms of poor health and living alone are consistent with the literature (Kiefer et al., 1985; Lee et al., 1996; Linn et al., 1979; Mui, 1996b, 1996c; Youn & Song, 1992). The findings suggest that elderly Korean immigrants, like other elderly groups, are vulnerable to psychological distress in the form of depressive symptoms (Burnette & Mui, 1996; Lee et al., 1996; Mui, 1993, 1996b, 1996c). Poorer perceived health is a significant predictor of depression. Previous studies on white and other ethnic elders found that older persons who rated their health as poor were more likely to be depressed (Kemp et al., 1987; Mahard, 1988; Mui, 1993, 1996b). It is unclear whether the poorer self-rated health in this group of Korean elders was a sign of physical illness or of a mental health problem because they might find the expression of physical problems culturally more acceptable. The data suggest that helping professionals need to be aware and sensitive to their clients' unspoken needs and that they need to provide information in terms of health education and preventive medicine.

Living alone is another significant predictor of depression among elderly Korean immigrants in the study. This is also consistent with a study of elderly Chinese immigrants (Mui, 1996b). One of the major reasons most elderly Korean immigrants, as well as other Asian elders, came to America was to be with their children (Koh & Bell, 1987). Living alone and apart from their children may be a sad, lonely, and disappointing experience for them. Korean culture places a strong emphasis on family togetherness and the interdependence of family members, placing a high value on family cohesion through an intergenerational household. It is a norm rather than an exception for adult sons and their families to live with their older parents, particularly so for the oldest married son (Hong & Ham, 1992; Koh & Bell, 1987). Therefore, an adult child's decision to move out and live apart from the aging parents is often a very stressful transition because it engenders great disappointment and shame. The splitting of the household could mean failure and embarrassment for all parties involved. Helping professionals need to be sensitive to the cultural meaning of the changes within a multigenerational family system and be able to provide supportive services to help elderly Korean immigrants accept and adapt to these changes. Furthermore, this finding strongly suggests counseling programs for younger Koreans planning to bring their parents to America. These programs can prepare and teach the Korean adult children about the adaptation process of their immigrant parents and explore practical ways to minimize parents' feelings of frustration and depression.

Coping resources, as expressed by perception of family help and number of good friends, are powerful factors in determining the overall quality of life for elderly Korean immigrants. Perceived dissatisfaction with the quality of help from family members and fewer good friends are associated with higher depression scores. In the present study, perceived dissatisfaction with family help was a significant variable in explaining depressive symptoms. Korean elders may have high expectations for family help, but the children of these Korean elders may not feel the same, due to differences in acculturation and family role expectations. More research is needed, both to replicate these findings and to examine the role of traditional norms of family help, filial piety, and care for the elderly. This research should be conducted in the context of the Korean intergenerational family and from the perspective of both Korean elders and their family members.

The number of good friends was the strongest factor in predicting better mental health of the Korean elderly immigrants and is consistent with Moon and Pearl's work (1991). In their study, the small size and lack of cohesiveness of the ethnic community had a negative relationship with feelings of alienation. It seems that elderly Korean immigrants may feel better if the size of their friendship network is larger. Obviously, more good friends would be comforting and might help to minimize adjustment problems; friends can also provide both emotional and instrumental support when necessary. New programs to help elders cope with their feelings of dissatisfaction with their children, facilitate the formation of a friendship network, and evaluate their unmet needs are important to improve their quality of life and adaptation ability.

Recent dramatic increases in the Korean population of the United States, and the aging of this population, guarantee that future service providers will be called upon to serve the mental health needs of elderly Korean-Americans. The most prevalent of these problems–depression–can be addressed effectively only by paying careful attention to the cultural values and expectations of this group. The present study suggests that helping professionals who provide treatment to this group should pay special attention to their clients' self-perceived health, living arrangement, size of friendship network, level of satisfaction with help from family members, and number of stressful life events. Consideration of these variables is essential to the design of culturally appropriate mental health interventions for elderly Korean immigrants.

Overall, the findings of this study are consistent with previous research (Lee et al., 1996; Mui, 1993; 1996b; 1996c; Pang, 1995); however, they must be interpreted with caution. The voluntary nature of subject participation limited the study because of self-selection bias. Older Koreans who are homebound and isolated are not represented in the study. The interpretation of the results is limited by its cross-sectional nature. Longitudinal studies are needed to determine the direction of the relationship between variables and how depression rate changes over time. Finally, the self-rated measures in the present study may have been affected by the Korean cultural norm of expression of feelings and emotions. It is not clear whether the depression was over- or underestimated. The findings of the present study are most appropriately generalized to Korean elderly immigrants who are participants of senior centers, live in urban settings, and are mentally competent.

REFERENCE

Aldwin, C.M. (1994). *Stress, coping, and development.* New York: The Guilford Press.

Allen, A. & Blazer, D. G. (1991). Mood disorders. In J. Sadavoy, L. W. Lazarus, & L. F. Jarvik (Eds.) *Comprehensive Review of Geriatric Psychiatry* (pp. 337-352). Washington D.C.: American Psychiatric Press.

American Psychiatric Association (1988). *Mental health of the elderly.* Baltimore, MD: Author.

Barringer, H. R., Gardner, R. W., & Levin, M. J. (1993). *Asians and Pacific Islanders in the United States.* New York: Russell Sage.

Berry, J. M., Storandt, M., & Coyne, A. (1984). Age and sex differences in somatic complaints associated with depression. *Journal of Gerontology, 39,* 465-467.

Blazer, D., Swartz, M., Woodbury, M., Manton, K. G., Hugges, D., & George, L. (1988). Depressive symptoms and depressive diagnoses in a community population. *Archives of General Psychiatry, 45,* 1078-1084.

Borden, W. (1991). Stress, coping, and adaptation in spouses of older adults with chronic dementia. *Social Work Research and Abstracts, 27,* 14-21.

Brink, T. L., Yesavage, J. A., Lum, B., Heersma, P., Adey, M., & Rose, T. A. (1982). Screening tests for geriatric depression. *Clinical Gerontologist, 1,* 37-44.

Burnette, D., & Mui, A. C. (1994). Determinants of self-reported depressive symptoms by frail elderly persons living alone. *Journal of Gerontological Social Work, 22*(1/2), 3-18.

Burnette, D. & Mui, A. C. (1996). Psychological well-being of three cohorts of older American women who live alone. *Journal of Women and Aging, 8*(1), 63-80.

Burnette, D. & Mui, A. C. (1997). Psychological well-being of the oldest-old Hispanics. *Journal of Clinical Geropsychology, 3*(3), 227-244.

Butler, R. N., Lewis, M. I., & Sunderland, T. (1991). *Aging and mental health: Positive psychological and biomedical approaches.* New York: Macmillan Publishing Company.

Cantor, M. H. (1979). The informal support system of New York's Inner City elderly: Is ethnicity a factor? In D. E. Gelfand & A. J. Kutzik (Eds.), *Ethnicity and Aging: Theory, Research, and Policy* (pp. 153-174). New York: Springer.

Chi, I. & Boey, K. W. (1993). A mental health and social support study of the old-old in Hong Kong. Department of Social Work and Social Administration, University of Hong Kong. Resource Paper Series No. 22.

Chiu, H. F. K., Lee, H. C. B.,Wing, Y. K., Kwong P. K., Leung, C. M., & Chung, D. W. S. (1993). Reliability, validity and structure of the Chinese Geriatric Depression Scale in a Hong Kong context: A preliminary report. Unpublished Manuscript. Chinese University of Hong Kong.

Ferraro, K. F., & Su, Y. P. (1999). Financial strain, social relations, and psychological distress among older people: A cross-cultural analysis. *Journal of Gerontology: Social Sciences, 54B*(1), S3-S15.

Gelfand, D. & Yee, B. W. K. (1991). Influence of immigration, migration, and acculturation on the fabric of aging in America. *Generations, 15* (4), 7-10.

Gibson, R. C. (1989). Minority aging research: Opportunity and challenge. *Journal of Gerontology: Social Sciences, 44*, S2-S3.

Gottlieb, G. L. (1991, November). Barriers to care for older adults with depression. Paper presented at the National Institute of Health, Consensus Development Conference on the diagnosis and treatment of depression in late life. Bethesda, MD.

Hong, G. K. & Ham, M. D. C. (1992). Impact of Immigration on the Family Life Cycle: Clinical Implications for Chinese Americans. *Journal of Family Psychotherapy, 3*(3), 27-39.

Husaini, B. A., Castor, R. S., Linn, G., Moore, S. T., Warren, H. A., Whitten-Stovall, R. (1990). Social support and depression among the black and white elderly. *Journal of Community Psychology, 18*, 12-18.

Ishii-Kuntz, M. (1997). Intergenerational relationships among Chinese, Japanese, and Korean Americans. *Family Relations, 46*, 23-32.

Jackson, J. S. (1989). Race, ethnicity, and psychological theory and research. *Journal of Gerontology: Psychological Sciences, 44*, P1-P2.

Kemp, B. J., Staples, F., & Lopez-Aqueres, W. (1987). Epidemiology of depression and dysphoria in an elderly hispanic population: Prevalence and correlates. *Journal of the American Geriatrics Society, 35*, 920-926.

Kessler, R. C., Foster, C., Webster, P. S., & House, J. S. (1992). The relationship between age and depressive symptoms in two national surveys. *Psychology and Aging, 7*(1), 119-126.

Kiefer, C. W., Kim, S., Choi, K., Kim. L., Kim, B., Shon, S., & Kim, T. (1985). Adjustment problems of Korean American elderly. *The Gerontologist, 25*(5), 477-481.

Koh, J. Y., and Bell. W. G. (1987). Korean elders in the United States: Intergenerational relations and living arrangements. *The Gerontologist, 27*(1), 66-71.

Krause, N. (1986). Social support, stress, and well-being among older adults. *Journal of Gerontology, 41*, 512-519.

Lapierre, S., Pronovost, J., Dube, M., & Delisle, I. (1992). Risk factors associated with suicide in elderly persons living in the community. *Canada Mental Health*, September, 8-12.

LaVeist, T. A. (1995). Data Sources for Aging Research on Racial and Ethnic Groups. *The Gerontologist, 35*(3), 328-339.

Lazarus, R. S. & Folkman, S. (1984). *Stress, appraisal, and coping*, New York: Springer.

Lee, J. A., Yeo, G., & Gallagher-Thompson, D. (1993). Cardiovascular disease risk factors and attitudes towards prevention among Korean-American elders. *Journal of Cross-cultural Gerontology, 8*(1), 17-33.

Lee, M. S., Crittenden, K. S., & Yu, E. (1996). Social support and depression among elderly Korean immigrants in the United States. *International Journal of Aging and Development, 42*(4), 313-327.

Linn, M. W., Hunter, K. I., & Perry, P. R. (1979). Differences by sex and ethnicity in the psychosocial adjustment of the elderly. *Journal of Health and Social Behavior, 20*, 273-281.

Loo, C., Tong, B., & True, R. (1989). A bitter bean: Mental health status and attitudes in Chinatown. *Journal of Community Psychology, 17*, 283-296.

Mahard, R. E. (1988). The CES-D as a measure of depressive mood in elderly Puerto Rican population. *Journal of Gerontology, 43*, P24-25.

Markides, K. S. & Mindel, C. (1987). *Aging and ethnicity.* Newbury Park, CA: Sage.

Moon, J., & Pearl, J. H. (1991). Alienation of elderly Korean American immigrants as related to place of residence, gender, age, years of education, time in the U.S., living with or without children, and living with and without a spouse. *International Journal of Aging and Development, 32*(2), 115-124.

Mui, A. C. (1993). Self-reported depressive symptoms among Black and Hispanic frail elders: A sociocultural perspective. *The Journal of Applied Gerontology, 12*, 170-187.

Mui, A. C. & Burnette, D. (1994). A comparative profile of frail elderly persons living alone and those living with others. *Journal of Gerontological Social Work, 21*(3/4), 5-26.

Mui, A. C. (1996a) Geriatric Depression Scale as a community screening instrument for elderly Chinese immigrants. *International Psychogeriatric, 8*(3), 1-10.

Mui, A. C. (1996b). Depression among elderly Chinese immigrants: An exploratory study. *Social Work, 41*, 633-645.

Mui, A. C. (1996c). Correlates of psychological distress among Mexican American, Cuban American, and Puerto Rican elders in the U.S. *Journal of Cross-Cultural Gerontology, 11*, 131-147.

Mui, A. C. & Burnette, D. (1996). Coping resources and self-reported depressive symptoms among frail older ethnic women. *Journal of Social Service Research, 21*(3), 19-37.

Olin, J. T., Schneider, L. S., Eaton, E. M., Zemansky, M. F., & Pollock, V. E. (1992). The Geriatric Depression Scale and the Beck Depression Inventory as screening instruments in an older adult outpatient population. *Psychological Assessment, 4*(2), 190-192.

Ouslander, J.G. (1982). Physical illness and depression in the elderly. *Journal of the American Geriatrics Society, 30*, 593-599.

Pang, K. Y. (1995). A cross-cultural understanding of depression among elderly Korean immigrants: Prevalence, symptoms, and diagnosis. *Clinical Gerontologist, 15*(4), 3-20.

Parmelee, P. A., Lawton, M. P., & Katz, I. (1989). Psychometric properties of the Geriatric Depression Scale among the institutionalized aged. *Psychological Assessment, 1*(4), 331-338.

Reifler, B. (1991, November). *Depression: Diagnosis and comorbidity.* Paper presented at the National Institute of Health. Consensus Development Conference on the diagnosis and treatment of depression in late life. Bethesda, MD.

Snowden, L. R. & Cheung, F. K. (1990). Use of inpatient mental health services by members of ethnic minority groups. *American Psychologist, 45,* 347-355.

Spitzer, R. L., Endicott, J., & Robins, L. N. (1978). Research diagnostic criteria: Rationale and reliability. *Archives of General Psychiatry, 35,* 773-782.

Sung, K. (1991). Family-centered informal support networks of Korean elderly: The resistence of cultural traditions. *Journal of Cross-cultural Gerontology, 6*(4), 431-447.

Tanjasiri, S. P., Wallace, S. P., & Shibata, K. (1995). Picture imperfect: Hidden problems among Asian Pacific Islander elderly. *The Gerontologist, 35,* 753-760.

Thompson, L.W., Futterman, A., & Gallagher, D. (1988). Assessment of late life depression. *Psychopharmacology Bulletin, 24*(4), 577-586.

U.S. Bureau of the Census (1991, April). Census and you. (Press Release No. CB91-100). Washington, DC: U.S. Government Printing Office.

Wallace, S. P., Villa, V., Moon, A., & Lubben, J. E. (1996). Health practices of Korean elderly people: National health promotion priorities and minority community needs. *Family Community Health, 19*(2), 29-42.

Wethington, E. & Kessler, R. (1986). Perceived support, received support, and adjustment to stressful life events. *Journal of Health and Social Behavior, 27,* 78-89.

Wong, P. T. P, & Reker, G. T. (1986). Stress, coping, and well-being in Anglo and Chinese elderly. *Canadian Journal on Aging, 4*(1), 29-36.

Yamamoto, J., Rhee, S., & Chang, D. (1994). Psychiatric disorders among elderly Koreans in the United States. *Community Mental Health Journal, 30*(1), 17-26.

Yesavage, J. A., Brink, T. L., Rose, T. L., Lum, O., Huang, V., Adey, M., & Leirer, V. O. (1983). Development and validation of a screening scale: A preliminary report. *Journal of Psychiatric Research, 17*(1), 37-49.

Youn, G. & Song, D. (1992). Aging Koreans' perceived conflicts in relationships with their offspring as a function of age, gender, cohabitation status, and marital status. *The Journal of Social Psychology, 132*(3), 299-305.

Diversity Within Diversity:
Research and Social Work Practice Issues
with Asian American Elders

Namkee G. Choi

SUMMARY. Asian American elderly form a heterogeneous group with respect to immigration history, ethnic/cultural background, socioeconomic position, and health and mental health status. This paper provides an overview of the internal heterogeneity within the Asian American elderly population and identifies those who experience multiple stressors affecting their quality of life. Then it discusses barriers to formal service utilization as well as strengths and deficits of informal support systems. To better serve Asian American elders with their multiple needs for health, mental health, and social services, increased funding is recommended for research on this group, diversification of social service programs in coethnic communities, and increased cultural competence in non-Asian social service agencies. *[Article copies available for a fee from The Haworth Document Delivery Service: 1-800-342-9678. E-mail address: <getinfo@haworthpressinc.com> Website: <http://www.HaworthPress.com> © 2001 by The Haworth Press, Inc. All rights reserved.]*

KEYWORDS. Asian American elders, culture, immigrants, heterogeneity

The 1980 and 1990 U.S. census data show that the number and share of Asian and Pacific Islander Americans (referred to as Asian Americans hereafter) in the U.S. population increased rapidly between 1970 and 1990. The

Namkee G. Choi, PhD, is Professor, Graduate School of Social Work, Portland State University, P.O. Box 751, Portland, OR 97207-0751.

[Haworth co-indexing entry note]: "Diversity Within Diversity: Research and Social Work Practice Issues with Asian American Elders." Choi, Namkee G. Co-published simultaneously in *Journal of Human Behavior in the Social Environment* (The Haworth Press, Inc.) Vol. 3, No. 3/4, 2001, pp. 301-319; and: *Psychosocial Aspects of the Asian-American Experience: Diversity Within Diversity* (ed: Namkee G. Choi) The Haworth Press, Inc., 2001, pp. 301-319. Single or multiple copies of this article are available for a fee from The Haworth Document Delivery Service [1-800-342-9678, 9:00 a.m. - 5:00 p.m. (EST). E-mail address: getinfo@haworthpressinc.com].

Census Bureau projects that this population will increase even more dramatically in the future. In the next decade, the Asian American growth rate, spurred by a high immigration rate, is projected to outpace those of whites, blacks, Native Americans, and Hispanics (U.S. Bureau of the Census, 1996).

The number and share of Asian Americans who are age 65 and older will increase at a rate even faster than the Asian American population as a whole. As shown in Table 1, the current number of Asian American elders is expected to double by 2010 and quadruple by 2030. By 2050, Asian Americans are projected to make up 6.3% (up from 1.8% in 1995) of the elderly U.S. population, as compared to 9.3% black and 17.5% Hispanic elders (of both white and black races). In fact, some researchers and government officials

TABLE 1. Population Projections by Race/Ethnicity and Age: 1995 to 2050 (In Thousands)

Year	Total	White	Black	Hispanic origin	Native American	Asian
All ages						
1995	262,820	193,566 (73.6)	31,598 (12.0)	26,936 (10.2)	1,931 (0.7)	8,788 (3.3)
2000	274,634	197,061 (71.8)	33,568 (12.2)	31,366 (11.4)	2,054 (0.7)	10,584 (3.9)
2005	285,981	199,802 (69.9)	35,485 (12.4)	36,057 (12.6)	2,183 (0.7)	12,454 (4.4)
2010	297,716	202,390 (68.0)	37,466 (12.6)	41,139 (13.8)	2,320 (0.8)	14,402 (4.8)
2020	322,742	207,393 (64.3)	41,538 (12.9)	52,652 (16.3)	2,601 (0.8)	18,557 (5.7)
2030	346,899	209,998 (60.5)	45,448 (13.1)	65,570 (18.9)	2,891 (0.8)	22,993 (6.6)
2040	369,980	209,621 (56.7)	49,379 (13.3)	80,164 (21.7)	3,203 (0.9)	27,614 (7.5)
2050	393,931	207,901 (52.8)	53,555 (13.6)	96,508 (24.5)	3,534 (0.9)	32,432 (8.2)
% Change in numbers						
1995-2010	113.3	104.6	118.6	152.7	120.1	163.9
2010-2030	116.5	103.8	121.3	159.3	124.6	159.7
2030-2050	113.6	99.0	117.8	147.2	122.2	141.1
65 years and over						
1995	33,543	28,665 (85.5)	2,644 (7.9)	1,505 (4.5)	129 (0.4)	600 (1.8)
2000	34,709	29,126 (83.9)	2,781 (8.0)	1,872 (5.4)	149 (0.4)	783 (2.3)
2005	36,166	29,737 (82.2)	2,957 (8.2)	2,298 (6.4)	170 (0.5)	1,004 (2.8)
2010	39,408	31,835 (80.8)	3,249 (8.2)	2,847 (7.2)	197 (0.5)	1,281 (3.3)
2020	53,220	41,445 (77.9)	4,651 (8.7)	4,735 (8.9)	275 (0.5)	2,113 (4.0)
2030	69,379	51,760 (74.6)	6,357 (9.2)	7,782 (11.2)	358 (0.5)	3,122 (4.5)
2040	75,233	52,924 (70.4)	7,020 (9.3)	10,804 (14.4)	410 (0.5)	4,074 (5.4)
2050	78,859	52,036 (66.0)	7,603 (9.6)	13,770 (17.5)	473 (0.6)	4,976 (6.3)
% Change in numbers						
1995-2010	117.5	111.1	122.9	189.2	152.7	213.5
2010-2030	176.1	162.6	195.7	273.3	181.7	243.7
2030-2050	113.7	100.1	119.6	176.9	132.1	159.4

Source: U.S. Bureau of the Census (1996, Tables I, J, and 2).
( ): Percentage of the total population of the year in the age category. Percentages do not add to 100 due to rounding.
Note: "Native Americans" includes Alaska Natives.
"Asians" refers to Asian and Pacific Islanders.

acknowledge that the real number and share of Asian American elders may well surpass the Census Bureau's enumeration (see Kauh, 1997). It is known that due to language barriers, ignorance, fear, and other inhibiting factors, many immigrants, especially elders, did not take part in the 1990 census.

Despite the dramatically changing demographics, the ethnogerontological research on Asian American elders has been limited to a relatively small number of studies based on relatively small, nonrandom samples drawn from geographically limited areas. Few surveys of nationally representative samples contain subsamples of Asian Americans elders large enough to allow meaningful analyses of the group (see LaVeist, 1995). For many subethnic groups of Asian Americans, even small-scale, exploratory studies are rare. Lack of an accumulated knowledge base means lack of understanding of this group of elders, with its diverse ethnic/cultural, socioeconomic, and other characteristics, and, thus, inadequate and ineffectual provision of services.

Asian Americans are one of the most internally heterogeneous population groups in the United States with respect to ethnic composition, immigration history, language and religion, and other sociodemographic variables. Of all Asian American age groups, the elderly present the most variations in these characteristics because a large proportion of them are foreign-born, first-generation immigrants and, thus, are more likely to adhere to the culture of their country of origin than are the younger generations, who were born here or have an easier time assimilating to the dominant culture. Given the heterogeneity of the Asian American elder population, existing studies based on small samples of one or a few ethnic groups in geographically limited areas are unlikely to be generalizable to other such groups, although they certainly represent important small steps toward building the knowledge base.

Under these circumstances, both researchers and practitioners face a daunting task of identifying strengths, deficits, needs, and culturally appropriate service-delivery models for the growing number of Asian American elders and their families. The purpose of this article is: (1) to provide an overview of the Asian American elderly population in terms of its diverse ethnic composition, health and mental status, and social service needs; (2) to identify barriers to utilization of formal services as well as strengths and weaknesses of informal support systems; and (3) to recommend directions for future research on and social work practice with Asian American elders and their families.

INTERNAL HETEROGENEITY

The term Asian Americans in the United States refers to a mosaic of at least 26 census-defined Asian and Pacific Islander subethnic groups, among them Chinese, Japanese, Filipino, Korean, Asian Indian, Vietnamese, Cambodian, Hawaiian, Samoan, Laotian, Hmong, Thai, and Guamanian. Some of these groups–Chinese and Japanese–began arriving in this country in the mid-1800s, while others–Filipinos, Koreans, Asian Indians, and Southeast Asians–arrived in large numbers only in the past three decades. (Although a small number of Filipinos established their permanent settlement in Louisiana in the late 18th century, Filipinos did not immigrate to the United States in large numbers until the early 1970s (see Agbayani-Siewert & Revilla, 1995)). The circumstances of their immigration also vary. In the 1800s, Chinese men and the Japanese were brought in as a temporary source of cheap labor to do harsh work; those who arrived after 1965 came to join their families and/or to find a better life; many foreign students settled in the United States instead of returning to their home countries at the end of their advanced studies; and still others came as refugees fleeing the persecution that resulted from political conflicts and other societal turmoil in their home countries. Because the U.S.-born have few language and other adjustment problems, they are naturally more structurally and culturally integrated in the mainstream. Similarly, the length of U.S. residence has also been found to be a significant variable determining the immigrants' level of structural assimilation and acculturation (see Yang, 1999). Also, those who immigrated voluntarily are likely to differ from those who did not want to do so in terms of their attitude toward the host country's customs and their desire to assimilate.

Not only did Asian Americans arrive in different time periods and under different circumstances, but they originated from different parts of the Asian continent and the Pacific islands, where entirely different languages are spoken and different religions and customs are practiced. Moreover, people from the same country often speak entirely different languages and practice different religions and customs. For example, the first-generation Asian Indian Americans identify themselves with particular regional-linguistic subgroups, not with the Indian national-origin group (Kar, Campbell, Jiminez, & Gupta, 1995/1996; Sheth, 1995). The same is true of Filipino Americans and the Indochinese subgroups, or those from Southeast Asian countries (Agbayani-Siewert & Revilla, 1995; Rumbaut, 1995).

Roughly mirroring the population shares of the subethnic groups among Asian Americans, the Chinese elder population is, numerically, the largest of all Asian American elder groups, followed, in descending order, by Filipino, Japanese, Korean, Asian Indian, Vietnamese, and Hawaiian. A majority of Asian American elders, including Chinese, are foreign-born, first-generation immigrants who arrived in the United States after the liberalization of the immigration law in 1965. In fact, almost all the Filipino, Korean, Asian Indian, and Southeast Asian elders came to the United States in the past two and a half decades. Previous studies report that most nonrefugee Asian American elders immigrated to be reunited with their children, who often were themselves recent immigrants still struggling to get established in the

United States. Although Asian American elders preferred to live in their home countries, they often viewed reunification with their children as the only way to retain family ties. Many duty-bound elders also came simply to help their children with (grand)child care and other household chores, to help the children succeed in the new country. Those who immigrated to the United States in old age in general, and the ones who did so reluctantly in particular, may lack the desire or find it difficult, structurally and culturally, to assimilate into the host country and, thus, tend to follow the customs of their country of origin (Cheung, 1989; Kauh, 1997; Kiefer et al., 1985; Lee, J. J., 1987; Wu, 1975). As a result, internal linguistic, religious, and other cultural diversity within the Asian American elder population is a magnified version of the internal diversity among all Asian Americans.

The emphasis on internal heterogeneity is not intended to deny the fact that these elders, especially those from the proximate parts of the Asian continent, such as the Near East and Southeast Asia, share common values and norms, such as extended familism, emphasis on one's obligation to family instead of to the individual, filial piety, respect for elders, and emphasis on the virtues of hard work, endurance, and self-reliance. Notwithstanding these shared values, norms, and other common cultural roots, Asian American elders also show extreme heterogeneity in socioeconomic characteristics, which may in turn effect differences in health and social service needs, level of available informal resources, and formal service utilization patterns.

Education and income: Using the 1990 census data, Tanjasiri, Wallace, and Shibata (1995) compared Asian American elders with their white and black counterparts in terms of education and income. Although Asian American elders, like white elders, were more likely to have completed high school or college than black elders, a much higher proportion of them (12.7%, in contrast to 1.4% of whites and 5.7% of blacks) were also found to have had no formal education. Those who immigrated from some Asian countries–notably India and the Philippines–during the first two decades, following the 1965 liberalization of the immigration law, tend to have more education than their U.S.-born counterparts (Agbayani-Siewert & Revilla, 1995; Sheth, 1995). As these highly educated immigrants have grown older, they have pulled up the average educational level for Asian American elders. At the same time, however, the influx, in the past three decades, of a large number of Asian elderly immigrants, who came mostly as parents of U.S. citizens or resident aliens or as refugees from countries where formal education had not been widely available or accessible until the last two or three decades, resulted in the concentration of a higher proportion of Asian American than white and black elders at the lower end of the educational strata. The proportion of those without formal education is especially high among foreign-born Asian American elderly women because, in their youth, educational opportunities for girls had been even more limited than for boys in their home countries. The combined effect of these recent elderly immigrants' lack of education and the relatively short length of their U.S. residency has been the inability to speak and write English and the inability to participate freely in employment or other productive and leisure activities outside their immediate family circles or ethnic enclaves.

As can be expected from the educational distribution, income distribution among Asian American elders also shows a bipolar pattern, albeit to a lesser extent than the pattern for education. That is, in 1990, a higher proportion of Asian American elderly married couples (27.6%) than their white and black counterparts (18.1% and 10.4%, respectively) enjoyed a family income of $50,000 or more, but twice as high a proportion of Asian American elderly married couples (10.1%) as their white counterparts (5.4%) had incomes below the poverty line (Tanjasiri et al., 1995). On average, Asian American elders, regardless of their marital status, are better off than black or Hispanic elders. But their standing relative to whites can be deceptive if only the average figures are considered, because a higher proportion of Asian American than white elders have incomes below the poverty line. This bifurcated income distribution among Asian American elders reflects the bipolar occupational and income distributions among the Asian American population as a whole. For example, according to data compiled from the March Current Population Surveys of the past 12 years, Asian American households, regardless of the household head's age, have had the highest median income of all race/ethnic groups. In 1997, the median income of Asian American households was $45,249 as compared to $38,972 for white households, $26,628 for Hispanic households, and $25,050 for black households. (However, per capita income for Asian Americans is lower than per capita income for whites. The conclusion is that the higher median income of Asian American households than that of white households owes to the greater number of earners in the average Asian American household.) But at the other end of the income distribution, the incomes of a higher proportion of Asian Americans than whites were below the poverty line (U.S. Bureau of the Census, 1998).

On average, Asian American elders who immigrated recently are more likely to be poor than their U.S-born counterparts because they are not eligible for Social Security or pension benefits due to lack of work history. Nor have they brought significant assets with them because the value of their assets, if they had had any, in their home countries could have been significantly lower than in the United States. Thus, it is not surprising that a much higher proportion of elderly immigrants than U.S.-born elders receive Supplemental Security Income (SSI) as their primary source of income (Cho, 1998; Hu, 1996).

Physical and mental health status: Data on mortality and most other indicators of health status show that Asian American elders, on average, have a longer life expectancy and are healthier than their counterparts in most other race/ethnic groups. As shown in Table 2, average annual death rates between 1994 and 1996 for Asian Americans of both genders aged 55 to 74 years were the lowest of all race/ethnic groups in the same age group. Even for the 75- to 84-year group, Asian Americans have significantly lower overall death rates than whites and blacks. More detailed data, in Table 3, on average death rates for three leading causes of death for elders, diseases of the heart, malignant neoplasms (cancer), and cerebrovascular diseases (stroke), show that Asian American elders aged 65 to 84 years have lower rates than whites and blacks in all categories.

Again, however, these favorable average figures belie internal heterogeneity in the health status of Asian American elders. For instance, using unpublished 1980 data maintained by the National Center for Health Statistics, E. Yu (1986) found that the age-adjusted death rate for foreign-born Chinese Americans was more than two times greater than that for U.S.-born Chinese. For elders 65-74 years old, the death rate for foreign-born Chinese was 5.78 times higher than that reported for U.S.-born Chinese. For elders 75-84 years old, the ratio was 1.88 (also refer to Morioka-Douglas & Yeo, 1990, cited in Wong & Ujimoto, 1998). The higher death rate among the immigrants implicates immigration as having negative effects on physical health. Overall, given the confirmed significant positive association between socioeconomic and health status, the bimodal education and income distributions among Asian American elders surely point to the presence of significant differences in mortality and morbidity rates and self-rated health among different groups

TABLE 2. Average Annual Death Rate 1994-1996 by Age, Sex, and Race/ Ethnicity (per 100,000 residents)

	Age			
Group	55-64	65-74	75-84	85+
Non-Hispanic white male	1,339.4	3,225.0	7,354.7	18,152.5
Black male	2,418.4	4,564.2	8,739.1	16,329.1
Hispanic male	1,045.1	2,307.9	5,078.0	11,609.5
American Indian male	1,346.3	2,685.4	4,713.7	7,789.3
Asian male	739.3	1,969.0	5,055.5	14,498.7
Non-Hispanic white female	795.5	1,940.8	4,863.5	14,665.2
Black female	1,334.4	2,808.7	5,798.3	13,348.2
Hispanic female	579.8	1,387.0	3,236.6	9,066.0
American Indian female	889.5	1,841.3	3,542.1	6,464.8
Asian female	449.3	1,076.4	3,233.0	9,981.9

Source: National Center for Health Statistics (1998, Table 37).

TABLE 3. Average Annual Death Rate 1994-1996 by Age, Sex, and Race/ Ethnicity for Three Leading Causes of Death and for Suicide (per 100,000 residents)

	Heart diseases			Malignant neoplasms		
Group	65-74	75-84	85+	65-74	75-84	85+
Non-Hispanic white male	1,089.5	2,622.1	7,177.1	1,082.0	1,820.5	2,785.0
Black male	1,447.4	2,838.2	5,856.3	1,509.9	2,434.6	3,273.0
Hispanic male	747.7	1,728.9	4,472.7	659.4	1,228.7	1,806.5
Native American male	876.6	1,568.6	2,671.0	692.5	1,015.9	1,172.8
Asian male	602.9	1,594.6	5,423.9	654.6	1,252.7	2,165.9
Non-Hispanic white female	528.1	1,696.1	6,340.9	702.6	1,071.8	1,428.6
Black female	921.6	2,139.3	5,546.2	794.9	1,148.1	1,489.3
Hispanic female	396.3	1,155.3	3,892.0	391.0	642.0	921.5
Native American female	482.2	1,043.4	2,257.8	452.1	689.0	692.0
Asian female	290.6	1,057.8	4,064.3	350.3	729.9	1,117.2

	Cerebrovascular diseases			Suicide	
	65-74	75-84	85+	45-65	65+
Non-Hispanic white male	142.8	509.0	1,552.7	24.9	39.2
Black male	292.3	684.6	1,347.7	11.3	14.1
Hispanic male	126.5	347.4	942.2	13.7	18.5
Native American male	144.5	314.1	705.0	13.7	11.8
Asian male	163.5	517.3	1,578.3	8.9	18.1
Non-Hispanic female	111.1	450.2	1,693.1	7.2	5.6
Black female	218.5	584.0	1,486.6	2.2	2.1
Hispanic female	91.1	282.1	864.8	2.5	2.4
Native American female	120.6	325.2	685.5	4.9	--
Asian female	108.8	403.4	1,358.4	5.1	8.1

Source: National Center for Health Statistics (1998, Tables 38, 39, 40, and 48).

of Asian American elders. A recent study that compared 223 Korean American elders with 201 non-Hispanic white elders in the Los Angeles area showed that 51% of the Korean American elders, in contrast to only 23% of non-Hispanic white elders, reported that their health was fair or poor, although the former group was younger (Moon, Lubben, & Villa, 1998). The Korean American sample elders, all of whom were foreign born, had significantly lower education and income than their non-Hispanic white counterparts. A study of 100 Chinese and Vietnamese Americans age 45 years and older in San Diego County also found that lack of English language skills and lack of use and exposure to English were associated with poor mental, physical, and functional health status (Morton, Stanford, Happersett, & Molgaard, 1992).

Nationwide prevalence studies of mental health problems among Asian American elders do not exist. Nevertheless, it is not difficult to estimate that the rate of depression, and of all mental health problems, may be quite high as the elders experience stresses associated with immigration and acculturation in addition to those associated with aging itself. Stressful life events, widow-hood or single life (i.e., loss of close persons), poor social support, physical illnesses (in themselves and problems due to the side effects of medications), and/or poor self-rated health have been found to be risk factors for depression among older persons (Baker, 1996; Dhondt & Hooijer, 1995; Gottfries, 1998; Husaini, 1997; Katona & Watkin, 1996; Lepine & Bouchez, 1998). Immigra-tion to a new country in one's later years and the struggle to adapt to a completely different culture definitely constitute some of the most stressful life events. Successful adjustment/adaptation to a new country and culture depends not only on a person's internal fortitude, good health, and cultural competence but also on external resources, including financial as well as family and community support. But a sizable proportion of Asian American elders, especially those at the bottom rung of the socioeconomic ladder, suffer from poor health, lack of financial resources, and poor English lan-guage skills. Elderly immigrants also suffer from lack of participation in meaningful role/leisure activities, difficulty in forming new friendships and other social relationships, and intergenerational conflict (due in part to differ-ent levels of acculturation among family members; Kiefer et al., 1985; Ne-moto, 1998; Wong & Ujimoto, 1998; Wu, F. Y. T., 1975). These multiple adjustment problems increase the elders' vulnerability to depression and/or anxiety disorders.

A small number of studies of depression among subethnic groups of Asian American elders confirm that it is especially likely to develop in the early period of immigration. The significantly higher mean scores in depressive symptom measures among Korean American elders were attributed to the subjects' relative newness as immigrants (Koh, S. D., Koh, T. H., Sakauye, & Lin, 1986; Kuo, 1984). Although recent studies of depression among both Korean and Chinese American elders found that social/emotional support from immediate family members (mostly adult children) and friends signifi-cantly moderates the stress level and may prevent depression (Lee, M. S., Crittenden, & Yu, E., 1996; Mui, 1996; Zhang, Yu, L. C., Yuan, Tong, Yang, & Foreman, 1997), the loss of identity, roles, status, and power to control their environment in the new country causes immigrant elders to be more susceptible to depression and anxiety than their U.S-born counterparts.

One indicator of the prevalence of depression is suicide rate. As shown in Table 3, Asian American elderly women had the highest suicide rate of all elderly women in 1994-1996. Earlier studies found some evidence of cohort effect in Chinese and Japanese women, meaning that the cohorts born later had lower suicide rates than the cohort born earlier (see Yu, E., 1986). The vital statistics data from the National Center of Health Statistics (1998) also show that the suicide rate among Asian American elderly women decreased from 13.6 in 1985 to 8.4 in 1996. Nevertheless, it was still the highest of all the elderly female groups in 1996. The average suicide rate for Asian American elderly men between 1994 and 1996 was also higher than that for black and Native Americans men, but lower than that for white men, and about the same as that for Hispanic men.

FORMAL AND INFORMAL SUPPORT SYSTEMS
FOR ASIAN AMERICAN ELDERS

As just shown, a large segment of Asian American elders appear to experience multiple economic and physical and mental health problems affecting their physical and psychological well-being. Despite indications of these multiple problems, Asian American elders are underrepresented among recipients of health and social services.

Barriers to formal service utilization: The underutilization of services by Asian Americans in general, and elders in particular, has been attributed to language barriers and cultural differences. The lack of English language skills restricts potential service recipients' exposure to necessary information on available programs (see Moon et al., 1998) and hampers their ability to go through the oftentimes-cumbersome processes necessary to obtain services. Inability to communicate in English also limits the elders' access to center-based services/programs, such as those provided by senior centers and adult day care facilities. Cultural factors, including Asian values of self-reliance and the reluctance and shame attached to bringing personal problems to strangers, are powerful inhibitors to these elders' seeking external help (Cho, 1998; Lee, J. J., 1987; Nemoto, 1998; Zhang, Snowden, & Sue, 1998). In addition, cultural beliefs and attitudes also affect perceptions of problems and modalities available for treatment of the problems, be they physical illnesses or mental disorders. For example, Asian Americans often hide a family member's mental illness because they attach a deep sense of shame and stigma to the illness, and they do not seek treatment from formal service providers until it becomes too severe and serious for the family to handle (Kang & Kang, 1995).

Also, lack of cultural sensitivity and competence on the part of some service providers from the dominant culture has generated distrust of the entire formal service network by Asian Americans. Asian American elders who have a low degree of exposure to the dominant culture are especially likely to feel uncomfortable and even distressed by their perception of cultural incompatibility between themselves and Anglo service providers (Cheng, 1997). Moreover, although blatant racial discrimination may no longer be tolerated in this society, the not-so-distant history of institutional and blatant discrimination and the continuing practice of subtle and aversive racism in many segments of society and even by some helping professionals can be a powerful deterrent to the Asian Americans seeking help from mainstream helping networks. Perception of such discrimination, as well as a sense of some Anglo/mainstream service providers' disrespect for and prejudice against Asian culture alone, would be enough to make Asian American elders feel humiliated and distrustful of the service system (Lee, J. J., 1987).

On a practical level, the elders may also simply find the services unacceptable by their cultural standards and, therefore, may refuse to use them. One example may be home-delivered meals. Unless ethnic meals are provided, the elders are likely to reject the service (see Choi, 1999). Another may be home health aide services. Unless the aide and the elderly client speak the same language, it would obviously be quite difficult for them even to communicate.

Although the cultural attributes are indeed significant barriers to utilization of formal services by Asian American elders, we must not forget that these elders may also not receive services because they are not allowed to do so under governmental policies and regulations. A study of use of mental health services by Asian Americans aged 50 years or older in Los Angeles County found that severity of illness as well as level of financial coverage (federal, state, local, and/or private sources) significantly influenced the level of usage (Harada & Kim, 1995). Since financial coverage can be influenced by government policies regarding health insurance (e.g., Medicare and Medicaid), the accessibility to services may be hampered or facilitated by such policies. The influence of government policies rather than culture as determinant of service use is quite obvious in the case of SSI. The 1996 welfare reform (the Personal Responsibility and Work Obligations Reconciliation Act) denies most new immigrants access to SSI for the first five years of their U.S. residency. If it were not for the restoration, by the 1997 Balanced Budget Act, of SSI eligibility to resident aliens who were receiving the benefit as of August 1996, many Asian American and Hispanic elders would have been cut off from their only source of income.

In conjunction with the influence of policies and regulations, another important barrier to service utilization by Asian American elders is the general lack of recognition, by the policy makers and service providers, of the extent and the specifics of the elders' needs. Due to the lack of empirical data generated from systematic research, both policy makers and service providers lack understanding of these elders' needs for health and social services. We know almost nothing about the needs of many subethnic groups of Asian American elders. Although the numbers of Asian Indian and Filipino elders are fast increasing, little research has been conducted on them. In the absence of empirical data, the myth and stereotype of the self-sufficient "model minority" persists, and the Asian American elders' predicament has not attained the status of a social problem warranting special appropriations and interventions. The number of Asian American elders in the population may have thus far been too small to attract political and social attention. With the number of Asian American elders rapidly increasing, the future should hold a more sympathetic attitude toward and more resources for them.

Strengths and problems of informal support network: Asian American elders rely on their extended families, especially adult children, to meet their economic and other needs. These elders are more likely than those of any other race/ethnic group to live with adult children and receive material, instrumental, and emotional support from them (Kamo & Zhou, 1994; Kauh, 1997; Lubben & Beccera, R. M., 1987; Osako & Liu, 1986; Yu. L. C. & Wu, S. C., 1985). In their comparison of non-Hispanic whites, Chinese Americans, and Japanese Americans aged 65 years or older from the 1980 Census of Population and Housing, Kamo and Zhou (1994) found that Chinese and Japanese American elders were disproportionately more likely to live in extended family households, particularly in their married children's homes, regardless of the elder's marital status, state of residence, and gender. They also found that the Asian American elders' foreign birth, longer U.S. residency, and lack of English use at home significantly increased their likelihood of living in their married children's home. In other words, Asian American elders who are most likely to have economic and adjustment problems are indeed taken care of by their children, and thus, they may not have to rely on formal services to meet their needs.

In fact, studies have found that living arrangement and the quantity and quality of interactions with their informal support system are often the most significant predictors of Asian American elders' psychological well-being/adjustment. Chinese, Korean, and Japanese American elders who lived with others (mostly children, as opposed to living alone) and had more frequent contact with and received emotional support from family members and friends were less likely to be depressed than those who lacked or were not satisfied with such support (Lee, M. S. et al., 1996; Mui, 1996; Nemoto, 1998; Zhang et al., 1997). A study of elderly Indochinese refugees also reported that those who lived with their elders had higher social adjustment scores than those with other living arrangements (Tran, 1991).

Sole reliance on children to meet their instrumental and emotional needs has its downside, though, for both elders and children. Elderly parents may feel that they are burdening their children too much, and the children, indeed, are likely to feel the pinch from the burden of support, be it housing, financial, instrumental, or emotional. It is also quite possible that the quality of their relationship may be laced with intergenerational conflict if the levels of acculturation differ between parents and children. A few exploratory studies of Korean and Chinese American elders show that they (especially women), in fact, prefer a separate residence, though in proximity to their children, rather than a coresidence with them (Kauh, 1997; Koh, J. & Bell, 1987; Wu, F. Y. T., 1975). This preference for independent living may be a sign of family conflict. In many cases, however, the elders do not want to burden their children, and they prefer living close to their peers and in their coethnic communities to living in the their children's suburban homes isolated from the people and activities of the coethnic communities (Kim, P. K. & Kim, J., 1992).

Studies have shown that Asian American elders indeed draw both instrumental and emotional support from their coethnic communities if the communities are located in proximity to their residence. The availability of ethnic religious and health care institutions, outlets for socialization and recreation with their peers, and other resources (e.g., grocery stores, restaurants, and beauty shops) in coethnic communities facilitates elders' adjustment to the new environment and definitely increases their sense of well-being and enhances their quality of life. J. H. Moon and Pearl's study (1991) of Korean American elders showed that those living in Oklahoma displayed a greater feeling of alienation than those living in Los Angeles. The authors attributed the difference to the presence of a large Korean community in Los Angeles and the lack of such a coethnic community in Oklahoma. A study of Vietnamese Americans aged 45 and older in San Diego also found that the extensiveness of the Vietnamese community may act as an effective buffer to the stress associated with the acculturation process (Morton et al., 1992). Asian American elders' tendency to seek help from their coethnic community may partially explain their underutilization of mainstream health and social services (Wong & Ujimoto, 1998).

A variety of social service programs serving ethnic elders have been established in coethnic communities. The best known of all may be the On-Lok program that started in 1972 in San Francisco's Chinatown and has since served as the model for the Program for All Inclusive Care for the Elderly (PACE). Ethnic senior centers, congregate meal sites, and assistance with applications for SSI and other welfare programs are also available in large coethnic communities in urban areas. Although these services are a god-send for Asian American elders who can utilize them, they are out of reach for those who are homebound or do not live near them. For the latter group, the choices are either utilization of mainstream services or sole reliance on family members. Most available data on service (under)utilization by Asian American elders (gleaned from the many small-scale studies discussed previously) indicate that most of them choose help from family members.

As mentioned briefly, informal support networks are not likely to be able to shoulder all the burden and stress associated with taking care of elders with serious physical and mental health problems. Asian American elders and their family members need to be able to utilize formal services that are culturally acceptable. Health care and social service providers need to be aware of the internal heterogeneity within the population of Asian American elders and be able to provide culturally competent services.

RESEARCH AND SOCIAL WORK PRACTICE ISSUES
FOR ASIAN AMERICAN ELDERS

This overview has identified the problems that Asian American elders face in economic, physical and mental health, and social support areas. The question that naturally follows is: what needs to be done to better serve Asian American elders? In this section, I attempt to answer the question by pointing out the future tasks to be accomplished in both research and social work practice arenas.

Research issues: As discussed, few large-scale empirical studies on Asian American elders have been done. This problem can be addressed in the following ways:

1. The National Institutes of Health (NIH), including the National Institute of Mental Health (NIMH) and the National Institute on Aging (NIA), need to provide funding for nationally representative sample surveys of Asian American elders of all subethnic groups. Although funding has been made available for ethnogerontological research by these funders, the projects they have funded for studies of Asian American elders have tended to be geographically as well as topically restricted. Nationally representative sample surveys, both cross-sectional and longitudinal and including all Asian American subethnic groups, are needed to allow comparative analyses of inter- and intraethnic differences in health, mental health, and social service needs.

2. Future nationally representative sample surveys of aging, health, and mental health need to oversample Asian Americans to allow meaningful analyses of interracial differences. (Blacks have been routinely oversampled for this purpose in many previous surveys, and the trend to oversample Hispanics has also begun to be seen in recent nationally representative sample surveys.) Considering that the Asian American population is the most rapidly increasing minority, it is only logical that future surveys include a meaningful, not just a token, representation of them.

In addition to investing in large-scale surveys and research projects, public and private funding sources need to continuously encourage small-scale studies of Asian American subethnic groups by making funds for such projects available. Limited as these studies may be with respect to their generalizability, they are still useful for increasing social service providers'/practitioners' as well as researchers' understanding of the subjects. The accumulation of the findings of such studies will also contribute to building the knowledge base and designing and providing culturally competent services. Especially for the Asian American subethnic elderly groups, such as Indians, Filipinos, and Indochinese, about whom little research has been done, exploratory studies may serve useful purposes for both practice and laying the foundation for bigger research projects in the future (e.g., by developing and testing instruments that will provide valid data on the ethnic groups and by determining which variables are significant).

Social work practice issues: To make services available, acceptable, and accessible to Asian American elders and their families, the following need to be done:

1. Social service agencies in coethnic communities or ethnic enclaves need to diversify their services in order to better meet the needs of their elders. Because they lack financial resources and/or manpower, multipurpose social service agencies in large coethnic communities provide community- and center-based services for ambulatory clients but are unable to provide many home-based services for those who are homebound. With the growing number of Asian American elders, however, the need for home-based as well institutional care for sick elders is rapidly growing (Beccera, H., 1999). Home health care, home-delivered meal programs, respite care, and friendly visitors, as well as adult day care and nursing homes, are needed to meet the long-term care needs of the growing number of ethnic elders and to reduce family members' caregiving burden and stress.

For elders who are well, recreational activities, job training and placement, and volunteer work opportunities are needed. In addition, services are needed to help elders who live alone maintain their independence; these include assistance with grocery shopping, transportation, and language interpretation. It is also important for social service agencies in coethnic communities to provide a forum for intergenerational activities to bridge the cultural gap between older and younger generations and promote mutual understanding. Recruitment of younger volunteers to assist the elders would be helpful.

2. Non-Asian social service agencies need to add Asian American content in the cultural sensitivity training of their staff. It is especially important for social service agencies located in areas that have a large Asian American community to have bilingual and bicultural staff, conduct needs-assessment surveys, disseminate information on services and programs targeting Asian Americans in the community, and engage in outreach services for isolated and homebound Asian American elders.

3. The reality is that Asian American elders and their families living in a predominantly non-Asian community will continue to perceive or experience barriers to utilizing mainstream social services. Satisfactory solutions to their predicament are not within easy reach, and social workers must continue to strive to come up with innovative means to help this group.

CONCLUSION

The rapid increase in the number of Asian American elders is one of the most significant demographic changes taking place in the United States. Despite this fast growth, the population of Asian American elders is one of the most neglected groups in terms of research on their needs and links to the formal service networks. Asian American elders are characterized by their internal heterogeneity in ethnic/cultural composition, socioeconomic status, and physical and mental health status. A large proportion of Asian American elders, especially those at the bottom rung of the socioeconomic ladder, suffer from lack of financial resources, poor health, acculturative stress as recent immigrants, and poor social support, both formal and informal. These multiple risk factors that Asian American elders face, on top of the challenge of aging per se, warrant increased attention from researchers, policy makers, and social service providers. More representation in nationally representative sample surveys as well as increased funding for large and small Asian American research projects are called for. Diversification of social services in coethnic communities as well as increased cultural sensitivity and competence in mainstream social service agencies are also recommended.

REFERENCES

Agbayani-Siewert, P. & Revilla, L. (1995). Filipino Americans. In P. G. Min (Ed.), *Asian Americans: Contemporary trends and issues* (pp. 134-168). Thousand Oaks, CA: Sage.

Baker, F. M. (1996). An overview of depression in the elderly: A U.S. perspective. *Journal of the National Medical Association*, 88(3), 178-184.

Becerra, H. (1999). For immigrants, agony over ailing parents. *The Los Angeles Times*, February 4. Al, A18-A19.

Cheng, B. K. (1997). Cultural clash between providers of majority culture and patients of Chinese culture. *Journal of Long-Term Home Health Care*, 16(2), 39-43.

Cheung, M. (1989, September). Elderly Chinese living in the United States: Assimilation or adjustment. *Social Work*, 457-461.

Cho, P. J. (1998). Awareness and utilization: A comment. *The Gerontologist*, 38, 317-319.

Choi, N. G. (1999). Determinants of frail elders' length of stay in Meals on Wheels. *The Gerontologist*, 39, 397-404.

Dhondt, A. D. F. & Hooijer, C. (1995). Iatrogenic origins of depression in the elderly: Is medication a significant aetiologic factor in geriatric depression? Considerations and a preliminary approach. *International Journal of Geriatric Psychiatry*, 10, 1-8.

Gottfries, C. G. (1998). Is there a difference between elderly and younger patients with regard to the symptomatology and aetiology of depression? *International Clinical Psychopharmacology*, 13(Suppl. 5), 513-518.

Harada, N. D. & Kim. L. S. (1995). Use of mental health services by older Asian and Pacific Islander Americans. In D. K. Padgett (Ed.), *Handbook on ethnicity, aging and mental health* (pp. 185-202). Westport, CT: Greenwood.

Hu, W. Y. (1996). Elderly immigrants on welfare, *Focus*, 18, 50-53.

Husaini, B. A. (1997). Predictors of depression among the elderly: Racial difference over time. *American Journal of Orthopsychiatry*, 67, 48-58.

Kamo, Y. & Zhou, M. (1994). Living arrangements of elderly Chinese and Japanese in the United States. *Journal of Marriage and the Family*, 56, 544-558.

Kang, T. S. & Kang, G. E. (1995). Mental health status and needs of the Asian American elderly. In D. K. Padgett (Ed.), *Handbook on ethnicity, aging and mental health* (pp. 113-131). Westport, CT: Greenwood.

Kar, S. B., Campbell, K., Jiminez, A., & Gupta, S. R. (1995/1996). Invisible Americans: An exploration of Indo-American quality of life. *Amerasia Journal*, 21(3), 25-52.

Katona, C. L. E. & Watkin, V. (1996). Depression in old age. *Reviews in Clinical Gerontology*, 54, 427-441.

Kauh, T. O. (1997). Intergenerational relations: Older Korean-Americans' experiences. *Journal of Cross-Cultural Gerontology*, 12, 245-271.

Kiefer, C. W., Kim, S., Choi, K., Kim, L., Kim, B. L., Shon, S., & Kim, T. (1985). Adjustment problems of Korean American elderly. *The Gerontologist*, 25, 477-482.

Kim, P. K. & Kim, J. (1992). Korean elderly: Policy, program, and practice implications. In S. M. Furuto, R. Biswas, D. K. Chung, K. Murase, & F. Ross-Sheriff, (Eds.), *Social work practice with Asian Americans* (pp. 227-239). Newbury Park, CA: Sage.

Koh, J. & Bell, W. (1987) Korean elders in the United States: Intergenerational relations and living arrangements. *The Gerontologist*, 27, 66-71.

Koh, S. D., Koh, T. H., Sakauye, K. M., & Lin, W. T. (1986). *The value scheme of Asian American elderly.* Chicago, Pacific/Asian American Mental Health Center.

Kuo, W. H. (1984). Prevalence of depression among Asian Americans, *Journal of Nervous and Mental Disease*, 172, 449-457.

Kurzeja, P. L., Koh, S. D., Koh, T., & Liu, W. T. (1986). Ethnic attitudes of Asian American elderly: The Korean immigrants and Japanese niseis. *Research on Aging*, 8, 110-127.

LaVeist, T. A. (1995). Data sources for aging research on racial and ethnic groups. *The Gerontologist*, 35, 328-339.

Lee, J. J. (1987). Asian American elderly: A neglected minority group. *Journal of Gerontological Social Work*, 9(4), 103-116.

Lee, M. S., Crittenden, K. S., & Yu, E. (1996). Social support and depression among U.S. elderly Korean immigrants in the U.S. *International Journal of Aging and Human Development*, 42, 313-327.

Lepine, J. P. & Bouchez, S. (1998). Epidemiology of depression in the elderly. *International Clinical Psychopharmacology*, 13(Suppl. 5), 57-512.

Lubben, J. E. & Becerra, R. M. (1987). Social support among Black, Mexican, and Chinese elderly. In D. E. Gelfand & C. M. Barresi (Eds.), *Ethnic dimensions of aging* (pp. 130-144). New York: Springer.

Moon, A., Lubben, J. E., & Villa, V. (1998). Awareness and utilization of community-long-term care services by elderly Korean and non-Hispanic white Americans. *The Gerontologist*, 38, 309-316.

Moon, J. H. & Pearl, J. H. (1991). Alienation of elderly Korean American immigrants as related to place of residence, gender, age, years of education, time in the U.S., living with or without a spouse. *International Journal of Aging and Human Development*, 32, 115-124.

Morioka-Douglas, N. & Yeo, G. (1990). *Aging and health: Asian/Pacific Island American elders*. (Working Paper Series No. 3) Stanford, CA: Stanford Geriatric Education Center.

Morton, D. J., Stanford, E. P., Happersett, C. J., & Molgaard, C. A. (1992). Acculturation and functional impairment among older Chinese and Vietnamese in San Diego County, California. *Journal of Cross-Cultural Gerontology*, 7, 151-176.

Mui, A. C. (1996). Depression among elderly Chinese immigrants: An exploratory study. *Social Work*, 41, 633-645.

National Center for Health Statistics (1998). *Health, United States, 1998 with socio-economic status and health chartbook*. Hyattsville, MD: Author.

Nemoto, T. (1998). Subjective norms toward social support among Japanese American elderly in New York City: Why help does not always help. *Journal of Community Psychology*, 26, 293-316.

Osako, N. M. & Liu, W. T. (1986). Intergenerational relations and the aged among Japanese Americans. *Research on Aging*, 8, 128-155.

Rumbaut, R. G. (1995). Vietnamese, Laotian, and Cambodian Americans. In P. G. Min (Ed.), *Asian Americans: Contemporary trends and issues* (pp. 232-270). Thousand Oaks, CA: Sage.

Sheth, M. (1995). Asian Indian Americans. In P. G. Min (Ed.), *Asian Americans: Contemporary trends and issues* (pp. 169-198). Thousand Oaks, CA: Sage.

Tanjasiri, S. P, Wallace, S. P., & Shibata, K. (1995). Picture imperfect: Hidden problems among Asian Pacific Islander elderly. *The Gerontologist*, 35, 753-760.

Tran, T. V. (1991). Family living arrangement and social adjustment among three ethnic groups of elderly Indochinese refugees. *International Journal of Aging and Human Development*, 32, 91-102.

U.S. Bureau of the Census (1996). *Population projections of the United States by age, sex, race, and Hispanic origin: 1995 to 2000* (Current Population Reports No. P25-1 130). Washington, DC: U.S. Government Printing Office.

U.S. Bureau of the Census (1998). *Measuring 50 years of economic change using the March Current Population Survey* (Current Population Reports No. P60-203). Washington, DC: U.S. Government Printing Office.

Wong, P. T. P. & Ujimoto, K. V. (1998). The elderly: Their stress, coping and mental health. In L. C. Lee & N. W. S. Sane (Eds.), *Handbook of Asian American Psychology* (pp. 165-209). Thousand Oaks, CA: Sage.

Wu, F. Y. T. (1975, June). Mandarin-speaking aged Chinese in the Los Angeles area. *The Gerontologist*, 271-275.

Yang, P. Q. (1999). Sojourners or settlers: Post-1965 Chinese immigrants. *Journal of Asian American Studies*, 2, 61-91.

Yu, E. S. H. (1986). Health of the Chinese elderly in America. *Research on Aging*, 8, 84-109.

Yu, L. C. & Wu, S. C. (1985). Unemployment and family dynamics in meeting the needs of Chinese elderly in the United States. *The Gerontologist*, 25, 472-476.

Zhang, A. Y., Snowden, L. R., & Sue, S. (1998). Differences between Asian and white Americans' help seeking and utilization patterns in the Los Angeles area. *Journal of Community Psychology*, 26, 317-326.

Zhang, A. Y., Yu, L. C., Yuan, J., Tong, Z., Yang, C., & Foreman, S. E. (1997). Family and cultural correlates of depression among Chinese elderly. *International Journal of Social Psychiatry*, 43, 199-212.

Index

Abbott, A.A., 266,278
Abe-Kim, J., 5,243-262
ABS. *See* Affect Balance Scale (ABS)
Abueg, F.R., 166,173
Abuse
    Filipino Americans, dating violence
      and, 115-133
    Indian American women, attitudes
      toward, 135-158
    Japanese American women,
      domestic violence and,
      201-224
    substance abuse, Asian/Pacific
      Islander (AP/I) women and,
      263-280
Academic achievement, adolescents
    historical perspectives of, 36-39
    introduction to, 35-36
    references, 47-48
    research methods, 39-40
    research results, 40-44
    research results, discussion of, 44-47
Acculturation and Vietnamese
    Americans, 225-242
Adjusted Goodness-of-Fit Index
    (AGFI), 72-74
Adolescents
    academic achievement, 35-48
    adoptees, Korean American, 65-82
    depression and, 49-64
Adoptees
    Chinese Americans, 19-33
    Korean American adolescents, 65-82
Adoption Law (1991), People's
    Republic of China, 19-33
Aeby, C., 65
Affect Balance Scale (ABS), 71-72
Agarwal, P., 138,155
Agbayani-Siewert, P., 4,115-133,203,
    233,304,316
AGFI. *See* Adjusted Goodness-of-Fit
    Index (AGFI)

Agoncillo, T.A., 118,131
Agtuca, J.R., 117-118,130-131,203,219
Akutsu, P.D., 54,64,88,98,100,114
Alcott, C.L., 115
Aldarondo, E., 204,221
Aldwin,C.M., 161,173,183,196,285,296
Allport, G.W., 86,97
Alpert, B., 105,113
Alvarez, M., 53,64
American Psychiatric Association (APA),
    165,228,239,249-250,285,296
Anderson, J., 201
Anderson, R.B., 265,279
Andreski, P., 228,240
Aneshensel, C.S., 208,220
Angel, J.L., 172-173
Angell, R.H., 166,175
Antonovsky, A., 88-90,97
Antrobus, J.S., 86,95,97
Anxiety, 162-164
APA. *See* American Psychiatric
    Association (APA)
Asai, M., 164,177
Ashcraft, N., 143,155
Asian American experiences
    (psychological aspects),
    research about adolescents
    academic achievement and, 35-48
    depression and, 49-64
Asian/Pacific Islanders (A/PI),
    substance abuse treatment
    and, 263-280
Cambodian Americans, Cambodian
    Killing Fields survivors,
    243-262
Chinese Americans
    adoptive parents and child
      identity development, 19-33
    young adults and network
      composition, social
      integration, and sense of
      coherence, 83-98

elderly, research and social work
    practice issues, 301-319
Filipino Americans, dating violence
    and, 115-133
Hmong Americans, cultural orient-
    ation of, 99-114
Indian American women, 135-158
introduction to, 1-6
Japanese Americans, women and
    domestic violence, 201-224
Korean Americans
    adolescent adoptees,
        psychological adjustment of,
        65-82
    independent self as requisite for
        well-being and, 179-200
    stress, coping, and depression
        and, 281-299
    mental health research about,
        current state of, 159-178
    sociodemographics and, 7-17
Vietnamese Americans
    acculturation, premigration
        traumatic experiences, and
        depression and, 225-242
    Hmong, cultural orientation of,
        99-114
Asian and Pacific Islander Center of
    Census Information Services,
    170-171
Asian Pacific American Community
    Fund, 35,39
Asian/Pacific Islanders (A/PI), research
    about women, substance
    abuse treatment and
    culturally-based treatment
    programs, 268-271
    historical perspectives and statistics
        of, 265-268
    introduction to, 263-265
    references, 278-280
    research methods, 271-272
    research results, 272-276
    research results, discussion of,
        276-277
Asiatic Exclusion League, 11

Astin, M.C., 204-205,217,220
Attitude Toward Women Scale
    (AWS), 143-144,146-152
Avison, W.R., 54,63,192,198,204,220,
    232,241
AWS. *See* Attitude Toward Women
    Scale (AWS)
Azaldua, G., 138,156

Bagley, C., 67-68,80
Baker Miller, J., 267
Baker, F.M., 306,316
Balanced Budget Act (1997), 311
Bargh, J.A., 182,196
Barner, H.L., 70,80
Barringer, H., 37,47
Baumeister, R., 182,196
BDI. *See* Beck's Depression Inventory
    (BDI)
Beccerra, R.M., 312,315,317
Beck's Depression Inventory (BDI),
    71-72
Beck, A.T., 71-72,80
Beckett, J., 117,131
Beiser, M., 229,239
Belensky, M.F., 267,278
Belknap, R.A., 205,220
Bell, W.G., 294,297,313,317
Bellah, R., 181,196
Bem, S.L., 116,131
Bemak, F., 166,173,244,260
Bender, D., 20-21,31
Bennett, J., 227,240
Bennett, L., 204,220
Bentler, P.M., 72-74,80
Berg, B.J., 215,220
Bergquist, K., 22,30-31
Berry, J.W., 53,63,139,156-157,184,196,
    226-227,235,239,287,296
Berthold, M., 11,17
Best, C.L., 205,222
Bhosley, G., 204,217,233
Blazer, D., 285,296
Boehnlein, J.K., 166,175,229,240,244,
    259-261
Boey, K.W., 284,286-287,296

Bogaarts, J., 21,31
Bohme, F., 8f
Bollen, K.A., 72,80
Bollini, P., 229,232,241
Bond, M.H., 111,114
Bonnett, D.G., 72-74,80
Boothby, N., 67,81
Borden, W., 285,296
Bornemann, T.H., 166,173
Bouchez, S., 309,317
Bourne, P.G., 164,174
Boyd, C., 264,278
Bradburn, N.M., 71-72,80
Brady, H., 37,47
Brady, M., 268,278
Brand, D., 36,47
Breslau, N., 228,240
Brewer, M.B., 182,196
Bridges, K., 164,174
Brief Symptom Inventory (BSI), 144
Brindis, C.D., 264,266,278
Brink, T.L., 291,296
Brisbane, F., 264,280
Bronfenbrenner, U., 88,97
Broom, D., 266,278
Brouwers, M.C., 170,177
Browne, C., 264,278
Brush, L.D., 128,131
BSI. *See* Brief Symptom Inventory
        (BSI)
Buhl-Auth, J., 226-227,242
Bureau of the Census, United States.
        See United States, Bureau of
        the Census
Burnam, M.A., 54,64,180,196,227,240
Burnette, D., 285-286,288,294,296
Burton, L.M., 171,174
Butler, R.N., 285,296

Cambodian Americans, research about
    Cambodian Killing Fields survivor
        experiences
    introduction to, 243-246
    references, 260-262
    research methods, 248-250
    research results, 250-258
    research results, discussion of,
        259-260
    somatization and, 246-248
Cambra, R.E., 163,174
Campbell, J.C., 204-205,220
Campbell, K., 149,156,304,317
Cantor, M.H., 285,296
Cantor, N., 183,198
CAPES. *See* Chinese American
        Psychiatric Epidemiological
        Study (CAPES)
Caplan, N., 229,240
Caplan, R.D., 183,196
Capsi-Yavin, Y., 229,232,241
Carlson, E., 244,260
Carmines, E.G., 71,80
CASA. *See* National Center on
        Addiction and Substance
        Abuse at Columbia
        University (CASA)
Castillo, T.B., 119,131
Casual modeling as psychological
        adjustment predictors, 65-82
Cecere, L., 21-22,31
Census, Bureau of (United States). *See*
        United States, Bureau of the
        Census
Center for Epidemiologic Studies
        Depression Scales (CES–D),
        49-64,161-168,186-196,
        231-239,284f
Central Intelligence Agency (CIA).
        See United States, Central
        Intelligence Agency (CIA)
CES-D. *See* Center for Epidemiologic
        Studies Depression Scales
        (CES-D)
CFI. *See* Comparative Fit Index (CFI)
Chan, R., 49
Chan, S., 10-11,16,100-101,113,118
Chandler, D., 244,261
Chant, S.H., 130-131
Chao, R., 167,177
Chavira, V., 20,32,68
Chen, Y., 52,64
Cheng, B.K., 310,316

Cheng, D., 167,174
Cheung, M., 247,305,316
Chew-Graham, C., 245-247,258-259,262
Chi, I., 284,286-287,296
Chin, V., 15-16
China Daily, 21,31
Chinese American Psychiatric
    Epidemiological Study
    (CAPES), 161,167-173
Chinese Americans, research about
  adoptive parents and child identity
    development
    implications for social work
      practice, 30-31
    introduction to, 19-21
    references, 30-31
    research method, 22-23
    research results, 23-28
    research results, discussion of,
      28-30
    single child policy and adoption
      law in China, 21-22
  young adults,and network composi-
    tion, social integration, and
    sense of coherence
    historical perspectives of, 85-88
    introduction to, 83-85
    references, 97-98
    research methods, 89-90
    research results, 90-94
    research results, discussion of,
      94-97
Chinese Exclusion Act, 11
Chinese Psychiatric Epidemiology
    Study, 168-169
Cho, P.J., 306,310,316
Cho, Y.G., 204,221
Choi, N.G., 1-6,301-319
Choy, M.H., 229,240
Chun, C.A., 164-167,169,174,178
Chun, K.M., 36-37,47,166,173
Chun, M.B., 37,47
Chung, D., 264,278
Chung, R.C., 100,113,166,173,205,
    233
Chung, W., 172,174

CIA. *See* United States, Central
    Intelligence Agency (CIA)
CIDI. *See* Composite International
    Diagnostic Interview (CIDI)
Civil Liberties Act (1988), 15
Clara, M., 129-130
Clark, M.L., 117,131
Clum, K., 201
Coherence, sense of among Chinese
    Americans, 83-98
Coleman, H.L., 144,157,184,197
Colleges and universities
  Columbia University, 265-266,281
  University of California, Berkeley,
    35,83
  University of California, Davis,
    135,137,146-147
  University of California, Los Angeles
    (UCLA), 115
  University of Michigan, 167,179
Collier, M.J., 87,95,97
Columbia University, 265-266,281
Commission on Civil Rights. *See* United
    States, Commission on Civil
    Rights
Comparative Fit Index (CFI), 72-74
Composite International Diagnostic
    Interview (CIDI), 167-168
Contextual Justification Scale, 121-127
Coolidge, C., 11
Coping and stress. *See* Stress and coping
Corbin, J., 272,280
Corin, E., 38,48
Corpi, L., 137,156
Council on Social Work Education, 263
Court cases, United States, *Doe v. State*,
    20
Covington, S.S., 267,278
Cowger, C., 65
Coyne, A., 287,296
Crittenden, K.S., 309,317
Croll, E., 20-21,31
Cross, S., 184,192-193,196
Cross-cultural studies
  adolescents
    academic achievement and, 35-48

depression and, 49-64
elderly, research and social work
practice issues, 301-319
historical perspectives of, 169-170
Indian Americans and European
Americans, 135-158
sociodemographics, 7-17
Crow, S.S., 265,280
Crystal, D., 36,47
Cultural competence and substance
abuse treatment programs for
Asian/ Pacific Islander
(A/PI) women, 263-280
Cultural orientation, Hmong
Americans, 99-114
Culturally-based substance abuse
treatment programs, 263-280
Current Population Survey, 12,306

D'Andrade, R.G., 182-183,196
D'Avanzo, C.E., 244,247,261
Daniels, R., 9-11,16-17
Dansku, B.S., 204,222
Das, A.K., 148,156
Das, V., 244-246,258,261
DasGupta, K., 137,149,156
Dasgupta, S.D., 138-139,143,146,156,
203,220
Dasgupta, S.S., 138,156
Dating violence, Filipino Americans
and, 115-133
Davidson, G., 117,133
Davin, D., 20,31
Davis, G.C., 228,240
de los Angeles Aranalde, M., 106,113
De Vita, C.J., 37,47,85,97
DeCambra, H., 265,278
Definitions of dating violence, 121-127
Delgado, M., 265,278
Demo, D.H., 204,220-221
Depression
adolescents, inner-city and, 49-64
Korean Americans, 281-299
research results, historical
perspectives of, 161-162

Vietnamese Americans, 225-242
Derogatis, L.R., 144,156,208,220
Dhondt, A.D.F., 309,316
Di Clemente, R.J., 205,222
Diagnostic and Statistical Manual of
Mental Disorders (DSM)
DSM-III-R, 287
DSM-IV, 165,228,239,249-250
Diener, E., 71-72,81
Dobbelaer, R., 86,97
Dobson, K.S., 169,176
Doe v. State, 20
Domestic violence
Filipino Americans, dating violence
and, 115-133
Indian American women, attitudes
toward, 135-158
Japanese American women and,
201-224
Donovan, J., 266,278
Doyle, H., 245-247,258-259,262
Drapeau, A., 38,48
DSM. *See* Diagnostic and Statistical
Manual of Mental Disorders
(DSM)
Dubois, B., 264,279
Dungee-Anderson, D., 117,131
Duran, B., 268,278
Duran, E., 268,278
Durvasula, R., 167,177
Dutton, M.A., 204,217,220

Eames, E., 143,157
Ebreo, A., 161,177
Ebrey, P., 128,133
ECA. *See* Epidemiologic Catchment
Area Study (ECA)
Economist, The, 21
Edwards, J.N., 204,220-221
Edwards, J.W., 165,174
Eich, E., 218,220
Eisenbruch, M., 244,260-261
Elderly
Korean Americans, stress, coping,
and depression and, 281-299
research and social work practice
issues, 281-299

importance of research about, 314-316
internal heterogeneity, 303-310
introduction to, 301-303
references, 316-319
support systems, formal and informal, 310-314
Ellison, C.G., 85,87,95,97
Eng, P., 148,154,156
Enomoto, K., 164-167,169,174,178
Ensel, W.M., 163,175-176
Epidemiologic Catchment Area Study (ECA), 164,167-168,228
Erikson, E.H., 51,63,67,81,86,97
Ertl, M., 117, 132
Escobar, J., 227,240
Eshleman, E., 208,221

Fabrega, H., 227,240
Fadiman, A., 100-101,113
Fairbank, J.A., 228,249
Family Violence Prevention Fund, 203
Fanon, F., 153,156
Faraone, S.V., 228,240
Feigelman, W., 66,68,77,81
Feld, S., 179
Felsman, J.K., 174,182
Femina, 137,156
Filipino Americans, research about dating violence and
introduction to, 115-116
practice and research, implications for, 130-131
references and literature review about, 116-120,131-133
research methods, 120-122
research results, 122-127
research results, discussion of, 127-130
Filteau, C.H., 138,156
Finkelhor, D., 205,220
Fiske, A., 181,196
Flannigan, A.Y., 4,115-133,203,233
Flaskerud, J., 128,131-132

Folkman, S., 285-286,297
Follingstad, D.R., 215,220
Folstein, M.F., 164-165,174
Fong, R., 2,5,20,31,263-280
Fong, S.L., 169,174
Foreman, S.E., 309,319
Foster, S.L., 85,97
Foy, D.W., 204,220
Frank, A., 163,176
Freeman, V.S., 37,47
Freud, S., 266,278
Friedman, M., 166,176
Froman, R., 244,261
Frye, B.A., 166,176,244,247,261
Fujimoto, Y., 35
Fukushima, K., 201
Futterman, A., 286,299

Gall, S.B., 8f,10f
Gall, T.L., 8f,10f
Gallagher, D., 286,299
Gardner, W., 182,196
Gaw, A.C., 164-165,174
GDS. *See* Geriatric Depression Scale (GDS)
Geist, R., 167,174
Gelles, R.J., 206,233
General Ethnicity Questionnaire (GEQ)
abridged version (GEQ-A), 105-112
American version (GEQA), 144-145, 149-152
Asian Indian version (GEQAI), 144-145,149-152
Hmong version (GEQ–H), 105-112
non-specialized version, 105-112, 144-145
Gentlemen's Agreement, The (1907), 11
GEQ. *See* General Ethnicity Questionaire (GEQ)
Geriatric Depression Scale (GDS), 286-296
Germaine, C.B., 183,196
Gerton, J., 144,157,184,197
Gey, F.C., 37,47

GFI. *See* Goodness-of-Fit Index (GFI)
Ghuman, S.P.A., 138,156
Gibbons, J.L., 5,225-242
Gidycz, C.A., 117,132
Gilandas, A., 129,132
Gill, O., 54,63,68,81
Gillespie, B., 208,218,224
Gilligan, C., 267,279
Giri, R., 181,198
Glenn, E.N., 9,12,16
Global Severity Index, 208
Goldberg, D.P., 164,174
Goldfeld, A.E., 228,240
Golding, J.M., 54,64,180,196,204,
    220
Gonzales, H., 264,279
Good, B., 245,248,261
Goodman, L.A., 204,220
Goodness-of-Fit Index (GFI), 72-75
Gottfries, C.G., 309,316
Green, B.L., 204,221
Green, J.W., 116,132
Greenberger, E., 51,56-57,64,161,173,
    183,196
Greenblat, C.S., 129,132
Greene, M.A., 184,196
Greenhalgh, S., 21,32
Grotevant, H., 20,29-30,32-33
Grove, V., 20,32
Growing Up Asian American (essay
    contest), San Francisco Bay
    area, 39
Guest, S.S., 194,198,229,241
Gupta, M.D., 139,153,156
Gupta, S.R., 304,314

Habenicht, M., 229,240
Ham, M.D., 294,297
Happersett, C.J., 308,318
Harachi, T.W., 143,156
Harada, N.D., 311,317
Harding, S., 272,278
Harvard Trauma Questionnaire
    (HTQ), Vietnamese version,
    232,237-239

Harvey, S.M., 266,280
Hause, E.S., 215,220
Hawaii, State Department of Health,
    266,268
Hayduck, L.A., 72,81
Hegde, R.S., 138-139,156
Helmreich, R., 127,133,143,158
Helweg, A.W., 138,156
Helweg, U.M., 138,157
Helzer, J., 228,240
Her, C., 100,113
Herskovits, M.J., 226,241
Hess, D., 99
Heterogeneity among the elderly,
    301-319
Hibbard, J., 266,280
Hiller, W., 245,262
Hing, B.O., 12,17
Hirschman, C., 37,47
Hmong Americans, research about
    cultural orientation of
        introduction to, 99-103
        notes, 112
        references, 113-114
        research methods, 103-107
        research results, 103-107
        research results, discussion of,
            109-112
Ho, C.K., 128,132,203,220
Ho, M., 119,132
Hoffman, K.L., 204,220-221
Hofstede, G., 181,197
Hogan, D.P., 172-173
Hohm, C.F., 205,221
Holamon, B., 203,222
Hollingshead, A., 55,56,64,89,97
Holt International Children's Service, 69
Hong, G.K., 294,297
Hooijer, C., 309,316
Hosmer, D., 125,132
Hotaling, G., 205,220
Hough, R.L., 227-228,240
Houskamp, B.M., 204,221
Hovanitz, C., 204,221
Howell, N., 218,222
Hsu, L.K.G., 164-165,174

HTQ. *See* Harvard Trauma
    Questionnaire (HTQ),
    Vietnamese version
Hu, W.Y., 306,317
Huang, B., 20,22,32,51
Huang, J.S., 83
Huang, L.N., 88,98,100,114
Hughes, M., 208,221
Human Rights Watch, 21,32
Hung, Y., 36,48,83
Hunter, K.I., 285,298
Hurd, K., 53,64
Hurh, W.M., 37,47,162,174,180,197
Husaini, B.A., 285,297,309,317
Hyun, K.J., 4,179-199

Ibrahim, F.A., 169,172,176
ICD-10, 168-169
Identity development, Chinese
    American adoptees, 19-33
Ima, K., 205,221
Immigration Act (1924), 16
Immigration Law (1965), 12
Independent self as requisite for
    psychological well-being
    and Korean Americans,
    179-200
Indian Americans, research about
    women, cross-cultural studies of
    historical perspectives of,
      137-139
    introduction to, 135-137
    notes, 155
    references, 155-158
    research about, importance of,
      154-155
    research hypotheses and
      objectives, 139-140
    research methods, 140-145
    research results, 145-154
Indian moves on Human Development,
    137,156
Indochinese Psychiatry Clinic (Boston,
    MA), 232
Ingersoll, B., 28-29,32
Inner-city adolescents and depression

description of, 51-52
introduction to, 49-50
references, 52-54,63-64
research methods, 55-60
research results, 60-62
research, importance of, 62-63
significance, 50-51
Innes, P., 128,132
Ino, S., 163,176
Inouye, D., 15
Interdependent Self–Construal Scale,
    199-200
*International Adoption and Child
    Abduction,* 20,31
Iwamasa, G.Y., 162,164,174

Jackson, B., 68,81
Jang, D., 219,221
Japanese Americans, research about
    women and domestic violence
    historical and statistical
      perspectives of, 203-205
    implications for practice, 219
    introduction to, 201-203
    other types of victimization and,
      211-213
    psychological distress and,
      213-214
    psychological distress and the
      role of victimization,
      216-217
    references, 219-224
    research measurement
      instruments, 206-209
    research methods, 205-206,
      217-219
    research results, 209-211
    research results, discussion of,
      214-216
Jasinski, J.L., 204,221
Jilek, W.G., 265,279
Jimenez, A., 149,156,304,317
Johnson, K., 20,22,32
Johnson, M.C., 162,174
Johnston, H.F., 50,64

Jones, L., 118,131
Jordan, B.K., 228,240
Joreskog, K.G., 72,81
Joshi, R., 148,157
Justice and Peace Commission
  (Mumbai, India), 135

Kakar, S., 137,156
Kamo, Y., 312,317
Kane, P., 20,32
Kang, G.E., 118,310,317
Kang, T.S., 118,310,317
Kanuha, V., 204,222
Kao, G., 38,47
Kaplan, H.B., 71,81
Kaplan-Meier (KM) estimator,
  208-211,218
Kar, S.B., 149,156,304,317
Karno, M., 227,240
Kasindorf, M., 36,47
Kaspar, V., 232,241
Katona, C.L.E., 309,317
Katz, I., 287,298
Kaufman Kantor, G., 204,221
Kauh, T.O., 305,312-313,317
Keefe, K., 167,177
Kemp, A., 204-205,217,221
Kemp, B.J., 285,294,297
Kemp, S.F., 148,156
Kessler, R.C., 168,204,208,221,285,
  287,299
Kiefer, C.W., 291,293-294,296,305,
  309,317
Kiernan, B., 244,261
Kihlplan, J., 183,198
Killing Fields (Cambodian) survivor
  experiences
  introduction to, 243-246
  references, 260-262
  research methods, 248-250
  research results, 250-258
  research results, discussion of,
    259-260
  somatization, 246-248
Kilpatrick, D.G., 205,222

Kim, D.S., 22,30-32,66-68,81
Kim, J., 313,317
Kim, K.C., 162,174,180,197
Kim, K.I., 37,47,204,221
Kim, L.S., 311,317
Kim, P.K., 313,317
Kim, S., 183,197
Kim, U., 37,47,139,156,226-227,235,239
Kimura, S., 35
Kincaid, D.L., 183,197
Kinzie, J.D., 166,175,229,240,244,261
Kirk, B.A., 163,176-177
Kirk, H.D., 66,81
Kirmeyer, L.J., 164,175,246-248,
  261-262
Kish, L., 185,197
Kishwar, M., 136-137,151-152,156
Kitanishi, K., 164,177
Kitano, H.N., 2,7-17
Kitayama, S., 87,98,180-182,196
Klatzkin, A., 21,23,31
Kleinman, A., 164-166,175,178,193,
  197,244-247,258,261
Kleinman, J., 193,197,229,245-247,261
Klopf, D.W., 163,174
KM estimator. *See* Kaplan-Meier
  (KM) estimator
Koh, F.M., 67,81
Koh, J.Y., 294,297,313,317
Koh, S.D., 309,317
Koh, T.H., 309,317
Kohlberg, L., 266,279
Korean Americans, research about
  adolescent adoptees and casual
    modeling
    historical perspectives of, 66-67
    introduction to, 65-66
    references, 80-82
    research about, importance of,
      79-80
    research methods, 69-72
    research results, 72-76
    research results, discussion of,
      76-79
    theoretical framework and
      literature review, 67-69

independent self as requisite for
    psychological well-being
    and
Interdependent Self-Construal
    Scale, 199-200
    introduction to, 179-181
    notes, 195-196
    references, 196-199
    research methods, 185-189
    research results, 189-192
    research results, discussion of,
        192-195
    research, importance of, 195
    theoretical framework of,
        181-185
stress, coping, and depression
    among the elderly
    introduction to, 281-286
    references, 296-299
    research methods, 286-287
    research results, 287-291
    research results, discussion of,
        291-296
Koss, M.P., 117,132-133,215,221
Koss-Chioino, J., 264,280
Krause, N., 227,240,285,297
Krishnan, A., 139,157
Kroll, J., 162,175,229,244,262
Kub, J., 205,220
Kuiper, N.A., 182,196
Kulberg, A.M., 85,97
Kulka, R.A., 228,240
Kumagai, A.K., 201
Kuo, W.H., 50,57,64,128,132,162-163,
        175-176,180,183,194,197,
        309,317
Kurasaki, K.S., 171,177
Kurtines, W., 106,113
Kwan, A.B., 85,98
Kyomen, H., 164,177

La Du, T.J., 72,81
Lachenbruch, P.A., 208,220
LaFromboise, T., 144,157,184,
        193-194,197

Lai, J., 163,169,175
Lai, T.A., 203,221
Lam, L.V., 35
Langan, P., 128,132
Langer, L., 244,259-260,262
Lapierre, S., 285,297
LaVeist, T.A., 303,317
Lavelle, J., 166,176,229,232,241
Lawrence, K.J., 204,220
Laws and legislation
    Oregon
        Measure 58, 20
    People's Republic of China
        Adoption Law (1991), 19-33
    United States
        Balanced Budget Act (1997), 311
        Chinese Exclusion Act, 11
        Civil Liberties Act (1988), 15
        Gentlemen's Agreement, The
            (1907), 11
        Immigration Act (1924), 16
        Immigration Law (1965), 12
        McCarran-Walter Act (1952), 12
        National Origins Acts (1924), 11
        Personal Responsibility and Work
            Obligations Reconciliation
            Act (1996), 311
        War Brides Act (1945), 11-12
        War Brides Act, amendment
            (1947), 11-12
Lawton, M.P., 183,197,287,298
Lazarus, R.S., 285-286,297
Lecca, P., 264,279
Lee, D., 219,221
Lee, E., 139,149,156-157,236,240
Lee, J.J., 4, 159-178,305,310-311,317
Lee, L.C., 172,175
Lee, M.S., 295-296,298,309,312,317
Lee, P.A., 2-3,35-48,56, 64,83-98,102,
        113,144-145,150,155
Lee, S., 38-39,47
Lee, Y.J., 3,38,48,83-98
Lee, Y.M., 180,197
Leff, J., 164-165,174
Legislation. *See* Laws and legislation
Lei, A., 4, 159-178

Lemeshow, S., 125,132
Leonard, K.I., 139,143,156-157
Leone, B., 20-21,31
Leong, F.T.L., 162,167,174
Lepine, J.P., 309,317
Leung, K.P., 166,176,229,237,240,242
Levav, I., 244,262
Lew, S., 106,113
Lewandowski, L., 204,220
Lewin, I.A., 205,220
Lewis, M.L., 285,296
Li, H., 21,32
Liddle, J., 148,157
Lim, D., 65
Lin, K.M., 100,113,165,175,205,223,
	229,241,244,262
Lin, M., 36,48,83
Lin, N., 163,175-176
Lin, T.Y., 165,175
Lin, W.T., 309,317
Lin-Fu, J., 186,197
Linden, W., 163,169,175
Lindholm, K., 53,64
Linn, M.W., 285,294,298
Linn, N., 161,177
Linton, R., 226,241
Liptak, K., 20,32
Liu, W.T., 312,318
Lock, M., 244-246,258,261
Locke, B., 208,222
Lonner, W.J., 169,172,176
Loo, C., 161,176
Lopes-Aqueres, W., 285,297
Lopez, E.M., 184,197
Los Angeles County Commission on
	Human Rights, 219,221
Los Angeles Race Riots (1994), 84-85
Lu, F., 236,240
Lubben, J.E., 308,312,317-318
Ly, T., 99

Macauley, D., 218,220
Mackenzie, T., 229,240
Mahard, R.E., 285,294,298
Makepeace, J., 116-118,132

Maki, M., 11,15,17
Mallick, M., 67,80
Mananzan, M.J., 119,132
Mangahas, F., 119,132
Mani, L., 147,157
Marcia, J., 20,32
Markides, K.S., 285,298
Marktrom-Adams, C., 67-68,82
Markus, H., 87,98,179-182,197
Marmar, C.R., 228,240
Marsella, A.J., 166,176
Marshall, L.L., 206,221
Marshall, W.E., 265,278
Martinez, C.R., 85,97
Masaki, B., 117,132
Masden, R., 181,196
Masuda, M., 229,241
Mattai, P.R., 138,157
May, C., 245-247,258-259,262
Maypole, D.E., 265,279
McCarran-Walter Act (1952), 12
McColm, M., 20-21,32
McCullough, J.E., 194,198,229,241
McDonald's Centrality Index (MCI),
	72-74
McDonald, R.P., 65,72-74,81
McEvoy, L., 228,240
McGoldrick, M., 67-68,81
McGonagle, K.A., 208,221
MCI. *See* McDonald's Centrality
	Index (MCI)
McIlwaine, C., 130-131
McLaughlin, D.G., 164,177
McNamara, J.R., 117,132
McRoy, R., 20,32
Measurement instruments
	Adjusted Goodness-of-Fit Index
		(AGFI), 72-74
	Affect Balance Scale (ABS), 71-72
	Attitude Toward Women Scale
		(AWS), 143-144,146-152
	Beck's Depression Inventory
		(BDI), 71-72
	Brief Symptom Inventory (BSI), 144

Center for Epidemiologic Studies Depression Scales(CES-D), 49-64,161-168,186-196, 231-239,284f

Chinese American Psychiatric Epidemiological Study (CAPES), 161,167-173

Chinese Psychiatric Epidemiology Study, 168-169

Comparative Fit Index (CFI), 72-74

Composite International Diagnostic Interview (CIDI), 167-168

Contextual Justification Scale, 121-127

Epidemiologic Catchment Area Study (ECA), 164,167-168

General Ethnicity Questionnaire (GEQ)
  abridged version (GEQ-A), 105-112
  American version (GEQA), 144-145,149-152
  Asian Indian version (GEQAI), 144-145,149-152
  Hmong version (GEQ-H), 105-112
  non-specialized version, 105-112,144-145

Global Severity Index, 208

Goodness-of-Fit Index (GFI), 72-75

Harvard Trauma Questionnaire (HTQ), Vietnamese version, 232,237-239

ICD-10, 168-169

Interdependent Self-Construal Scale, 199-200

Kaplan-Meier (KM) estimator, 208-211,218

McDonald's Centrality Index (MCI), 72-74

Multigroup Ethnic Identity Measure (MEIM), 70-71

National Violence Against Women Survey (NVAWS), 201-224

Omnibus Personality Inventory (OPI), 162-164

Parent-Adolescent Communication Scale (PACS), 70

Parental Acceptance-Rejection Questionnaire (PARQ), 70

Research Diagnostic Criteria (RDC), 287-296

Root Mean-Square Residuals (RMR), 72-74

Rosenberg Self-Esteem Scale (RSE), 71

Satisfaction with Life Scale (SWLS), 71-72

Sense of Coherence Questionnaire, 89-90

Short Portable Status Questionnaire (SPMSQ), 286-296

Social Participation and Integration Questionnaire (SPIQ), 89-90

State-Trait Anxiety Inventory (STAI), 71-72

Structural Equation Modeling (SEM), 65-82

Symptoms Check List (SCL)
  Symptoms Check List, 90-item (SCL-90), 167-169
  Symptoms Check List-90R (SCL-90R), 207-209

MEIM. *See* Multigroup Ethnic Identity Measure (MEIM)

Meinhardt, K., 225,227,242,244,262

Mendoza, R.H., 106,113

Mental health research on Asian Americans, current state of
future directions for research, 171-173
introduction to, 159-161
references, 173-178
research methods
  cross cultural studies, 169-170
  sample and population studies, 170-171
research results
  anxiety, 162-164
  Chinese American Psychiatric Epidemiology Study, 167-169
  depression, 161-162

Post-Traumatic Stress Disorder
(PTSD), 166
somatic problems, 164-166
Merton, R.M., 183,198
Metsch, L.R., 266,279
Miley, K., 264,279
Miller, J.B., 267,279
Mindel, C., 285,298
Misra, G., 181,198
MMPI, 167
Moes, D., 105,113
Mokuau, N., 265,269-270,279
Molgaard, C.A., 308,318
Mollica, R.F., 166,176,228-229,232,
237-238,240-241,244,249,
262
Moon, A., 308,310,313,318
Moon, J., 293,295,298
Moore, J.L., 229,240
Morelli, P.T., 5,243-262,265,278
Morello-Frosch, R., 219,221
Morera, O.F., 161,177
Morioka-Douglas, N., 307,318
Morishima, J., 172,177
Morss, J., 37,47
Mortensen, H., 99
Morton, D.J., 53,63,308,313,318
Mosher, S., 20,32
Mowbray, C., 201
Mui, A.C., 5-6,21,32,281-299,309,312,
318
Multigroup Ethnic Identity Measure
(MEIM), 70-71
Murphy, J., 105,113

Na Wahine Makalapua Project
(Hawaii), 263,268-377
Nagata, D.K., 172,176
Nakaoka, S., 2,7-17
Nandan, Y., 143,157
National Asian Pacific Legal
Consortium, 205,219,222
National Center for Health Statistics,
307-309,318

National Center on Addiction and
Substance Abuse at Columbia
University (CASA), 265-266
National Comorbidity Study (NCS), 168
National Household Survey on Drug
Abuse, 265-266
National Institute on Aging (NIA),
314-315
National Institute on Drug Abuse,
265-266
National Institute on Mental Health
(NIMH), 99,135,159,201,206,
225-243,314-315
National Institutes of Health (NIH),
314-315
National Organization for Women
(NOW), 152
National Origins Acts (1924), 11
National Research Center on Asian
American Mental Health,
167,243
National Violence Against Women
Survey (NVAWS), 201-224
NCS. *See* National Comorbidity Study
(NCS)
Neff, J., 203,222
Neider, J., 100,113,163,172,178
Nelson, C.B., 208,221
Nelson, E., 204,222
Nemoto, T., 309-310,312,318
Networks, Chinese Americans, 83-98
Neufeld, J., 117,132
NFI. *See* Normed Fit Index (NFI)
Ngo, D., 5,225-242
Nguyen, S.D., 164-165,174,229,241
NIA. *See* National Institute on Aging
(NIA)
Nicassio, P.M., 194,198,229,241
Nicholson, B.L., 100-101,113
Niedenthal, P.M., 183,198
NIH. *See* National Institutes of Health
(NIH)
NIMH. *See* National Institute on
Mental Health (NIMH)
Nisbett, R., 181,196

NNFI. *See* Non-Normed Fit Index
(NNFI)
Noh, S., 192,198,232,241
Noller, P., 53,64
Non-Normed Fit Index (NNFI), 72-74
Normed Fit Index (NFI), 72-74
Norris, F.H., 205,222,228
NOW. *See* National Organization for
Women (NOW)
Nugent, S., 100,114
Nunes, J., 264,279
NVAWS. *See* National Violence
Against Women Survey
(NVAWS)

O'Hare, W.P., 37,47
O'Melia, M., 264,279
Oka, B.J., 163,174
Okazaki, S., 37,48,161,163,176,181,
184,198
Olin, J.T., 286-287,298
Oliver, J.E., 37,47
Oliver, J.M., 5,225-242
Olivira, J., 263-280
Olson, D.H., 70,80
Omnibus Personality Inventory (OPI),
162-164
On-Lok program (San Francisco), 313
Ono, M., 265,278
Open Family Communication Scale, 70
OPI. *See* Omnibus Personality
Inventory (OPI)
Orne, M.T., 105,113
Osako, N.M., 312,318
Ouslander, J.G., 285,298

PACE. *See* Program for All Inclusive
Care for the Elderly (PACE)
PACS. *See* Parent-Adolescent
Communication Scale (PACS)
Padilla, A., 53,64,118
Paglinawan, L., 269-270,279
Pang, K.Y., 295,298
Paranjpe, A.C., 137-138,157

Parent-Adolescent Communication
Scale (PACS), 70
Parental Acceptance-Rejection
Questionnaire (PARQ), 70
Parents, adoptive (Chinese Americans),
19-33
Parmelee, P.A., 287,298
PARQ. *See* Parental Acceptance-
Rejection Questionnaire
(PARQ)
Patton, M.Q., 171-172,176
Paulus, D.L., 169,176
Pearl, J.H., 293,295,298,313,318
Peasvento, B.H., 228,240
Peng, C., 35
Perceptions of and attitudes toward
intimate violence, 121-127
Perry, P.R., 285,298
Personal Responsibility and Work
Obligations Reconciliation
Act (1996), 311
Peters, S.D., 215,233
Peterson, E., 228,240
Pettigrew, T.F., 85,98
Philleo, J., 264,280
Phinney, J., 20,32,68,70,144,157
Piaget, J., 266,280
Pillai, A.K.B., 143,157
Poisson, S.E., 85,98
Pokorny, A.D., 71,82
Polek, D.S., 215,220
Ponton, L.D., 205,222
Poole, C., 244,262
Population growth, 7-17
Post-Traumatic Stress Disorder
(PTSD), 166,173
Powers, D.A., 85,87,95,97
Prathikanti, S., 148-149,157
Premigration traumatic experiences
(PTE) and Vietnamese
Americans, 225-242
Program for All Inclusive Care for the
Elderly (PACE), 313
Psychological adjustment predictors
and casual modeling, 65-82

Psychological well-being and the
    independent self, Korean
    Americans, 179-200
PTE. *See* Premigration traumatic
    experiences (PTE) and
    Vietnamese Americans
PTSD. *See* Post-Traumatic Stress
    Disorder (PTSD)
Publications
  articles
    *Indian Moves on Human
        Development*, 137,156
  books
    Race Matters, 84,98
    *Second Generation Japanese
        American Problem, The*, 11
    Warrior Lessons, 154
  serials and periodicals
    China Daily, 21,31
    Current Population Survey, 12,
        306
    Economist, The, 21
    Femina, 137,156
    San Francisco Examiner, 84-85,
        98
    Statistical Brief, 14
    U.S. News & World Report, 37
  web documents
    *International Adoption and
        Child Abduction*, 20,31
Pukui, M., 269-270,280
Psychological abuse and dating
    violence among Filipino
    Americans, 115-133
Psychological Violence Subscale,
    122-127

Quervalu, I., 264,279

Race Matters, 84,98
Radloff, L.S., 52,57,60,64,231-232,241
Rao, K., 205,222
Rath, B., 166,175
Rawlings, E.I., 204,221

RDC. *See* Research Diagnostic
    Criteria (RDC)
Redfield, R.E., 226,241
Redress Movement, 15
Refugees, Hmong Americans, cultural
    orientation of, 99-114
Regier, D.A., 168,176,208,222
Reif, W., 245,262
Reifler, B., 285,299
Reinhartz, S., 272,280
Reitz, M., 29,32
Reker, G.T., 293,299
Research Diagnostic Criteria (RDC),
    287-296
Resnick, H.S., 205,222
Ressler, E.M., 67,81
Revilla, L., 304,316
Rew, L., 183,197
Reynolds, W.M., 50,64
Richels, K., 208,220
Richie, B.E., 204,222
Rickard-Figueroa, K., 106,113
Riley, C., 229,240
Riley, N., 20,22,33
Rimonte, N., 118,132
RMR. *See* Root Mean-Square
    Residuals (RMR)
Roberts, C., 52,64
Roberts, R.E., 52,54,63-64,231,241
Robins, L.N., 168,176,208,222,228,240
Rock, A.F., 208,220
Rodriquez-Giegling, M., 162,176
Rogers, T.B., 182,196
Rohner, R.P., 70,81
Roland, A., 143,157
Ronningen, B., 101,113
Root Mean-Square Residuals (RMR),
    72-74
Rosenberg Self-Esteem Scale (RSE), 71
Rosenberg, E., 29,33
Rosenberg, M., 71,81
Rosser-Hogan, R., 244,260
Rousseau, C., 38,48
RSE. *See* Rosenberg Self-Esteem
    Scale (RSE)
Rubin, G., 266

Rumbaut, R.G., 244,304,318
Russell, D.E.H., 205,218,222
Rutledge, L.L., 215,220
Rutter, C.M., 208,220
Ryan, L., 218,220

Sack, W.H., 166,175
Sackett, L.A., 204,217,222
Sagar, H.A., 86,95,98
Sakauye, K.M., 309,317
Salzinger, S., 86,97
Sam, D., 184,196
SAMHSA. See United States,
        Substance Abuse and Mental
        Health Administration
        (SAMHSA)
San Francisco Examiner, 84-85,98
Santos, R., 117-119,132
Saran, P., 146,153,157
Sarason, S., 85,98
Satisfaction with Life Scale (SWLS),
        71-72
Saunders, B.E., 205,217,222
Saunders, D.G., 204,222
Schaberg, L., 100,114
Schlenger, W.E., 228,240
Schliebner, C.T., 266,280
Schluter, T., 203,222
Schmitz, P.G., 183,198
Schneider, B.H., 38,48,85,98
Schofield, J.W., 86,98
Schooler, J., 29,33
SCL. See Symptoms Check List (SCL)
Searle, W., 183,198
Second Generation Japanese
        American Problem, The, 11
Sedlack, A.J., 215,222
Seipel, M., 183,198
SEM. See Structural Equation
        Modeling (SEM)
Sense of Coherence Questionnaire,
        89-90
Shah, N., 138,146,153,157
Shay, J., 259-260,262
Sheffield, C.J., 205,222

Sheth, M., 304,318
Shibata, K., 305,318
Shin, K.R., 183,198
Shintani, T., 270,280
Shook, E.V., 269-270,280
Short Portable Status Questionnaire
        (SPMSQ), 286-296
Sigel, R.S., 85,98
Sigler, R., 128-129,133
Silverman, A.R., 66,68,77,81
Simeone, R.S., 163,175-176
Singelis, T.M., 181,198
Singhal, S., 138-139,157
Siu, P., 9,17
Sluzki, C., 53,64
Smith, A., 85,98
Smith, C., 205,220
Smith, D., 229,240
Smith, E.J., 66-68,82
Smither, R., 162,176
Smukler, M., 202,233
Snowden, L.R., 164,167,178,310,319
Snyder, H.N., 86,98
Social integration, 83-98
Social Participation and Integration
        Questionnaire (SPIQ), 89-90
Sociodemographics, 7-17
Soldevilla, E., 128,131-132
Solomon, M., 194,198,229,241
Somatization
    Cambodian Killing Fields survivors
        and, 243-262
    research about, historical
        perspectives of, 164-166
Somes, G., 105,113
Song, D., 294,299
Song-Kim, Y.I., 203,222
Sopetta, M.A., 106,113
Sorbom, D., 72,81
Sorenson, S.B., 204,206,222
South Asian Women's Alliance, 135,
        146-147
Southeast Asia Action Resource
        Center, 100
Sowell, T., 37,48
Spain, H., 166,176

Spence, J., 127,133
Spence, T., 143,158
Spencer, M.B., 67-68,82
Spielberger, C.D., 71,82
SPIQ. *See* Social Participation and
    Integration Questionnaire
    (SPIQ)
Spitzer, R.L., 287,299
SPMSQ. *See* Short Portable Status
    Questionnaire (SPMSQ)
Srinivasan, S., 4,135-158,171,177
STAI. *See* State-Trait Anxiety
    Inventory (STAI)
Standfield, D., 153,158
Stanford, E.P., 308,318
Staples, F., 285,297
Stapp, J., 143,158
State-Trait Anxiety Inventory (STAI),
    71-72
Statistical Brief, 14
Steinbock, D., 67,81
Stevens, A., 266,278
Stiles, J., 37,47
Storandt, M., 287,296
Straus, M.A., 206,233
Strauss, J., 20-21,33
Strauss, S., 272,280
Stress and coping, Korean Americans,
    281-299
Strong, E., 11,17
Structural Equation Modeling (SEM),
    65-82
Suarez, K.E., 116-117,133
Substance Abuse and Mental Health
    Administration (SAMHSA).
    See United States, Substance
    Abuse and Mental Health
    Administration (SAMHSA)
Substance abuse, Asian/Pacific Islander
    (AP/I) women and, 263-280
Sue, D.W., 50,64,160,163,170,176-177
Sue, L., 50,64,160,176
Sue, S., 4,37,48,50,64,159-178,310,319
Suinn, R.M., 106,113
Sullivan, W., 181,196
Sundberg, N.D., 170,176

Sunderland, T., 285,296
Sung, K., 293,299
Surrey, J.L., 267,278
Sustento-Seneriches, J., 128,133
Suzuki, B., 36-37,48
Swidler, A., 181,196
SWLS. *See* Satisfaction with Life
    Scale (SWLS)
Symptoms Check List (SCL)
    Symptoms Check List, 90-item
    (SCL-90), 167-169
    Symptoms Check List-90R
    (SCL-90R), 207-209
Szapocznik, J., 106,113

Ta, K., 100-101,113
Takaki, R., 136,158
Takeuchi, D.T., 37,47,50,64,160,168,
    176,202,205,233
Tan, D.L., 36,38,48
Tan, J., 117,133
Tanaka, J.S., 72,81,161,177
Tang, J., 36,48
Tanjasiri, S.P., 305-306,318
Taylor, K., 100-101,113
Tazuma, L., 229,241
Telles, C., 227,240
Telles, C.A., 204,222
Templin, T., 205,220
Tessler, R., 23,33
Theidon, K.S., 264,266,278
Thoennes, N., 202,233
Thomas, N., 205,220
Thompason, T., 265,280
Thompson, L.W., 128,286,299
Timm, J., 244,260
Tipton, S., 181,196
Tjaden, P., 202,233
Tolman, R.M., 204,206,217,233
Tompar-Tiu, A., 128,133
Tong, B., 161,176
Tong, Z., 309,319
Tongyonk, J., 164,177
Tor, S., 229,232,241,244,262
Toukmanian, S.G., 170,177

Tran, T.V., 5,162,177,225-242,312, 318
Traumatic experiences and Vietnamese Americans, 225-242
Treatment for substance abuse, Asian/ Pacific Islander (AP/I) women and, 263-280
Triandis, H.C., 65,119,133,180, 198-199
True, R., 161,176
Truong, T., 229,232,241
Tsai, J.L., 3,36,48,56,64,83-114, 144-145,150,155,162,175
Tsang, M., 3,83-98
Tseng, W., 164-165,177
Tsukada, N., 201
Turner, R.J., 204,220

U.S. News & World Report, 37
Uba, L., 128,133,169,173,178
UCLA. *See* University of California, Los Angeles (UCLA)
Uehara, E.S., 5,202,217,233,243-262
Ujimoto, K.V., 172,178,307,309,313, 318
UM-CIDI. *See* University of Michigan version of the Composite International Diagnostic Interview (UM-CIDI)
United States
    Bureau of the Census, 8-17,37,50, 84,100,118,180,202,210, 233,301-303,305-306,312, 318
    Central Intelligence Agency (CIA), 100
    Commission on Civil Rights, 203, 233
    Committee for Refugees, 229,241
    Department of Health and Human Services
        definitions of origins of persons, 265-266
        Office of Refugee Resettlement, 228-229,241

Substance Abuse and MentalHealth Administration (SAMHSA), 265-266
United Way of Greater Los Angeles, 15
University of Michigan version of the Composite International Diagnostic Interview (UM-CIDI), 167-168
Universities and colleges. *See* Colleges and universities
University of California, Berkeley, 35, 83
University of California, Davis, 135, 137,146-147
University of California, Los Angeles (UCLA), 115
University of Michigan, 167,179
Unschuld, P., 259,262

Vaglum, H.P., 229,242
van deVijert, F., 237,242
Vang, T.F., 163,172,178
Vargas, L., 264,280
Vega, W., 54,63,226-227,242
Verma, L., 67,80
Vietnamese Americans, research about
    acculturation, premigration traumatic experiences, and depression and introduction to, 225-228
    mental health status of refugees, 228-229
    psychological consequence of trauma experiences, 228
    references, 239-242
    research hypotheses, 229
    research methods, 229-232
    research results, 232-235
    research results, discussion of, 235-239
    research, importance of, 239
Hmong Americans, cultural orientation of
    introduction to, 99-103
    notes, 112
    references, 113-114
    research methods, 103-107

research results, 107-109
research results, discussion of, 109-112
Vigil, P., 106,113
Villa, V., 308,318
Violence, dating. *See* Dating violence
Visweswaran, K., 136,158

Waid, W.M., 105,113
Wald, R., 266,280
Walker, L.E., 215,233
Wallace, S.P., 305,318
Wan, C.T., 36,48,83
Wang, A., 2
Wang, L., 20,22,32
War Brides Act (1945), 11-12
War Brides Act, amendment (1947), 11-12
Ward, C., 183,198
Ware, N.C., 165,178
Warheit, G., 226-227,242
Warrier, S., 203,220
Warrior Lessons, 154
Watkin, V., 309,317
Watson, K., 29,32
Watson, R., 128,133
Weiss, D.S., 228,240
Well-being and the independent self, Korean Americans, 179-200
Wells, M., 117,131
West, C., 84,98
Westermeyer, J., 100,113-114,163, 172,178
Wethington, E., 204,221,285,299
White, J.W., 117,133
Whitmore, J.K., 229,240
WHO. *See* World Health Organization (WHO)
Wing, D.M., 265,268,280
Wisniewski, N., 117,132
Wodarski, J., 1
Women
    Asian/Pacific Islanders (A/PI), substance abuse treatment programs for, 263-280

Indian Americans, cross-cultural studies of, 135-158
Women's Resources and Research Center, 135
Wong, L., 117,131
Wong, M., 37,47
Wong, P.T.P, 172,178,293,299,307, 309,313,318
Wong, S.L., 3,49-64
Wong, Y., 99
Wood, J., 67,82
Wooding, S., 53,64
World Health Organization (WHO), 168
Wu, F.Y.T., 305,309,313,318
Wu, S.C., 219,312
Wurf, E., 182,197
Wyatt, G.E., 215,218,233
Wyshak, G., 166,176,229,241

Xenos, P., 37, 47

Yang, C., 309,319
Yang, K.S., 111,114
Yang, P.Q., 9,17,304,318
Yap, J., 119,133
Yeo, G., 307,318
Yi, J.K., 266,280
Yick, A.G. *See* Flannigan, A.Y.
Ying, Y.-W., 2-3,35-49,54,57-58,60, 64,83-102,112,114, 144-145,150,155,162,178, 232,242
Yoon, D.P., 3,65-82
Yoshihama, M., 5,201-224
Youn, G., 294,299
Young adults, Hmong Americans, cultural orientation of, 99-114
Young, A., 246-248,261
Young, L., 67-68,80
Youtz, D., 23,33
Yu, E.S.H., 307,309,317,319
Yu, L.C., 309,312,319
Yuan, J., 309,319
Yum, J.O., 183,197

Yun, G., 36,48
Zane, N., 163,167,177-178
Zeff, S.B., 127,133
Zeller, R.A., 71,80
Zhang, A.Y., 164,167,178,309-310,
    312,319

Zhang, X., 88,98,100,114
Zhao, S., 208,221
Zheng, Y.-P., 165,168,178
Zhou, M., 312,317
Zimmerman, C., 204,222